The Lonesome Plains

Death and Revival on an American Frontier

NUMBER SEVEN:

WEST TEXAS A&M UNIVERSITY SERIES

JERRY CRAVEN, GENERAL EDITOR

The Lon

Death and Revival on a

some Plains

merican Frontier

Louis Fairchild

TEXAS A&M UNIVERSITY PRESS COLLEGE STATION

∞ The paper used in this book meets the minimum requirements
of the American National Standard for Permanence of Paper for
Printed Library Materials, z39.48-1984. Binding materials have
been chosen for durability.

"Shield of Achilles" copyright © 1976 by Edward Mendelson,
Wil1956 by W. H. Auden, from *W. H. Auden: Collected Poems*
by W. H. Auden. Used by permission of Random House, Inc.

"Saddle Song" from *Cow Country,* by Edward Everett Dale.
Copyright © 1942 by the University of Oklahoma Press.
Reprinted by permission.

Library of Congress Cataloging-in-Publication Data

Fairchild, Louis.
The lonesome plains : death and revival on an American frontier /
Louis Fairchild.— 1st ed.
   p. cm. — (West Texas A&M University series ; no. 7)
   Includes bibliographical references and index.
   ISBN 1-58544-182-1 (cloth : alk. paper)
   1. Frontier and pioneer life—Texas, West. 2. Texas, West—
Social life and customs—19th century. 3. Texas, West—
Religious life and customs—19th century. 4. Pioneers—Texas,
West—Social life and customs—19th century. 5. Pioneers—
Texas, West—Psychology. 6. Loneliness—Texas, West—
History—19th century. 7. Solitude—Texas, West—History—
19th century. 8. Funeral rites and ceremonies—Texas, West—
History—19th century. 9. Camp meetings—Texas, West—
History—19th century.   I. Title. II. Series.
   F391 .F26 2002
   976.4—dc21
                                                2001006555

FOR

My Family

AND

In Memory of
Jonah Boyd

Having been asked many, many times what was the hardest thing to bear in the life of a pioneer I never hesitate to answer for to me of all the things that a pioneer woman had to endure, loneliness, was the most trying. It's the one memory that time can never cure.

Temple Ann Ellis

Many a time when I was a child and lived 'way out in the country, I'd sit on the fence and wish to God that somebody would ride by on a horse or drive by in a buggy—just anything to relieve my loneliness. Loneliness consumes people. It kills 'em eventually. God help the lonely.

Sam Rayburn

Contents

List of Illustrations   *xi*

Acknowledgments   *xiii*

Introduction   *xv*

Chapters

1. Brave Cheers But Many Tears: Departure   3

2. Over the Threshold: All Things New   13

3. Fearful Solitude   27

4. Such a Country as This: Loneliness   41

5. The Insecurity of Life: Sickness and Accidents   59

6. Death's Visitation   73

7. Neglected and Forgotten: Lonely Graves in Lonely Places   87

8. The Sounds of Entombment   107

9. Meeting Time   129

10. Camp Meetings—Half-Vacation   143

11. Camp Meetings—Half-Revival   169

12. Fellowship of the Lonely   197

Notes   *211*

Bibliography   *283*

Index   *315*

List of Illustrations

Wagon train to Plainview   *6*

Dorothy Scarborough   *24*

Canyon City, Texas   *36*

Amarillo, Texas   *38*

West Texas windmill   *49*

Lonely West Texas line camp   *55*

Saloon in Old Tascosa, Texas   *56*

Boot Hill tombstone   *110*

A cowboy funeral   *112*

Camp-meeting bound wagon   *151*

Camp-meeting campsite   *152*

Texas camp meeting   *154*

A cowboy cooks dinner outdoors   *162*

Cowboys cooking outdoors   *163*

Camp-meeting mealtime   *164*

Children at a Texas camp meeting   *203*

Acknowledgments

The people, resources, and facilities of West Texas A&M University helped make this book possible. The James and Mary Elizabeth Cornette Library was a mainstay. Funding was provided by the Killgore Research Center, and I am grateful to directors of the center for their support: Drs. James D. Woodyard, Falvius C. Killebrew, and Vaughn C. Nelson. Drs. Gary R. Byrd, Norman Theodore "Ted" Guffy, Killebrew, and Brian Lotven approved adjustments in my teaching schedule to allow time for writing.

The archivists of the Research Center of the Panhandle-Plains Historical Museum, Canyon, Texas—my gold mine—could not have been more courteous and helpful. Thanks to Claire Kuehn, Betty Bustos, Cesaria Espinoza, Mica Loyd, and Dulcinea Almager. Michael Grauer, curator of art, shared his time and expertise. Personnel of the Southwest Collection, Texas Tech University, Lubbock, were always responsive. Jim Bradshaw guided me through holdings of the J. Evetts Haley Historical Center and the Nita Stewart Haley Memorial Library in Midland, Texas. I am especially appreciative of the hospitality shown by Mrs. Rosalind Haley. The Museum of Texas Tech University; the Texas Collection, Baylor University, Waco, Texas; the A. Webb Roberts Library and the Bowld Music Library, Southwestern Baptist Theological Seminary, Fort Worth, Texas; and the Center for American History, the University of Texas at Austin, provided assistance. The Panhandle-Plains Historical Society permitted me to expand on material previously published in the *Panhandle-Plains Historical Review*.

Dr. Garry L. Nall read early drafts of the manuscript and was a generous reservoir of information about West Texas and the Panhandle. Myrna Raffkind also read the manuscript and, as always, was uniquely interested and supportive.

Finally, a word of gratitude is reserved for those who granted me interviews. These West Texans were a special people.

Introduction

It was a bitter March afternoon in 1987 as I drove to my three o'clock interview with Roy Ransom outside of Claude, Texas. An oncoming blizzard made the sky leaden, and I listened with concern to the radio for weather updates. I did not want to get caught in heavy snow or icy conditions driving a small car with poor traction.

Mr. Ransom, a native West Texan born near Amarillo in 1904, had given me directions by phone to his ranch, noting a final cutoff from the farm road. As I pressed along, fewer and fewer houses appeared on the thinly populated landscape. Occasionally, an abandoned farm implement lay rusting in one of the fields. The blacktop became a dirt road, but I continued on, hoping for my turn. The road crossed through an opening in a barbed-wire fence into a remote pasture, then became two shallow ruts. Farther along the ruts leveled out under green sprigs of hearty prairie grass, sure signs that few people came this way.

Stopping the car and stepping outside, I saw no sign of life save a solitary white farmhouse, far away in the distance. There were no bounds to the expanse before me. The land seemed to roll forever in swells of brown and gray. Never before had I felt so isolated and alone as I stood surrounded by miles upon miles of unbroken, barren plains.

It was just such a scene that greeted many West Texas settlers a century ago.

Retracing my route, I found a house where someone directed me to the cutoff. It was around five o'clock when I reached the Ransom spread, just in time to see a pickup truck disappearing over the rim of the canyon. Mrs. Ransom said her husband had to take feed to his cattle in anticipation of the blizzard. I would have to return another day.

BORN ON THE SOUTH PLAINS IN COLORADO CITY IN 1903, Marcia Caldwell was another West Texas native. Marcia was seventy years old when she completed her master's degree in history at West Texas State University. In a 1984 interview I asked whether a death in her childhood years tended to bring people in the community together. "More than any other one thing," she responded, "unless it was in the summer when they had those revivals."

"They did such good visiting," she told me, "when they were in the process of helping somebody in sickness or death, if death came on. The neighborliness of it was just unbelievable because farmers were so isolated in their ordinary lives. I don't know just how you felt, whether you were hungry for neighborliness, neighbor contacts, but you sure did devour it whenever you had [the opportunity.]"[1]

In a later interview I asked Marcia if children ever played outside during a summertime revival. "There may have been little children that played. I don't know." She then paused and reflected: "I don't guess I've ever talked to you about how lonely I was when I was growing up—and I, of course—I had to sit by my mother."[2]

Marcia Caldwell's loneliness was typical of the responses many early settlers had to the plains of West Texas. It was a time and place of prevailing isolation, and this book will explore the loneliness often ensuing from that solitude, as well as various features of two occasions settlers found for social contact. Hungering for neighborliness, people came together in times of misfortune—sickness, accident, and death. They gathered at religious services.

In the introduction to Joanna Stratton's *Pioneer Women: Voices from the Kansas Frontier*, Arthur M. Schlesinger, Jr., observes that history is in the main lived by the unknown and the forgotten.[3] Stratton describes her book as a history based not on interpretations of annalists or recollections of statesmen, but rather a personal account of the pioneer experience described by those for whom "'history' was nothing more than daily life."[4]

To document details of daily life in the beginning decades of plains settlement, this book gives voice to people like Marcia Caldwell. The experience of these early residents is known through their language, expressions of experience, and a primary purpose is to preserve this language. Their word pictures become the strands of the tapestry. The contributions of annalists—as well as those of novelists, poets, and lyricists—are included, and although material from neighboring regions is on occasion cited, the voices are primarily those of people who lived in the West Texas area during the latter and subsequent decades of what Walter Nugent calls the frontier-rural period of American social history.[5] Nugent dates this period from 1720–1870 but allows for the continuation, or conjuncture, of frontier-rural social patterns into the early twentieth century, particularly in regions outside of New England and the Middle Atlantic states.

The accounts included in this book are taken principally from two phases of development in frontier-rural West Texas, both of which were driven by a craving for land: the ranching frontier and the farming frontier.[6] With suppression of the threat from nomadic Indian tribes, cattle ranchers and sheepherders became in 1876 the first permanent settlers in the region, eager to capitalize on the vast, uninhabited grasslands.[7] The cattle industry thrived until the late 1880s when weather conditions and a depressed beef market necessitated other, more profitable uses of the land. Railroads entered the Panhandle at this time, providing an alternative to animal-drawn wagons and making possible the movement of larger quantities of household goods, draft animals, and farming equipment.[8] To recoup some of their losses, ranchers were ready to sell land at bargain prices to eager farmers, and West Texas newspapers, immigration associations, land promoters, and the railroads launched active campaigns to promote this land of "Health, Wealth and Happiness."[9] The result was a mass migration and land boom in one of the last regions of the United States to be settled by farming families, a boom lasting from 1890 to 1917.

The interview and manuscript files in the research Center of the Panhandle-Plains Historical Museum in Canyon, Texas, include many accounts of early West Texas settlers. The Southwest Collection, Texas Tech University, in Lubbock, and the J. Evetts Haley Collection, Nita Stewart Haley Memorial Library, Midland, Texas, also provided archival material. Some eighty-five early Panhandle and South Plains residents who were born in the late nineteenth and early twentieth centuries participated in recorded interviews. The dates of birth of these interviewees ranged from 1887 to 1910, and the average year of birth was around 1900.

The archival and recorded interview materials focus on the plains region of West Texas, and these sources are complemented by published reports on life in this section of the country. In so far as it relates to the topics in this book, published material from other regions may be included in the text or endnote section.

ACCOUNTS OF PIONEER LIFE ARE A RECORD OF PERCEPTIONS, and as Joseph Conrad has noted, "There is a quality in events which is apprehended differently by different minds or even by the same mind at different times. Any man living at all consciously knows that embarrassing truth."[10] John L. Allen discusses competing views of the Great Plains in the nineteenth century—the desert-garden continuum.[11] For some it was the Great American Desert; for others, the Garden of the World. Allen likens the mind to a mirror that reflects what it perceives. The reflected image of geographic reality is determined by the condition of the mirror, how it has been warped or cracked or otherwise altered by personal and collective experience.

"All images—and this is particularly true of regional images or patterns of belief about the nature and content of a definable area—are distorted and discolored by the quality of the minds in which they have been lodged."[12]

To be sure, different minds apprehended events and experiences on the early plains differently, sometimes paradoxically. Members within any given family, for instance, seldom saw life the same way. They had unlike perceptions, individual points of view. Little on the frontier coalesced. "Like the pictures in a kaleidoscope, vision was shattered into myriad forms and unfamiliar shapes."[13] Even though both men and women participated in the same historical events, their experiences and feelings about those events were not necessarily the same. The West was seen differently through the eyes of women, and there was diversity of experience and perception even among women.[14]

These accounts are also a product of human memory, the task of which, like the study of history, is unearthing the past and disclosing it to the present.[15] This is not a passive process of recovering and reproducing details of the past. Memory is creative and often subjective. People frame events of yesteryears into narratives and thereby simplify those events and give them new meaning.[16] Written documents themselves are often an unreliable guide to past reality.[17] Documents such as diaries and personal letters are subjective by their very nature, as are oral histories, relying as they do on the interaction between interviewer and interviewee.[18]

People do not remember in isolation.[19] Discussions with others shape memory, and institutions such as the church, government, and media are powerful forces in determining what people remember. On examining collections of pioneer interviews and memoirs dating from the 1890s to the 1950s, Barbara Allen was struck by the fact that the reminiscences all sound alike.[20] Despite differences in locale, time period, and personal experiences, the same themes and the same general story seemed to emerge. Old-timers, she concluded, would reminisce at reunions and other functions, and out of their conversations evolved a consensus of which experiences were crucial, defining categories of pioneer experience. The publication of these accounts shaped later interviewers' notions about what questions to ask, and the questions themselves reinforced memories for certain events.

Memory is also influenced by the actual events themselves, and there should be agreement between memory and documented facts concerning the past. Narratives about the past are not to be judged simply as narratives, but as nonfictions.[21] Oral history becomes factual only to the extent it is corroborated.[22] Oral history is not a re-creation of historical events. It is a record of perceptions.

Allowing for the contributions of selective perception and memory, there remains sufficient agreement in the pioneer experience to permit generalizations about frontier life for both men and women.[23] Frontier conditions undoubtedly differed, but they also corresponded, lives and behavior shaped by comparable social forces.[24] John Washington Lockhart, born in Alabama in 1824, traveled to Texas with his family when he was sixteen. Upon graduating from medical school in 1847 he opened his practice in the southeastern Texas community of Chappell Hill, and his letters and other writings record the social history of life along the Brazos River over the last half of the nineteenth century. In 1879 Dr. Lockhart wrote an article for *The Galveston Daily News* about camp meetings in early Texas and said in concluding: "These were the good old times we once had in Texas, and applies with equal propriety to all other frontier states, for we are all of the same stock, only a little removed from each other, perhaps on account of less favorable conditions—cast in rougher molds, perhaps."[25] Looking back on frontier towns in Nebraska, another pioneer reached a similar conclusion: "It is sufficient to recount experiences in but one of these villages for customs were similar in all of them."[26]

Loneliness is an underlying current in this book, and although much has been made of the loneliness and trials of plains life, we are reminded that generalizations on these topics must be made cautiously. Small communities of settlers began to dot the frontier landscape, and some individuals were not lonely. Accounts of loneliness and hardship require careful dating.[27] Nonetheless, of all the late-nineteenth-century agricultural frontiers, western Texas was probably the most isolated and the most lonesome, and this condition persisted well into the twentieth century.[28] Interview files from the Panhandle-Plains Historical Museum's Research Center contain repeated references to West Texas isolation and loneliness at the end of the nineteenth century and beyond. It was in the early twentieth century that one West Texas pioneer remembered God as her nearest neighbor.[29] Warding off isolation and loneliness were major considerations in 1907 when C. W. Post founded his model West Texas community on the South Plains.[30]

Elizabeth Porter Seymour was one of the early plains settlers who recalled her bouts of loneliness. An Iowan, she settled with her husband and infant in Nebraska in 1872. Greeting her were a small cottonwood house and living conditions she described as dreary, but the most savage blow came a few months later when their child contracted cholera. The young mother was ignorant of treatment remedies, and the long distance from a doctor resulted in a delay that was fatal. Fellow settlers were the distraught parents' only resource. Although widely scattered, "they were kind and neighborly, as a rule—ready to help each other in all ways, especially," Mrs. Seymour wrote, "in sickness and death."[31] There was a sense of interdependency and loyalty among pioneers. People felt responsible for one another, and caring for one's neighbor was both a duty and a privilege. Going to the aid of an individual or a family in distress was one form of social contact, one opportunity to break the onerous feelings of isolation and loneliness.

Religious services were another opportunity for contact with seldom-seen neighbors. Big meetings, protracted meetings, brush-arbor meetings, and camp meetings were terms variously and interchangeably used for summertime revivals, occasions highly anticipated for their spiritual and social significance. It was the camp meeting, however, that best filled the social void, and camp meetings were popular in Texas until after the turn of the century. Farmers were the ones primarily attracted to these meetings in the later years, but town folk, those with close neighbors, also turned out in large numbers.[32] Such a gathering was the highlight of the year, and for some, the camp meeting was not religion, it was simply friendship. H. G. Bedford arrived in Fort Worth from Kentucky in 1850, and he recalled early camp meetings in northwestern Texas. "In nothing," he wrote, "was the friendship of the people more exemplified more [*sic*] than at these gatherings."[33]

TOTAL ISOLATION IS DIFFICULT FOR THE MODERN MIND TO CONCEIVE, BUT on the West Texas frontier it was a known and sometimes formidable reality. Susan E. Newcomb and her husband, Samuel, lived in the Fort Davis area in the 1860s. She despaired that her closest neighbor was eighteen miles away, that in her desolation time passed so slowly, and she longed for the day when she could visit a friend and go to church. Repeated entries in her 1867 diary not only captured the desperation in her lonely life, but foreshadowed the experience of others to follow:

> SUNDAY MAY 5TH/67. . . *I am lonesome Oh: very lonesome. . . I actually think that it is almost a sin for a person to live where they scarcly ever see anyone, and are always lonesome. We have been living here over a year and there has been one woman to see us, only one.*

> FRIDAY JUNE 14TH 67:—*Weather warm and dreary—Water scarce and bad—The stoutest hearts grow weary—And merriest hearts grow sad—here alone in the wild wilderness of western Texas.[34]*

The Lonesome Plains

Chapter 1

Brave Cheers But Many Tears

Departure

Many dear friends gathered to see us off. The tender "good-byes" were said with brave cheers in the voices, but many tears from the hearts. . . . Amid the waving of handkerchiefs and the lingering "God bless you" the stage rolled away.

Phoebe Goodell Judson

PHEBE KERRICK WAS A YOUNG TWENTY-ONE-YEAR-OLD IN 1898 when she stepped off the train from Illinois into the harsh cold and wind of a Texas Panhandle winter. The diminutive, former college science teacher and bride-to-be of pioneer Panhandle physician Dr. William Arthur Warner found herself in such a stark, remote land that she would later claim the people who followed in the settlement of West Texas were the bravest American pioneers of the twentieth century. She could only imagine the fortitude of those pioneer mothers who had preceded her.[1]

Early-nineteenth-century explorers of the Texas Panhandle and Llano Estacado found these southern regions of the Great Plains desolate wastes, totally unsuited for cultivation.[2] Barren, uninhabited solitudes, they were destined to remain uninhabited forever.[3] The Panhandle and southern plains of West Texas remained primitive and largely unsettled until the latter nineteenth and early twentieth centuries in part because the region still suffered under its image as the southernmost portion of the Great American Desert.[4] For the first half of the nineteenth century, and in some sections of the country following the Civil War, the existence of an immense desert east of the Rockies was a reality in the minds of most people at that time.[5] As late as 1908 William Hard, freelance writer and pioneer radio news commentator, stated that the American people were then witness to one of the most heroic and spectacular victories over the forces of nature ever achieved by civilized man—the conquest of this great desert.[6] The plains was one of the great terrors, one of the great wastelands of the world. When our ancestors gazed westward across the Mississippi and Missouri, they literally took it for granted that they were looking at a desert. Whereas today we see names like "Nebraska," "Oklahoma," "Salt Lake City," and "Fargo," our forebears saw on their maps in bold, forbidding type the words, "Great American Desert." Farmers would take one look at the treeless terrain and conclude that land not fit to grow trees was not fit to grow anything. It was a useless expanse of dried prairie grass, thorny cactus, gnarled mesquite, and flying sand. Hard was convinced that the conquest of this sterile American desert was a miracle, a feat more important even than the Panama Canal, then under construction. It was "perhaps the greatest achievement in American history." The great desert was "roused . . . from its swoon of brooding centuries."[7]

Distances were generally not as far, travel was faster and less hazardous, and separations not necessarily as permanent when West Texas was settled toward the end of the nineteenth century. By 1910 a railroad was serving all but four of the twenty-six counties in the Panhandle.[8] Nevertheless, for many turn-of-the-century settlers an apprehensive view of West Texas was not uncommon. Heading southwest into this wild and unsettled land was an uncertain and hazardous step into the unknown. Even in 1902 a wagon trip of fewer than two hundred miles across Texas was like feeling one's way in the dark, never knowing what might be encountered next.[9] One 1882 newcomer from

England confessed that her interest in the western United States had been stimulated by reading romantic western stories, but when she reached her destination in the "terribly wild" Texas Panhandle she felt she was on the very western edge of the world.[10]

In light of the perceived risks, family and friends might put up all manner of discouragements and obstructions to dissuade migration. J. T. Griswold arrived in Texas in 1891, straight out of an Alabama college. He believed that this was where he wanted to begin his preaching ministry, but when he shared his dreams with fellow students they reacted with alarm: "You are crazy, boy! That is nothing but a desert. There are no people out there, and why throw away your life? You will either starve to death or freeze to death."[11] Mrs. N. S. Bagwell was eleven years old when her family left Tennessee for Texas in 1878, and the comments she heard were grim: Go to Texas and you might be killed.[12] In 1888 friends cautioned Isaac N. White about leaving Kansas for Texas with five daughters. Taking so many girls to a land where there was no one but cowboys was irresponsible.[13]

Mary Blankenship and her husband, sharecroppers near Stephenville, Texas, left in 1901 to relocate on the South Plains near Lubbock. She remembered the friends and family who saw them off, how they wished them Godspeed but predicted that they would be back in three months. Some friends were more generous and gave them a year, but few thought they would stay the course. "All had heard of the loneliness of the country in which we were to take our stand to live and die."[14]

Although nineteenth-century American farmers were predisposed to moving, as were job-seeking urban youth of the same era, like other Americans they were accustomed to being a part of a region, a small community or kinship network.[15] They shared common values, social activities, customs, and traditions. Births, weddings, and deaths were community experiences. They knew one another's tragedies. Families called upon each other in times of crisis. They prayed together; they celebrated together. Leaving such a harbor was understandably wrenching.[16]

Wagon train to Plainview area, circa 1904.
Courtesy Research Center, Panhandle-Plains Historical Museum

It was not easy to leave family homesteads. Recollections of home conjured up memories not only of those who sat around the hearth, but also of those who slept in death.[17] It was excruciating to leave the graves of family, especially those of children. There was regret over having to abandon personal keepsakes and possessions of sentimental value. Wagons were no more than ten to fifteen feet long and four to five feet wide; the wagon box two to five feet deep.[18] All of the family's necessities for traveling and settlement had to fit into this limited space, so items to be packed were carefully selected. There might not be room for family heirlooms and treasures. One 1900 West Texas settler said people think that just because someone was a pioneer they ought to have lots of antiques. But in a wagon they carried only those goods required to live, nothing unnecessary.[19]

Distant travel in a loaded wagon was not easy. A slow, tiresome ordeal plagued with hardships, it tested the mettle of even the stoutest pioneer.[20] Shorter trips of fewer than two weeks could also be wearisome due to illness, the weather, flies, mosquitoes, and other discomforts.[21] Many had to travel after harvesting and disposing of crops on the land they were leaving, yet before it was too late to erect some kind of shelter, plow and seed their new fields.[22] This meant that they were invariably en route between November and February, the coldest months of the year.

Gracy Henderson was a child when in 1888 his family moved from Central Texas to the Panhandle: "I can still feel the jog, jog, jog and the creak, creak, creak of the wheels; 'going out west' wasn't all that Pa had pictured."[23] Mary Brothers grew up on the Pecos River in

New Mexico. The sound of the "clop, clop, clop" of the horses was not to be forgotten. A turn-of-the-century wagon trip of only sixty miles, she wrote, could seem like a thousand. "The idea that life in the open—all meals prepared over a campfire, your bed on the ground—is a big picnic is a very erroneous one."[24]

What Phebe Warner found most difficult to imagine, however, was the break early settlers were forced to make with family and home. "Have your ever tried," she asks, "to picture in your imagination and feel in your soul what such partings must have meant to our pioneer mothers?"[25] The journey began in an emotional void like death itself, and it was this sense of finality that made the moment of last good-byes so troublesome.[26] Few could ever expect to return to scenes of their childhood and youth. There were no hopes of returning home for Christmas or going back for the funerals of loved ones, so leave-takings were poignant occasions.[27] Some of the most graphic accounts of parting come from diaries and journals of mid-nineteenth-century overland migrants. The emotions of overlanders like Lodisa Frizzell or members of the Scott wagon train, Mrs. Warner would have found almost impossible to comprehend.

Lodisa Frizzell crossed the plains for California in 1852. She is an often-quoted pioneer who recalled the moment of separation. "Who is there that does not recollect their first night when started on a long journey, the wellknown [*sic*] voices of our friends still ring in our ears . . . & that last seperating [*sic*] word *Farewell!* sinks deeply into the heart. It may be the last we may ever hear from some or all of them. . . . there can be no more solemn scene of parting only at death; for how many are now sleeping in death on the lonely plains whose Farewell was indeed their last."[28]

Catherine Scott Coburn was thirteen years old when in 1852 her family and four other families left Illinois in an Oregon-bound wagon train. Throughout the winter preceding the April morning when the trip began, the fingers of women and girls were busy preparing additional stores of bedding and blankets, stockings and sunbonnets, hickory shirts and gingham aprons. "Ah! the tears that fell upon these garments, fashioned with trembling fingers by the flaring light of tallow candles; the heartaches that were stitched and knitted and woven into them." She wrote about that trying morning of final good-byes, about the men with their forced show of indifference walking beside sluggish oxen, though from time to time the back of a brawny hand was brushed quickly across the eyes. She described quietly weeping women and sobbing children, their flushed, tear-streaked faces peering through the opening in the wagon covers. An aged grandfather stood at his gate as the wagons filed past, one trembling hand shaded his eyes, the other clutched a red handkerchief.[29] It was to be a journey, Coburn wrote, that promised no return.

TURN-OF-THE-CENTURY MIGRATION TO WEST TEXAS WAS NOT SO final, the option to retrace one's steps and return home a more realistic possibility. In August of 1902 David and May Scott and their four children left Stephens County, Texas, for Floyd County in West Texas. May was in poor health and the high winds, strangeness, and vastness of the bleak plains were too much for her fragile nerves. In short time she was besieged by homesickness and longed to return to the family and familiar surroundings left behind. The Scotts, therefore, made plans to move back to Stephens County as soon as school was out the following spring, only months after arriving. An epidemic of whooping cough, however, led to the death of an infant, and this tragedy changed the life course of the family forever. Mrs. Scott suppressed her longing for family and her aversion to the new country. She understood that life would be difficult, but there was now one thing that rooted her forever to these desolate plains. She would never forsake the tiny, freshly dug grave in the small Floydada cemetery.[30]

A family's decision to leave forever their secure web of family, friends, and community was traumatic not only for them but also for those left behind. Guilt and sorrow made it difficult to forget images of downcast faces, and that final scene of parting could haunt many waking and nighttime hours to follow.[31] Friends and neighbors might come from miles around to say their last good-byes. It was a common practice for friends to ride along with migrants and their wagon for the first several miles in a kind of extended good-bye expression. In some cases this gesture might continue for several days.[32]

Dora Merrill Stroup's family left San Saba County, Texas, in 1888 to settle near what is today Quitaque, Texas, and she remembered how hard it was to say good-bye to friends and neighbors. Her family had been gone for three days when a good friend and his small daughter, Dora's playmate, rode into their camp. He had not come to wish them well when they left because he could not bear to see them part. Shortly thereafter, though, his regret over not having bid farewell became too great. He took to the trail to see them one last time. As the neighbor prepared to return home, he asked Dora if she thought she would ever see her young friend again. Dora Merrill could not speak, but only wept.[33]

Lillian Schlissel observes that it was generally the women who apprehended leave-taking, a feature less common in the diaries of men.[34] Julie Jeffrey also notes that men were less likely to dwell on separations.[35] She suggests that perhaps the long hours of riding in the wagons contributed to women reminiscing. Men had the constant distractions of the trip—herding cattle, maintaining wagon and team, fording rivers—that allowed less time for indulging in yesterday.[36] They were in their element—the out of doors. Women, on the other hand, were displaced from the private, domestic sphere that had enveloped much of their lives in established communities.[37] It was more tormenting for them to be wrenched from the homes and household duties so integral to their identities. Then too, women were socialized to anticipate the experience of loss. They married and moved away, leaving behind family and friends, and it was permissible for them to own up to their feelings.[38] Men were expected to be stoic.

Nevertheless, men were not spared the anguish of what would be a lifelong separation from friends and relatives. They too endured the pangs of homesickness and the scenes of final farewells, and some records describe their emotions and sense of loss as the wagons began to roll.[39] The diary of James Baker, a mid-nineteenth-century migrant from Virginia and later Texas schoolteacher, spoke of the tears and farewells of "tenderhearted parents and friends," probably never to be seen again.[40] Charles Warren recalled the longing of his father, a blacksmith who arrived in the Texas Panhandle in the summer of 1889, dreaming of fields blessed with golden harvests. Regardless how promising dreams of the future were, though, there was always regret over leaving friends made by years of association. "Father was suffering such pangs of remorse at this time."[41]

> *When I think of my own native land,*
> *In a moment I seem to be there;*
> *But alas! recollection at hand*
> *Soon hurries me back to despair.*[42]

Loneliness and homesickness were often commingled emotions. Gilbert Fite maintains that the loneliness so often associated with western farms has been frequently misunderstood. He concedes that in some isolated regions pioneering families seldom saw their neighbors, but this was more the exception than the rule. Most settlers were not lonesome because of insurmountable distances from neighbors. They were lonely because they desperately missed loved ones and friends back home.[43]

Homesickness, this soul mate of frontier loneliness, was almost universal in the Texas Panhandle during the late nineteenth and early twentieth centuries. Dr. Warner began his medical practice in Claude, Texas, in 1897 and for several years was the only doctor in Armstrong County. Trips in a one-horse buggy to isolated cow camps and farms often involved distances of thirty-five miles. Phebe Warner recalled a comment he frequently made after one of these long and difficult calls to see female patients: "These women are not really sick, they are just homesick."[44]

Men were subject to the same malady. On May 25, 1907, William Tanner, southwestern cowboy and Oklahoma Territory homesteader, recorded in his diary: "Sitting on a high red hill so homesick and lonesome I could cry."[45] To be homesick for the home one no longer had was the worst of all possible torments. "Thinking of it was like hearing the clods fall on the coffin of the one dearest to you."[46]

THE DISTRESS OF SEPARATION WOULD CONTINUE TO SHADOW SETTLERS AS each wagon was loaded and each train boarded. Arriving at journey's end, adjustment to the plains of western Texas was no doubt affected in part by the lingering sorrow of last good-byes.

> *Home! Home Who can that place forget,*
> *Though severed far by sea or land,*
> *The wanderers eye is often wet,*
> *As thoughts bring back the household band,*
> *And though afar our feet may roam,*
> *Our hearts untravelled cling to home.*[47]

Chapter 2

Over the Threshold

All Things New

Nostalgia crept over us as we watched the cedar covered mounds of hills be-
hind us give way to this level plain land that had lured us away from our
beloved woods, our home folks and our comfortable living. In just eight days,
old things had passed away and all things had become new. We suddenly re-
alized that we were a very young group of pioneers removing ourselves by slow
transportation and communication from our native habitat. None had expe-
rienced this new life before us. We had stepped over the threshold into a new
world.

Mary Blankenship

RELOCATION AND SEPARATION FROM THE RELATIONSHIPS AND
familiarities of home are often associated with significant stress.
There is the strain of facing new physical conditions and customs as
well as developing new friendships. All moves, in varying degrees,
force individuals to cope with a loss of the old and known, to adapt
to the unfamiliar, and to contend with the stresses created by both
demands.[1]

Although major migrations require equally major psychological
and social readjustments, the relocation itself may be less significant
than characteristics of the individual, and perhaps even more impor-

tant, the characteristics of the new surroundings.[2] Once relocated, the individual must establish and maintain a relatively stable relationship with this new environment, especially the social or interpersonal environment.[3] But adaptation also involves bonding with the physical conditions. Resettlement requires making peace with a new land.

Craig Miner writes of the psychological impact caused by a group's sudden departure from a known locale followed by a long, difficult journey and arrival in an entirely new region.[4] One effect is a heightened sensitivity to first impressions of the new surroundings. First impressions and the arrival scene occupy a prominent place in reminiscences of pioneer women who settled on the plains, and this prominence reveals the power of their initial reactions to the new environment.[5] These first impressions had, undoubtedly, a powerful influence on early adjustment and how both men and women coped with feelings of longing and loneliness.

Despite competing desert images, West Texas, in the minds of some, was a land of magic and charm, a frontier of romance, adventure and fortune. In reality, however, the land proved kind and bountiful to some, but cruel and deceptive to others.[6] Many who sowed were not fortunate enough to reap.[7] The history of the early Texas Panhandle and northwestern Texas is one of trial and error, hope and disappointment, success and failure.[8] Like the rest of the western frontier, the land was both compelling and repelling.[9] The J. A. Willis family migrated from Illinois to west of Wichita Falls, Texas, in 1890. T. Guy Willis recalled that his dad was entranced by the new land and always spoke of Texas as God's country, but for his mother it seemed more like Satan's.[10] Willa Cather was nine when her family moved from Virginia to Nebraska in 1883. One of the nation's distinguished writers, acclaimed for her accounts about prairie life, Cather remembered Nebraska as both the happiness and the curse of her life.[11]

Pleasure was a common first reaction to West Texas. W. B. Clark, a Tennessee schoolteacher with a flair for expression, arrived in West Texas in 1890. He climbed the eastern caprock and was greeted by the "rapturous scene" of an incredibly level plains spreading before him like an enormous green carpet. The setting sun "painted one of those georgious [*sic*] pictures so ravishing in its marvellous [*sic*] beauty. The cool breeze fanned our pallid cheeks and the pure fresh air sent the blood racing through our [v]eins, and animated us with fresh vigor and exalted hopes.

"We had apparently merged into a new world; nothing approaching unto it had ever dawned upon our eyes. It is impossible to describe the sensations and emotions we experienced."[12]

Sheltering West Texas was a dome of the bluest sky and brightest stars some of the settlers had ever seen. Sunrises and sunsets were in full, unobstructed view. Elizabeth Ann Spikes, born near Dallas in 1878, moved to the plains when she was a young girl. Following her marriage to Temple Ellis the couple settled on a remote and lonely 1890s South Plains ranch near Lubbock, and she later became one of the first public school teachers in West Texas. Ellis described the grandeur of the sunrise as a picture beyond compare. It left her with the feeling that she had arrived in a land of make-believe where she might at any moment awaken to see the land and its beauty, like a child's fairy tale, vanish forever.[13] The opposing end of the day was equally spectacular. Maude Smith Galloway, a native of Missouri, settled near what is now Claude, Texas, in 1909. Despondent from the move, she stepped outside one evening and observed the sun sinking in the west. The prairie sunset was the most splendid she had ever seen. "I felt that it gave me a promise of a brighter day. I had the faith to believe that the Good Lord who had painted that sunset would give me the courage to meet the challenge and he did."[14] There was a primitive peace and beauty in the stillness of a western twilight.[15]

ED TRIGG, A MISSISSIPPIAN BY BIRTH, SPENT MUCH OF HIS EARLY years in Ellis County, Texas, but arriving in West Texas in 1889 at the age of twenty-eight with a couple of health-seeking friends was an occasion for celebration. When he saw the beautiful country, the fertile plains alive with antelope, he pulled off his hat and waved good-bye to the long sack and cotton patch. It was the dream of a young man come true.[16] For his companions, though, beauty was less in the seen than the unseen—the clean, dry air.

It was a common nineteenth-century belief that diseases often resulted from contaminated and moisture-laden air, and if bad air could account for poor health, then clean air ought to be an effective remedy.[17] Because physicians knew of dependable medications for so few serious diseases, many had greater confidence in healthy climates than in specific medicines.[18] Extended journeys or changes of residence were recommended for even the most hopeless of cases.[19] Sea voyages and overland trips were two types of travel prescribed, but these therapies were expensive and inconvenient. For some, relocation seemed the only alternative.

Travelers and explorers in the first half of the nineteenth century returned home with praise for the healthy climate of the plains, and by the late 1830s the sanative benefits of the Great American Desert were acclaimed by patients and doctors alike.[20] The healthfulness of plains travel was eagerly advertised to the rest of the nation in medical treatises, travelogs, and newspaper articles.[21] The clean air was said to enhance health and ward off the chills and fever of malaria, so common in the Mississippi Basin. Certainly it would offer hope to the tubercular sufferers in the eastern sweatshops and slums.[22] Railroad companies promoted the West as a panacea for all kinds of physical ills.[23] By mid-century, then, doctors were pointing families with frail and sickly children and even their sickest patients to the plains, mountains, and deserts of the west.[24] It was a desperate attempt to save lives, a prescription of last resort.

Although California and Colorado were first choices for health seekers, the broad stretch of prairies, plains, and deserts ranging from lower California to San Antonio became popular for its climatic relief. It is estimated that up to twenty-five percent of those who settled in the Southwest in the nineteenth century did so for reasons of health, a motive second only to land in attracting settlers, and by the turn of the century health seekers were as thick as home seekers in the Texas Panhandle.[25]

West Texas, with its perennial sunshine, arid atmosphere, constant temperatures, and mild seasons became a haven for those seeking improved health.[26] One youth had finished high school and was on his way to college when he got to "coughin'." His dad sent him to find work on a West Texas ranch.[27] The ranch cure, a combination of high, dry air and rigorous, outdoor work, was regarded by some as the treatment of choice for men with tubercular disease. "It will make a new man of you" became a confident promise, but as increasing numbers of sufferers hastened to try this manly cure for themselves they became no small problem for the ranchers.[28] Working cattle ranches could not be casually transformed into working health resorts. The tide of sick even created problems for the state.

Much of Texas enjoyed the reputation of favorable climates. Claims about the health-giving virtues of the state had been promoted as early as 1828.[29] Texas became such a popular destination for victims of pulmonary disease that a 1909 issue of the *Journal of the American Medical Association* sounded the warning—"Consumptives Unwelcome in Texas."[30] An official release from the state's chief health officer served notice that Texas could no longer cope with the tuberculosis problem. So many victims had been sent to the state that native Texans were contracting the disease, and public health was endangered.

Texas was so healthful, some joshed, that it was almost impossible to die in the state. Travelers approaching San Antonio, so one story went, met three disconsolate-looking fellows hurrying from the city. Asked what was wrong and where they were headed, the men said they had met with reverses—they wanted to die, and they were going someplace where they *could* die.[31] Maybe it was the pure, dry air, or possibly the lime in the water that led people to say nobody ever died in West Texas, "They just 'dried up and blowed away.'"[32] In 1890 it was boasted there was no cemetery and no graves in Potter

County, Texas, and only one grave could be found in adjoining Randall County.[33] People liked to say the country was so wonderful and so healthy that no one could die a natural death. With such hope and opportunity, death should have no place.[34]

The most convincing evidence about western climates came from the recovered sick themselves. Some, regarded by eastern friends as hopeless and soon to be claimed by respiratory diseases, returned to their homes after only a brief trip west and astounded everyone with their new-found health.[35] Folks would arrive bed-ridden in advanced stages of illness and with every expectation of dying.[36] Not only did they survive, but many lived to make significant contributions to the region. Dabney White came to West Texas in the 1880s "with lungs that were bleeding and a head without any hope therein of ever getting well. Others came here with similar minds and bodies."[37] White enjoyed a complete recovery, however, became a Texas Ranger, and lived to write about his experiences many years later. Herbert Timmons's ailing father thought he had come to West Texas to die, but he became so preoccupied in establishing a new home that he forgot about his failed health and enjoyed a full life for another thirty years.[38] "People who came here to live, died," one Panhandle health seeker said, "and those who came here to die, lived."[39]

For Wallace Stegner it is not hills and mountains that are eternal. Creation abhors an elevation as much as it detests a vacuum. No sooner is a knoll upraised than the erosive forces of nature begin wearing it down. "Eternity is a peneplain."[40] Some newcomers found the eternal peneplain of West Texas to be not an occasion of beauty and happiness but a valley of despair. The general character of the plains was one of sadness, even melancholy, a land that appeared grieving over something forever lost.[41]

> *I can imagine quite easily ending up*
> *In a decaying port on a desolate coast,*
> *Cadging drinks from the unwary, a quarrelsome,*
> *Disreputable old man; I can picture*

A second childhood in a valley, scribbling
    Reams of edifying and unreadable verse;
But I cannot see a plain without a shudder;—
    "O God, please, please, don't ever make me live there."[42]

Galloway said settling in the Panhandle was one of the hardest moments of her life to that point. She stood in the door gazing on the remote horizon and thought of the women who had preceded her, living in covered wagons and dugouts. They would not have considered her a pioneer, but she certainly felt like one. While standing there preoccupied, the first coyote she had ever seen came within a few yards of the door. He looked around as if surprised, as though these settlers had encroached on his domain. "He raised his head and let out the most weird and hysterical howl I had ever heard. I thought, 'Why didn't you let me do that? I have more to howl about than you have.'"[43]

Opal Berryman was the eight-year-old daughter of a pioneer preacher who settled in West Texas in 1905. She wrote of her first staggering view of the Llano Estacado. No tree worthy of the name could be found on the knotty fabric of earth, and every indigenous plant of any size was covered with spines and thorns. In order to survive, small animals were forced to take refuge underground.[44] It was a neglected, stubborn, forgotten land.[45] The vast emptiness of the Llano Estacado could even leave a fearful first impression.[46] The observation was made in more than one document that on the open plains there were more rivers and less water, more cows and less milk or butter, and you can see farther while observing less than in any other place on earth.

S. B. Fedric described himself as a sap oak boy straight from the pine hills of Mississippi who found the Texas Panhandle in the 1870s uncertain and risky, a forlorn, lonesome, and desolate waste.[47] C. E. Cheyne remembered his first view of the plains in the 1880s after he left Montague County in northern Texas. People, he said, did not think very favorably of the plains in those days. "The general idea was that a country was not much good where a man could ride a horse all day without getting a drink of water. . . . These plains were a barren, lonesome-looking country the first time I saw them with nothing much except horses, cattle, antelopes, jackrabbits, and coyotes living on them."[48] Bald, somber, a treeless infinity, Kansas was described by Willa Cather "as naked as the back of your hand."[49]

Perhaps some of the initial uneasiness with West Texas, as was true of the broader plains, derived from a feeling of insignificance. The land seemed to convey an attitude of indifference. One mid-nineteenth-century overland traveler felt like a mere speck as she crossed the enormous breadth of the plains.[50] Describing the northern plains, Stegner says: "The world is very large, the sky even larger, and you are very small."[51] With its obscure, receding horizons and limitless distances, the plains conveyed to settlers the impression that they were rather inconsequential. Even today, David Dary says, men ponder the vastness, the silence and solitude of the plains and question why it affects them as it does. It is a question that may remain forever unanswered.[52] In a paper presented to a 1922 Fourth of July celebration, Mrs. T. W. Tomlinson recalled settling in Swisher County, Texas, in 1893 and her first reaction to the lonely-looking country. "One was made to feel," she said, "that we were such a small atom in this great universe, and could fill such a small part of the vacant space around us."[53]

Elizabeth Hampsten suspects that for some northern plains women houses became a fortification against the great out of doors.[54] Presumably, their fears of the awesome space made it more difficult to think about venturing out into the open. There was a certain security within the tight, cramped enclosure of the dwellings, a protection from the intimidating sweep beyond the walls.

West Texas was a country of equally staggering distances. V. H. Whitlock, a native of the Staked Plains of western Texas and eastern New Mexico, observed that a rider could cover mile upon endless mile toward the obscure, distant horizon, yet never reach it.[55] One woman became disheartened after she left a small West Texas community in 1896 to continue her trip in the Panhandle. She soon discovered that the country was simply becoming larger and larger and there was absolutely nothing to be seen other than a limitless sea of grass.[56] It was like being absorbed in an earthly infinity. Mitch Bell, Briscoe County, Texas, rancher, said his first impression in 1884 was of a land "Plenty wide open for a seasoned plainsman, but for a bug-eyed tenderfoot—Well, it just didn't have any boundary at all."[57]

A. C. Greene describes the "washed-out looking eyes" of fellow West Texans, eyes accustomed to focusing on vastness.[58] Nellie Spikes had earlier noticed that same look in the eyes of old West Texas settlers attending a 1936 reunion. It was a distant, faraway gaze acquired from a lifetime on the prairies, eyes habituated by years of staring out over wide expanses of grass.[59]

In a 1927 interview, American artist John Noble recalled the plains of his native Kansas. One looked out into space, on and on and on, almost beyond time itself, and all that could be seen was the rise and swell of the land. There was always more and more grass—"the monotonous, endless grass."[60] Noble's interview included a discussion of his developing awareness that the vastness and overwhelming power of the prairie was in its magnitude much the same as the sea. Not only Noble's Kansas, there was also Nebraska:

> *In her horizons, limitless and vast*
> *Her plains that storm the senses like the sea.*[61]

There was a visual and psychological relationship between plains and ocean. In 1968 our family moved to Amarillo from Galveston, where we lived only a couple of blocks from the beach. Our oldest daughter, Amy, was not yet four years old, and at one point on Texas Highway 70, between Abilene and Turkey, she looked out of the window at the vast expanse of treeless terrain and wanted to know, "Is that the water?" It was in prairie schooners that settlers crossed this sea of wind-troubled grass, undulating and swaying like waves in a storm, so little wonder that the musty canvas and rolling motion of the wagon could contribute to bouts of dizziness and nausea akin to sea sickness. Like the ocean, the plains could be a veritable panorama of nature in its wildest meteorological moods.[62] Hamlin Garland, a native of the Iowa prairies, was aware of the brooding potential within this range of tempers:

> *The plain has moods like the sea;*
>
> *It grows dark; like the sea*
> *It holds no shelter.*[63]

In such an environment the settler could feel as lonely as a ship missing at sea, as cut off from the world as one stranded on some lonely, distant island lost in the ocean.[64]

Settlers were tortured by the unrelenting winds, a feature shared in common with the sea.[65] Incessant. Wearying. Invariable. The West Texas wind blew furiously, month after month. Like the winds of the greater plains, it wailed "like a woman in woe."[66] It howled like wolves of the night, muttered and growled "like a lion in lair."[67] Duff Green, a northeastern Texas native who migrated to West Texas in 1889, wrote of the volatility of the wind when it went on a rampage and lost its reason of course and direction.[68] It was a pushing, shouldering wind; one that stiffened the hair and rattled the eyes. Inescapable, the settler had to lean against it, squint into it.[69]

> *Do you fear the force of the wind—*
> *The slash of the rain?*
> *Go face them and fight them;*
> *Go hungry and cold like the wolf,*
> *Go wade like the crane;*
> *The palms of your hands will thicken,*
> *The skin of your forehead tan,*
> *You'll be ragged and swarthy and weary,*
> *But you'll walk like a man!*[70]

For many women, though, the West Texas wind was anything but ennobling. It was the sound of isolation and loneliness. "On the plains where the wind like a mourner moans," it was the sound of grief.[71] Scorched by the sun's rays the wind became a veritable "furnace breath," causing railways to buckle and apples to bake in the trees.[72] The temperature in this driven heat reached upwards of 140 degrees in the sun and well-nigh choked off their breath.[73] It marred their complexions.[74] It left their modest dwellings disheveled. It broke their nerves.

The combination of sand and wind could be overwhelming. Berryman remembered sandstorms rolling over the horizon, trying to beat the life out of every living thing.[75] Born in Hood County, Texas, in 1875, Lou Caraway Stubbs moved to Lubbock in 1891. Some of the West Texas sandstorms were so strong that windmills were laid flat by their force. A pioneer physician told her that the day after one of these storms there were certain women who became emotionally distraught. They would walk the floor weeping, and the doctor would be summoned to give them a calming sedative.[76]

Dorothy Scarborough never forgot her mother's vivid account of battling the 1880s West Texas elements, and these recollections provided the inspiration for her controversial 1925 novel, *The Wind*. In her story the wind becomes a demonic force set on rending its victim to pieces, a terror that might lash by day or night. It materializes as a black stallion with streaming mane and hoofs afire, speeding across the open plains. Deathless. Defiant. "A phantom, riderless horse, whom no mortal would ever ride—that no lariat flung by human hand could capture! His proud neck arching, his eyes glancing flames, he raced . . . across the sand—supernatural, satanic, the wind of the North!"[77]

Once the winds at last paused in their stampeding, when the dust had settled and the din subsided, there followed a vacuum of stillness as the prairie resumed its accustomed silence.[78] The hush was unnerving, the silence eternal. Combined with the solitude and sadness of the land, this unbroken quiet became oppressive and maddening, bearing down on the spirit like a heavy weight on the body. The deep silence exacerbated loneliness, and under the burden of

Dorothy Scarborough
when she was an English
instructor at Baylor
University, 1900–16.
*Courtesy the Texas Collection,
Baylor University*

these depressing circumstances men felt like crying aloud in a feeble
attempt to break out of the still. "Often they did so."[79]

> *So the plain lies, hushed and dumb as death,*
> *Songless and soundless.*[80]

Nightfall seemed to amplify the stillness. Concealing the prairie
under a blanket of dense, charred blackness, it brought an even
deeper sense of solitude.[81] Temple Ann Ellis wrote of days of utter
loneliness and nights of maddening melancholy. In *Road to Destiny* she
described settlers from East Texas arriving on the plains, their wagon
stopping at sunset. The darkness and the loneliness of the land cast

its spell, and following supper it seemed that for no reason at all everyone became strangely quiet. Tired children were tucked in their
bedrolls, then older members of the family sat silently around smol-
dering embers of the campfire, each lost in thought, all feeling homesick and very lonely.[82]

Some of the softer, gentle sounds of night were reassuring: the
swishing of tall prairie grass, the "chirr" of the crickets, the lowing of
the herd. Other sounds, though, were unsettling. The howling of the
wolves was unearthly, leaving a chill in the darkness. John Lyles, a native of Archer County, southwest of Wichita Falls, Texas, could remember few sounds more terrifying than the nighttime cries of a
downed calf being eaten alive by wolves.[83] One early West Texas
settler remembered lonely nights and the yelping of a coyote on a
neighboring hill, the discord of his yelps resounding for miles. In the
solitude of the night, he said, it became a discordant cry from illim-
itable space, sounding as though all the evil spirits of darkness had
gathered in augmentative council.[84]

IN 1872 J. H. TICE PUBLISHED HIS OBSERVATIONS OF TRAVELS
through Kansas and Colorado made the preceding year. At the close
of one long, weary day riding the rails he logged his final comments
before retiring. It was becoming dark and a thick dusk had settled on
the plains. The loneliness of the landscape, the somber appearance of
the sky masked by the grayish haze became unsettling and left a
vague sense of restless anxiety. As the pall of darkness settled around
him, Tice saw the engine, like a monster spewing smoke and flame,
reflecting shafts of light off the heavy haze. All else was but impene-
trable gloom and darkness. "I felt as though we had left the coasts of
light, and Milton's description of the arch fiend's flight through the
domains of Chaos vividly recurred to me:

> '*On he fares, through a dark,*
> *Illimitable ocean, without bound,*

Without dimension; a vast vacuity, where
Length, breadth, hight [sic], time and place are lost.'"[85]

Crossing the threshold into the severe world of West Texas, some pioneers found little comfort for their lonely, homesick spirits. Lonely settler was indifferently received by an equally lonely land.

Chapter 3

Fearful Solitude

This is solitude—anxious, fearful solitude! "O, God forsake us not utterly!"

Miriam Davis Colt

ARRIVING IN FORT WORTH IN 1850, H. G. BEDFORD FOUND THE country for hundreds of miles to the east very sparsely settled. Farther west there was no one for thousands of miles. "Everybody you met were glad to see you and you were glad to see them. We didn't meet people often enough to get tired of them, and in this wild and unsettled country we were a sort of mutual protection to each other."[1]

The landscape was much the same in 1879 when James Nunn, Sr., and his brothers began driving cattle from Washington County to Scurry County in West Texas: "the only settlers here then were buffalo hunters and supply people—there was 'no nothing' here but grass, prairie dogs, buffalo, coyotes, lobo wolves, and some wild cats and bears. We turned our cattle loose on free grass among the buffalo."[2] Over the entire year Nunn saw only three women. "Women had terrible times in those days," he said. "It was thirty miles to the nearest doctor, and there were no schools, churches or 'no nothing.'"[3]

Western Texas and eastern New Mexico were two of the last

regions in the United States to be settled, and along with Colorado were meagerly populated until the early twentieth century.[4] Home seekers bound for West Texas in the late 1800s had to know they would be locating in sparsely settled territory, but few were prepared for the total emptiness that awaited them. Consequently, isolation would prove to be one of the most dreaded realities of the southern plains, even more dreadful in the entombing cold of winter.[5]

The first federal census of the Texas Panhandle conducted in 1880 recorded 1,607 residents, a population distributed over 25,610 square miles.[6] The 1876 Texas legislature sectioned off twenty-six counties in the Panhandle, and although only one of these counties, Wheeler, had organized in 1880, census numbers were, nevertheless, reported along these legislated lines.[7] No one lived in six of the counties. Seven counties had populations of from 3 to 25, and nine other counties contained but 28 to 100 residents. Only four counties recorded more than 100 people, with Wheeler County boasting a grand total of 512.

People might know not only everyone living in their own county, but everyone in adjoining counties.[8] John Robert Henry came to Texas from Mississippi in 1883, and he claimed to know at one time every man, woman, and child in nine counties. "Now I don't even know who in hell lives across the street from me."[9]

Men were the first attracted to the Southwest, and some found the barren openness to their liking.

> *I liked my fellow man the best*
> *When he was scattered some.*
> *When my old soul haunts range and rest*
> *Beyond the last divide,*
> *Just plant me on some strip of west*
> *That's sunny, lone and wide.*[10]

Women, however, were more reluctant to set roots in such isolated conditions, as Nunn discovered.[11] W. M. Graham could remember but two women in the Crosby County, Texas, area around 1877 and neither was a permanent resident. One was on her way to New Mexico and the other was from California with her husband buying buffalo hides for robes.[12] An 1879 Fourth of July ranch picnic near the current community of Chillicothe, Texas, was attended by five women, all the women within the three-county area.[13] The population of the Texas Panhandle in 1880 included only 400 females, many of whom were children, and a man might take mischievous pleasure in introducing his wife as the best-looking woman in the county, when she was, in fact, the only woman in the county.[14]

Ed Baird heard stories of the opportunities for a young man on the plains, so in 1883 he went west to practice his trade, cow work. Baird regretted that he was not an artist so he could paint a picture of the first woman he ever saw in the Panhandle, which was in 1887. She was the wife of the bookkeeper for the Pancake Ranch, and "We were hoo-dooed when we first saw her! The first one I had seen in four years and for some of the boys it numbered ten years."[15]

In 1895, no more than a dozen women could be found in some counties of the Llano Estacado, and in other sections of West Texas women might go for months without seeing another woman.[16] Following her marriage in 1900, Sarah Willoughby lived on the Rocking Chair Ranch in Collingsworth County, Texas, and for two years she never left home. During this entire period she saw no one except family members and an occasional cowboy who might drop by for a meal.[17]

Young, single women were even more rare, like "Angel's visits, few and far between." The H. A. Russell family came to the Panhandle in 1879, and the caption under a photograph of the family published over fifty years later indicated that Molly, the oldest child, was the only girl in ten counties.[18] In 1880 there were only 40 single females between the ages of fifteen and thirty in the entire Texas Panhandle.[19] There were 550 single males (one was a widower) in this same age range, making for a 1:14 ratio of females to males. In Armstrong County there were few single girls within a radius of three hundred miles, and this population pattern continued into the early 1890s.[20]

J. W. Bradly arrived on the plains in 1887, and looking back across fifty years he could still recall not only the few families that had girls, but also the exact years when those families had arrived.[21] Claude Neelley was ten when his family settled near Olney, Texas, in 1879, and he spoke of the youthful excitement created by the arrival of a new family with two young girls. "Back in those days our gregarious instincts were ever alert for contacts with others of our kind."[22] Given the limited presence of young women, it is not surprising, therefore, to learn that cowboys would ride miles out of their way just for the pleasure of a brief glimpse at a girl.[23]

Having close neighbors, male or female, was in some areas of West Texas an unknown luxury, and Temple Ann Ellis offered one explanation for how this early isolation evolved. Most men who arrived in the late nineteenth century came to build up what was popularly called a stock farm. To do this the rancher selected a remote section as far from settlement as possible. He wanted ample open range away from roads or freight trails, hoping to insure that no one would ride by and intentionally or unintentionally disturb his herd. Everyone wanted unlimited free grass where fences were not required to keep their cattle from mingling with those of neighboring ranches. It is easy to see, Ellis concluded, how this pattern isolated ranching families.[24]

Even though the closest families might live thirty to forty miles away, they were called neighbors.[25] Agnes Cleaveland referred to their "twenty-miles-away neighbors" in New Mexico.[26] The Matador Ranch was fifty to sixty miles from her home in Blanco Canyon, but Elizabeth Smith still spoke of Mrs. Harry Campbell of the Matador as a good neighbor.[27] One cowboy reminisced about the distances between folks: "To look back on it now it was a lonesome land. Our nearest neighbors were: T Anchor Ranch—25 miles, Goodnight headquarters—35 miles, Clarendon—45 miles."[28]

Mary Blankenship was forewarned of the isolation that awaited her on the South Plains in 1901, but there were times when she and her husband thought that they were the only people inhabiting the earth. The solitude almost panicked them into returning home and left her with endless hours and days "to be still and know God," her one refuge.[29] Some plains settlers felt even beyond the reach of God.[30]

Toward the end of the century the distances between homes had narrowed to more like five to twenty-five miles, but even though neighbors might be closer, they still had relatively little contact.[31] People living within fifteen or twenty miles of one another were often unaware of the others' presence, the discovery at times made only after a chance meeting on the open range.[32] Gatherings would attract settlers from a broad area. John and Maggie Weatherly settled in Hutchinson County, Texas, in January, 1898. A Fourth of July picnic six months later attracted about forty people, the entire population of Hutchinson and Carson Counties. It was there they met their closest neighbor for the first time.[33] Months might pass before neighbors were seen again.

James Vardy, a native Texan who first visited the Panhandle in 1878, recalled people taking what today would be called a vacation. They would spend a day and night with one family then move on to the next house until they made the rounds.[34] For the most part, though, visitors were a rare and welcome treat.[35] In 1900 Charley Cowan and his family moved to a ranch north of Miami, Texas; their nearest neighbor lived eight miles away. One year they had only two visitors over the entire year.[36] Sallie Matthews's family settled on a distant ranch so far removed from any road that if anyone came, it was solely for the purpose of visiting them.[37] She described a relative's isolated ranch in the Davis Mountains, a ranch named "South Africa" because it was so remote.

Children were especially excited by visitors. Eula Cave remembered the covered wagons that camped as late as 1922 by the side of their house in Olton. "They would get their water from our well and I loved playing with their kids."[38] These wagon trains that stopped over were one of the biggest events in the lives of isolated children. Travelers swarmed all over the place, making innumerable demands—wanting to cook biscuits on the stove, asking for milk, butter, and vegetables. They consumed every drop of milk, sweet and sour, and every ounce of butter. Tomorrow, however, there would be more milk and more butter, but it might be months before there would again be anyone with whom to socialize.[39]

Children were not the only ones excited by a new face. Pioneers have been labeled ill-mannered inquisitors who showed little respect for privacy as they sought to relieve the isolation of their lives.[40] Frank Coe came by wagon train from Missouri to New Mexico in 1871, settling on the Ruidoso River between Lincoln and Roswell. Wilbur Coe remembered his father keeping a saddled pony tied to a cottonwood tree for use in an emergency. Any time a traveler rode by and failed to stop, Mr. Coe would jump on the pony and overtake him to find out the latest news. If the traveler proved interesting enough he was invited back to the house to camp and stay a spell while Mr. Coe "simmered" him under the shade of the trees. He would find out where the stranger was from, where he was headed, and what he hoped to find when he got there—all matters of interest to an isolated pioneer family.[41]

Nunn said strangers were always treated kindly because settlers were so happy to see anybody ride up—"even a dog from home looked good to us."[42] Ella and Tom Bird were so isolated that they were glad to see anything that resembled the shape of a human being. She recalled that her husband was so lonely at times he would say, "I would be proud to see even one of our old neighbors' dogs come in." Once in a while when out riding they would come across fresh wagon tracks. Excited, they followed the tracks for several miles, hoping to overtake the wagon and see who it was.[43] A passing traveler once commented that he did not understand how anyone was able to survive such total seclusion and solitude. If it were he, he would forget how to talk.

If plains isolation made for embarrassing inquisitiveness, it also made for generous hospitality.[44] The country was famous for its graciousness. The door was always open, regardless of the time—day or night. Henry Frye, Wheeler County, Texas, pioneer, had been gone for several weeks looking for cattle when late one night Lulu Frye, his wife, heard someone calling: "Hello, hello." The caller was Charles Goodnight, the first rancher to start large-scale cattle feeding in the Palo Duro Canyon in 1876. Goodnight and a companion had traveled all day, their team was exhausted, and they too were given out and famished. They needed something to eat and a place to sleep. Although it was midnight, Mrs. Frye was so glad to see them that she cooked their supper and apologized for not having anything better to serve. She sent them to sleep on the split-pole, prairie-hay bed, and next morning they boasted it was the best bed and breakfast they had ever enjoyed. "They went on their way and I felt almost lonely enough to cry. That was just how welcome visitors always were in those days."[45]

Settlers had few close neighbors and saw so few strangers because of the scope of the territory, an expanse that often resulted in a degree of isolation virtually impossible for contemporaries to grasp.[46] The 1880 Texas Panhandle, for example, with its 26,000 square miles and 1,600 residents had a per square mile population density of only .06 person.[47] Density in 1890 was only .37 person per square mile and in 1900, .83.[48] Ira Taylor, born in 1896 and the last known living hand from the XIT Ranch said, "They just had two kinds of time them days, sun time and railroad [time], and we went by sun time because we's closer to the sun than we was the railroad."[49] When interviewed in 1984, Joe Sheldon had resided in the Panhandle longer than any other living person. Shelton recalled talk of somebody moving to Hereford, Texas. "I remember that real well, and I asked 'em how far it was. I's just a little ol' kid. Told [me] it is a hundred miles. Well golly, I thought a hundred miles was clear out of the world."[50] One early-day cowboy remembered the distances covered on horseback: "I tell you ma'm it was a long way between drinks."[51]

Because of the distances and travel conditions, people tended to remain homebound. Tom Black's mother died when he was born in 1897, and he was sent to live with an aunt in Altus, Oklahoma. Black was fifteen before he ever saw a crowd of more than fifty people. "The way it used to be out here in this country, a feller never got five miles

from home. Hell, . . . you didn't get five miles from home in ten years.
Then we didn't have bridges across the river. Hell, there wasn't no
bridges anywhere. If you couldn't swim or ride a horse or walk across
or go across with a team swimming the water or something you didn't
get across. They didn't have no roads either." Black remembered one
day-long, fifteen-mile trip to Silverton, Texas, in the early 1900s.
There was a crowd around the courthouse, the biggest crowd he had
ever seen. As a young country boy who had never been to town,
"It looked to me like, *oh my*, something big happening here. About
seventy-five people I guess. All the people in the county were there."[52]

Alabama-born Sarah Coleman, an 1892 Panhandle arrival, was
another who remembered travel conditions. Settlers would have to
strike out across the prairie and trust their sense of direction. There
were no landmarks other than the wind-swept hills, and they all
looked alike. Mrs. Coleman became so bewildered whenever she did
leave home that she seldom ventured out.[53] Travel in West Texas was
difficult, in part, because the region remained much like it was when
first settled in 1876, a veritable "cartographic void."[54] Henry Boydstun brought his family from Johnson County, Texas, to the Panhandle in 1889. An account of their trip provided by his daughter
makes clear just how easy it was to get on a wrong road or find oneself
on a trail that would eventually play out, ending up nowhere out on
the open plains.[55]

Distances of forty or fifty miles by current standards might seem
rather insignificant, but as noted, trips in a wagon were not to be taken
lightly. Those who did travel saw few signs of human existence along
the way.

> *Down a lonely road, through a lonely land*
> *With seldom a clasp of [a] friendly hand.*[56]

Houses were as scarce as a hen's teeth, so a traveler crossing West
Texas was lucky to see any kind of dwelling during an entire day.[57]
One pioneer remembered moving from Temple, Oklahoma, to Floyd

County, Texas, in two covered wagons in 1908. The journey lasted seven days, and there were days they never passed a dwelling or saw another person. The only people they usually chanced upon were freighters hauling supplies.[58] Before moving to West Texas in 1884 George Hunt had lived several years on the prairies of Iowa and Kansas, so he had some familiarity with the appearance of the greater plains. West Texas was different, however, due to the enormity of the territory and the fact that there were almost no settlements. Apart from his small South Plains colony, there was not one farmhouse, church, or school building—not even a fence—across the surrounding plains.[59]

Towns or trading posts were often so far away that pantries were replenished only once a year, and toward year's end entire areas might run short of provisions.[60] In some sections, one of these trips might take from eight to fourteen days.[61] Runs to resupply the Frying Pan Ranch were made every six months, and under normal conditions it took ten days for the wagons to go and return. However, trips often took three weeks when the wagons had to wait for the Canadian River to recede.[62] Women typically remained at home when these drives were made, but whether they went or stayed, either option was anticipated with dread, as a real hardship.[63]

Provision runs of even shorter distances were not made casually. Joe Gibson, a 1901 native of Guthrie, Texas, said, "If you could picture living—even as we did—eighteen miles from the place where you bought your groceries and such like . . . having one, two, three, four neighbors is all that you have and our father went to town to get meat and things only when we had to have 'em."[64]

Frontier towns were by any standard modest, often little more than a small cluster of rickety, unpainted buildings. The "town" closest to Ira Ott consisted of only three or four houses.[65] Another report indicated that what was called a town might consist of fewer than half a dozen dugouts.[66] Recollections of towns with only ten to twelve houses were common, and a small frame building—little more than a shack—might have a hand-painted sign identifying it as a general

Canyon City, Texas, 1890.
Courtesy Research Center, Panhandle-Plains Historical Museum

store, hotel, or saloon. Blacksmiths and livery stables were typical businesses; in rare instances there might be a courthouse or a bank. One old-timer described frontier towns as simply a group of three or four houses, one store that carried general merchandise, one or two saloons, a blacksmith shop, and some sort of name tacked on the whole to inform folks that it was supposed to be such and such a town.[67]

These towns offered few attractions for women. They were for men, and there was little for women to do once the grocery shopping was completed.[68] The men could stand around and visit about politics and other topics or entertain themselves by pitching horseshoes and

dollars. Or, men could sit on boxes inside or in front of the stores and whittle on just about anything they could get their hands on.[69] Saloons were popular establishments, but these were sites for male socializing.[70]

If the range defined itself as what Philip Rollins called "he country in pants," then the stores in town might have appropriately borne the sign, "For Men Only."[71] Stores were a man's world. Shelves were stocked with men's items—work clothes, socks, gloves, underwear— but there were few garments for women. When a merchant received a single bolt of calico, the good news rapidly spread from ranch to ranch.[72]

Amarillo, Texas, 1895.
Courtesy Research Center, Panhandle-Plains Historical Museum

The absence of regular mail service contributed to the sense of isolation. People were cut off from their families as well as their neighbors, and this often led to anxiety about being forgotten.

> My friends, *do they now and then send*
> *A wish or a thought after me?*[73]

Ranch mails were always small, regardless how infrequent their delivery or how large the outfit. For most cowboys, letters were so rare that Edgar Bronson reported seeing men slowly turn and study an unopened envelope for half a day, wondering who it was from and what it contained.[74] There are reports of people going three, four, five months without mail or any news of the outside world.[75] N. F. Locke,

1880s Texas Ranger, put it in broader context: "Many times I have gone for ten years at a time without being in a church. I have gone as much as six months without getting any mail, and equally as long without seeing a decent woman."[76]

Sending a letter was likewise difficult. Often the only option was to ask a traveler going a certain direction to carry the mail and leave it at a designated store or ranch.[77] Young children were recruited to ride miles to deliver mail or messages, and "put a kid on a horse" was the formula for sending messages back and forth between ranches in one section of New Mexico.[78]

While the rest of his family waited in Seymour, Henry Boydstun and his oldest son, Riley, continued on to Carson County, Texas, where they began digging a dugout in preparation for the family's arrival. The emotional toll on her parents of the slow, irregular mail service was recalled by their daughter, Ora. Mrs. Boydstun would receive a letter every few days from her husband, begging her to write. All the while she was writing as fast as she could, but he was not receiving the letters. Riley commented that his father would come out of the post office without a letter, looking as though he were leaving a funeral. Their mother was tearful and frightened, imagining someone was stealing his mail and planning to kill both her husband and son, thinking possibly they had money. She had it in her mind that cattlemen and cowboys were awfully rough people, maybe intent on keeping these settlers out. "I never will forget the last letter she got from father. He was so torn up that he said in his letter, 'My God, Mary, why don't you write and let me know how your are?' Well, my mother just walked the floor and yard, and cried day and night."[79]

A SINGLE, SOLITARY EVENT OR CIRCUMSTANCE CAN AFFECT A PERSON'S mood for brief or extended periods of time, but it is equally true that state of mind is often a function of cumulative experiences and conditions. Following her father's death from an accidental gunshot wound in 1882, Agnes Cleaveland's mother bought a remote ranch southwest of Albuquerque. Cleaveland told how a couple of their horses learned to open the kitchen door and thrust their head inside for a biscuit. The horses' behavior, she suggested, was motivated by more than simply the need for a treat. "In our extreme isolation all living things seemed to want to stick together."[80] This sense of isolation was in itself enough to make for intense bouts of forlornness and depression. Compounded, however, by lingering sadness over leave-taking and reactions to the barren, uninviting surroundings of the plains, the settler became vulnerable to one of the most difficult challenges of frontier life—"the lonely homesick hours for which there was no remedy."[81]

Chapter 4

Such a Country as This
Loneliness

SATURDAY JUNE 22ND 1867:—. . . *Such a country as this I almost wish I had never seen it, if I had wings to fly I would abandon it forever, it surely is the last place on earth for a woman to live, or any one else. I dont believe it ever was intended for civilized people. . . . As my companion pressed me to his bosom and bade me goodby, I could hardly restrain my feelings, and as soon as his back was turned on the dwelling, I let the tears come freely that had been almost blinding me all day.*

Susan E. Newcomb

SPEAKER OF THE HOUSE SAM RAYBURN WAS SPENDING AN EVENING in his apartment with friends when the discussion turned to farmers and the rural way of life. Born in Tennessee in 1882, Rayburn's family had moved to Texas when he was five years old, settling on a farm near Bonham. He mostly listened until someone made a disparaging comment about farmers who spent what appeared to be too much time riding around in their automobiles. Visibly moved, Rayburn leaned forward in his chair. He said that when he went home to Bonham and saw farmers' cars parked around the courthouse square, their women-folk and children walking around window shopping or talking with neighbors, he was glad to see it even if they did not have a dime to their name. "Many a time when I was a child and lived 'way out in the country, I'd sit on the fence and wish to God that somebody would ride by on a horse or drive by in a buggy—just anything to relieve my loneliness. Loneliness consumes people. It kills 'em eventually. God help the lonely. That's why I'm glad to see farmers have cars and use 'em."[1]

There was much about the frontier plains that was disagreeable—the vacant distances, the weather, the unremitting toil, the apprehension, the constant dangers, the "savageism."[2] Many, however, found their most difficult challenge in coping with the dreadful isolation and loneliness, a challenge that called for their final reserve of moral stamina.[3] Addressing a younger generation, one pioneer was straightforward: "You, who have had no life experience, can have no conception of what the word lonely means."[4] Questioned repeatedly about the ordeals of pioneering the South Plains, Temple Ann Ellis was likewise unequivocal: loneliness was the most difficult challenge facing the pioneer woman. "It's the one memory that time can never cure."[5] For more than one frontier woman, loneliness was the "vacuum in their hearts."[6]

In literary references to the northern prairies, a land "empty as nightmare," loneliness and land are often conjoined, the inhabitants little more than solitary, vertical objects on an endless stretch of flat horizons.[7] Opal Berryman remembered as a child being very, very lonely, and it seemed impossible to separate her loneliness from the harsh, borderless West Texas landscape.[8] After living for six years on the extreme frontier of Texas, Susan Newcomb records a desperate hope that God will stretch forth His benevolent hand over the wild and destitute country and allay her enduring loneliness.[9]

The land spawned two great evils, thirst and loneliness, and the latter was a kind of social thirst, an incessant yearning for companionship, for someone to talk to.[10] Mary Blankenship remembered the absence of life and always being "starved for company and thirsty for conversation."[11] Jennie Holcomb was born in Collingsworth County,

Texas, in 1892. After at age six losing both parents within a five-month period, life in the country with an older sister's family was very forlorn. "I remember one time we had planned to go to a neighbor's and spend the day, and it was awful cold and the wind blowing. And there was a little tree out in the yard and I thought, 'Now, if I can take a string and go around and tie those limbs together we can go.' That was just my thought. I wanted to go. We went such a little."[12]

A POPULAR IMAGE OF THE WESTERN FRONTIER IS THAT OF A LONELY woman, separated from home and family, depressed by the isolation and untamed nature of the west.[13] Yet, literal isolation was more perceived than real. Isolation and loneliness are not the same. One can be lonely in a crowd. Pioneering women were seldom cut off from all human contact, being in the company of husbands, children, and possibly hired hands. On the trail there were others in the party. Still, they were lonely. They missed family and friends, but on a frontier opened and populated primarily by men, they longed for the nearness and companionship—the conversation—of other women.[14]

Pennsylvania-born Abbie Bright was twenty-one and single when she decided to see the West. She visited her brother in Kansas in 1871 and while there took 160 acres as an investment. At one point in her trip she was waiting to cross a swollen river, and because the wait might entail several days she was invited to the home of a woman who lived nearby. The woman was very friendly because she had not seen another female for weeks. Tired, Bright went to bed. After sleeping but for a short time, though, she was awakened by her host: "You have slept long enough, I am lonesome for some one [*sic*] to talk to."[15]

This need for female companionship—and nurturance—was especially acute in times of sickness. Bright's diary included the dispirited entry: "To be ill and not see a woman for a week—is hard luck."[16] Mary Boydstun lost her infant son shortly after his birth, and this sad event was then compounded by a period of infirmity during which time female company was almost nonexistent. Apart from her mother staying with the family during the weeks of her convalescence, it was more than a year before Mrs. Boydstun saw another woman.[17]

Harriette Andreadis finds a collection of women's private writings from nineteenth-century Texas often joyless.[18] Isolation and loneliness were common themes, and combined with the perceived indifference and emotional distance of their affectionless husbands, these women concluded that they, themselves, must be to blame for their miserable state. Feelings of powerlessness, depression, self-castigation, and self-denigration were pervasive. They faulted themselves for failures to live up to what were undoubtedly impossible expectations. Isolated and without resources, there were no female kin for support.[19]

The wretchedness of her lonely life and possibly some of the self-depreciation noted by Andreadis may well have led Susan Newcomb to identify with the sufferings of Christ. Her emotions seemed to well up uncontrollably as she expended herself in the words of a popular hymn:

> *Alas! and did my Saviour bleed?*
> *And did my Sovereign die?*
> *Did He devote that sacred head*
> *For such a worm as I?*
>
> *Was it for crimes that I have done*
> *He groan'd upon the tree?*
> *Amazing pity! grace unknown!*
> *And love beyond degree!*
> *Well might the sun in darkness hide,*
> *And shut his glories in*
> *When Christ the mighty Maker died,*
> *For man the creature's sin.*[20]

Often aggravating loneliness was the monotony of daily life, a perception that seems to span age and sex. Rayburn's childhood on the Texas farm was one of isolation and bitterness, and the slightest break

in the routine was of immeasurable relief.[21] A trip to the small town of
Bonham was exhilarating. Margaret Armstrong was fifteen and living
in Jack County, Texas, when she began her diary. In one entry she
recorded the event of her sister's thirteenth birthday, but added that all
days were alike in her lonely country existence.[22] The farm was hum-
drum, her days like being buried alive. A collection of letters written
by a Kansas homesteader in the late 1870s notes the tedium and slow-
ness of life, even for men.[23] William Tanner's journals make repeated
references to long, slow days, one day being much like all others.[24] The
predictability might leave the faithful diarist frustrated in attempts to
think of something new or different to record.

Andreadis elaborates on the bone-numbing drudgery and boredom, quoting from the diary of Henrietta Embree: "what a sameness
is my life—its to bed and the same worn, tired sleep—and up, feeling
worse than when I went to bed the night before . . . next morning—
Same is the first thing that welcomes me—*Same! Same!! Same!!!* and
persues [*sic*] me wherever I turn my eye—Shaw such monotony, it is
enough to drive one to despare [*sic*]. . . ."[25]

Hamlin Garland knew well the confinement and monotony of
the plains woman's life:

It was a human habitation.
It was not a prison. A prison
Resounds with songs, yells, the crash of gates,
The click of locks and grind of chains.
Voice shouts to voice. Bars do not exclude
The interchange of words.
  This was solitary confinement.

  The sun up-sprang,
Its light swept the plain like a sea
Of golden water, and the blue-gray dome
That soared above the settler's shack,
Was lighted into magical splendor.

To some worn woman
Another monotonous day was born.[26]

Interminable work and countless privations exacerbated the tedium. The plains callused settlers to hard work. It was a demanding land, a land that required the "big nerve," the "guts and determination of a giant."[27] Ira Taylor was persuasive: "It wasn't no forty hours. It was from can to can't. [You were supposed] to work just as long as you could see—and then a little longer."[28] For many settlers, frontier life operated on a fourteen-to-sixteen-hour day, seven-days-a-week schedule, quite possibly making the theme of endurance the most recurring feature of women's diaries.[29]

Women yearned for a sanctuary where the work was at last all done, and Richard Bartlett suggests that the hymns they sang as they went about their chores reveal this longing.

When at last life's day is ending,
 As the ev-'ning draweth nigh,
And our sun is slowly wending,
 Down behind the western sky.
'Twill be sweet to think of pleasures,
 That shall never know decay,
In that home of joy and splendor,
 Just beyond life's twilight gray.

Then the chorus:
Rest, sweet rest, and joy and gladness,
 Comes when toil, when toil is o'er,
Sweetest resting Comes when toil is o'er,
 'Twill be joy and rest eternal,
On the other shore.[30]

Sick and depressed, Miriam Colt watched the sun go down and asked herself, "Can this be the same sun that shines upon our Northern friends, who are enjoying blessings and comforts they know not how to appreciate?"[31] Edith Duncan Pitts wrote about the trials of her mother, Sarah Kay Duncan, and maintained it would be impossible to imagine the hardships and privations endured by West Texas women.[32] A canyon neighbor used only one needle for seven years. If a neighbor died, she did not have a dress to wear to the funeral. Another woman hung her only dress over a chair when she went to bed, but a spark from the fireplace ignited it and she had no other. The next morning she ripped apart a mattress tick to make something to wear. There were hundreds of such incidents.[33]

The world beyond the farm or ranch was the province of men. Women were homebound, men moved about.[34] They had more opportunities to get away, to ride freely across the plains. A popular image of the western frontier, on the other hand, would depict women not only as lonely, but close to home—bending over an open fire, sewing, nursing a baby or aiding the sick.[35] As indicated, the small towns offered them few attractions, and their work and responsibilities were confining. Anna Mae McManigal remembered people saying, "I knew your dad but I can't remember your mother." This was because, she explained, "Your mothers never went anywhere [and] I know why . . . I said, 'Well, she's home baking cookies and laundering.'"[36]

Joe Killough was fifteen when in 1888 he traveled by train to meet his brother in the Texas Panhandle. At one point, looking out of the window at the barren terrain, he began to cry. Years later Killough acknowledged the loneliness and confinement of women and how seldom they got to town, but another of his observations would surely generate more controversy: "We never had any discontented wives. Evidently it made them happier to have plenty of work to do and never leave home for weeks at a time."[37]

Small children and the difficulty of travel restricted women to the homestead, and because family supplies were generally hauled in by the husband and father, women and children never left home for months on end.[38] Some women might get to town but once or twice a year, sometimes not even that often. After settling in the Hereford,

Texas, area in 1891, it was seven years before one woman went to town. When she did finally go it was to have a tooth pulled.[39] For another settler, a celebration meant the opportunity to go with her husband to the small town of Mobeetie, Texas—once every two years.[40]

Sometimes it seemed to women like men were always on the road while they were left at home, alone, tending children.[41] Ella Bird remembered the dread of her husband taking a long trip and how lonely it was for her and their two children.[42] One three-month absence seemed like an eternity.

Just how material a husband was for daily companionship is seen in the 1889 diary of Emma Burns, wife of Rollie Burns, cattle driver, rancher, and cofounder of Lubbock.[43] Of her 365 brief entries, 227 focus on her husband; whether or not he is home and sometimes his activity for the day. Fifty-eight percent of her entries begin with his name: "Roley [*sic*] is home[,] raining," "Roley was home all day," "Roley worked around home," "Roley came home," "Roley has gone to line camp," "Roley branded horses."

Wives of cattle drovers spent months of anxious waiting for their husbands to return. It was rare for these women to receive a letter or other news about the trail drive, so they were often concerned about their husbands' safety.[44] Mary Blankenship granted that these drives were hard on men and cattle, but she felt they were hardest on the women left behind. "I climbed the new windmill tower many times for a lookout during their three week trip. The heavy solitude seemed unbearable without a man on the premises in such foreboding times."[45] Susan Newcomb's diary pulls together a number of factors contributing to her loneliness: "A man that drives cattle can't stay at home with his family much. The time passes slow and lonsome [*sic*] with me while he is gone."[46] At another point she writes about "the long lonsome [*sic*] days that I will have to spend here during this season. I would not mind staying if my companin [*sic*] could stay here with me. but [*sic*] he will be gone weeks at a time after his cattle."[47]

Reminiscing about early-twentieth-century farm life in West Texas and New Mexico, Maggie Lee Holden said, "We were not

West Texas windmill.
Courtesy Research Center, Panhandle-Plains Historical Museum

lonely, but were just happy in a sad sort of way."[48] For some, though, the loneliness was far more distressful. A main character in Dorothy Scarborough's novel comments that cowpunchers can find relief from their loneliness by going into town ever so often, enjoying a high lonesome and losing money at poker. "But the women can't do that, poor calicoes. They got to stay bottled up, and its liable to bust 'em, sooner or later."[49]

Without relief from the pressure of loneliness, if only for a brief time, Ellis feared she would lose her sanity. "Believe it or not, I have found myself seeking the company of cattle, I would go out to the watering places and stroll among them touching them, rubbing their hips, talking to them about their calves, asking questions which I knew they couldn't answer. Their contentment though served as balm to my tense nerves."[50] One Kansas pioneer found refuge among the flock of "wistful-faced" sheep, lying down among them for companionship when she was alone.[51]

Often Ellis climbed the windmill tower and scanned every direction, "hoping against hope that a glimpse of someone, just anyone, as they rode across the range would come into view. The sight of a human being though they were riding away from you rather than toward you would have a tendency to relieve the tenseness."[52]

Molly Goodnight took comfort in the three chickens brought to her in a sack by a cowboy. "No one can ever know how much pleasure and company they were to me," she said. "They were something I could talk to, they would run to me when I called, and follow me everywhere I went. They knew me and tried to talk to me in their language."[53] Miriam Colt was undoubtedly only one of many who found consolation in a pet. "I take little Sambo dog with me sometimes, when I go for water; for his pat, pat, pat, along in the path behind me, is another sound added to my own tread; he is really a great deal of comfort for me, makes the way seem much shorter."[54]

One woman found horseback riding a relief for her loneliness, and the firing of a shotgun relieved others, especially when the men were away.[55] Another pioneer tried to conceal her nostalgia from her husband. Longing for music, she pretended that her husband's desk was a keyboard, playing on it as though it was a piano or an organ.[56]

Although daily chores were tedious and wearisome, they could also be a distraction from loneliness. Margaret Armstrong's diary included a brief entry in December, 1873: "This is a lonely life we dont [*sic*] see a person once in six months, if we did not have a lot of house work to do we would be at a loss how to kill time."[57] Large families also provided relief.[58]

Writing about his itinerant, covered-wagon boyhood in early-twentieth-century West Texas, Paul Patterson recalled an older brother's comment. One day the brother pointed from the wagon to an abandoned nester's shack and said, "it's haunted. Full of ghosts and boogers." A second older brother agreed: "Sure enough! . . . Either that or rafters chuck full of crazy women!" Still to be convinced, the youngest asks, "Why all crazy women up in them rafters, and no crazy men?"

"Men like it out here. And don't go crazy. . . . Women don't, and they go loco from pure lonesome."[59]

As suggested, the writings of men, especially those with families, were less likely to give vent to their loneliness or homesickness.[60] There were, however, those exceptions. The diaries of William Tanner contain recurring references to his chronic loneliness.[61] He was lonely whether he was in camp, in Athens, Georgia, in Oklahoma Territory or Abilene, Texas. When in Georgia he was lonely for Texas; in Texas he was lonely for either Georgia or the Oklahoma Territory. His loneliness was associated with the weather: cold, rainy, cloudy, hot, windy. He was lonesome when herding cattle, when planting or chopping cotton, gathering grapes, reading, writing, sleeping, or sitting up with the corpse of a neighbor.

Like women, men were especially vulnerable to the depressive effects of loneliness when ill. This relationship between state of health and mood becomes evident in the 1871 diary of T. C. Oatts:

TUSDAY 8″ OF AUGST

All well except I have a Boil in my nose which is very painful . . .

WENSDAY THE 9″ OF AUGST

All well except my nose have some little fever in concequence of the boil in my nose.

THURSDAY AUGST 9ᵀᴴ [*SIC*]

Not so well this morng I have bin quite sick to day Same hed ake and my bowels out of order.

FRIDAY AUGT 11

Only Tolerable well

SATURDAY AUGT 12

Onley Tolerable well . . .

SUNDAY 13TH OF AUGST

Onley tolerable well stil complaning of Boils
Some hed ake . . .

MUNDAY 14TH AUGUST

Onely tolerable will this morng some little hed ack and my boils is
veay painful

TUSDAY 15TH AUGST—

Only tolerable well . . .

WENSDAY 16TH AUGT

Stil complaining feal quite lonsom to day . . .

THURSDAY AUGT 17

Stil complaining to day got some medisen from Doct More felt some
better about 12 oclock got a letter from my wife this eavOning feal
revived very glad to heare from Home [sic][62]

Life on the range is often thought of in terms of romance, freedom, and adventure, but for the cowboy it was forsaken, hard work.[63] A hand might operate miles from the ranch house, and an occasional visit by the foreman or ranch owner only accentuated his solitude. Arriving in West Texas in 1889 where he worked on the XIT Ranch for six years, J. H. Weems could remember none of the cowboys he knew ever carrying six-shooters. He could recall no gunfights. "They [*sic*] boys were all too glad to see one another."[64] Walter Posey was ten years old when his family moved to Floyd County, Texas, in 1891. In addition to herding cattle, he and his father drove sheep across West Texas. Asked whether they encountered trouble from the cattlemen, Posey said that boys on the ranches were all so lonesome they were glad to see anybody. They would follow his wagon all the way across a ranch just to eat with him, talk, and lie around the wagon.[65]

Mrs. Claude Boone recalled her father, Jacob Weaver, catching Texas fever around 1889 and the six-week trip from Kansas to Texas. Shortly after arrival her mother gave birth. "In the next few weeks cowboys stopped by to see us . . . but what they wanted was to see the baby. Some had not seen a little baby in twelve years and when they held him in their arms tears ran down their faces."[66]

Records from the Spur Ranch in West Texas indicate that some men would begin work on the first of the month and quit within one or two weeks. Some of these departures were due to the rugged nature of the work, others to homesickness.[67] One old cowhand suggested that the song "When the Work Is Done This Fall" was composed by cowboys longing to return home after the seasonal chores were finished.[68]

The remote, monotonous vigils of the cowhand often left him "as taciturn as an Indian."[69] His reserve and closed-mouth tendencies, especially with strangers, resulted in communication that was at best terse. Philip Rollins preferred the term "sentiousness," writing: "So adverse was the man of the Cattle Country to unnecessary words that he often advised a discursive conversationalist to 'save part of your breath for breathing.'"[70] Rollins further contended that a cowboy sauntering across a wooden floor sounded like a knight in full armor, the jangle intentionally created to stave off the loneliness of total isolation.

Although the wrangler was not long on conversation, he talked continuously to his mount. A man's horse knew his most private and innermost secrets.[71] However tight-lipped he might be with outsiders, he shared all of his secret thoughts with his horse, and this, according to Rollins, almost humanized some of the mounts.[72]

Possibly contributing to puncher's loneliness was a certain sense of anonymity. Ben Mayes was a cowboy in Tom Green County, Texas, from 1880–1904. Despite limited typing and spelling skills, he was able to get his point across:

> *no cow Boy had Mr to his name if he dident hav nick name it was Just Plain old Bob or Jack or what ever his name might Bee or was called By the Brand he worked*
>
> > *there is Boys I usto Bee well aquaninted with By there nick name if*

I Should meat them now wouldent know any other name I met man the other day I hadent Saw for thirty five years he came up to me and Says guess you dont know me

I Says Sure I do this is the South concho cow Boy we usto call Shady But for the life of me I couldent tell your other name for you Know lots of us Went by nick names when We knew one another

and he Says you havent got the Best of me in that way I always knew you By the name of V as you worked for that outfit and we had to get aquainted again

I told him my name and he Says in all the time he Knew me he never heard my name called

he Says my name is Bill Gardner and as up to date I had to call old Shady Mr Gardner"[73]

C. R. Smith worked with men on the XIT for six months at a time and never knew their names. "No one asked a man's name or where he was going. You called him Slim, Slew Foot, Pieface, Red, or whatever he looked like."[74] When a rider rode up to a ranch he was given a nickname, and the name usually stuck. No one ever knew a man's real name.[75] Something as insignificant as a man's name did not amount to very much in those days.[76]

JOHN NOBLE SPOKE OF LONELINESS AS A FATAL DISEASE. HE AND his father were once bringing sheep from Mexico when they encountered a man near Las Vegas, New Mexico, who had lost his way. He was in a terrible state, afflicted with a deadly case of loneliness. Born on the plains, Noble explained, one became accustomed to them, but for the newcomer the plains could be demoralizing. There was nothing but the rise and swell of land and grass—monotonous, endless prairie. Expecting to see something different on topping the next rise, a stranger traveling across the prairie would get his hopes up, but the monotony and disappointment were terrible. "'He's got loneliness!' we would say of such a man. Sometimes, if he couldn't get away, the

Lonely West Texas line camp.
Courtesy Research Center, Panhandle-Plains Historical Museum

lonely man would shrivel up and die. And this fellow whom we picked up at Las Vegas had it. He died in the night."[77]

Line camps were the most lonely assignments on the range. Coleman Jones began driving cattle at age ten, and while working for J. C. Powell he asked Powell why he never allowed a man to stay in camp by himself. Powell explained that one summer he left alone in camp a man named Johnson. Every time he carried him food Johnson would ask if he could return to the ranch headquarters for a few days because he was so lonesome. Powell would joke with him and kid that real cowboys never got lonesome. One day he stopped by the camp and looked in the window. He saw Johnson walking the floor and talk-

Saloon in Old Tascosa, Texas.
Courtesy Research Center, Panhandle-Plains Historical Museum

ing to himself, all the while whirling his six-shooter on his forefinger. Powell went inside, and he and Johnson sat down, drank coffee, and talked for about an hour. Johnson seemed to relax, and Powell went back to the ranch. A few days later a neighboring rancher dropped by and told him he went by the camp and although Johnson's horse was there, he could not find Johnson. Neighbors gathered and searched the range but never found the man. Two or three years later a skeleton with a bullet hole in the head was found in a small mountainside cave. The spurs and gun had Johnson's initials on them. Powell believed that if he had only let Johnson come back to headquarters for a few days this tragedy would never have happened.[78]

LIKE WOMEN, MEN SOUGHT RELIEF FROM THE PLIGHT OF THEIR isolation.[79] C. R. Rister wrote that during wintertime the cowhand was a creature of "monkish abnegation," but come spring when his tongue was loosened by hard liquor and his eyes glazed by the excitement of saloon and gambling hall, he succumbed to wild excesses.[80] Pent-up emotions were released with the abandon of an irresponsible child.[81] Matthew "Bones" Hooks came to a similar conclusion. Born in 1867 to former slaves, Hooks was a noted bronco buster and one of the first black cowboys in the Panhandle to work alongside whites. He pointed out that men often spent up to eighteen months on the open range, seeing maybe only six or eight other men over this entire period. When they came to a town consisting of little more than a saloon, a wagonyard and nothing to do but drink whiskey, naturally they became wild.[82]

There were, however, ways other than saloons and whiskey, climbing windmills, or firing shotguns for people to break out of their solitude. They came together in times of misfortune. Sickness, accidents, and death were occasions for contact with neighbors.

Chapter 5

The Insecurity of Life
Sickness and Accidents

To say that life then and there was insecure is to describe altogether too feebly a state of society and an environment wherein Death, in one violent form or another, was ever abroad, seldom long idle, always alert for victims.

Edgar Beecher Bronson,
The Red-Blooded Heroes of the Frontier

FRONTIERS ARE INHABITED BY THE YOUNG.[1] MOST OF THOSE WHO crossed the continent in the nineteenth century were between the ages of sixteen and thirty-five, physically fit and healthy.[2] Men were in their prime, their bodies and minds toned for the hardships of the road and the rigors of the land. Women likewise enjoyed the strength of youth, but this stage in life included their best years to conceive. Pregnancy, childbirth, and the care of small children, therefore, compounded the ordeals of women traveling cross-country by wagon.

The Texas Panhandle of the 1880s was a country of young people. The average age of those listed in the 1880 census was only twenty-five (twenty-six for men and twenty-one for women).[3] "Young people would come in," one settler stated. "There wasn't no old people coming in much."[4] Another noted that his father was thirty-five. "Old people wouldn't have moved in here to settle a new country."[5]

Twenty-two percent of these pioneers were Spanish-speaking, having come from New Mexico and Colorado. The Anglo-American families had mostly migrated from Colorado, New Mexico, and Kansas.[6] Thirteen percent of the region's population was foreign, originating from Europe, Latin America, and the British Empire.[7] Arkansas, Louisiana, Tennessee, and Mississippi became major suppliers of settlers, and shortly after the arrival of the railroads, land agents began promoting the West Texas plains in earnest.[8] Inquiries were received by land offices from a wide range of locations, but primarily from the Midwest and East Texas.[9] W. P. Soash, who headed one of the more successful land companies, had agents operating out of Iowa, Missouri, South Dakota, Nebraska, Wisconsin, Illinois, Indiana, and Minnesota, as well as Texas.[10] These were the principal regions and states that contributed the rush of new landowners in the early twentieth century.

Youth and resilient health served these early West Texans well, and this combination, along with the sparse population, made death a rarity.[11] A neighbor's passing was a "a little outstanding," no less than "a real event."[12] It was even difficult in some sections for a new doctor to establish his practice.[13] Dr. Henry Hoyt became a cowpuncher for the LX outfit because in the thinly settled Panhandle there were so few calls for his services. "He told us 'there was not much doing in his profession, since nobody was ever sick and nobody died except with their boots on and the undertakers were doing the most of the business—they would hustle the victim out to Boot Hill before the doctor had a chance.'"[14] Addie Whitcomb's father had been in the furniture and undertaking business in Arkansas before arriving in Amarillo around 1890. Upon arrival, though, he was forced to become a building contractor because "never anybody got sick or died. . . ."[15]

One South Plains settler was fifteen years old when in 1916 an old pioneer died, but he could recall no other deaths in the small community over the next six years.[16] Funerals were so infrequent that a young person might never attend a burial or see a corpse until their teen years.[17] Lavert Avent, a Central Texan born in the mid-1890s, came to the Panhandle in 1911. He described the local cemetery as so small that "you could put all the graves there was out there in a space as big as this house pretty near then. Sure wasn't many graves there."[18]

There were, of course, places and circumstances that were an exception. Although deaths might not occur in one's immediate vicinity, people were aware of others dying in adjacent communities.[19] There were also individual exceptions. Jennie Holcomb, mentioned earlier, was six when she lost both parents in 1898. Her father died of pneumonia, and a few months later her mother was taken by measles. To attend school she lived for a while with a family in town, and during this time the man of the house was killed in a horsing accident.[20] Large extended families might suffer numerous deaths, making funerals all-too-common affairs.[21] Death also became more familiar as years passed and the population increased. Avent remembered when the flu hit West Texas in 1918. The weather was cold and wintry, and "O Boy, I tell you people died like sheep with the rot then."[22]

People, for the most part, operated on the assumption they would not become seriously ill, and isolation protected settlers from new and more virulent infections.[23] Various reports suggest that serious illness was not often witnessed. Claude Biddy was fourteen when in 1909 he went to work on a ranch for $25 a month. "It seems to me," he said, "people weren't as prone to be sick as much as they are today[.] back [*sic*] then it was mostly broken bones and we set them as good as a doctor could have done. If we did get somebody really ill though we'd put them in the wagon and drive them Twenty-five miles to old Doctor Alexander."[24] When the child in one remote Panhandle family was asked what their mother did for a doctor when they got sick, the boy replied, "We never get sick."[25]

Ranch hands were variably described as jovial, hard, husky— and supposedly—seldom sick. Fred Scott, a native Kentuckian, signed on with Charles Goodnight in 1881 and worked with him for eighteen years. Scott said there were no sick cowboys. After one became accustomed to range life he would be very healthy.[26] Another observer agreed and found this durability remarkable when the privations and exposures of cowboys are considered.[27] Sallie Matthews, daughter and wife of West Texas cattlemen, wrote that she and her family were seldom sick, and she too found their health exceptional given what they had to eat.[28] The poverty and isolation of frontier life made for a restricted diet, staples often limited to little more than salt pork, beans, cornbread, soda biscuits, molasses, and milk.[29] Occasionally there was some variety of wild game. For Agnes Cleaveland, meals consisted of meat—"first, last, and always"—and when in season, potatoes. Sourdough biscuits, beans, sowbelly, and dried fruit rounded out the menu. For a touch of luxury, there were canned goods. "Any diet at all was the important thing," though. "To become choosy about it was not in good form."[30]

IN SPITE OF YOUTHFUL HEALTH AND THE CLIMATE—AND POSSIBLY the failure to recall serious illness—advanced medical conditions and the hard years took their toll. Going west was not always therapeutic. Those who helped promote the legend of western health all too often ignored the grim reality of countless hastily dug trailside graves. The West's reputation was perpetuated by successes only, the recovery of but one invalid enough to mask many times that number of failures.[31] The travel guides' promises of good health went unfulfilled for countless migrants as they succumbed to the most common causes of death—the infectious diseases: tuberculosis, malaria, dysentery, typhus, typhoid fever, pneumonia, measles, and epidemics of small pox, yellow fever, and cholera.[32]

E. C. Abbott related the poignant account of nursing in a hotel room one of the boys from his outfit. The young man was a bookkeeper who had gone west for his health—"He had t.b., bad"—but he finally died in Abbott's arms.[33] Andy Adams spun a story about a young consumptive advised by doctors to pursue a physical outdoor life. He joined the outfit with the mark on his brow, but there was to be no escape. "He wanted to live, and struggled hard to avoid going. Until three days before his death he was hopeful; always would tell us how much better he was getting, and every one could see that he was gradually going."[34] Similar true accounts were common. The disease of many tuberculars was too grave for them to survive the long trip either to or across the plains.

By the time the healthy young were in their thirties even the most sturdy would likely have had a bout of fever, suffered through one of the contagious diseases, or begun showing the consequences of too much hard liquor, fried and greasy food, stress, or childbearing.[35] Because of the scarcity of vegetables, dysentery and scurvy were common.[36] Some sicknesses went unexplained. "People died and nobody knew what caused it."[37]

Although Potter and Randall Counties in Texas had no cemeteries in 1890, that situation soon changed. Over a ten-year period from the last of the 1890s through the early 1900s, Amarillo, a city that by 1925 spanned the boundary between these two counties, reported the highest death rate for any town its size in the United States.[38] The principal cause of death was tuberculosis, followed by typhoid fever. Typhoid reached near epidemic proportions, and the cause was attributed to poor sanitation. Sanitation, however, was a little known or understood concept on the frontier.[39]

John Crudgington, an Amarillo newcomer in 1904 at the age of ten, thought back on sanitation and the outdoor toilet in relation to health in early Amarillo. With clouds of germ-bearing houseflies swarming every residence with an outhouse, "It is now a wonder that the epidemics of typhoid fever were no worse than they were. There is probably no doubt that this source of filth contributed to the increase of the virulence of all the contagious diseases."[40]

Hester Cash, at age fourteen was another who came to the Panhandle in 1904, and she attributed many deaths to the absence of hygiene.[41] Morning toilet for the wrangler, as an example, was limited to putting on his hat.[42] Ed Lord asked one old cowhand if he ever took a bath. The response was "no" because he had never gotten dirty enough to need one.[43] LaVerne Hanners remembered an elderly cowboy say he had no gray in his thick black hair because he never washed it.[44] Her mother would enforce hygiene, however, calling the boys in from the bunkhouse every Saturday and making them bathe and put on clean underwear. "I can't imagine how our small kitchen must have smelled with three or four unwashed cowboys, five nasty little kids, and perhaps, in a box behind the stove, a few baby chickens."[45]

ALICE TUBB, LIKE OTHER SETTLERS, FOUND SICKNESS, OF ALL the privations and hardships on the early plains, the most distressful.[46] Born in England, Mrs. Tubb came to the United States with her husband and six children in 1881. After six years in Kansas, they settled in Hemphill County, Texas. This dread of illness and disease was, in part, a legacy of the wagon trains where sickness became one of the most frightening adversaries of the road, that "sinister threat."[47] Once homes were established, though, it persisted as among the most fearful realities of pioneer life, the dreaded visitor in every cabin and dugout.[48]

Although pregnancy and childbirth are natural and normal events, they represent one of the literal meanings of "disease" in the sense they involve the "absence of ease," inconvenience and trouble.[49] For frontier women, to be pregnant was to be sick, and childbirth certainly was no incidental experience.[50] Miscarriages, stillbirths, and birth complications exacted a dreadful toll on their strength and spirits.[51] The possibilities of maternal death were so high that one can only imagine how young women envisioned the conjugal bed.[52] Highly romantic or sentimental views of marriage were quickly dispelled by repeated and difficult childbirths endured with little or no professional help.[53] Frontier cemeteries are dotted with more than one weathered tombstone bearing the words, "Mother and Child," an inscription undoubtedly suggesting a tragic story.[54]

Distances were great and trails dim, so a summoned doctor was not likely to find the mother in time to assist in the delivery.[55] Neighboring women were quick to gather around and offer assistance, but they too could be handicapped by distance. When it came time for C. N. Cosby to "knock on the door," his mother was alone with two small children. Fortunately, a preacher passing through stopped and assisted with the birth—"His name was Nelson and I got his name."[56] The importance of somebody, maybe anybody with any degree of maturity, being present at this critical time cannot be overstated. "To be alone at such a moment was a dreadful fate to be avoided."[57]

Child mortality was a nineteenth-century given, so fear of losing children was not an unknown or idle emotion. Among Midwestern farming families, one out of five children died before their fifth birthday.[58] The experience of Gladys Deitiker's grandmother was not exceptional. She had twelve children, but only five ever reached adulthood.[59] A. C. Greene stood on a cemetery plot in Hood County, Texas, where he observed two full rows of graves entrusted with the lost children of one man's two marriages. "The frontier drew heavily on the infants, and every old graveyard offers waves of brothers and sisters."[60] Charles and Maggie Brown moved twenty-four times in twenty-six years, leaving behind six grave markers to children buried in the rocky soils of Colorado and New Mexico.[61] Maggie's own parents had lost six children; Charles's mother and father, four.[62] Children could choke on everything from a collar button to a cotton seed. They could be scalded by water tipped off the stove or poisoned by a swallow of kerosene used to light the stove. They fell into caldrons of boiling water and tripped into raging fireplaces and campfires. Snakebites could be fatal, horses lethal. Deitiker spoke simply to the problem: "So many things could happen to children. They didn't know why."[63]

The kinds of injuries and the causes of sickness and death, like those shadowing children, were as far-ranging as the territory itself: the collapse of a sod house roof, the puncture of a rusty nail, a dragging skirt ignited by flames from burning trash, the bite of a tick, the glancing blow from an ax, a mother with infant in arms jumping from a moving wagon, the swift kick of a mule, the long fall from a windmill, the bite of a rabid polecat, a flash of lightning, a rattlesnake slipping under the sleeper's warm cover at night.

Frank Collinson, an Englishman born in 1856, arrived in San Antonio at age sixteen and later became a legendary West Texas buffalo hunter, frontiersman, and cattleman. Collinson recalled little or no sickness on the frontier, but he frequently served as a pallbearer and helped bury many victims of violence.[64]

Firearms were a frequent cause of serious injuries and death as settlers moved into and across the plains. Guns lacked newer safety features found on side arms today, and many emigrants were unfamiliar with weapons.[65] Fatigue and carelessness often contributed to a man's accidentally shooting himself or someone else.[66]

Some shootings were not accidental. On a ranch, it was a rare individual who got along with everyone, and some men got along with no one. As a result, friction between ranch hands was common.[67] Fatigue, and possibly boredom, could have contributed to trigger-quick reactions. In town, this conflict could be as bad—or worse. Around the turn of the century guns were the fourth leading cause of death in Amarillo, a town with an overall staggering death rate.[68] The bars in Amarillo were popular haunts for cowboys seeking relief from the drudgery and isolation of range life, and as in all early western towns, bullets often became clinchers in arguments.[69]

Wagon accidents were a common cause of injury or death.[70] Teams might lurch, hurling an unsuspecting passenger beneath the large and unforgiving wheels. On the trail, fatigue and carelessness accounted for many injuries to adults. Children became increasingly bold in jumping off or onto moving wagons, and adults became increasingly tolerant because it would save the driver the trouble of having to stop the team. But to stumble, lose balance, or have clothing snag on some part of the wagon could make for irreversible tragedy. If not fatal, injuries could leave the victim bedridden for months or disabled for a lifetime.[71] Ella Dumont stepped into a buggy and the horse bolted, throwing her to the ground, crushing her ankle, and "tearing my foot just half off."[72] She was in bed for six months before she could stand and put any weight on the foot. It was six years before she could walk without crutches. When Andy and Mary Blankenship considered purchasing their first automobile they recalled their many narrow escapes from accidents involving horses and buggies. It would be safer, they thought, to own a car.[73]

Handling domestic animals often resulted in injuries. Children were knocked down and hurt by loose livestock, and brushing too close to a tethered mule or horse might result in a reflexive, brutal kick. Breakaway horses, runaway teams, and stampeding herds were causes of broken bones, dislocations, and concussions.[74] On the open range, the pedestrian was at constant risk from all of the cattle, but the cows posed a special danger. Philip Rollins alleged that the range cow was more dangerous and unpredictable than even the grizzly.[75]

Among those identified as jovial, hard, and seldom sick—the cowhands—health had to be a major concern. One aspect of ranch life the hands did not like to think about, but often had to face, was sickness and accidents. Numbers of men on the Spur Ranch could be laid up with dysentery and diarrhea, and there were occasional cases of typhoid fever and pneumonia.[76] Critical illness was regarded as a serious matter because it took several days to get a doctor, but even with medical help the prognosis was not encouraging—"When you got bad sick then you usually died."[77]

Accidents on the Spur seemed endless. The difficult, strenuous work made the men poor physical risks, almost continually subject to serious injury and possible death. Cowboying was not as exciting or romantic as the popular literature of the day portrayed. It was the work of men engaged in mortal combat.[78] Dock McCoy started punching cattle in 1885 at age fifteen, and "When you signed up as a cowboy, you took your life in your own hands."[79]

R. M. Dudley worked on the XIT Ranch until 1896 when he quit to become a wolf hunter. Dudley would have welcomed the opportunity to relive some of his past experiences on the XIT, but not all. The many accidents, dangers, and other disagreeable features, he said, were no temptation.[80] After detailing his multiple painful injuries, one range veteran spoke with conviction: "Believe me, . . . the life of a cowboy is no bed of roses."[81]

Most men had to forego more demanding range chores after ten or fifteen years. Old cowboys were rare. One former cowpuncher said, "For a man to be stove up at thirty may sound strange to some people, but many a cowboy has been so bunged up that he has quit riding that early in life."[82] Sleeping out in the open and neglecting health or injuries often made for a gimpy cowboy, one who would spend the rest of his life nursing abused health.[83] Georgia-born Alfred "Babe" Moye became a West Texas trail driver in the 1870s. Moye later described his few surviving cowboy chums as "sore-footed and dragging, but still full of life."[84]

As a child, Wilbur Coe admired the cowboys with their scared, rope-burned hands and weather-beaten faces, their lips swollen, dried, and cracked by wind and sun.[85] His one wish was that he could hurry and grow up to become a member of this elite group. Cowmen were plagued with boils, and they commonly had running sores on their hands from rope burns or pricks from mesquite thorns.[86] The image of the cowboy as a handsome lover has been dispelled as a myth. Rather, the typical cowboy more than likely limped, had a crooked nose from being broken at least once, nursed a hernia, and had one or more gnarled fingers that had never set properly following a fracture. There were gaps from missing teeth, and those that remained were full of cavities and yellowed from tobacco juice.[87]

Trail drovers were especially vulnerable to illness due to overwork and lack of sleep.[88] Fatigue could dull attention and make for careless slips. Abbott believed the worst hardship when driving cattle was the loss of sleep. On a calm night they might sleep five hours, one hour if the weather was rough.[89] Need for sleep would become so overpowering that in order to stay awake the men sometimes rubbed tobacco juice in their eyes—"It was rubbing them with fire."[90] Following one particularly long and exhausting effort to control cattle in stormy weather, a trail partner rode up beside Abbott and made the weary comment: "Teddy, I am going to Greenland where the nights are six months long, and I ain't agoing to get up until ten o'clock next day."[91]

The most dreaded danger on the cattle trail was the stampede, or "stompede" as it was likely called by the drover.[92] Frightened herds might stampede as many as eighteen times in a single night, and although a minor runaway might scatter the herd only a few miles, a bad one could last a week and in extreme cases cover hundreds of miles. Most stampedes occurred at night when it might be so dark that a rider using both hands was unable to find his nose. Abbott remembered the instant danger even in daytime when a deep coulee opened up suddenly and unexpectedly in front of a rider. The thought of what could happen at night was awful. "It was riding at a dead run in the dark, with cut banks and prairie dog holes all around you, not knowing if the next jump would land you in a shallow grave."[93]

Drownings at river crossings were common, the result of wagons' or ferries' overturning, a tired teamster becoming entangled in the harness, or someone on foot being swept away by cold, turbulent waters.[94] These crossings were also especially hazardous on cattle drives. Trying to move a herd of cattle across a wide and rushing river was perilous to both horsemen and cattle, and graves at river crossings were not uncommon.[95] Milling herds could leave a rider unhorsed in a watery melee of thrashing hoofs and sharp, slashing horns. Wayne Gard speaks of the judgment, courage, and quick thinking required for this critical part of the drive. When a cowhand wanted to give a special compliment to one of his trail partners, he called him "a man to ride the river with."[96]

If the hazards of the range did not fell them, the perils of the bottle might. It has been quipped that the three R's of the cowboy were "riding, roping, and roaring drunk."[97] Around the turn of the century in Amarillo, alcoholism was the third-leading cause of death.[98]

"Of course," Mitchell Jones pointed out, "getting mixed up with horses was one of the main ways of injury then."[99] Cleaveland spoke of their utter dependence on horses.[100] They were everywhere, indispensable in everyday life, for to be without a horse in West Texas was like being overboard at sea, prey to whatever risks the plains might present. On horseback, though, man became a superior, confident being who could rule nature and prevail over any hostile environment.[101] Horses were also recreational and involved in many daily activities of children.[102] Some of the fondest memories of pioneer childhoods involved horseback riding.

At the same time, horses were dangerous, and, in part, because of the nature of the beast. Many descended from Spanish stock and were frequently referred to as mustangs or broncos, terms suggesting their unbroken and potentially violent disposition. Wild and wiry, tough and mean, some horses could never be cured of their tendency to buck.[103] It was as though they held a permanent grudge against anything human, and the rider was never absolutely safe until the horse had been ridden to a state of exhaustion.[104] Rollins calculated that two horses out of a hundred were chronically addicted to the habit of pitching; one in five hundred was an outlaw that would almost buck in its sleep; and maybe one in ten thousand enough of a man-killer to deliberately jump on the thrown rider's prone and prostrate body.[105]

Each cowboy's mount consisted of from eight to ten horses, and of these, four or five were well trained, the rest broncs.[106] Dock McCoy remembered that when a new man started out on a ranch the hands cut out a remuda for his use. "You didn't ask if they'd pitch," he said, "you knew they would, but you had to ride 'em."[107] Riding bucking horses was not something that was optional, it was a matter of necessity, and every ranch had at least one or more outlaw horses "as bad as ever wore hair."[108] These horses were so intimidating that many times some poor boy would stand quaking in his boots after everyone else had mounted.[109]

Horses, of course, were often docile and would act like a kitten when mounted, but even with apparently quiet horses it was prudent to be cautious.[110] One never really knew exactly what to expect next, and it was this uncertainty that made climbing into the saddle so dangerous.[111] Creatures of habit, range horses tended to behave well so long as conditions were familiar, but anything unusual could frighten the animal and make it unmanageable. The flipping of a bandanna, the flapping of a woman's skirt, the opening of a parasol, the playful, childish slap with a bonnet, or a darting dog or rabbit could unnerve a horse, sometimes with deadly consequences.

Not to be overlooked is incompetent horsemanship. An inept rider might at any moment send even a horse long since broken and thoroughly mild-mannered into spasms of "equine violence."[112] No self-respecting steed would tolerate indefinitely an incompetent horseman, and some riders seemed to invite bucking. It was said of a man with little riding aptitude that he could not even ride a covered wagon, and certainly "nuthin' wilder than a wheel chair."[113]

Joe Shelton spoke of the "rough horses" with which cattlemen were forced to work. "They're just really mustangs, and sometimes the horses threw 'em and drug 'em or maybe they'd fall and kill 'em that way."[114] Horses pitching, dragging, or falling with a rider were three common causes of injuries and death. Shelton also suggested a fourth—collisions with cattle. One pioneer cattleman would have agreed, writing in 1915 that "Every rider of the range, even to this good day, knows the result of such a collision—a cloud of dust, horse, cow and man, all in a heap, and when the dust had cleared away, the boy with blood issuing from ear, nose and mouth, when picked up was found to be more dead than alive."[115]

Broken limbs resulting from riding misadventures were commonplace and regarded as an inconvenience, accepted matter-of-factly and with the recognition that it could have been much worse.[116] The many injuries of J. Evetts Haley, West Texas and Oklahoma cattleman and southwestern range historian, were cited by his wife Rosalind: "Six broken legs. Thirty-two broken bones. Ribs? O Lord! I don't know. [He] counted up to nine and stopped counting."[117] One man's right leg had been broken three times, his left leg twice, and his right wrist once, yet he modestly regarded himself as fortunate: "I ain't bin hurt bad yet. But some day, I reckon, I'll get it."[118] Years ago, I can remember someone saying in an interview: "Bad things could happen with horses."

FAYE LEWIS REMEMBERED THE HAZARDS AND SHADOWS OF EARLY plains life in South Dakota. After one potentially perilous incident, she and her brothers returned home and related the event to their parents. Their mother burst into tears, and later they overheard her despair to their father: "There are so many dangers in this country; more than we ever knew about before we came!"[119]

As in South Dakota, there were many unknown and unanticipated dangers in West Texas. What Nannie Alderson said about horse mishaps in Montana could be said about frontier plains life in general: "Terrible things could and did happen. . . ."[120] When terrible things did happen on the West Texas plains, people came together. It was an occasion to help—or to mourn.

Chapter 6

Death's Visitation

*It don't matter how rough men are—I've known 'em that never spoke with-
out cussin', that claimed to fear neither God, man, nor devil—but let death
visit camp an' it puts 'em thinkin'. They generally take their hats off to this old
boy that comes everywhere an' any time. . . . He's never welcome, but you've
got to respect him.*

Rawhide Rawlins,
in *Trails Plowed Under*
by Charles M. Russell

FAXON, OKLAHOMA, 1902, WAS A SMALL COMMUNITY OF TWENTY
families with an additional four families living on nearby homesteads.
Happy and contented, the residents had little reason to suspect pend-
ing misfortune. Then one Saturday night, sometime between midnight and dawn, death struck three times. Albert Gilles was awakened
by his father at daybreak Sunday morning and informed of the deaths.
Much had to be done. "Death was something the town neither con-
templated or prepared for. We had none of the appurtenances for a funeral. There were no caskets, no undertaker, no cemetery, and no
minister."[1]

Henry and Rosa Ise lost their first infant shortly after settling in western Kansas in 1873, and the response by neighbors was immediate. As in Faxon, there were no provisions for a burial or funeral. It had never occurred to the young parents that such arrangements might be necessary.[2]

Blanche Rutherford remembered death's first visit to her small West Texas community in 1911. The people had so little acquaintance with this "master of confusion and turmoil" they did not know how to proceed.[3] That same year, C. M. Thomas, owner of a furniture store in Canyon, Texas, reported that he had not taken his hearse out of the barn for nine months. During this period there had been only one death from natural causes and only one by violence in the whole county.[4] An undertaker for nine years, Mr. Thomas had never seen so few deaths.

When death did visit the frontier, there were none of the amenities of civilization to lessen the impact, few comforting distractions to cushion the reality.[5] As in colonial times, homes were small and with little privacy or opportunity to shield family members from the dying or dead.[6] They could not have isolated death from life had they so desired. Bodies were not cosmetically enhanced to preserve lifelikeness, so people were forced to see the dead as they were.[7] Born in Nebraska in 1904, Adelheid Albers migrated with her family to the Texas Panhandle in 1908. She was five years old when her grandfather died, and they simply laid him out on the table to cool. "That's hard for kids!"[8]

The happy death of a good nineteenth-century Christian was something that was supposed to occur in the bosom of the family.[9] Such closeness made dying and death highly personal as family and friends waited anxiously at bedside to offer what little treatment and comfort they could. Nevertheless, surrounded by all the love and devotion a family could summon, death remained a shocking and difficult experience, maybe life's major event.[10] Certainly, life's bitterest hour.

Death phrases of the day were vivid and graphic.[11] Up close and unadorned, death was the mystery of all mysteries, the cruel curse of a grim and ruthless monster. It was the destroyer, the "insatiate

Archer."[12] A dark, hovering angel of doom, death would stretch forth its relentless and untimely hand and leave the wretched victim convulsing helplessly in its chilly grasp. It was that dreaded summons, "that cold couch from which no traveler ere returns."[13] For Miriam Colt it was a stern decree, a cruel fate that forced her to look upon the lifeless body of her only son, "frozen into marble by the icy hand of death."[14]

In the idiom of the West, death was that long, dark trail, the end of the trail, the Great Divide. A person approaching death was "picking at the Kivvers (Covers)," and a dead cowboy was one who had "sacked his saddle."[15] When a cowman returned home by train following a lengthy trail drive he customarily put his saddle in a grain sack to be checked at the station. In death he was now on that long return trip to his eternal home. A mysterious journey not fully understood, it followed a dim trail to a distant, murky beyond.[16] Mrs. Colt tempered mystery with hope when she wrote of the "shadowy, misty path that veils from the vision of mortals the glorious view of immortality."[17]

Death was something fearsome, in part, because people felt so defenseless. Gladys Deitiker remarked that often there was no doctor, and in the clutches of this most critical and final of crises, the sense of helplessness could be overwhelming.[18] Born in Central Texas in 1901, Lois Prichard's family moved to Snyder, Texas, when she was seven. Mrs. Prichard spoke of her grandmother's frightening nosebleeds. She would nearly strangle to death, and her mother worried, knowing that some morning she would awaken to find her dead. "Oh, it was frightening. My mother had such horror of her strangling to death and nothing she could do about it." Her grandmother died in the home. "Mama had gone in to see about her that night and she had taken her some cake and some buttermilk. And she had eaten part of that cake and some of the buttermilk, and there was the glass on the table."[19]

Death was especially frightening because it could strike so suddenly, like lightning in a summertime storm.[20] Hazel Walsh, born near

Crowell, Texas, in 1900, was a child when a young boy died unexpectedly, and then a youth drowned in a nearby lake. "The suddenness of it was the thing that frightened me because they were so alive and they were gone."[21]

Catherine Porter's father died abruptly in Kansas in 1886 at the age of forty-three. "[Mother] had just extinguished the light when father began to breathe rather hard and strangely. Before she could light the lamp and call brother, he was gone."[22] Conducting the funeral service of a cowboy killed by his falling horse in a roundup, the preacher reminded those standing around the open grave of the unexpectedness of death. Little did the poor boy dream "that he was ridin' right into the bog of eternity!"[23] The mourners were left uneasy when again cautioned that at that very moment "the pale rider o' death may be lookin' you over, and takin' down his rope for a final throw, an' you don't know over whose head the tug'll fall."[24] Recalling her New Mexico childhood, Eva Henderson spoke of a young man trampled to death when his horse stumbled and fell in a stampede. That very afternoon he had drawn his wages and written to his mother he was coming home.[25]

Ad Spaugh, son of a Kansas farmer, left home at fourteen to become a cattle driver in the 1870s. At the end of one tiring trail day the haggard men ate their supper then sat on their heels around the fire. Some sprawled on the grass, resting on their elbows. They reminisced about other drives and about bad horses ridden, and before the glow of the embers turned gray there might be a hymn or two. There was a sense among the men that death always rode close at hand, and relentless nature—hard and indifferent—was never far behind. "Lives were snuffed out, tragedies enacted, harsh dramas unfolded—yet the drive went on."[26]

Isolated graves gave mute testimony to sudden deaths on the range. One of Andy Adams's tales was of his outfit coming on the fresh grave of a man killed when his horse fell backward, accidentally discharging his gun. There was nothing to distinguish this grave from hundreds of others on the trail. It was just the latest. Around the campfire that night, the men became thoughtful, and some were moved to share their experiences. This accident, they agreed, could have happened to any of them, but it seemed awfully short notice to a cowboy enjoying life.[27] The doleful lyrics of many a cowboy song spins the tale of sudden death snatching some unsuspecting trail hand when he is far from home and far from family.[28]

He was a youth far from home,
With friends he chanced to be;
No kindred nor relation,
To know his agony.[29]

Susan Newcomb's melancholy mood pervades her diary entries regarding the frailty of life:

SATURDAY DEC 30TH/65:— *This year will soon be past and gone. one [sic] more day and another will take its place. And who knows how long it will be before some of us will be called upon to go, leave this world of trouble and sorrow!*

SUNDAY DEC 31ST/1865. *I have been permitted to live to see the last day of the year eighteen hundred and sixty-five but how many more days I may live to see it is hard to tell life is very uncertain but death is very certain.*[30]

One of the factors that reminded early New Englanders of the nearness and reality of death was the religion of the day.[31] Clergymen routinely preached on the topic, and a death in the congregation was seized as an opportunity to remind the living of sin's toll. The terror of death was seen as one way to inspire godliness, and children were frequently targeted for this grim message. It was a pulpit technique destined to endure. Boone McClure, first full-time director of the Panhandle-Plains Historical Museum, attributed the fear of death in his day to this very theme. "It seemed to me that nearly every sermon preached was that you're gonna [die] and if you don't live right why you're not going to heaven. We were taught that death was coming to everybody, and if you lived a good life there was nothing to worry about and if you didn't, you better change your ways. . . . It was almost a threat hanging over you."[32]

These sermons left a lingering impression. Ira Taylor was afraid of the way the preachers would screech about death and going to hell—"and one thing and another." It was enough, he said, "to put a kid's mind to studying about things like that."[33] E. C. Abbott recalled the loud hellfire and brimstone sermons that could be heard for a mile. "We'd all go to hell, the way they looked at it. If they were right there was no hope for me. You know you ride around alone at night, looking at the stars, and you get to thinking of those things."[34]

Ruth Lowes worried because the pronouncements at church were that everybody was a sinner, and sinners would burn forever in hell, something she desperately wanted to avoid.[35] Her distress about death was not easily dismissed, and she recollected a favorite childhood book containing a picture of "Babes in the Woods," a Grimms' fairy tale. "These two babes were walking through the woods and they died and the birds came and put leaves on them, covered them up with leaves. And I remember when I looked through that book, the pictures, I knew where that was and I always held the pages together so I wouldn't see that picture. All the other pictures I liked, but here I was coming to that story about babes in the woods so I'd do this."[36]

For some, death was not a dreaded end but rather an inevitable event to be approached courageously and endured with dignity. They were fatalistic folk, believing something simply happened or did not happen, and there was not much to be done about it either way.[37] Looking back over many years, Henderson was one of the philosophical ones. "So many lives come and go . . . that I begin to understand: life is nothing but a coming and a going. We are born and we die."[38] Born in Oklahoma Territory in 1901, Lee Matney grew up on an isolated West Texas ranch. His family had few neighbors and few contacts with death, and under these circumstances most people seldom thought about the matter. "I think they knew it was inevitable so why give it any thought. They didn't worry too much about that."[39] The average cowhand, though, might well see a companion die with his boots on and in a very unpleasant way, so for many, thoughts of death and the hereafter became strangely familiar concerns.[40]

In one 1866 military diary written en route to New Mexico the entries regarding death were as cursory and undistinguished as were references to setting up camp or the number of miles marched on a given day:

> JUNE 18—. . . *Still in camp mud bound. I had one man die today of pneumonia. Gains Creek is ahead three miles but impassible. We must wait for it to go down.*
>
> JULY 15—. . . *We saw large herds of buffalo today, and a part of a herd broke through our train, completely scalping one of the drivers. He will die. We camped near some strange looking large mounds this evening, they are composed of shells.*
>
> JULY 22—. . . *Today we passed a wagon capsized. It evidently belonged to some venturesome trader who had been murdered by the Indians as we found his scalped body and the bodies of two women, also mutilated a few steps from his wagon. We buried all. We are camped opposite the Natural Mounds.*[41]

Pioneers were well acquainted with death in the natural life cycle, because in rural, agricultural settings there was constant exposure to animal deaths.[42] "People who have grown up in cities, towns, and populated communities," C. N. Cosby said, "don't understand how much kids learn about people from animals. It dawned on us pretty soon that . . . animals lived like people lived, and our cats and our dogs died and we saw them die and our horses and our cattle died, and we knew what death was all about. It was a saddening, it was a bereavement, and children reacted to it."[43]

Ed Ramey spoke to the certainty of death, but also to the inevitable apprehension. "The general public," he said, "has always known that you was born to die and there's no reason of being afraid of death. But you're never ready for death. Regardless of [how] young or old, you're never ready for death."[44] Mr. Cosby agreed that there were no illusions about a deathless life. "We had friends and we had enemies, and we had life and we had death." At the same time they steeled themselves to such things and learned to endure it.[45]

One woman died only three weeks after arriving in Amarillo in 1887, but her deathbed scene was in all likelihood not typical: "Grandma was only fifty-eight when she passed on. . . . They told us that she wasn't scared of dying. Before she passed on she said, 'Death has no fear for me, it's just like stepping from one room into another.' She then started to sing and she sang until she died."[46]

Philosophical though they were, the settlers' discomfort with death was suggested by the way they talked about—or avoided—the subject. It was mentioned reluctantly, guardedly, and in low tones, but even then, seldom with children.[47] Mrs. Albers said that parents "didn't explain things to kids . . . No, my parents never prepared us for anything like that. They just taught us to take things as it came. They didn't talk to us about anything. They just raised us."[48]

Some children were curious; others were not. Edna Bridwell asked about death—"'Where do they go when they die?' 'Well, how do they get to heaven?'—and things like that." Her mother responded briefly and in evasive terms. "I think they were afraid it would disturb we younger ones so very much that I think they shielded us. They protected us from the idea of death because they knew it would bother us—or they felt like it would. And it would have."[49] George Moore said that if other children were like him, "they'd push it away. They didn't want to talk about it. That was kinda my thinking. I may have been a misfit, but I couldn't help from flinching from death thoughts. I usually stood behind my mother when they's lowering the coffin, the casket, into the grave."[50]

Ruth Lowes was of the opinion that death seemed to be a part of life that was, paradoxically, removed from life. People did not know how to talk about it because they lacked the vocabulary, an understanding of just what death entailed.[51]

THERE WAS A DIVINE ORDER TO LIFE. LIFE AND DEATH UNFOLDED according to a celestial plan, and God was the plan's benevolent, all-knowing architect. On her eighteenth birthday, the derivation of life was for Susan Newcomb incontrovertible.

> *Eighteen years of my short life is past and gone. And how many more I will be permitted to live is not for me to know. it [sic] may be many and it may not be one. No one knows but the Great ad [sic] Good [sic] who gave us the breath of life, and who will take it away in his own good time.*
>
> *It has been God's will that I should live to enjoy the sweet bright flowers of eighteen summers, and the cold white snows of eighteen winters . . . my self and all of my relations have been graciously spared by the wise prividece [sic] of God.*[52]

God was the caring, loving Father; the good and faithful Shepherd.[53] Compliant and unquestioning resignation to His will was expected, because whatever God did, God did well.[54] Even the most untimely and unexpected death could be apprehended as an occasion for glorifying God and finding reassurance: "Certainly, 'The Lord hath given, and the Lord hath taken away. Blessed be the name of the Lord'. . . . We can not determine what is best for us here and yet we may be assured that if we love Him supremely and our neighbor as ourselves all things will work together for our good."[55]

As difficult as it was to see his small son take flight to "Heavenly climes," Charles Hazelrigg, pioneering Nebraska and Oklahoma preacher, bowed obediently to the will of the One who always knows best.[56] The Reverend R. F. Dunn became in 1881 the first circuit rider in all of West Texas. His young daughter died in 1885, and he wrote of her spirit leaving the suffering body "to live in the presence of Him who said, 'suffer little children to come unto me, and forbid them not.' and [*sic*] we dare not refuse the Savior the pleasure of taking his little ones to their home in glory."[57] Who dared object when the Lord called for a flower on earth to be plucked for the garden above? Who dared protest when angels with airy wings bear upward to blissful bowers a young child to blossom in heaven?[58] It was not beyond comprehension that because children were so very special, God might well desire them prematurely for His own loving and fatherly arms.[59] "Here rests Mary Hamilton, aged 14" read the tombstone inscription in Dodge City, Kansas. Then chiseled below:

> *Weep not for me my parents dear,*
> *I am not dead, but only sleeping here.*
> *I was not yours alone,*
> *But God's who loved me best, and took me home.*[60]

It was this assurance of "home" that undergirded the bereaved, for without such hope many would have found it not worth the effort to live.[61] The death of her son compelled Mrs. Colt to lament: "O my God! My God! Why is this? my hopes all blasted—my bright anticipations ended. . . ."[62] Yet, even in the throes of despair, not to be forgotten was the anticipation of an immortal home, a reassurance she stroked boldly with her pen: "HOME *to die no more.*"[63]

Although the death of the Dunn child cast a shadow over her earthly home, God's house became for the Reverend Dunn more enticing than ever.[64] The sadness of death could not dampen his confidence in a spiritual life beyond the cold tomb. There would be a heavenly reunion. The diary of the Reverend Hazelrigg expressed his faith in meeting his young son again. The child's body was not destined to lie evermore below a heavy mound in the desolate graveyard. Such a belief would make life intolerable. "Oh, I would not take worlds for that hope . . . and one day he shall not be with us where we are but we shall be with him where he is."[65]

It may well be that deaths of plains children, with no doctors, hospitals, or immediate comfort from minister and sometimes friends, were more devastating than any other hardship of settler life.[66] The staunchest of faiths were tested by the death of a child, and loved ones were left with unanswerable questions as to the mysterious purpose

of that brief life on earth.[67] Attitudes about these deaths were anything but objective, and the sentimentality surrounding children's
deaths often bordered on maudlinism.[68]

The conflicting emotions aroused by the finality of death and the
hope of heaven is reflected in the behavior of one father. He mourned
that upon burial his young daughter would be shut away from the sun
for so long, but at the same time he placed in her tiny hand a note exhorting God to give her to the care and keeping of "some very motherly angel."[69] More than one West Texan undoubtedly experienced
the bereaved confusion of Ella Dumont on the death of her daughter:
"Why, oh, why must our hearts be rent asunder and laid bare at thy
feet when we have lived a Christian life to the best of our knowledge
and understanding? Why with all thy power were we not made strong
in mind and with all fortitude to bear these things?"[70]

The "whys" of death left some mourners disconsolate, others
skeptical or angry. On the death of her infant, Rosie Ise received a letter from her father exhorting her to resign herself to God's will. She
would find consolation, he wrote, in chapter one and verse eight of
First Samuel. That night Mrs. Ise read the suggested verse. In fact,
she read the First Book of Samuel in its entirety, but when she laid the
Bible aside and glanced across the room at the bed where she had so
often put the child to sleep, she felt more abandoned than since the
day he was buried.[71] In 1856 Mrs. Colt stood for her last farewell before the side-by-side graves of her husband and son, both dead within
six months after leaving New York:

> *How can I say, "Thy will be done,"*
> *When all's so dark beneath the sun?*
> *The cup's been rais'd—the dregs are drain'd;*
> *A life I've liv'd—I'm sorrow stain'd!*[72]

In 1861, the first year of the Civil War, Dave McCormick was six
years of age when his father died, leaving behind an indebted farm
and a widow with six children, the oldest a bed-confined invalid and

the youngest only a few months old. The preacher prayed for the family and said it was all for the best. Perhaps his mother was convinced by the words of the preacher, but the young boy thought that she needed her helpmate and the children needed their father. He could do them more good on earth than in Heaven: "I have not changed my way of thinking as yet. My Mother had a hard struggle, it being war. . . . They tell you the Lord knows best. . . . Maybe so."[73]

Opal Berryman remembered the death of a local child and the school-house funeral conducted by her father. She was not to be pacified by his words of comfort, addressed primarily to the parents of the dead child. Sitting beside her mother, resentful and rebellious, she watched the people as they filled every seat and the spaces next to the walls. Hats in hands, others stood outside by the windows. She admired her father, handsome and wise, but "I couldn't figure how it was that God had him so fooled. It seemed to me Father was being deliberately blind to the dirty trick God had pulled on the Kelsos."[74]

Death left some individuals inconsolable—and unforgiving. E. C. Abbott never got over the death of his childhood idol, a nineteen-year-old brother who died in southeastern Nebraska in the early 1870s. They buried the young man in the cemetery in Lincoln—"and the wind blowed my hat in his grave." Abbott claimed this death left him an infidel. He asked his mother if God could have kept his brother from dying. She said yes. God was all-powerful and could have prevented it had He so chosen. "So I said: 'I'll never go in one of your damn churches again.' And I never have. The family stuffed me full of all that religious bull when I was a kid, but I never had any more use for it after I was growed, and in that I was like the rest of the cowpunchers. Ninety per cent of them was infidels."[75]

Emerson Hough described a group of bereaved cowpunchers, just as inconsolable but less defiant, who had brought back to camp the body of a young cowboy killed by a storm-panicked herd. Their tired, worn faces appeared hard and grim in the early light of the morning sun. Some stood holding the bridles of their mounts, others leaned against the wagon or sat on the tongue. No house was near. It was a hundred miles to the nearest ranch, two hundred to a town. There was no minister, no church. "Not one hypocrite is to be found in this knot of rude men, and as none has professed any religion before, so none does now."[76] Following breakfast the cook's shovel was used to dig a grave. The young man was buried wrapped in his blankets with his hat over his face, his boots and spurs placed as they were when he slept in life. There was no service.

Although fictional, Andy Adams's account of the foreman who drowned while swimming a herd of cattle across the North Platte was inspired by a common event. Adams, his herd already safely across the river, was helping the second outfit when he heard a shout of panic. Some unsaddled cowboy was struggling in the turbulent water, and the terrified scream was a desperate cry for help. The men scouted the river until darkness without finding the body. It was a night of muffled conversation, and the next morning small groups of men huddled around the wagons in silent contemplation of the sad event. The body was finally recovered some eighteen hours later, placed in a tarpaulin and carried to camp. "When the corpse had been lowered to the ground at our camp, a look of inquiry passed from face to face which seemed to ask, 'What next?'"[77]

DEATH IN A COMMUNITY CONTEXT REQUIRES A RESPONSE. THE RESPONSE may be simple, much like the one described by Hough—a hastily dug grave, blankets, a hat placed to protect the face, boots and spurs in place, and no service. But in other circumstances, as was the case in old Faxon, "There was much to be done."

Chapter 7

Neglected and Forgotten

Lonely Graves in Lonely Places

The little child had to be put away in a lonely grave by itself on the wide, silent prairie. . . . The arrangements for the funeral were very simple and of the most primitive and inexpensive character . . .

During the half century that has elapsed since that day, [I] have attended many funerals and witnessed many sorrowful scenes in connection with them, but I have seen none that impressed me as that did. It seemed to me a cruel thing to bury her in the solitary waste, alone in the brooding silence of mighty nature, there to remain forever, to be first neglected and then forgotten.

Isham Reavis

LEE "LEEMAC" MCMURTRY, AN OLD-TIME COWBOY WITH SIMPLE tastes and little polish, would have sacrificed almost anything to work around cattle.[1] One of McMurtry's last requests before he died in 1994 was to be buried in a homemade casket. His daughter enlisted the help of her woodworking business associate, and within twenty-six hours the project was completed. It was a rectangular box, not ornate, because it had to be built in a hurry.[2] A homemade casket—a reversion to the past.

IN CONTEMPORARY AMERICAN SOCIETY DEATH AND DYING ARE increasingly isolated from public view, resulting in a social distancing from the dead.[3] Responsibilities for the deathbed, coffin making, grave digging, and other funeral arrangements have been assumed by professionals. Hospitals and mortuary facilities have become proficient at insulating people from death's disruptiveness, so common in small, preindustrialized societies.[4] It is rare for the typical person to see an untreated body, and dealing with a corpse—a common domestic responsibility in the nineteenth century—has disappeared.[5]

Along with this increase in social distance, community involvement has diminished. Local ties are limited due to frequent changes of residence, diversity of work, and sometimes by the deliberate search for anonymity. Consequently, the absence of community along with an emphasis on individual interests have led to a certain detachment from the problems of others, including their deaths and their dead.[6] Unless it is an important figure who has died, participation in and interest in funerals are restricted to family and immediate friends.[7] Grief is more personal, less communal.

As indicated, there were no provisions for allaying the realities of death in early West Texas. It was an event that occurred within the family. There were no institutions to house the final days of the dying, no professionals to be assigned last rites. Those who died away from home were either returned to the home or buried on the spot.

> *There was once a cowboy funeral that I many times recall,*
> *A bad hoss killed a feller on a beef work late one fall.*
>
> *There were no automobiles then, and we was far from trains*
> *In that rugged piece of country where the canyons break the plains.*
> *We had to make a buryin' to finish the affair,*
> *Well, the best time was the present, and the closest place was there.*[8]

The only death specialists were family, friends, or maybe an occasional passerby.

Even though settlers might be widely dispersed, deaths and burials were a community affair, and if death had been preceded by sickness, neighbors were usually already there and helping.[9] After Albert Witt was paralyzed from falling off a South Plains windmill in 1885, neighbors came from ten to twenty miles to help care for him until he finally died.[10] Willie McClary, a lifelong resident of Moore County, Texas, spoke of the loyalty among neighbors and its importance in the sparsely populated Panhandle.[11] People shared an instinct for survival and were bound by strands of interdependency, an interdependency especially apparent in times of crisis.[12] Everybody always helped everybody else, "More kindly if there was sickness or a death."[13]

Every household felt such a sense of responsibility that it might not even be necessary to send for help. Neighbors came without being asked. One Texas pioneer recalled a woman walking into the home in which there was sickness, hanging up her bonnet, and saying to the neighbor who had sat up all night: "'Mary, you go home. I have cooked enough for Jack and the children to last through tomorrow at dinner. . . .' She did not ask 'Can I help?' but walked in and took charge. That was the spirit of the frontier."[14]

When sickness or an accident led to death, the response was so total that the family had nothing to do except grieve. Neighbors did everything.[15] "In death, why, they just took over."[16]

One of the first responsibilities following a death was the laying out of the body. "That meant," according to Ira Taylor, "after they died, why get 'em ready to bury. And they'd lay 'em out on a table or slab or something around right where they died. Wasn't no place to take 'em. They dressed 'em, shaved 'em if they had to be shaved. My daddy used to be a barber and I know he shaved dead people. It was a neighborhood deal if anybody died 'cause that was the only people there was to take care of 'em."[17] Although it was generally the neighbors who washed and clothed the body in an attempt to make it presentable, there were times when the family itself had to perform these melancholy duties due to the scarcity of people.[18]

Lilian Bell, who with her sheep-rancher husband came to the Texas Panhandle in 1894, said that nursing often entailed preparing the dead for burial, and just as nursing was primarily a female function, even so was the laying out of bodies.[19] There were other death-related services more likely performed by women, such as lining the coffins and making the shrouds. Men, on the other hand, made the caskets, dug the graves, and transported the bodies.

Laying out included placing the body on a cooling board. Anything flat could serve this function—a door, a partition of a wall, the dining table, or planks placed across a couple of saw horses—to cause the body to lie flat.[20] In the early twentieth century more practical cooling boards resembling ironing boards with fold-up legs were available in some small towns.[21] While on this flat surface, the legs were straightened and the wrists crossed over the breast and maintained in this position until the corpse grew rigid.[22] A body left straight by rigor mortis was more easily prepared for burial and more easily managed at the time of burial than one that had contracted.

One way of preserving the body until burial was to keep the face, and possibly the hands, bathed in a liquid. A cloth soaked in vinegar, chloroform, or a solution of soda water helped deter discoloration, allowing the body to retain its natural color.[23] Camphor, another commonly used solution, was administered with a camphor rag. "See," Mrs. McClary explained, "that's the way we kept 'em from turning blue. We'd squeeze a cloth out of camphor and put over their faces."[24] The appearance of Ed Lord's dead child was conserved by sponging her off with whiskey.[25]

After the body was washed, the hair combed—

They have parted back the tresses
From her young and lovely brow—[26]

a neighbor might be called on to make a burial garment, sometimes staying at the task through the night.[27] This shroud or wrapper, "the last garment of the living," would be of the best fabric available, but

even then it was much like everything else, of the coarsest description.[28] If a town were nearby, burial clothes might be purchased.
When three LS Ranch cowboys were killed in an 1886 gunfight, ranch
manager J. E. McAlister and his wife went to town and bought the
finest black suits they had. "We got everything nice, including white
shirts. I know how those boys were buried," Mrs. McAlister said. "I
bought the clothes."[29]

Preparing and dressing the body was a sign of respect, because
even in death a body was to be treated with dignity.[30] Mary Ada May,
a native of Michigan, came to Texas in 1875 and married a cowboy in
Tascosa in 1887. She bristled at the accusation people were buried cal-
lously. "I never knew of anyone who didn't have a decent burial in
Tascosa. They were washed and dressed in clean clothes and some
body [*sic*] always read a scripture [*sic*] at the grave."[31]

Respect was also apparent in the care taken in moving the body.
Margaret Fullerton Frost recorded her experiences growing up in
southwestern Oklahoma in the first decade of the twentieth century.
Her father moved to Oklahoma from Iowa in 1900, hoping the sunshine, along with rest and good food, would work a miraculous cure on
his tuberculosis. One of the hands accidentally shot himself, and a
wagon was sent to the field for the body. "Mama snatched blankets
and a pillow to put on top of the straw the men put on the bed of the
wagon. The men added a big square of canvas."[32] Back at the ranch,
they pushed the wagon into the barn to get it out of the rain. Blanche
Rutherford's memory was one of a coffin being lifted onto their hack
for its trip to the grave site, and as was customary, placed on her
mother's heaviest and softest quilt.[33] Emerson Hough told about the
limp body of a young cowboy killed in a stampede being lifted to the
grieving trail boss sitting astride his horse. Taking the dead boy in his
arms, reins hanging loosely over the saddle horn, he rode slowly, holding his burden carefully across his lap. Saying nothing till he neared
camp, he muttered simply, "It's too d—d bad!"[34]

The final phase of laying out was to place the body on an article
of household furnishing that served as a bier until the time for burial.

Children were laid out on something as unlikely as a trunk or the cabinet of a sewing machine.[35] An adult would be placed more typically on a table or a bed. Under circumstances when burial was delayed—by snowbound conditions, for example—the body might be kept in a separate room or shielded by a blanket or other form of curtain hanging from the ceiling and draped around the casket.[36]

It was a neighborly ritual to sit up with the corpse. Marcia Caldwell said the family was never left alone with their dead.[37] Although sitting up became a courtesy shown the family, something to relieve their oppressive solitude, the practice originated out of necessity.[38] In the beginning it was a precaution to keep animals, especially cats, away from the body.[39] "You had to fight the cats off," Jess Barker said. "Oh, they were really anxious. Something about that corpse—I don't know. I guess they got an odor, but the idea was that they would eat it if they could get to it."[40] Boone McClure remembered asking his father why they sat up with the body. "He says, 'Well, they have to fight the rats off.'"[41] Ira Ott agreed it was because of the rats and mice. Pet Ott elaborated: "In those days there was animals and even the dogs and the animals could get in the places where they were."[42]

Born in 1879, Mary Ella Peters lived in various Texas and Oklahoma locations before moving to Amarillo in 1925. She told of harassment by cats while sitting with the corpse of a neighbor's baby. The father was delirious with grief, the mother so exhausted she could not stay awake. There were numerous holes in the small house, and cats started to creep through these openings to get at the body. Mrs. Peters took a broom and fought the cats off until midnight when the men who were making the casket arrived.[43]

Ed Lord recounted the grim experience of searching for a windmill greaser who had been missing for several days. He rode up to the little shack, "opened his door and seen at a glance he was laying in his bunk dead. He had a couple of weeks growth of beard on his face, (perhaps he did not even shave over a couple of times a month anyhow) and he was all bloated up. His two pet cats were eating him one on each side of his neck. I got a couple of pieces of baling wire and tied them around their necks and hung them both up in a tree that was growing near the door."[44]

Another concern was some means of protecting the body at the time of interment, although at the most primitive level a burial could proceed without any covering or wrap at all. These burials were more likely on the trail or under conditions demanding haste.[45] Alfred Moye told of hunting for stampeded beeves when he and fellow cowhands came across the corpse of a cowboy who had died in some unknown manner. They had to bury him on the spot, so they dug a hole and rolled him in with but little ceremony.[46] "Our hearts were sad," Moye said, "when we left that poor unknown boy out there under the sod of that lonely prairie, many miles from a habitation."[47] On other occasions and under different circumstances, though, an burial with no coffin could be a sign of indifference or even contempt, there being no pretense at protection. Frank Collinson recalled a fatal stabbing at a gaming table and the subsequent capture and lynching of the murderer. The next morning the stabbing victim was wrapped in a wagon sheet and "lowered" into his grave, but the killer was "rolled" into his grave—minus a shroud.[48]

If the body could not be protected, an attempt would be made to at least cover the face. Hough's account of covering the cowboy's face with his hat was cited in the preceding chapter. In another case a cloth was placed over the face.[49]

Some kind of fabric, full-body wrap was typical when a coffin was unavailable. Alexander Majors, nineteenth-century freighter, promoter of the pony express, and stage coach operator, observed that early expeditions in the West were made on horseback and the best the men could do in case of a death was roll the body in a blanket.[50] "Out on the plains," Joe Shelton said, "out with the chuck wagons where they's doing ranch work, they'd dig a grave, they'd wrap 'em in the blanket. They would just wrap him in a blanket and laid him away. Most everybody had a blanket."[51] Mack Jones left Illinois for Kansas in 1882 and over the next several years worked on a number of ranches from Kansas to New Mexico. He was in Lipscomb County,

Texas, when the great cattle herds would come through on their way to Wyoming. Drovers often rested these herds several days before moving on, and on one occasion when a cowboy was killed by lightning the response was simple. "We wrapped him in his blanket and put him down in his grave and covered him up."[52] More than one blanket would be used if they were in the cowboy's gear—"We wrapped him in his blankets, an' put him to bed." Victims of the range or trail would be buried in their clothes, just as they died.[53]

Baylis Fletcher's outfit drove a herd of longhorns up the Chisholm Trail from Victoria, Texas, to Wyoming in 1879. Fletcher noted that a common item tied to the cowboy's saddle was his slicker, and this might be used as his "only winding sheet."[54] A wagon sheet, the heavy canvas used as covering on the prairie schooners, was another common alternative.[55] The sheet might be torn into wide strips and wrapped around the body from head to foot.[56] Bodies were also frequently rolled in tarpaulins before burial.[57] Frank Collinson mentioned wrapping a body in a buffalo hide, and J. Frank Dobie made reference to a green cowhide.[58] If the body was that of a woman, a more feminine shroud such as a clean white linen tablecloth or a bed comforter was deemed more suitable.[59]

Coffins were of at least three types: improvised, homemade, or purchased. A large trunk, an Arbuckle's coffee shipping case, or an empty cracker box could provide the wood, be modified, or used in its existing state to house the body of a child.[60] Packing, goods, and wagon boxes were other crates that could serve the purpose, but in some instances these sundry containers were less than adequate.[61] In 1877 Motley County, Texas, a corpse placed in a box long enough to accommodate only a portion of the woman's body had to be buried with her feet protruding.[62] After digging a grave without assistance, one mid-nineteenth-century Kansas father contrived a coffin for his son by placing boards in the bottom of the hole in the form of a coffin. He stepped down into the open grave, lowered the body, and after covering it with a sheet arranged boards over the body as a cover.[63] Another blanket-shrouded body was placed on a layer of hay in the bottom of the grave and protected above by two-inch thick boards taken from wagons.[64]

Simple wooden coffins were generally made by friends, neighbors, or relatives, but in some cases this sad task fell to the immediate family. C. N. Cosby recalled the death of his small sister. "Dad went out—and he was a carpenter, had tools and had some lumber—and he went to work and made a little casket. I remember how sorry I felt for Daddy making a little coffin and putting little sister in it. And then Mother and the girls dressed it out with material and covered it with cloth—nice little bed for her."[65] Mary Shearer related her mother's account of migrating to Texas in the 1830s. A young child in the family died on the trail, and the father took an ax, went into the woods and cut down a tree. Out of the trunk he made a small coffin for the child. A stranger who happened by fastened down the lid, following which her father and brother dug the grave. Mrs. Shearer quoted her mother: "There, far away from home and friends, with dim forebodings of a clouded future, we buried our baby."[66] For loved ones within hearing distance, the coffin-making sounds of hammers and the rasping of saws had to be torture.[67]

If he could do no better, the coffin maker would simply make a kind of rude box.[68] "It couldn't make a very good-looking job," Shelton said, "but it beat nothing."[69] Mourners seated at a funeral service could not from their seat see the deceased because of the coffin's shape—"they were a square box and you had to go up and look straight down in there to see 'em."[70]

Lumber was at a premium, so material for coffins had to be taken where it could be found. On the trail or range the top sideboards on a wagon could be pulled off and used in an emergency.[71]

Early coffin makers had no choice but to use irregular grades of wood like puncheons, bark, rough pine, or cottonwood. Wood that the migrants brought with them or purchased for other purposes might have to be requisitioned for a casket.[72] Wardrobes, cupboards, and other pieces of furniture would be torn apart for their material.[73] Walls, partitions, and floors of barns, sheds, grain rooms, and houses yielded their timber. Water troughs for the animals were a common source of lumber.[74] V. H. Whitlock watched as hands made a casket from heavy cypress boards hauled in to build a water trough. "Uncle George said that kind of lumber would make a good coffin, being practically waterproof and slow to decay."[75]

Marcia Caldwell remembered open caskets sitting on saw horses at the grave site, the top boards nailed on just prior to burial.[76] In one case they made the casket too short and could not get the dead man's knees to bend, so the men took an ax and broke the legs, making them more manageable. Bob Beverly wrote of ranch hands ripping planks from the kitchen floor to build a coffin that turned out far too short, so one of the boys left and returned with an ax to "chop" off the man's legs. Fortunately, they finally worked the old man onto his side and doubled up his legs so the body would fit.[77]

Although roughhewn, coffins were not made carelessly. The builders would do their best, and everything taken into consideration, the individual was put away very respectably.[78] Dora Stroup tells of the makeshift funeral and burial of an unknown cowboy whose body was discovered lying along an ancient wagon trail, but they did the best for him with what they had.[79] Under more normal circumstances rugged wood would be planed or scraped smooth with glass, sawed, and fitted together so as to taper at the foot or maybe take on an oval shape.[80] Lavert Avent's dad and a neighbor always got the job of building caskets for area families. "They'd get about three one-by-twelve boxing plank and they'd take a sheet, they'd put some cotton in there and tack that sheet around on it. It looked real nice. They'd kind of slope it and make the foot of it a little narrower and the head a little wider up there. They'd taper off. Wouldn't be just a box."[81] Ira Ott's older cousin was a cabinetmaker, and when somebody died he would go to the home, measure the body, then work through the night to build a pine box. "Dad used to say he didn't see why he didn't make them boxes in advance, but this old man thought they had to fit."[82] Sawmills made available more finished lumber like black walnut or various native woods, and then coffins were cut to more exact measurements. Similar to those built by Mr. Avent and his neighbor, they were triangular, wider at the shoulders and more narrow at the feet.[83]

The casket might be padded with cotton batting covered with a white cloth like muslin or velvet, but in most cases they used whatever cloth was available because the small West Texas towns allowed for few choices.[84] If available, lace would be scalloped around the top inside edge of the coffin; maybe a row of flowers would provide a decorative border. A white cashmere shawl, underskirt, sheet, or other household domestic could be used to soften the hard wood.[85] A feather pillow, sometimes trimmed in black, might be placed under the head.[86]

It has been pointed out that women were the ones most likely to line the coffin. Bertha Doan Ross was the first white child to live in Wilbarger County in northern Texas where in 1878 her uncle established a trading post at a crossing on the Red River. When there was a death, cowboys usually made the wooden caskets, and Ross' father, who helped operate the post, supplied lawn and laces the women used for a lining.[87] In some circumstances, however, the clumsy fingers of cowboys had to provide these finishing touches.[88]

The coffin could be covered with fabric like black calico or black plush, perhaps dove-gray for adults but white for babies and small children.[89] When Ed Lord's baby daughter died under the collapsed roof of their house, an old carpenter made a casket and the women of the community lined it and covered it with velvet. "It wasn't all alike, but it was all they had."[90] Coffins were also painted black, and the rough pine boards of the first casket in Garden City, Kansas, were blackened with shoe polish.[91]

If a friend or neighbor did not donate his services, a carpenter or area woodworker might be paid to build a coffin. When lightning killed a man in his outfit, one rancher drove his wagon some thirty-five miles to Canadian, Texas, to have a coffin made. Unfortunately, on the return trip the casket was submerged during a river crossing and appeared ruined. The girls of a family living in a nearby one-room log house, however, removed the fabric, washed and pressed it, and re-lined the coffin.[92]

Once the population started increasing, store owners saw the need to have a supply of ready-made caskets on hand, and these items became a source of curiosity for the locals, accustomed to seeing only the homemade variety.[93] Early store-bought coffins, however, were very crude affairs in comparison to those available today.[94]

There were no ready-made, store-bought graves on the plains, nor were there professional grave diggers—"You just took your pick and shovel."[95] The pick, long-handled shovel, grubbing hoe, and maybe a crowbar for truing up the corners were "the sometimes sad utensils" required for the difficult task of digging out a grave. Boone McClure helped dig a few graves, "and boy, that was hard digging! There'd probably be three or four that'd go do the digging, but your space, you see, was barely over six feet long and about six feet deep."[96] Not just hard, the task could be painful. Albert Gilles remembered the difficult digging outside of Faxon. The soil had never been disturbed, and "Sometimes it seemed the pick actually bounced back when I tried to drive it into the red earth. I remember wondering to myself if the great buffalo herds had not helped to pack the earth, because it seemed so solid."[97] Digging in sun-baked soil was like breaking through concrete, and in frozen ground, like cutting through iron.[98] The men who dug graves in blizzard conditions, all the while fighting the punishing wind and snow, are justifiably esteemed as "heroes unsung by poets."[99]

At times the only alternative was to dig a shallow grave, and the cowhand who died on a cattle drive was usually laid away in such a grave.[100] When one cowboy was killed in a stampede the men took a broken-handled shovel and buried him on a nearby rock-covered hillside. They dug a little ground from beneath the body, slipped his saddle blanket under him, and finally covered the grave with rocks. "That was the best we could do," E. C. Abbott said. "The ground was hard and we didn't have no proper tools."[101]

Frank Collinson reminisced about digging a shallow grave because of the frozen ground. They finally rolled the body into the hole,
no more than a foot deep, and covered it with brush. A week later
when the ground had thawed, one of the men returned to the grave
and covered it more securely. With warmer weather, though, the coyotes succeeded in scratching him out, and some hunters who found
the bones had to rebury them.[102]

In other instances bodies were simply left on the ground and
covered with earth, but these bodies were soon uncovered, leaving
body parts exposed and passersby horrified.[103] But generally emigrants and early settlers would take great precautions to protect a
grave. The soil would be pounded as firmly as possible and "cruel
stones" piled on top. Rocks, large pieces of timber, and even cactus
might be put in graves, just over the corpse, in a futile attempt to ward
off marauding wolves and coyotes.[104] Determined wolves were known
to make their den in a grave, and wolves and coyotes could be seen
growling and scratching at a grave even before the burial party was out
of sight.[105]

> *They have gone the long dim trail,*
> *Down the shadow of the vale,*
> *O'er their lone graves the lean*
> *Coyotes sigh.*[106]

It was not the thought of coyotes peacefully sighing over one's
grave that was so worrisome, but the idea of being consumed by wild
animals that westerners found so traumatizing. The words to the
mournful ballad—"O bury me not on the lone prairie, Where the wild
coyotes will howl o'er me"—left a distinct image in the minds of early
plains dwellers. Easterners had thoughts of a lonely but peaceful
grave with sounds of coyotes yelping in the distance. The wrangler
saw these coyotes fighting over his remains.[107]

A. C. Greene notes that small, burrowing creatures could also
invade a grave, "blindly going after something sensed rather than

known," but wild animals, large or small, were less threatening to the grave than domestic ones, knocking over headstones and trampling sacred soil.[108] Opal Berryman remembered their square and bare cemetery with only a four-strand fence of rusty barbed wire protecting graves from the vandal hooves of a thousand cattle.[109]

Van Doney Burrus's family was living in Floyd County, Texas, when her six-year-old brother died from diphtheria in 1907. "The neighbors came in as they always do in pioneer country and the men . . . made the little coffin or casket and one of our neighbor friends made the little clothes for him. They lined the little pine box with nice white cambric inside and covered the outside with heavy black woolen cloth. . . . We went, and the neighbors did, in wagons, the family together, and some of our girl friends. Father took an extra wagon and team with wire and posts to fence his grave before we went away from there. It was in a pasture, and he knew stock would tromp and paw that fresh dirt that very night and he couldn't stand the thought of that."[110]

One grave might be enclosed with bois d'arc and twisted barbed wire, another by a small wooden fence, and if enough large stones were nearby, a rock fence might be constructed.[111] Most plains graves, however, were not protected by any kind of enclosure, and for many range-hardened punchers this was probably just as well.

> *Let cattle rub my headstone round,*
> *And coyotes wail their kin,*
> *Let horses come and paw the mound,*
> *But don't you fence it in.*[112]

Graves might be personalized, like the one with a hole "rounded out" in the center containing a man's knife, tobacco, and pipe.[113] Another trailside grave was surrounded by a pen of cottonwood poles enclosing a rocking chair with the name of the dead woman carved on it.[114] In many cases, however, older graves were identified by neither fence, mound, nor marker.[115] When Indians had been a threat, every attempt was made to conceal or obliterate the grave for fear it would be recognized and plundered for the clothing. Once exhumed, the body was then left exposed and even more vulnerable to scavenging animals.[116]

The natural tendency would be to mark a grave site in order to be able to find it again, and this was frequently done on both the wagon and cattle trails.[117] Mourners left rudely hewn wooden markers, the name of the deceased whittled out with a pocket knife.[118] The endgate of a wagon would be shaped into a headboard and the name and date of death burned in or daubed on with tar axle lubricant.[119] If a tree were nearby, a name could be cut into the trunk.[120] A rock or two might be all that was left to identify the spot, but if there were time and a slab of stone, words would be crudely chiseled into what was hopefully a permanent tablet.

No matter what marker the mourners might devise, though—be it a piece of wood or even a pile of rocks—no monument could withstand the relentless abuse of the elements.[121] Headboards with "rainwashed epitaphs" in cowboy scrawling would in time lean wearily under the weight of years.[122] Slabs of wood that once bore legends became "gray and wordless."[123] "Sandstone sentinels" wasted away from decades of rains and freezes—"Sentinels, but not too faithful, carrying now only an enticing line or so. . . ."[124]

> *The face*
> *Is gone. Years and*
> *Rain—the victors. Where are they*
> *Who strove to image here your face*
> *Forever?*[125]

As the plains became established and as emigrants became permanent residents, bodies were buried within the protective radius of a home or ranch where graves could be maintained.[126] Fresh dirt would be heaped on the graves, the headboards straightened, a few wildflowers placed in memory of the dead.[127] Graves were also clustered in a cemetery under the guardianship of a small town, protected from animal and plow.[128] Greene speaks to the continuity of graveyards in West Texas, where the frontier touches hands with the present. These cemeteries, some of the first public sites marked off, are all that remain of many a vanished community. "The tide of cities receded, leaving cemeteries to mark its retreat. The oldest cemeteries of West Texas have that gray, deserted corner where the burial started, nameless stones set at head and foot."[129] Opal Berryman never forgot the bereaved father standing at his son's grave, vacantly gazing beyond the desolate cemetery. There was no tree, no shrub to soften the bleak mounds of impassive earth.[130]

For wagons on the move or cattle on the drive, there were generally no communities of tombstones, no gray fields with bleak humps of earth in which to bury the dead. People desperately wanted to leave their dead next to another grave so the newly buried would not be so lonesome, but too often this was not possible. Dora Stroup recalled the four cedar posts and three strands of barbed wire guarding a solitary mound on a hill—the lone cowboy's grave, as it was then called. No one ever knew where he was from or who he was.[131]

One ranch grave site, so remote and obscure that passersby would miss its presence, was marked by a sandstone slab. Beneath a nearly illegible name (seemingly "Williams") were chiseled the words:

Born 1860–Died Oct. 1880
—Cowboy—
Horse Fell on Him[132]

Young people strolling along a riverbank in Archer County, Texas, discovered a grave with a weathered headstone. "Cowboy" and "last word" were all that remained to be deciphered.[133]

Ralph Allred attended a small one-room school house out of Fort Worth, and on the acre-size school yard was a single grave. "It was our playground, but that was the only grave there was there. It was just made out on the prairie. It's there yet."[134]

Near the little village of Cloverdale
There stands a lonely tomb.
Nearby the cows are browsing
And the lonely nightbirds call
It is there my memory wanders
When the evening shadows fall[135]

A factor contributing to this sense of loneliness, even in death, was the vastness of the plains. What anguished one mother when she buried her child on a colorless winter day was that the grave seemed so tiny and pitiful against the boundless prairie. The appearance of grass every spring became a consolation because it covered the grave and made it look less like it did on that sorrowful day.[136]

John Clay, a Scot who became a well-known nineteenth-century cattleman, wrote about ranch life in the Northwest. He never forgot the sentimental dirge sung by Texas cowboys one harsh winter night. They were snowbound in a one-room log cabin, and the boys sang by flickering candlelight. "It rings in my ears yet. The solemn moan of the winter wind blended with the quartette [*sic*]."

It matters not, I've oft been told,
Where the body lies when the heart grows cold;
Yet grant, Oh grant this wish to me,
O bury me not on the lone prairie.
O then bury me not on the lone prairie,
In a narrow grave six foot by three,
Where the buffalo paws o'er a prairie sea,
O bury me not on the lone prairie.[137]

This was a song frequently sung during night riding when boys were guarding the herd. They always felt lonely after the cattle were bedded down and all that could be heard was the mournful howl of the coyotes. "Every cowboy had a horror of being killed and buried out on the lone prairie," according to Frank Exum. "They could not imagine anything that could be worse than their remains being placed out on some lonely hill on the frontier where nobody would ever come by."[138]

Some, though, were able to find comfort in a prairie burial. The previous chapter referred to the hand killed in Rawhide Rawlins's outfit. Some of the men wanted to take him to Dodge City and have a box made for the body, but Old Spanish reminded them that Longrope was a prairie man, and even though the prairie was a little rough at times, she had always been a good foster mother. "'She cared for him while he's awake; let her nurse him in his sleep.' So we wrapped him in his blankets, an' put him to bed.

"It's been twenty years or more since we tucked him in with the end-gate of the bed-wagon for a headstone, which the cattle have long since rubbed down, leavin' the spot unmarked. It sounds lonesome, but he ain't alone, 'cause these old prairies has cradled many of his kind in their long sleep."[139]

My home is my saddle
My roof is the sky;
The prairies I'll ride
Till the day that I die.
I'll live on the prairie
Till life shall have passed
And lie down to sleep
In her bosom at last.[140]

LONELY GRAVES ARE UNFREQUENTED, DESOLATE GRAVES THAT WITH TIME are destined to be neglected, forgotten, and lost forever. They are as unknown on the great ocean of plains as are those of sailors buried at sea.[141] They have become part of a vast prairie-grass burial ground stretching across the country, last resting places where not even small plots of swollen earth remain to mark the sites.[142] The day eventually came when farmers planted corn over the abandoned bodies, and railroads dug up their nameless remains.[143] Joe Shelton would not have been surprised "for 'em to dig up a grave anywhere. I imagine a lot of wheat fields around you've got some graves in 'em. . . . They'd bury 'em and they'd never go back there and nobody back there's to do anything about it."[144]

For the few who could go back, graves were in all likelihood never found.[145] Some of the most poignant scenes in plains literature would have to be those of aged settlers returning to bygone homesteads, looking but unable to find the graves for which they were searching. Craig Miner includes the account of Mrs. John Cole's return to the Kansas homestead she and her family settled in 1878. She saw remains of the house and found fragments of a special cupboard, but seeing the knoll where the house had stood was not enough. Off she continued, walking round and round, looking for yet another mound—a small grave where they had buried one of their children in those difficult bygone years. "Time, however, had done its work and there was no sign of it—nothing to mark that amid the activities of that hopeful homestead, a life had flickered briefly and been swallowed without a trace."[146]

V. H. Whitlock was a child when westward-bound homesteaders, battered by a nighttime winter storm, stopped their wagon. The father wearily asked if they could bring their seriously ill infant out of the cold into the house. His mother hurried the small family inside and did what she could—the nearest doctor was a hundred miles away—but the baby died during the night. Next morning cowpunchers shoveled a path through the snow to a pasture behind the corral. There they dug a grave. It was a sorrowful scene when the griefstricken parents continued their journey west, leaving behind their child buried there on the bleak prairie. "Every time I hear that old cowboy song, ''Neath the western skies on the Lone Prairie,' I see that father and mother sitting in the spring seat of their wagon as they drove away, looking back at that little grave in our horse pasture." Decades later Whitlock returned to the site of this West Texas ranch house, but there was no sign of the small grave in the pasture where a baby belonging to a family of young home seekers was buried more than seventy years ago.[147]

> *A sadder search you'd hardly plan*
> *Than a brother seeking a brother's bones,*
> *Seeking the grave of a murdered man,*
> *On the plain where the wind like a mourner moans;*
> *Seeking a skull that the wolves have gnawed,*
> *Bones that the keen-eyed fox has pawed!*[148]

The Sounds of Entombment

By an open grave the mourners crowded around. . . .

[They] seemed much like dumb, animated monuments. No music. Not a voice could be heard. The only sound—muffled scufflings of hesitating, respecting feet through the prairie grass! From the faces of the men you could judge that the end of things had come for them and theirs. Women appeared ready to cry and boys and girls clung to their parents. The coffin was lowered. The first hopeless clods fell dully upon it. Flowers and sprigs dropped into the forlorn cavity.

Stuart Henry

J. C. ESTLACK WAS WORKING FOR THE TURKEY TRACK OUTFIT near Artesia, New Mexico, when Shady Davis, a cowboy from a nearby ranch, was thrown from his horse and dragged seven miles, his right hand entangled in the rope tied to his saddle horn. The cowboy was killed and mutilated beyond description, so it was decided to hold a quick funeral. There being no people anywhere near other than the men at the scene, the cowboys wrapped the body in the newest tarpaulin, dug a grave, and lowered the corpse into the ground. At that point one of the men suggested that someone should say something. "It really looked awfully crude to bury a friend without a word being said. Tom Cotten, a lanky puncher, took off his hat and said from the head of the grave, 'I'll say this, Shady was a damn good feller.' Nothing more was said and the lonely grave tops the hill where cowboys have kept the fence up for more than thirty years."[1]

Between 1876 and 1883 E. C. Abbott helped bury three sidekicks killed while working cattle. One man's body was so badly trampled in a stampede that supposedly the only thing recognizable was the handle of his six-shooter. Another was killed "deader than hell" when his horse ran off a thirty-foot embankment. The outfit took off the rest of the afternoon to bury him, and after the grave was dug, one of the fellows said: "Somebody ought to say something. Don't nobody know the Lord's Prayer?" Abbott volunteered but got only as far as "Thy will be done" when he got to thinking about his own dead brother and had to quit. "You know why. I was kind of rattled anyhow."[2]

Born in 1860 the son of a Kansas railroad builder, Fred E. Sutton in the early 1880s became the first Sooner to lay claim on land in north-central Oklahoma. Witness to the lawless days of the Oklahoma and southwestern frontiers, Sutton told about attending the burial of a cowboy shot during a quarrel on a bank of the Cimarron. As the men stood around the grave, hats in hands, someone commented that Bill had been a decent sort of fellow, and it was a shame he had to be buried like a dog without even a song.[3] At that point one of the cowboys solemnly began to sing all nine verses of "The Cowboy's Dream," a favorite across cow country. Sung to the tune of "My Bonnie Lies Over the Ocean," it began:

Last night as I lay on the prairie,
And looked at the stars in the sky,
I wondered if ever a cowboy
Would drift to that sweet bye and bye.

Roll on, roll on;
Roll on, little dogies, roll on, roll on,

Roll on, roll on;
Roll on, little dogies, roll on.[4]

There is consensus among various social sciences that mankind is a species that buries its dead with decorum, and in American culture there is a long-established tradition of burying the dead with ceremony.[5] The funeral is not a single event, but rather a series of phases or experiences through which the survivors pass: removal of the body to prepare it for burial, visitation, the funeral rite, the procession, and finally, committal. In West Texas, visitation was accompanied by laying out of the body, sitting up, arranging for a coffin and grave, bringing in food, and performing chores, as well as offering condolences. Unless the person was buried on the site, the procession would be a brief journey by foot or wagon. If there were a ceremony, it might precede committal or be the same event, but, in keeping with one of the historical functions of funerals, the survivors were generally compelled to have some kind of rite to honor the deceased and to give witness to the life lived.[6] Something needed to be said. A passage of Scripture needed to be recited. A song needed to be sung.

There were instances, to be sure, where the dead were buried without any sort of service, borne away "without prayer, requiem or knell, and laid [in a] narrow home. . . ."[7] One West Texan said her brother died at birth, and "Of course they didn't have a funeral, they just buried him."[8] A burial might proceed without a single word spoken.[9] While working for the Two Circles Bar Ranch a cowboy died after his horse fell on him. A woman in the area conducted a funeral service that became memorable because such a ceremony was so unprecedented.[10]

Sutton told about the burial of four cowboys killed in a Tascosa, Texas, gunfight. No lumber was available for coffins, so each body, boots on and clothed as it was when shot down, was simply wrapped in a blanket and lowered into the grave. Time was not even taken to wash the faces of the men, and one, especially, was caked with dried blood because he had been shot in the face. "There was no ceremony of any

Boot Hill tombstone,
Old Tascosa, Texas.
Courtesy Research Center,
Panhandle-Plains Historical
Museum

kind," Sutton said. "There was no one in Tascosa qualified to deliver a sermon. I feel sure there was not a Bible or prayer-book in town."[11]

Mrs. Mickey "Frenchy" McCormick, one of Tascosa's original inhabitants, made similar comments to a *Kansas City Star* reporter when he asked to see Boot Hill, burial site at the time for thirty-two men. "There wasn't a preacher within 200 miles and I do not believe there was a Bible any nearer," McCormick said. "There wasn't a soul in Tascosa who could pray, so we all tried to look as solemn as we could as we buried them."[12]

In spite of these unceremonious burials, the impulse to in some way honor the dead was compelling. Although crude and simple, funerals of men who died on the range were deeply moving. According to Philip Rollins, an open grave, somewhere out on the plains, would be surrounded by a small cluster of tight-lipped men. After the blanket-enfolded body was lowered gently into its resting place, there was a pause. Each man desperately wished that something appropriate might be said, either to God or about the dead, but none felt equal to the task. As they stood nervously around the grave, perhaps someone uttered a quiet expletive. If so, the requirement that something be said had been satisfied. If nothing was said, one of the men would glance at the shovel, but "Whether by the ending of the spoken words or by the recognition of the spade, the signal for the filling of the grave had come."[13]

Rollins's depiction also included a commonly mentioned feature of early range grave sites—the ponderous silence. On the range, it was the strained, uncomfortable reserve with which most American men of the era cloaked their deepest feelings.[14] The stillness was much the same in town. Stuart Henry described the scene at an Abilene, Kansas, funeral where mourners crowded around an open grave like "dumb, animated monuments." There was no music or speaking. "The only sound—muffled scufflings of hesitating, respecting feet through the prairie grass!"[15] The terms cemetery, graveyard, and silence almost seem synonymous. Marguerite Wallace Kennedy, an Arizona teacher during the early days of statehood, married a rancher and wrote about Arizona ranch life. She was taken by the stillness at the grave site, noting it was like a world removed.[16] Even at committals where there was a simple service, still a strange, unbroken silence seemed to pervade.[17] The words of the preacher were uttered against the backdrop of a hush, the kind of still that hovers over the presence of death.[18]

The observations of Rollins, like those of McCormick and Sutton, also referred to the difficulty often encountered in finding someone to conduct a service. This was especially true if the death

A cowboy funeral.
Courtesy Research Center, Panhandle-Plains Historical Museum

occurred unexpectedly in a remote area and burial was immediate. Under these circumstances, anything said or any act of ceremony might require prompting, and then it was often contributed hesitantly. On a cattle drive or out on the range, the wagon boss likely assumed responsibility for the burial and any last words.[19] A soiled and tattered Bible would have been stowed in the chuck wagon for just such an occasion.[20] Albert Thompson told about two cowboys killed in a gunfight and the "simple obsequies" that followed. As neighbor-

ing outfits gathered, the men, far from friends and home, were committed to earth. A Bible was borrowed, and the wagon boss selected a chapter. "'There ain't no preacher on this 'ere range,' he stated, 'an' if there was we'd surely round him up an' bring him in to do the job. There bein' none, it falls to me . . . I now proceedes with the verses.'"[21]

Joe Shelton could never recall a preacher presiding over an early-day range burial—"It [was] too far off, but he'd come later on and preach the funeral."[22] Most frontier settlements had no resident minister, so it was weeks, months, and in some cases years before a preacher who had moved in, a circuit rider on his rotation, or a cleric just passing through could be recruited to hold a belated service.[23] Word of these services would sometimes circulate for weeks in advance, attracting large gatherings.[24]

Writing about early days on the South Plains, Nellie Spikes told of a young man's remark that some old codger was going to have to be shipped in so a graveyard could be started. This very same youth was later killed while taking his gun off the wagon and it accidentally discharged. It was his body that started the local cemetery. "It was such a sad, sad funeral. As there was no preacher, his sister read the Scripture and prayed the prayer."[25]

A family member might well be the one required to control emotions long enough to say a few last words. Jessie Loomis Gilbert came with her parents to the Panhandle in 1890 where her father plowed the first field in Sherman County. When her brother was shot to death by a friend, her father conducted the service.[26] Marie Barbier Hess was two years of age when her family left France for Texas in 1882. Her mother died in Mineral Wells in 1884, and six years later the father and children moved to the Panhandle. Two months after arriving Mr. Barbier died, and it was Hess's sister who prayed the graveside prayer for her father, the only words spoken.[27]

Members of the community—a sainted person, a religious woman, or a layman recognized for devoutness—conducted many funerals. "Most of the time we buried the people without a preacher," Willie McClary said, "but there was always, usually, some religious person—well, my grandfather was one of 'em. I'd put him up against any preacher for knowing the Bible."[28] It might be the oldest man who was asked to say a few words, as in Joe Shelton's small community where an old man who lived by the cemetery always "gave a little service."[29]

It was not unusual for a child or young person to play some part in the ritual. For the funeral of a neighbor's child, Ad Spaugh suggested the preaching be assigned to one of the young cowboys in his outfit. "His paw' a regular minister, an' it'll be jest about the same thing to have him as to have a real parson."[30] In some cases a husband and wife might collaborate in these last rites.[31]

Western-bound wagons passing through unfamiliar communities or ranches were often dependent on a virtual stranger to conduct a funeral service, but grief and sympathy could make for instant bonding. Though they would never meet again, travelers and locals probably never forgot those brief and sad moments together around an open grave.[32]

A qualified sojourner was sometimes pressed into service for a local death. Dora Merrell Stroup's mother was summoned to the F Ranch by another mother whose child was desperately ill. While she got ready, one of the men caught a horse and cinched on a sidesaddle. Carrying her small son in her lap, she was off to see to the child. There was nothing Mrs. Merrell could do, however, and the little girl, Molly, died. That night a stranger stopped at the ranch for a meal and place to sleep, and on learning of the child's death he went into the kitchen to visit with Mrs. Merrell. He inquired about local funeral customs and was told there was no one to hold a funeral. Only one man prayed in public and that was the old man who was making the coffin. He was not well, and it doubtful he would attend the funeral. Mrs. Merrell wished aloud that someone would read a passage from the Bible, but they did not even have a Bible. "'Mrs. Merrell, I always carry my Bible with me,' the stranger said. 'I will read a few verses and say a prayer if they want me to.' Mother told him she would find out. They said they would be glad for him to do it."[33]

ALTHOUGH SOME EARLY WEST TEXAS AND SOUTHWESTERN FU-
nerals have been described as brief, heedless affairs, most funerals in settled sections and along the cattle trails were neither thoughtless nor neglectful.[34] They were simple ceremonies consisting of maybe a few words, a Scripture-reading, a prayer, a song, and possibly a sermon. Some rites were so brief as to consist of only one of these fea-

tures—"One man said prayers and that's all. It was awful sad too."[35] Other services may have included but a couple of the rituals—"My brother was buried . . . with only a song and a prayer."[36]

On the cattle trails, it could be a cursory, though sincere, comment about the deceased with no ceremonial significance whatsoever—"Shady was a damn good feller," for example. Rollins recorded the simple, hesitant words spoken at the burial for one man killed in a stampede: "It's too bad, too bad. Tom, dig a little deeper there. Hell, boys, he was a man." The burial was completed with a parting farewell: "Bill, we boys leave you to God and the mountain. Good-by, Bill."[37]

If several mourners gathered for a funeral, someone would read "a little bit of an obituary," but not delve extensively into the person's biography.[38] Alma Pafford recalled, "They would read the history of the person they were having the funeral for, when he was born and where he lived. Kind of giving a little light history."[39]

Scripture reading was almost always a part of any graveside ritual.[40] Some remembered a Bible verse or verses in general, but others identified specific passages—the Twenty-third Psalm, Chapter Fourteen of the Gospel According to Saint John, or the Lord's Prayer.

Songs were sung by one or more individuals or by all of those in attendance. William Timmons stood with four others beside a shallow-grave burial at which no words were spoken, the only sounds coming from a song sung by one of the men, a rich baritone.[41] Local singing groups, those who sang at community gatherings, often provided the music, or it was "those ol' ladies that thought they could sing [who] would sing some songs or something."[42] In 1894 English traveler Mary Jaques wrote about ranch life in Texas based on her two-year stay in the state. She observed a graveside service in Junction City and commented on the beautiful and impressive hymns, unfortunately marred by the nasal tones of those who participated.[43] Kennedy acknowledged that the voices of those who joined in the singing were untrained, yet she found them sincere and plaintive.[44]

These songs, according to Mildred Winkleman, were always "sad songs, of course—'When the Roll is Called Up Yonder I'll be There'—hopefully!"[45] "Nearer, My God, to Thee," "In the Sweet Bye and Bye," "Shall We Gather at the River," "Work for the Night Is Coming," and "Safe in the Arms of Jesus" were some of the other gospel songs sung on such occasions.

Dora Stroup and her sister were asked to sing at the funeral for Molly. "Molly would want you and Jane to sing a song," their mother had said. "We were just children and we did not know what to sing. We decided to sing 'Hark the Voice of Jesus is Calling.' Jane and I stood by the casket with our calico dresses on and our sunbonnets and sang:

> *Hark the voice of Jesus calling,*
> *Who will go and work today.*
> *The fields are white;*
> *The harvest waiting,*
> *Who will bear the sheaves away?*
> *Loud and long the Master calleth,*
> *Rich reward He offers free;*
> *Who will answer, gladly saying,*
> *'Here am I, send me, send me'?*

The stranger read his scripture [*sic*]. I do not remember what it was. He said a sweet prayer. Then the casket was lowered in the grave. Jane and I felt like we had done so badly, but Father said when we got home that we had never sung so pretty in our lives. This made us feel good."[46]

Catherine Porter recalled the "so inadequate" service for her father. A neighbor girl tried falteringly to lead the singing of Psalm Forty, one of her father's favorites:

> *I waited for the Lord my God,*
>   *And patiently did bear,*

At length to me he did incline
　　My voice and cry to hear.

He took me from a fearful pit
　　And from the miry clay
And set my feet upon a rock
　　Establishing my way.

He put a new song in my mouth
　　My God to magnify,
Many shall see it and shall fear
　　And on the Lord rely.[47]

The songs on these occasions were not necessarily religious in nature. More than one cowhand was undoubtedly buried to a mournful cowboy ballad, usually performed with such quavering voice that few hearers were left unmoved.[48] Some of these songs indulged in homesickness or romantic sentimentality, but a few touched on religion. In "The Cowboy's Dream," also known also as "The Great Roundup" and "The Dim, Narrow Trail," a cowboy, reclining on the prairie, gazes above at the nighttime stars and ponders that sweet bye and bye.[49]

In contrast to the extravagant funeral practices in England, those in colonial America were rather simple affairs involving little ceremony.[50] Time, however, led to more elaborate services, and by the early eighteenth century the funeral sermon had become established. The gathering of mourners was a chance to preach, the minister's great opportunity to make an impression. A funeral would put those around the casket in a receptive mood, it being one occasion they were likely to listen.[51] More than simply a ceremony, the funeral was an event for both the living and the dead.[52] Even the righteous could benefit from a refresher on the inevitability of death, so preachers would not want to miss this great moment before a small but attentive assembly.

Early plains burials, however, were sparsely attended affairs. When one of three elderly bachelor brothers died, George Tucker helped another brother dig the grave. No one was at the burial except Tucker and the two surviving brothers.[53] Three children—Marie Barbier, her brother and sister—and a neighbor were the only four who stood beside the grave of their father.[54] Several estimates placed the number that might be present at a frontier funeral at around a dozen, and this would have been a crowd.[55] In some communities, fifteen to twenty families could be represented, and if the service were in a small church, the building might be filled.

With established communities and more people in attendance, services became longer. "Some of 'em would kind of make a sermon out of it," Hobart McManigal said. "There'd be people [there], I guess, that don't get talked to any other time."[56] Hazel Walsh spoke of funeral services as including "songs and Bible reading and sometimes *too* long a sermon."[57] It seemed to Boone McClure as though the minister preached two sermons due to the fact he talked so long at the cemetery. "You'd get out there in the freezing weather and take your hat off out of respect for the dead and then the preacher would stand there and just preach another sermon and you'd nearly freeze to death."[58]

Services for the dead were often so grievous as to have few redeeming features. "Funerals today," according to South Plains native Bill Collyns, "are more on the line of a celebration, [an] occasion honoring the deceased. They're much more helpful to the family and mourners attending the services today. They've gotten away from the longer services. They're usually more brief. They used to last an hour or more at times."[59] Pet Ott attended a funeral that continued for some two hours. "This preacher was trying to save him I guess, but it was a terrible thing. It wasn't a comforting thing, what you'd expect when you'd go to a service."[60] Marcia Caldwell said they used to talk about preaching them into heaven. "If they didn't think they made it on their own, why the preacher could preach 'em into heaven."[61]

Not all funeral sermons were disagreeable. Jaques seemed impressed with the funeral service she attended, even though the "address," like the hymns, was spoiled by the nasal quality of the delivery.[62] When one preacher came to town to hold a belated service for a settler buried earlier, a collection was taken following the service. The cowboys were so impressed with his sermon that the hat was filled with silver dollars.[63]

AS NOTED, PEOPLE GENERALLY DIED AT HOME. IF THEY DIED elsewhere the body was more than likely returned to the home or buried on the spot. The body of one young cowboy killed by lightning was carried to a nearby cabin for the night. The parents and children moved outside where they slept and cooked over a campfire. The next day the family and a few cowboys were the only ones present for a brief service during which the father read a Scripture, sang a hymn, and offered a prayer.[64]

"Much, much of the time," Willie McClary said, "[the service] was held in the family home," but Gladys Deitiker emphasized that funerals were *always* in the home, "and the casket would be open and there was this awful dread of that room, that living room, where the casket had been for maybe two days—open. The room was never quite the same to you." The mother would be tired, and the father maybe emotional, so "you not only had this shock to yourself but this body lying over there in this open casket."[65]

Whether a service was held in the home, a church, or at graveside, viewing of the body was a tradition and a social expectation. If the body were in the home, Caldwell said, "part of going in was to look [at the body]," and this meant "all the way down to the feet too."[66] In a church, the mourner who did not go down to the open coffin was conspicuous.[67] It was against her will, but Ruth Lowes got caught up in the crowd walking past a casket, and the result was a mental picture of the man that lingered for days. "Sort of worried me. I somehow thought, 'Now what would happen to me if my mother died and was put in a box like that.'"[68] She later learned to turn her head when filing past a casket. After her grandmother died in the home, a neighbor tried to pressure her to step inside the room to see the body. "I didn't want to go. And I didn't."[69]

The funeral for Tom Black's aunt was held in her home, and people congregated around in the yard. "Wasn't room in the house for 'em. Hell, the whole house wouldn't be as big as this living room. So they stood around out there and the preacher would stand there in the door and deliver some kind of a funeral sermon or something."[70] It was common for as many as possible to group inside the house, others standing in the yard.[71] Marguerite Kennedy described people crowding into the living room, while some looked in from the dining room, others from the porch.[72]

At the end of the day their infant died, Henry and Rosa Ise slept the sleep of total exhaustion in the same room with the body and the neighbors who volunteered to sit as watchers. The funeral was held the following day, and Henry placed boards on chairs, boxes, and nail kegs arranged along the walls of the room. Those unable to find room on these boards sat on the bed. Everyone seated, a neighbor stood in the door and read a brief passage from the Gospel of Matthew: "Then were there brought unto him little children, that he should put his hands on them, and pray: and the disciples rebuked them. But Jesus said, 'Suffer little children and forbid them not, to come unto me: for of such is the kingdom of heaven.'"[73]

The service for the emigrant child on the Whitlock ranch was held in the living room. Mrs. Whitlock read a chapter from the Bible, then accompanying herself on the organ, sang a hymn. Finally, the small company of grievers knelt on the floor in prayer.[74]

Unless a person were buried at the site where death occurred, the body would have to be moved from the house to the grave; and if the burial plot were within a short distance the coffin was carried by men on foot. The small coffin for the emigrant child was carried by cowhands from the Whitlock house to the nearby horse pasture.[75] Two men picked up the Ise infant's casket, and the rest of the procession followed out to the corral for the burial.[76] If the coffin held an adult and the walk to the grave site was longer, covered difficult terrain, or proceeded up a slope, extra men might have to step in to assist with the burden.[77]

Bodies carried to more distant graves required the use of that hearse of the plains, the wagon.[78] George Tucker recalled the poignant sight of two wagons on the distant horizon headed for town to bury his uncle.[79] Although it was often the neighbor with the best wagon who volunteered his services, who actually provided this transportation was also a matter of convenience.[80] The funeral for Lee Matney's father was out in the open at the burial site. "They hauled him over there in a wagon. The ranch down there that was adjoining us, they wrote us a note and said they'd send us a team and horses to take him over there."[81]

The coffin could be slipped onto the bed of a wagon with little difficulty, but if a hack or carriage was used the back seat would have to be unlocked and lifted out.[82] The casket containing a small child might be cradled in the laps of a couple of mourners seated in the wagon. It was apparently not uncommon for the coffin to be placed on and covered by quilts, certainly protected by a wagon sheet or tarpaulin in case of rain.

The funeral cortege could consist of the wagon followed by mourners on foot, or be composed of a slowly moving train of hacks, surreys, buggies, wagons, and riders on horseback.[83] In some instances, because of road conditions or weather, men would have to remove the coffin from the wagon and carry it the remainder of the way by foot.[84] Kennedy remembered the obscure path to their small family graveyard as a trail "so grown over in spots, so covered with rocks, so whipped by wind and sand that its very existence seemed of the past rather than the present."[85]

Mary Jaques described the Junction City service as especially picturesque. Participants arrived in every variety of gay attire, the women in large sunbonnets and simple but colorful costumes.[86] The deceased was a relative stranger in town, a recently arrived consumptive who had hoped the dry air would restore his health, thus one reason for the festive air and the absence of funereal gloom. But far from being colorful and picturesque, the funeral scene more typically was one of a sad little body of people standing in the dusty grass, singing age-old gospel hymns, and hearing the preacher proclaim with sober finality: "Dust to dust, ashes to ashes."[87] Funerals were spoken of as somber, morbid, sad, frightening. "It was solemn business, a dreary business, a sad thing. Everything was sad."[88] "Funerals," Joe Shelton said, "bothered me, scared me—other kids too. [We] didn't understand."[89]

Kennedy is of the opinion that the face of a true Westerner is often expressionless—a poker face. Hurt is buried deeply, any emotion choked off before it reaches the surface.[90] To Philip Rollins's way of thinking, however, "Nature seems to have invented various horrid sounds for the final leave-takings of the several species of her animal subjects."[91] The prevailing hush that settled over early prairie funerals was often ruptured by the open and evident sounds of ineffable grief. Nineteenth- and early-twentieth-century deaths, especially those involving children, were events calling for public and vocal expressions of grief.[92] Ruth Cross came to Canyon, Texas, in 1927 from Wichita, Kansas, and she was startled by the "wailing—actual wailing—and crying and carrying on—physical expression of [emotion]."[93] "Somewhere in my childhood," Hazel Walsh thought back, "I remember people always crying and moaning and taking on at funerals. It seemed to me as if they wanted people to know they were suffering. They took on a great deal. My father hated it and I think he brought us up not to show much emotion."[94] Louise Gibson was another bothered by this behavior. "They'd put on a show. Sometimes . . . you could hear them all over town."[95] Mildred Winkleman concluded, "They didn't mind crying so people could see 'em and hear 'em. . . . I think it was just all right for everybody to make a big cry."[96]

Asked if people responded to death emotionally, Marcia Caldwell's response was instant and emphatic: "*Yess!* That was a part of it, to give the neighbors and friends an exhibition of your grief. I can't remember but one man who was hysterical, but women were pretty apt to do it. And I don't know to what extent they did it because it was expected of 'em, but I have heard criticism of 'em because they didn't—thought that they weren't affected. . . . Hysteria was synonymous with grief and lack of it was synonymous with not caring."[97] Friends and neighbors looked for vivid signs of bereavement. "Public opinion made people show grief whether you felt it or not," Mrs. Walsh said. "[They] expected people to mourn and show grief."[98] For this reason, these visible and audible demonstrations seemed the proper thing to do.[99]

Men too could display deep emotion.[100] Gladys Deitiker could recall "big men with their face in their hands, just sobbing, and it seemed so pitiful."[101] For the most part, though, men more successfully suppressed the emotions of grief. They were expected to be mentally tougher, less emotional.[102] Obviously, more manly.[103]

In *A Ranchman's Recollections*, Frank Hastings, manager of the SMS Ranch in Stamford, Texas, shared the moving account of the final hours of Johnnie, a boy in one of his outfits. It was, Hastings confessed, the saddest experience of his life. Kicked in the head by his horse, the young man developed a blood clot, but rather than have the doctor trephine the skull, the decision of the other men was to anxiously wait, anxiously watch. The frontier dreaded the surgeon's knife. Men on the frontier had seen their comrades lie unconscious for days and weeks at a time then recover, but they had also seen death follow valiant surgery. When finally contacted, the word from the boy's father was in agreement—"Wait." It was a stressful, exhausting night during which the doctor did not leave the young man's room. "The boys had followed me about," Hastings wrote, "like children; they would squat on their heels along the hall while I was in the sickroom, and when I came out there was that mute appeal, with never a word, but just the anguish of soul, crying for a word, a look of hope." Having left word that he was to be called if there were any change, the summons finally came: "'Frank, come! Johnnie is about to go.' Then we all gathered about the bedside, a band of stoics, not a tear from hearts bursting with grief, and Johnnie passed into the Great Beyond."[104]

ALTHOUGH THE TRADITION WAS APPARENTLY ON THE WANE IN the early twentieth century, one expression of grief that did seem the sole province of women was the wearing of black, generally for a year and primarily following the death of a husband.[105] Disapproval was cast at women who donned gay colors too soon after their husbands were "put away."[106] Deitiker remembered one woman whose husband "loved" to see her in pretty, bright dresses, and those were what she always wore. She appeared at church in a red dress the Sunday following his death and said, "This is exactly what he would have wanted me to do. He didn't like black [and] I don't have anything black."[107] Ella Dumont lapsed into a deep depression, weeks of emptiness and gloom, following her daughter's death. She sat in perfect idleness by the hour, having heart for little else other than to mourn. Her grief was to take a lifelong course: "at the time of Baby's death, I assumed a black costume, and from that day till this, twenty-four years, I have never worn anything but black. A few times of late I have tried to wear a light touch of color, but I never feel right until I have discarded it."[108] Elizabeth Hampsten could well have had the likes of Mrs. Dumont in mind when she writes: "Parents grieved unendurably at the deaths of children, and mothers most of all."[109]

UNENDURABLE FOR MANY WAS THE FINAL ACT OF COMMITTAL— the filling of that forlorn cavity, the grave. There was, on the one hand, the ceremonial gesture of someone stooping down, picking up a handful of loose soil and dropping it on the casket below. There was no minister in town to conduct a service for the young girl mentioned in chapter 7, so some of the women asked Isham Reavis to read the service for the dead from *The Book of Common Prayer* of the Episcopal church. Maybe it was because he was young and impressionable,

Reavis surmised, but he could never escape the image of that humble funeral procession, mourners following on foot the two-horse wagon "in which reposed all that was mortal of one of those little ones, whom the Master said was typical of the Kingdom. . . ."[110] Nor could he escape the peculiar feeling of sadness with which he scattered a handful of cold dirt on the coffin below and pronounced the final words: "Earth to earth, ashes to ashes, dust to dust."[111]

The actual filling of the grave was more than a gesture, however. Boone McClure described the procedure: "While the family was still sitting there they'd start throwing the dirt in. In those days you'd take turns. Four or five men'd pitch dirt in, and they used the long-handled—you just called 'em grave shovels or a round, pointed long-handled spade. They'd pitch the dirt right in and to me that was kind of an uneasy feeling to hear the dirt going into that grave. You'd hear the dirt hitting on there. They could get the [grave] filled in five or ten minutes."[112] That, Bill Collyns admitted, was a very emotional experience.[113] For Gladys Deitiker, it was the most gruesome part.[114] The sound of earth striking the coffin was one that could haunt memory for a lifetime. Miriam Colt found words inadequate to express her reaction: "Oh! language is too feeble to describe the deep anguish that was smothered deep down in my heart; so deep that my whole being was paralyzed with a mountain's weight of bitterness, as I heard the pebbly dirt rattle down upon the coffin's lid—it seemed to me as though all nature was being rolled together, and I the only one left to hear the dismal sound."[115] Opal Berryman noticed the father wince as the first scoop of clods "thudded" on the box containing his young son's body.[116] The mother, almost in a trance, gazed far to the west, appearing not to hear the final work of the spade.

Blanche Rutherford buried her mother in 1930, and she too could speak to this final act. When they began using the shovels she felt herself losing control. The custom of the family leaving before the grave was filled was a recent practice, but it was unacceptable to her family. "Mama never approved of half-done jobs. We felt that she would want her children to stay by her till everything was properly finished. As kind neighbors poured in the dirt, first gently, then more hurriedly, I wanted to cry out to them to stop. I realized I must get a hold on myself."[117]

Gladys Deitiker thought back on the wobble of the casket in its straps as men strained to lowered it gently into the grave. And then there was all of the dirt, "and the dirt wasn't covered up, you know. There was something final having it filled, as torturous as it was. Still there was a finality. You'd finished. You had finished."[118]

Chapter 9

Meeting Time

*I have said a number of times when I die and go to Heaven, and the time comes
for the Camp Meeting to start, I am afraid I will want to run off and come
back to attend the meeting.*

*There are hundreds of others just like myself, that wouldn't miss the meet-
ing for anything except sickness, or conditions over which we have no control.*

Joe M. Evans,
The Cowboys' Hitchin' Post

APPROACHING WEST TEXAS OUT OF FORT WORTH, THE TRAVELER
is suddenly and unexpectedly put adrift on what A. C. Greene describes as "a billowy ocean of land." Lone windmills and grazing cattle occasionally dot the landscape, but with few houses or people in
view and only an occasional road or tree, the overwhelming impression is one of solitude. Waves of land unfold immutably in every direction. It is an excessive land, a land under an even more excessive
sky, and "The loneliness of the high sky makes men see God."[1]

The prairie has been portrayed as the very repository of things
spiritual.[2] There is something in the far-flung openness that capti-
vates and holds the imagination, creating a sense of wonder at the

power and scope of the Infinite.[3] Edith Duncan Pitts spoke of her mother's first reactions to the beauty of the West Texas plains and the power of the sunsets to inspire a sense of harmony with infinity.[4] The average cowhand, Ramon Adams acknowledges, was not the church-going, hidebound type, but in his own way he knew God had something to do with nature: "Bein' a lover of Nature, it was hard for 'im to disbelieve that some higher Bein' didn't have somethin' to do with the creation of things."[5] Even a self-styled infidel such as E. C. Abbott confessed that while riding alone at night and looking at the stars, one's thoughts tended to drift to things eternal.[6] The devout cowboy might even become reverent under the influence of a western nighttime:

Oh Lord, I've never lived where churches grow. . . .

I know that others find You in the light
That's sifted down through tinted window panes,
And yet I seem to feel You near tonight
In this dim, quiet starlight on the plains.[7]

Not only the vastness of the plains, but the raw and inscrutable powers of nature seemed at times to overwhelm settlers, instinctively turning them to religion.[8] Independent and self-sufficient though they were, there was a certain reassurance in the thought of an all-powerful Creator, ever-present and ever-watchful over His flock, sufficient for any adversity. The possibility of sudden and unexpected death made the question of one's eternal destiny a matter of intimate concern.

Beyond the forces of nature, there were those stern and exacting demands of daily life.[9] Reports abound of an existence that was Spartan, uncompromising, and wearisome. The numbing routine became torture and monotony a precursor to madness.[10] Addressing the severity of pioneer life in Nebraska, one woman added, "This is no fairy tale."[11]

These hardships and uncertainties made many settlers keenly aware of a need that they themselves could not supply, a need that could be met only by a higher power. The isolation, monotony, and inadequacy found in Harriette Andreadis's nineteenth-century Texas women were to some degree vicariously relieved through the lives of their husbands and children. But possibly their greatest source of comfort was derived from religion.[12] The frontier church, where it existed, represented the message of a personal and caring God, a place of comfort and hope in a drab and difficult world.[13]

To be sure, some pioneers' spiritual and religious sentiments were moved by neither the galactic scope of the plains nor the perils and toils of early plains life. Some were even defiant.[14] No amount of high sky would inspire them to see God. No amount of hardship would drive them into the arms of religion. In fact, the untamed frontier so overwhelmed some settlers that they were preoccupied with material matters almost to the exclusion of things spiritual.[15] Life was a seven-days-a-week struggle for bare existence, draining settlers of all energy and leaving few reserves for spiritual concerns.[16]

Ranchers' wives were especially conscious of a religious void in early West Texas. They were not ignorant of life in the saloon-infested towns nor were they naïve regarding cowhand behavior, but if a woman resided on a ranch where her husband held a position of authority, she could take advantage of her status to encourage Christian conduct.[17] In the absence of churches and preachers, these women often held religious services on the ranches, reading selected passages from the Bible or teaching a lesson based on one of the religious publications to which they subscribed.[18] Annie McAllister, of the LS Ranch, received periodicals like the *Christian Herald* and the *Texas Christian Advocate*, which she placed in the bunkhouse for the cowboys to read.[19]

Molly Goodnight encouraged boys on the JA Ranch to discontinue their work on Sundays and come to the ranch headquarters for a brief devotional. They sang hymns from memory or from the few hymnals on hand and rounded out the service with a prayer. Anytime a preacher was passing through she invited him to linger and visit for several days.[20]

Some of the ranchers also respected the Sabbath. Gladys Deitiker recalled her childhood on the Matador Ranch. "The only way I knew it was Sunday—there was no church and we lived thirty miles away—I knew it was Sunday because my father would get over in the corner with the Bible, and he'd sit there and read it. He wouldn't say a word about it. He'd just do it. And that meant it was Sunday. There was no going to church if you lived on a ranch."[21]

The arrival of farming families complemented the religious sentiments of these ranching pioneers. Farmers were tied to the land and less migratory than earlier frontiersmen—buffalo hunters, ranchers, cowboys, and sheepherders.[22] They wanted to make permanent settlements and enjoy the benefits of churches, schools, and nearby towns, so long as they were not the wilder cowboy towns.[23]

Despite their isolation, some parents were unwilling to forgo their children's religious development while they waited for the coming of churches, so they took it upon themselves to instruct them in basic Biblical teachings.[24] Mrs. John Harvey's 1885 childhood home in the Panhandle was so remote that there was no opportunity to attend church, but her mother would not let Sundays lapse as just another day of the week. "Every Sunday morning our mother saw that each child was washed and dressed in fresh clothes and she superintended a Sunday school with just her own family present."[25]

Itinerant preachers passing through provided Bible study as well as spiritual encouragement.[26] Some came walking, but most arrived on horseback or by buggy and would hold preaching services at a ranch or farm. Cowboys might gather around a wagon or campfire on the range, or the rancher might invite them to attend a service at his home. Farmers lived closer to one another than did the ranchers, so the appearance of a preacher called for the arranging of a service and inviting neighbors to attend.[27] Worshipers would bring a picnic basket dinner that they spread out after the preaching, making the trip a social as well as a religious event. They also planned for the next gathering, to be held at the home of some other family.[28] "When they went from house to house," according to Joe Shelton, "the preacher when he'd wind up his sermon he'd always ask 'em, he'd say, 'Now, is there anybody that [wants] to have this meeting a month from now. I'll come back again if you do.' . . . A dozen or so people could get in those houses, but they'd be kind of crowded all right, but they could get in there."[29]

If a meeting were to be held in her home, it was the responsibility of the woman to have everything ready—a clean house and extra food.[30] Shelton spoke of his stepmother's preparations: "She'd put in two or three days of polishing up things around there agetting ready, and I suppose the other women did too."[31]

Circuit riders followed itinerant preachers, and settlers could anticipate more regular services, despite the lengthy intervals.[32] Other preachers, like the Reverend W. B. Bloys no doubt, served both a local church and the area mission field. In 1887 Bloys established the Presbyterian church at Fort Davis, but he also carried his message to the surrounding territory in West Texas.[33] At any hour of the day he might stop at a shack to visit the family, baptize the children in whatever faith the parents wished, hold a service, and inquire about directions to the next ranch.

Frontier itinerants and circuit riders were a mighty institution for Protestantism in Texas, but another potent force, unsurpassed in social and evangelistic excitement, was the camp meeting.[34] A remarkable institution, it was the most spectacular and dramatic event in frontier religious life, regarded by some as the greatest occasion of the day.[35] For a people socially, emotionally, and spiritually starved, this holy extravaganza brought them together with all "the impact of atomic fusion."[36]

Some of the characteristic features of camp meetings, such as emotionality and open-air preaching, date back to the earliest days of Christian evangelism.[37] The Wesleys were preaching in open fields in England as early as 1739, and in America, preaching in wooded clearings was popular in the closing decades of the eighteenth century.[38]

Meetinghouses, when they could be found, were often too small to hold large groups, and besides, there was something inspirational about religious services conducted in the outdoors, worshipers surrounded by the drama of nature. The proper setting for a religious happening was not some building with barricading roof and walls shutting out God's sunshine and breezes, but the virgin woodlands with their singing birds and fragrant blossoms.[39]

History does not disclose exactly when and where American camp meetings originated.[40] Similar gatherings for men have been traced back to Virginia in the early days of the Revolution, and forest meetings were held in the Carolinas in the 1790s. These outdoor services were not that unusual, however, because it was rather simple for frontier people to make camp at an occasion that was to last several days. For men and women who had made long journeys over difficult trails, the prospect of camping out was nothing novel.[41]

Commonly cited as one likely origin was an 1800 meeting in Gasper River, Kentucky, conducted by Presbyterian minister James McGready, a grave man with tremulous voice and small, piercing eyes. McGready was responsible for the congregations in three small communities in Logan County, and between 1789 and 1799 accounts of his power over audiences and the emotional intensity of his services began circulating throughout the backwoods of southwestern Kentucky.[42] Reports traveled by word of mouth about the vivid emotional displays and scenes of wild excitement. People were so overtaken by McGready's sway that they would tremble and quake and fall helplessly to the ground, remaining there as though felled by death; others groaned and prayed and cried aloud for mercy. As news spread that unusual excitement was to be found at these meetings, great crowds began to flock to them.[43] Therefore, when advance notice was given in 1800 of a service to be held that July in Gasper River, one of McGready's three charges, several hundred inhabitants from settlements near and far headed for Gasper River by wagon, horseback, and on foot, some reportedly coming from a hundred miles away.

Such a multitude necessitated two adjustments destined to become regular features of camp meetings. First, the small country church in Gasper River could not possibly seat the throng of worshipers, so men cleared away the brush from around the tiny church and built a preaching stand and simple log benches.[44] Open-air preaching became the heart of camp meetings. Second, for a stay of several days the people needed shelter and meals. The number of incoming participants was too great for the small community to accommodate, so many of the visitors came equipped with tents and provisions—"cold pork, slabs of corn bread, roasted fowls, and perhaps whiskey, too"—to last out the three-day event. This gathering was later recognized as the first camp meeting.[45]

From these early beginnings the camp meeting became an ever-evolving institution, one shaped by the prevailing intellectual mood of place and time.[46] Destined to follow no uniform pattern of development as it fanned out across the country, it was at any given time orderly and mature in one area, primitive and disorganized in another, a reflection of the population and social conditions of the particular region.[47]

DESPITE THIS UNEVEN DEVELOPMENT, CHARLES JOHNSON IDENtifies three stages of change through which camp meetings evolved. The first phase, boisterous and youthful, was characterized by poor planning, disorder, high-tension emotionalism, physical excitement, and some immorality.[48]

In part, physical emotionalism and excitement had their place, serving as confirmation of true religious experience.[49] They were not just excess trappings, so they had to be convincing. Considerable suspicion was cast on the religion of anyone who joined the church simply on a profession of faith, a statement that they thought they had been saved. Other members of the church wanted visible evidence.[50] Jessie Robinson remembered, "They'd always say, 'Well, I know he was saved because he showed it in his face, and he'd break forth and sing.'"[51] If some enraptured woman felt inspired to break out spontaneously in song or prayer, that was proof of the spirituality of a service, and other members of the congregation would respond with hearty amens. A row of trembling, weeping, singing "derelicts-brought-to-port," kneeling before the altar at the close of the evening was sure proof of a successful meeting.[52] Nevertheless, the emotionalism during this first period of camp-meeting development tended to be extravagant, leading to the criticism that the camp meeting was nothing more than "one long orgy of excitement."[53]

This heightened pitch of agitation was apparent from the din of utterances, noises, and loud ejaculations that resounded throughout the campgrounds—holy laughter, barking, singing, shouting, sobbing, wailing, groaning, and piercing shrieks. John Lockhart recalled a sermon in which the preacher painted an especially horrible picture of the eternal damnation awaiting the condemned. At the climax of the sermon a low wailing was emitted by one of the women in the congregation, and as others joined in the mourning it sounded like "the sighing of maddened winds off the desert of despair."[54] Camp-meeting noises reminded another observer of "the roar of Niagara," and for others the moaning and crying was likened to the dying sounds of wounded on a battlefield.[55]

There were also dramatic bodily and animal-like manifestations.[56] Acrobatic and muscular behavior included a range of nervous exhibitions—dancing, jumping, spastic jerking, falling, and rolling, tossing, and writhing on the ground.[57] Men jerked as though they would be scattered into atoms; the long hair of women snapped and cracked like a whip. Some threw themselves around as if battered by a stormy sea; others fell like trees toppled from the force of strong winds.[58] The fallen lay as soldiers slain in battle, and they might remain there for hours, motionless and apparently breathless.[59] Others trembled and convulsed, their extremities cold to the touch.[60]

These frenzied exhibitions were stimulated by the trademark features of the services: impassioned preaching, intense exhortations, earnest prayers, and lively singing.[61] The importance of message and messenger cannot be overstated. A stirring sermon in the hands of a fervid preacher was a powerful tool. The style of preaching incited emotions to such a pitch that the very intensity of experience demanded some form of outward expression. The terrors of hell were portrayed so vividly that even the unimaginative were alarmed, while the more convicted behaved as though they actually felt the suffering described.[62]

The social, intellectual, and psychological characteristics of the people and their times were also significant. The deprivations and harshness of life that existed on all frontiers created pressures that demanded catharsis, and the camp meeting was for many a socially accepted "emotional jumping-off place."[63] It provided a vigorous loosening up for a people often far too stolid and reserved, maybe purging unhealthy spiritual and mental debris. Regardless, it was the one type of hysteria permitted of sane and sensible people.[64]

Numerous worshipers were vulnerable to the kind of behavioral contagion described by Lockhart. One West Texas old-timer recalled the close of a service and the preacher's asking if anyone in the audience cared to express a word of testimony. A stranger stood and began to speak: "The more he talked the more fervent he became, and was soon shouting, 'Hallelujah! Praise the Lord!' The same religious fervor seemed to sweep over the congregation, and pretty soon several were shouting and singing and clapping their hands."[65] When people were converted, or "got religion," they often came up shouting, and that provided the occasion for relatives and friends present to do likewise.[66] The mere suggestion of an emotional discharge could send a whole congregation into fits, but women and children responded most readily.[67] Many services had this potential for chain-reaction hysteria and fanaticism. They just needed someone to provide the initial spark.

The physical setting could also contribute to a heightened state of emotionalism. "Awe-inspiring" were the nighttime services at one wooded meeting, the congregation surrounded by a veritable circle of fire. Candles were attached to trees back in the shadows, while the remains of suppertime campfires smoldered around the perimeter. To the rear, and on either side of the congregation, were some half dozen large platforms, eight to ten feet high, made of heavy tree trunks. Covered a foot deep with damp earth, they held roaring fires fueled by full-length logs. The furious popping and snapping of the flames, the wild sparks, the dense smoke, and the ghostly shadows that skulked along the edge of darkness beyond this flickering circle of light, all united to make the setting eloquent of awe.[68]

In addition to the excitement, camp meetings were dogged by disorder—immorality, rowdiness, and brawling—but such distractions were inevitable given the diverse character of the audiences. The mix included not only Christians and conscientious seekers, but also the dissolute and irreligious—troublemakers, hucksters, and lovers.[69] Great quantities of liquor—"jugs of inspiration"—were often sold near the grounds, so jokes were popular about the confusion between corn spirits and the Holy Spirit.[70] A camp meeting was also a perfect opportunity for bullying and harassment by local ruffians, and these rowdies often turned out in force.[71] Many participants attended, no doubt, out of curiosity and others were simply in search of a good time, having few, if any, religious motives.[72]

Camp leaders found it necessary to be on the watch for sparking and "buggy-riding or skylarkin'" among the young folks. In spite of their best efforts, though, the cavorting of some of the youth in the surrounding woods produced a crop of "woods colts" nine months later.[73] The distinction between religious love and romantic love could become easily confused under nighttime moon and stars. A common accusation was that as many souls were likely conceived, or "begotten," at a camp meeting as were saved, and as late as 1946 the phrase "camp-meeting babies" still persisted in East Texas.[74]

THE SECOND STAGE OF CAMP-MEETING DEVELOPMENT WAS distinguished by better planning, more effective audience control, and a notable decrease in emotional excess.[75] Meetings became smaller and more carefully organized with respect to frequency, length, and order of service. They were announced from pulpits and advertised in religious periodicals and area newspapers. Organizers laid out campgrounds with various permanent and semi-permanent structures, and meetings became less inclusive and more denominational. They became more of a way for religious denominations to gain new converts and not so much a spontaneous response to widespread feelings of need.[76]

THE FINAL PHASE OF THE CAMP-MEETING PHENOMENON WAS ONE of gradual decline, but even as its beginning was obscure, so was its demise. Different regions of the frontier followed dissimilar calendars of settlement, and so the life span of the camp meeting varied across the country. Camp meetings reached their greatest influence in Texas following statehood in 1845, a time period of increasing Protestant domination.[77] They flourished across the state, especially among the Methodists, and the frontier nature of Texas contributed to their longevity.[78] But as elsewhere, camp meetings slowly lost much of their popularity. Increasing population density made for established communities, and improving transportation brought these communities closer together. Social life in the towns grew more refined and varied. West Texas settlers brought with them singings, quilting parties, picnics, literary societies, and dramatic clubs, and these activities created less need for the social aspects of the meetings.[79] Church buildings erected in the towns increasingly became the center of social life, and it was no longer necessary that people come from a large area in order to make a religious meeting worth the effort.[80] Then too, church buildings made possible the more sedate indoor protracted meetings, "the disease that withered the camp meeting vine."[81]

Protracted meetings grew out of the camp meetings in Kentucky and Tennessee in the early nineteenth century, and, like their predecessors, lasted from early morning to late night for three to four days, participants taking time out for little more than to eat and sleep.[82] The primary purpose of these protracted meetings was to stimulate a fresh interest in religion among the church members that, in turn, might lead to a revival and attract those outside the church. Originally, this protracted phase referred only to those few days that immediately preceded but were a part of the longer meeting, the revival. Over time, however, the term "protracted" came to suggest a long meeting of three to four weeks, held in the evenings only. "Revival meeting," or simply "revival," later became the terms of choice, used indiscriminately for all such evangelistic efforts.[83] Although closely akin to camp meetings, revivals were held in small towns rather than on the far reaches of the frontier and in churches rather than outdoors (unless it was a brush arbor meeting). Because they generally served a closer population, extensive preparations and extended leave-taking were not required.

"CAMP MEETING," "PROTRACTED MEETING," AND "REVIVAL meeting"—as well as "brush arbor meeting" and "big meeting"—are terms often used interchangeably when discussing the frontier-rural era of West Texas. All of the various forms of religious meetings appeared to coexist in the region at that time. Into the twentieth century, however, while camp meetings began to decline, church-based protracted meetings and revivals became common. Sharing features common to Johnson's second stage of camp-meeting development, all of these events involved more planning and order. Certain hallmarks of the camp meetings were retained, like the ardent, evangelical preaching, zealous singing, food, and fellowship. Although mischief was popular, there was less of the more serious rowdiness and disruption by scoffers and agitators. Gross emotional histrionics and physical demonstrations were not customary, although a marked tendency toward emotional worship persisted.[84]

The West Texas territory was so vast and settlers so often isolated that all of these gatherings would have, as was said of the camp meeting, "appealed to many universal human urges, opened the door to many opportunities, and fulfilled many immediate needs."[85] Those needs were one part spiritual and one part social, and just about any religious gathering became widely anticipated as an occasion that promised to be "half revival and half vacation."[86]

Chapter 10

Camp Meetings—
Half-Vacation

Soon the occupants begin to arrive. They came "afoot and horseback," riding single or double. On carts and wagons are loaded bedding, cooking utensils and children. Dogs have not been invited, but they come anyway, and make themselves too familiar for comfort, and are all sizes and breeds, from the long-eared deerhound to the common cur. The camp ground begins to assume the appearance of a picnic on a large scale; horses neigh as the newcomers arrive, babies cry, children shout and play and a hum of good-natured conversation, inquiries and greetings all combine to make a vivid and realistic picture in this setting of living green.

J. N. Morrell,
"Happy Days on the Frontier,"
Frontier Times, 1943

LOCATION WAS AN IMPORTANT CONSIDERATION IN PLANNING A camp meeting, and in general, this meant a large section of open land and a temperate climate.[1] One camp-meeting manual suggested three basic criteria for selecting a site.[2] First, the encampment should be held in a friendly neighborhood, one accessible to the religiously inclined and protected, as much as possible, from disrupters. Second, adequate water and grassland were needed to support the crowd and to water and graze the livestock.[3] In West Texas, if a natural supply of water were not available, meetings were held near some neighbor's house or on a ranch where an earthen tank or windmill would guarantee water.[4] Finally, the location should convey a proper camp-meeting atmosphere when the grounds were cleared. In forest regions, this meant that when the scrub and smaller trees were removed, limbs of the remaining large trees should form a natural canopy over the site. The hoped-for effect was a wilderness cathedral that contrasted with the gloomy darkness of the dense forest.[5]

Although it was not possible to create a forest cathedral in West Texas, it could nonetheless be proclaimed that "God's outdoors is one of the best places in which to worship."[6] The territory was not without spots of inspirational beauty. The unobstructed high sky, the infinite stretch of the land, the sunrises and sunsets, the starlit heavens—all provided fitting backdrops for a spiritual retreat. Sallie Matthews described the evening scene near the Davis Mountains when they topped a hill overlooking the campgrounds. She thought the sight glorious. "The lovely valley with its groves of live-oak trees nestling under the shelter of rugged mountains, with the soft shades of evening coming on, was a view to delight the eye of an artist."[7] Carter Matthews recalled encampments in the 1920s: entire families slept under the stars in Ceta Glen Canyon of the Panhandle. "The rustling of the leaves on the trees, the trickling of water over the rocks, the night sounds of birds were very soothing. You were at peace. Problems forgotten. It was often punned that our religious batteries were being recharged. It was life at its best each year."[8]

A grove of trees was a choice site because of the shade it provided. Cold temperatures and possible West Texas snows prohibited extended outdoor worship in winter, so camp meetings and revivals were warm-weather events.[9] These meetings could occur anywhere from late spring to late fall, but they were less successful in the summer when the heat was excessive.[10]

A primary consideration was the agricultural calendar, and using this as a guide, the end of summer was the most convenient time.

August was the most popular month—despite the lingering summertime heat.[11] People had sown their crops by this time of the year and had more leisure time to enjoy.[12] Ira Taylor explained: "People generally commenced to laying their crops by—we always tried to—after the crops was put in and growing—get our crop laid by by the fourth of July and then maybe in August is when they'd have these protracted meetings. When you laid by, that's when you got done with the hoeing and the plowing. . . . From time the crops were laid by till you started gathering, why then you had nothing to do but feed the horses and keep the chores up."[13] It was a good time to catch up on some of those neglected jobs—fix the fences, mend the barn, repair the stalls.[14]

It was a point in the year when the family could batten down the homestead for a few days or couple of weeks and take off. Reports as to how long the gatherings would last vary from a few days to a month.[15] Four-day meetings eventually became the rule, starting on Thursday and continuing through Sunday, but a big meeting would continue through two weekends.[16]

Cows and calves were put out together in the pasture. "They'd always have plenty of water out for the stock, and they could graze," according to Taylor. "You didn't have to feed 'em in the summertime. . . . You could throw out enough feed for the chickens to last a week or two and somebody'd ride by and see after 'em for you."[17] Texas-born Joe M. Evans grew up in the Davis Mountains where his parents helped found the Bloys camp meeting in 1890.[18] When the time came for a camp meeting, like Ira Taylor said, the milk-pen calves were turned out with the cows, water troughs were filled, and a sack of corn was slit open and left in the corral for the chickens. Everything was readied for a ten-day absence.[19]

For cattlemen, demands of the herd dictated when they could participate. One meeting opened on the third Sunday in August in order for it to end before the fall roundups.[20] Ranchers participating in the Bloys encampment agreed that they had to begin after branding and before the cattle-shipping season.[21]

Other practical matters dictated the timing of a meeting, or a particular service. August allowed time for rains to green the grass so that horses and mules could be turned loose to graze.[22] During the first ten years or so the Reverend Bloys always brought his almanac to planning sessions. He wanted a time when there would be a full moon, making it more convenient to move around.[23] Preaching scheduled to begin at midday was welcomed by those coming in for only one service, because many families had no clocks or watches.[24]

CAMP MEETINGS, OR REVIVALS, DEVELOPED IN VARIOUS WAYS. Itinerant preachers were aware of the slack period in an agricultural community and of the opportunity to strike up a revival. "They'd come through," Marcia Caldwell said, "and get with somebody who was kind of important in the community or a bigwig in the church, if there was a place where they really had memberships."[25] One pioneer couple just happened to meet up with a Baptist minister and invited him to their home for a week of preaching.[26] About fifteen neighbors from the surrounding area got up early each morning and rode over on horseback or in wagons to attend an eleven-o'clock service. On the final Sunday an all-day meeting was held, and some twenty-five attended.

Camp meetings required more foresight. The Reverend Bloys always met with area ranchers before their annual encampments. As churches were established, the minister and church members would plan and organize in cooperation with other area churches.

Once a site was selected and the time determined, it then became a matter of informing area residents. If a service were to be held at a home, word would go out that a preacher was coming, and the people would gather to hear him.[27] In much the same way, word circulated about a camp meeting or revival. The Reverend P. H. Gates, early-twentieth-century bookkeeper turned West Texas preacher, said that it always mystified him how the news got around, but if there were to be a dance, word traveled mighty fast.[28] Likewise, news about a religious event would spread quickly across the territory, and as one settler said, "To hear of a dance, wedding, or any sort of entertainment [including a camp meeting or revival] was tantamount to receiving an invitation to attend."[29]

Learning of a camp meeting might simply be a matter of chance. "You'd meet some cowboy or somebody or ride up on it," Taylor said, "just stagger up on it and not even know it was there until you get there."[30] But generally, people closest to the planning—and this included the preacher—carried the word to neighbors, and they in turn told others. News of an 1886 camp meeting in Menardville (now Menard), Texas, was orated about because there was no newspaper.[31] Opal Berryman's father had large posters printed that publicized the upcoming meeting, and when the posters were ready she and her father distributed them about town, placing one in each window of the bank and tacking several on the board fence around the lumber yard. The barber welcomed them to "Stick 'em up in front of them bottles of bay rum" in his window, and then volunteered: "I'll hep [*sic*] you drum up a crowd."[32] Larger, more successful meetings were advertised in religious periodicals and through local channels. If churches were established, clergy would announce regularly from every pulpit weeks in advance that a camp meeting would be held at such and such a place, commencing on Thursday before the third Saturday in August. All were cordially invited to attend.[33]

Birtie Taylor remembered the grueling farm work before a meeting. "Mother and Daddy'd just work like everything—and worked us kids. We had to get the crops and everything ready by the time we had a revival. That was the deadline to meet. I don't know why, but people worked to kind of that point, just like people working to take their vacations."[34] For Mitchell Jones, it was like getting ready for a fishing trip. "People used to get in the wagon and go on a fishing trip and camp out. They always carried plenty of food and they had a good time."[35]

Camp meetings were guaranteed to provide excitement and a good time, and in some sections it was *the* social event of the year, attracting the year's largest crowd.[36] Even the grandest Fourth of July celebration paled in comparison.[37] Anticipated by children as one big, ten-day picnic, it would become for some the momentous occasion of their lives.[38]

These gatherings were one of the few times during the year when women could relax and enjoy several days of socializing. Freed from the drudgery of housework and cooking, many served only simple, cold meals that they had put together in advance at home.[39] Nevertheless, Texans were fond of saying that camp meetings were hell for women but a paradise for children and dogs.[40] The prepared meals were only one of their responsibilities in getting the family out-fitted for the trip.[41]

A family might spend weeks making ready, and many of these details fell to the woman.[42] "Clothing," according to Pet Ott, "was a problem. We didn't have clothes like we do now. You had to think of three or four days of wearable clothing. I can [remember] being sure everything was clean and ready to go."[43] Louise Gibson said, "The mothers and the daughters had to really get those clothes together to last, you see, because they'd have no way to do the laundry like we do now from one day to another. And that was a big job!"[44] For a large family, a big job indeed. Ordinary laundering could consume an entire day—maybe more. Mothers washed the colored clothes one day, scrubbed and boiled whites the next.[45] Daughters helped in the weeks of sewing to insure that each member of the family would have enough intact garb to last through the meeting.[46] The clean and mended clothes were then folded and placed in a trunk, soon to be loaded on the wagon.

The final few days were spent in the kitchen—smoking hams, frying chickens, and baking bread, cakes, pies, and cookies.[47] Opal Berryman went out with her father one early Saturday morning, gun-nysacks in hand, to look for cow chips to fuel the stove. Her mother was baking for the Sunday meeting, and more chips were needed than could be found in the depleted areas close to town. Upon returning home the kitchen looked like a commissary. On the table sat three cinnamon-sprinkled apple pies and a tall white cake, "fuzzy" with coconut. Her mother was baking tea cakes, and two chickens lay nearby, dressed and ready for frying.[48] John Lockhart listed all the good things "the old sisters" had prepared and carefully packed in boxes, ready to satisfy not only hungry family but friends and strangers as well.[49] Canned goods, watermelons, cantaloupes, beans, corn meal, slabs of home-smoked bacon—all might be found packed in boxes, tubs, or wicker baskets, sitting on the floor next to the door. Joe Shelton said, "They'd bring in these groceries in tubs. They'd be in big ol' wash-tubs. They'd set it down and the women'd pick the dishes up out that ol' tub to put around."[50]

Mary Blankenship's small community church stood apart and alone on the West Texas prairie, but it erupted with life on Sundays.[51] Saturday was devoted to preparing for an all-day Sunday service, and these preparations provide a time-lapse picture of the activities likely involved in getting ready for a camp meeting. Blankenship baked cakes, pies, and bread for the dinner. She cleaned chickens for frying early Sunday morning while she cooked breakfast. Clothes were pressed with a flat iron; shoes and boots blacked and maybe half-soled; hair "home cut"; water carried in and heated for the family bath in the washtub by the kitchen stove; and hair washed and rolled on stocking or kid curlers. Up Sunday morning before daybreak, her husband milked the cows while she made breakfast and packed their dinner in the same tub used the night before. They carried suggans for the youngsters' naptime, cane-bottom chairs for the women to sit on while riding in the wagon, an umbrella for shade, and feed for the horses.[52]

In addition to the food, they hauled barrels of water.[53] "Drinking water's what they's for," Albert Byars said. "We watered the team out of a tub. Everybody'd bring his own water."[54] Sacks of feed were included for the horses and mules, maybe a crate of chickens, a cow or goat tied behind the wagon. Extra bedding—suggans, blankets, quilts, pillows—diaper bags, lap robes, tarpaulins, tents, and chairs were items loaded. Pots, kettles, ovens, and other kitchen utensils were carried. To prevent breakage, chairs, tables, and lighter items were placed on top of the wagon.[55] After all the packing and loading, the home could almost appear barren because so much had been removed.[56]

When the morning finally came to hitch up the team the excitement was probably akin to that felt by Opal Berryman on the opening day of their meeting: "It was as though we had been holding our breaths for this Sunday morning."[57] The wagons had been put in traveling shape, and some of the men had built on the back end of their wagon a large chuck box to store the food.[58] The wheels were greased for at least a four-day trip, because many families would have to travel forty to fifty miles.[59] M. K. Little was holding a meeting on the South Plains when a covered wagon rolled up around dusk and a roughly garbed man climbed stiffly down. "Are you that Methodist preacher I've heard about?" The Reverend Little replied that he was a Methodist preacher. "Well, man, help me then. I've got my wife and four children out here in this wagon. None of us are Christians and we have driven more than 50 miles to come to these meetings."[60]

Ranching families lived as distant as seventy-five miles from the Davis Mountains campground; Sallie Matthews described their ninety-mile trip to this site.[61] One pioneer remembered the dread of having to camp on the banks of Limpia Creek and wait for the waters to subside following a heavy rain, thus extending an already long trip; and this was a stream they had to cross thirty-one times through the Davis Mountains before reaching the grounds near Fort Davis.[62]

The Matthews and Evans families would stop toward evening time and spend the night, camping out at one of the ranches along the way. Next morning, the host family would hitch up, fall in with their guests, and together they would wagon down the trail until nightfall, then camp at another ranch. This scene was repeated the next morning, and by the time they reached the campgrounds a considerable assembly was in tow.[63] Matthews said that they arrived with 130 riders in their entourage, including wagons, buggies, hacks, and buckboards.[64]

On arrival, wagons were parked, the teams unhitched and staked or led away to pasture. The men cleared an area for the tent or arbor, if one were to be built, and gathered wood to start a fire. At one meet-

Camp-meeting bound wagon.
Courtesy The Center for American History, The University of Texas at Austin

ing several wagons were backed up, side by side in a semicircle near the campfire with the chuck boxes on the back of the wagons nearest the fire. Families were then assigned a nearby spot on which to set up their tents.[65] Upright posts were set firmly in the ground and whatever material the campers brought for the purpose was stretched over the posts for the tent.[66] Straw might be scattered over the ground, and when the work was finished a temporary home was ready for occupancy. One father and his sons first pitched their tent and then built, as was customary in early Texas meetings, a small brush arbor for the family. They dressed in the tent and served meals and entertained visitors under the arbor.[67]

Camp-meeting campsite.
Courtesy Research Center, Panhandle-Plains Historical Museum

Berryman watched with fascination as covered wagons rolled in and disgorged their camping supplies. Bedrolls and tents were pitched to the ground beside the wagons. Endgates were let down on a folding leg, opening the chuck cupboard behind it and creating a table for the cook. The cupboards contained shelves of food, and pots and skillets hung beneath the wagon. Trunks stashed under the wagon seats contained clothing; hats were pinned between the bows to the inside of the wagon sheets. A canvas canteen of water usually hung beside the driver, and along with a sack of oats for the horses, a shotgun or rifle lay under the seat.[68]

Horses whinnied and snorted as new rigs entered the grounds, and campers already situated drifted over to extend a welcome, maybe help with the unloading. In large coops, chickens cackled and fluttered. The air was soon heavy with the scent of animals and camp-fire smoke. Men encountered one another and exchanged greetings as they gathered wood and went for water. Women assisted one another in setting up their sites, and excited children took little time in gravitating to their kind.

"It was completely informal," Carter Matthews said. "'Hello Bill. I haven't seen you. How are you?'—and all that sort of stuff. Just downright friendship. Not religion. Just friendship."[69] Joe Shelton said that people would meet who had not seen one another for months. "I remember one thing they used to say—ol' fellers. One ol' feller come up and maybe get out there and say, 'Tom, well how are you getting?' And ol' Tom'll say, 'Oh, tolerable. Just tolerable.' I never could figure out what 'tolerable' was. I'll never forget that."[70]

For someone living in West Texas, it was not that difficult to renew friendships or make new acquaintances by the end of the first day or two, because there would not be that many people present. Western Texas and Panhandle religious gatherings were fewer in number and more modestly attended because the area was so sparsely populated.[71] The first camp meeting held in 1886 in Blanco Canyon brought together thirty people from three counties.[72] Various reports suggested that the number attending an outdoor meeting or night-time revival might range from only twenty to thirty-five people.[73]

There were, however, meetings that attracted a larger crowd. During the 1880s, a camp meeting site in Young County, Texas, extended for half a mile.[74] Timmie Brown visited a meeting around 1904 on the Slaughter ranch in the Texas Panhandle. It was a Sunday, "and to me it was lots of folks. It was a big gathering for this isolated area. But we just spent the one day. My eyes were just so big looking at the trees and the people and the water and things like that."[75] Carter Matthews figured possibly 200 people attended Palo Duro Canyon Baptist Association encampments in the early twentieth century, with maybe 150 of those camping out.[76] By 1923 a Bloys service could

A Texas camp meeting.
Courtesy The Center for American History, The University of Texas at Austin

attract 1,500 worshipers.[77] Generally, though, any West Texas gathering of 50 to 60 people was regarded as a good turnout around the turn of the century.[78]

Settlers attending these events came from various religious backgrounds. Union churches were interfaith, cooperative efforts, and until the first decade of the twentieth century most religious happenings in West Texas were union. "Denominations didn't cut much figuring," C. B. Witt noted. "We weren't sectarian."[79] There was a spirit of religious cooperation and fellowship, and one worshiper would scarcely know to what church another belonged.[80] For the first several years the Reverend Bloys was the only preacher at the Davis Mountains camp-

grounds, but, in time, ministers from four denominations came to share in the preaching. It was only incidental that Bloys himself was a Presbyterian. "He belonged to every denomination. He wore a Joseph's coat of many colors, a real mantle of Christianity."[81]

THOSE WHO ATTENDED PLAINS CAMP MEETINGS WERE MOSTLY families intent on worship and fellowship. Men did not sit around a campfire drinking coffee or go off to pitch horseshoes during a service. "No siree," Evans exclaimed, "we didn't get a chance to go to church but three or four days in a whole year and when we came on the grounds it was for one purpose, to attend every service and listen with respect and reverence."[82] The kinds of disorder and disruption so characteristic in the early history of camp meetings were not common. Outside troublemakers and serious troublemaking were generally rare.

The Reverend Bloys allowed no selling or bartering on the grounds. Everything was free and meals could not be bought.[83] In some instances there were lemonade stands with popcorn and candy, and eventually some campgrounds had commissaries or booths where ice, bread, and other basics could be purchased, as well as ice cream and cold drinks.[84] Wilbur Coe was fourteen when he decided to make some extra money at a New Mexico camp meeting, so he went to the trading post and got cases of strawberry, lemon, and orange soda, two buckets of gumdrops, a large sack of mixed cookies, cans of sardines, one bag of crackers, and another of peppermints. The clerk also "knocked the dust and dead flies from a box of old, dry 'three-fer' cigars'" and handed it to him. Coe set up a stand near the river where he could keep the drinks cool and soon had twenty-five dollars stuffed in Bull Durham sacks. This business venture continued for several years—until Coe became more interested in girls than in making money.[85]

Vendors, though, did not prey on camp meeting attendees as in earlier times. Whiskey peddlers did not work the fringes of the campgrounds. Plains meetings did not become trading marts for food or housewares or other items, and there were no barbers, doctors, lawyers, or photographers moving in and out of the crowd trying to drum up business.[86] The gatherings were not feeding grounds for hucksters.

Nevertheless, even as the "everybody's picnics" were open to all comers, there was an everyone-is-welcome spirit about religious gatherings, and people of differing character and motives would show up.[87] Loose people, strange people, renegades, men who had been drinking—these were but a few who would make an appearance. Opal Berryman, though a child herself, was totally mortified to look around and see the saloon keeper's children in the congregation.[88] Some in the audiences were said to have barely escaped hanging in Texas only because they got up earlier in the morning and rode faster horses than the law.[89] There were those too wild to come under the tent, and those too shy.[90] W. H. Patrick described a congregation at one revival that he maintained was typical of the day and time. Sitting a few rows behind him was "Jim J," manager of the gambling house at a local saloon. Another gambler, "Pappy K," was not far away. "Indian Joe, part Mexican, part Indian, and part something else," who was a short time later killed in a card game, sat near the door. "Also present," Patrick continued, "were quite a contingent of females (social standing not mentioned) among whom were Annie, Kate, Pin Head, Scarface Lizzie, Boomer Jane, Rabbit, Goggle Eye and others with probably less euphoneus [sic] names."[91]

Curious individuals or small groups might ride over to visit a camp meeting and maybe spend the night. One West Texan told of the experiences he and a party of young folks had traveling to the Young County meeting and spending the night. Upon arrival they sauntered up and down the thoroughfare-like center of the grounds. They visited, stopped at the lemonade stands: "The music, with instruments of all kinds, was a great attraction."[92]

That some in attendance had other motives is apparent from the comments of one cowhand: "At these camp meetings we'd kill a beef and stay two or three days at a time because we would come a long way. Everybody cussed and got drunk, they was all good."[93] One camp meeting, a tradition for several years, was finally discontinued because "boys" began to attend who had been drinking.[94]

It appears, however, that mischief was more likely in the indoor protracted meetings or brush arbor revivals not necessarily associated with camping out. People of all types had easier access to these services that were in or just outside of town. Much of this misbehavior has been described as devilment or innocent jokes committed by local young blades, those "male creatures . . . that were in long pants."[95] It was as though every boy felt under some moral compulsion to pull pranks at these meetings.[96] "As we began to grow older," T. Guy Willis confessed, "a protracted meeting, under an arbor, was as good as a circus for us boys. To get us herded in was a job for both parents, to hold us there was almost impossible. We would pretend to get sleepy and lay under the benches. Then when the old folks closed their eyes for prayer, we wiggled out, and the fun began."[97] "But we never did tear up nothing," Ira Taylor added. "Playing tricks on people is about the only thing. . . . We never did do anything to hurt anybody, that'd cause 'em to get hurt or something like that."[98]

A commonly reported antic—"One trick we got spanked for," according to Willis—was to switch babies from one wagon to another during the nighttime service. When the hour got late, parents often made a pallet in the wagon for their babies and sleepy toddlers, but under cover of darkness pranksters would steal these youngsters to different wagons. Parents later climbed into their darkened wagons, not thinking to check children's faces, and would be on the road or back home before discovering that they had the wrong child. Caldwell remembered a couple of "terribly excited" parents coming to their house late one night. "My dad went out there and talked to 'em, and 'Naw,' he didn't have anybody in his wagon at all. But they made such a big-to-do about it."[99]

Common targets of mischief were wagons and horses left out in the night during a service. The front and back wheels of a buggy were reversed, the buggy whip stolen, or the reins covered with a dose of axle grease. They would turn the saddle backward on a horse, cut the strings off a saddle, or steal the bridle reins. A paste of flour and water could create a blaze face or change a dark horse to a paint in short order, causing no small confusion at service end.[100]

There were rowdies who always found something funny in every sermon, laughing, snickering, or shooting paper wads.[101] In an arbor meeting, boys could reach up and pick the hard, dry berries in the brush overhead and then shoot these at the preacher.[102] Pepper thrown into the air caused the audience to cough and sneeze.[103] When snuff was sprinkled liberally down the aisle and the women's long skirts dragged on the dusty floor or ground stirred the air, many of those sitting nearby erupted in fits of sneezing.[104]

H. G. Bedford thought back on all the fun ordinary bad boys had at the expense of the pack of dogs milling around a camp meeting. Accompanying horses and livestock were regular onlookers at outdoor functions, and it was not unusual to hear the bawling of cows and neighing of horses during a worship service.[105] Dogs, however, were more than casual observers. Because of wild animals, everybody kept dogs—and generally in large numbers.[106] Traveling a far distance to a meeting meant that families had to bring with them just about everything they owned, and this included their dogs.[107] However, when all the dogs were assembled they were in excess, and an unwelcome annoyance, fighting or otherwise causing distractions during a service.[108] Evans recalled a time in New Mexico when a Great Dane appeared on the grounds, unclaimed and unknown by any of the campers. During an invitation the preacher was pleading with the congregation, "Come on, come on." Apparently recognizing the command, the large dog obediently walked down the aisle to the preacher, thereby leading to a premature benediction—and in all probability to no small amount of amusement.[109]

After a pack of dogs created havoc by chasing a wildcat through the campgrounds, the Reverend Bloys announced at the following service that there would be no more dogs, and from that date forward dogs were never present.[110] Other preachers likewise insisted that dogs be left at home: "Tie 'em up if necessary. We don't want dogs running up and down in this arbor and interfering with the Lord's work."[111]

At this particular meeting, however, dogs were chasing around, and Bedford discreetly took out his pocket knife and chopped off the tail of a dog that, unfortunately, happened to crawl under the boy's bench. To be sure, the service was disrupted. But all the time, young Bedford sat "loking [*sic*] as serious as one of the penitents at the anxious seat . . . I think I looked serious enough outwardly, but inwardly I had fun all through my clothes."[112]

Some of the stunts were not so innocent. Ira Taylor told of grown boys starting a fire in the hay at one service that continued far too long. He also remembered the cowboy preacher who became annoyed by a child's squalling in the congregation. "So he hollered out, 'Some of you take that heifer out and let that calf suck.'"[113] The angry men slashed the preacher's tent and ran him out of town. "He called hisself a cowboy preacher but he wasn't no cowboy. A cowboy wouldn't have done that."

Scuffles could break out at camp meetings and revivals. "You know," Ira Ott said, "in them days everything was settled with a fight."[114] He recalled a man who carried to his grave the imprint on his ear of an adversary's teeth, the scar of an after-service fray. Uproarious revivals, civic gatherings, and dances so often ended in serious fights that it was sometimes hard to know where sociability ended and the antisocial began.[115]

Plains camp meetings and revivals continued the honored tradition of providing opportunities for romancing. Occasionally some of the girls would not come in under the arbor but keep to the back, or they would linger near the door when the boys were outside.[116] None of the "nice girls," however, would do this, and those who did were not respected—at least by the nice girls inside. The Reverend Bloys visited each tent nightly following the last service to inquire about the comfort of the family, but also to watch for any foolishness among the young people.[117]

THE PREPARATIONS, THE TRIP, ARRIVING AT THE GROUNDS, SEEing the people, courting, the music, the mischief—all were a part of the vacation emotion and excitement. In addition, settlers got to indulge in their historic enjoyment of outdoor camping.[118] Everyone enjoyed camping trips, and they were a treat even for those living in agricultural regions whose work kept them out of doors. There was something exhilarating about sleeping in the open air with nothing but the stars overhead.

"These ol' boys," Joe Shelton said, "still had their ol' tarpaulins they used in cowboy days. I had one of 'em myself. Their beds would be rolled up inside of it and some of those ol' tarps are ten-foot wide and twenty-foot long, and they'd fold back over and cover up—it would come clear back up over your head and cover up your clothes too if you wanted to. They'd roll that bed out and they'd just leave it through the day and let the sun hit it."[119] The men folk would sleep around their wagons near the fire or make a pallet under the wagon. If it started raining they could head for the wagon or tent, or they could roll up their bed, put on a slicker, and sit on the bedroll until it stopped raining. Women and small children slept in the wagon, in a tent, or under a small arbor the men built when setting up camp.

Joe Evans recalled what it was like as a child to sleep on the hard ground with only a quilt under you and one for cover. "We didn't need too much cover with four or five boys fightin' and kickin', keeps up enough exercise to stay warm. There wasn't anything to bother us except vinegaroons [*sic*], stinging scorpions, pole cats and occasionally a rattlesnake. We didn't have much to do to get ready for bed except pull off our hats. We were all barefooted and we slept in our clothes. When they called breakfast, we came out of there like a bunch of hungry hound dogs when somebody pours out a bucket of clabber and hollers 'heah.' As soon as we ate we grabbed our ropes and stick horses and took off. We stayed out and played until Brother Bloys hollered, 'Come to Church.'"[120]

Although much of the food had been prepared in advance, open-air cooking was another special feature of camp life. Posey Bonds said that the campfire was just like a branding fire. "They'd get up the next morning and cook their bacon [and] eggs on that fire like we used to do with the cattle wagon."[121] Women in sunbonnets and cooking aprons bent over hot, smoking campfires with pots, frying pans, kettles, and Dutch ovens preparing food that was remembered by Taylor as the best. "That ol' food cooked out on that ol' campfire, that wood smoke—boy! And them ol' sourdough biscuits that high."[122]

Spending all day in the open, sleeping in bedrolls or under tents,

A cowboy cooks dinner outdoors.
Courtesy Research Center, Panhandle-Plains Historical Museum

the aroma of outdoor cooking—all contributed to hearty appetites.[123] At some point in the day, the preacher or campground organizer would tell the people: "'Now folks, all of you feel free now to go to your camp or wagon or wherever you're going to fix food for your families.' Sometimes there'd be maybe two or three families set food together, just right on the ground, maybe on a wagon sheet or something like that."[124] Joe Shelton said that there would be the "darndest lot of stuff to eat you ever saw. . . . They'd come out with those ol' red checkered tablecloths and spread 'em out, and there's just a little of anything you wanted to eat."[125]

Opal Berryman ate with her aunt and uncle after they arrived in

Cowboys cooking outdoors.
Courtesy Research Center, Panhandle-Plains Historical Museum

their wagon. It was a supper that included thick beefsteaks and hot biscuits cooked in Dutch ovens.[126] But generally, roast beef was rare in the summertime because of the lack of refrigeration.[127] The most popular item on the menu at one meeting was a quarter of beef wrapped in a wagon sheet brought by Wilbur Coe's dad from the ranch, but sometimes ranchers would bring calves to barbecue, belling and hobbling the animals until time for slaughter.[128] If that meat supply became exhausted, the men could always go out and round up a steer they then butchered. There were so many cattle grazing in the area that no one seemed concerned to whom the animal belonged.[129]

Evans said that meals always consisted of meat and bread for breakfast, bread and meat for dinner, then back to meat and bread for supper. Wild animals were one of the sources of this meat.[130] Men always carried their Winchesters, and on one trip Evans's father and

Camp-meeting mealtime.
Courtesy Research Center, Panhandle-Plains Historical Museum

another man killed nine antelope. They loaded the carcasses into the wagons—among all of the children—and drove onto the camp-grounds with enough fresh meat for the entire meeting. There was nothing better to eat, Evans insisted, than a nice fat antelope steak, fried in a Dutch oven over an open fire with plenty of hot biscuits and dough gravy. Joe Shelton spoke of the game birds—the prairie chickens, quails (which they would trap), and ducks. "Sometime they'd try to fish a little bit, [but] the little ol' fish didn't amount to a hill of beans you'd catch out of those little mud holes out on the creek."[131]

In the early days of the Bloys camp meeting everybody did their own campfire cooking. But as the crowds grew, eating arbors were built and camp cooks employed. The long tables under the arbors were laden with grape, plum, peach, and apricot preserves, the finest

yellow butter, sweet milk, buttermilk, and cream for the coffee—
"and such coffee. No one can boil a pot of coffee like the plainsman."[132] A dinner- or suppertime meal under one of these arbors always included the West Texas standard of good food: roast beef and
gravy, chili con carne with frijoles, fried potatoes, stewed corn, hot
buttered biscuits, stewed apples, plum preserves, and, always, hot,
steaming coffee.[133]

Evans stated that over the years some of the most outstanding
preachers in the world had preached on the campgrounds, with digni-
taries and celebrities from across the country in attendance. He was
convinced, though, that when awards were given out in heaven the
cooks would stand proudly alongside those great preachers and leaders to share equally in after-life commendations.[134]

Preachers were always special guests at mealtime.[135] One participant remembered how his extended family would cooperate to prepare a large table of food on Sundays when the crowds were greatest.
The table would have to be filled several times before all of the visiting friends and family members could be served. He stood off to one
side and wondered if there would be anything left when it came time
for the children to eat. Three or four preachers dined with the family
on these Sundays, "and it seemed to my boyish appetite that they
would get the largest helpings and the choicest morsels. . . . I would
always make a resolution before the meal was over, that when I
reached man's estate, I would be a preacher and thereby get to eat at
the first table."[136]

Lillie Byars remembered her mother and a friend arguing over
who was going to take the preacher home for dinner. "Yeah," Albert
added, "but generally, of course, the folks, the grown people was that
way, but the kids, they didn't much want the preachers to come home
with 'em because they had to wait till the old folks, the elderly all got
through before we got anything to eat. We had to eat the leavings."[137]
Fried chicken was invariably served when the preacher ate at a parish-
ioner's home, so although children knew what to expect for dinner,
they also knew that all they would get was the neck or that part of the

chicken "last over the fence."[138] More than one child probably grew up unaware that there was anything at all to eat between the neck and the drumstick of a chicken.[139]

THERE WERE COMPARATIVELY FEWER WEST TEXAS CAMP MEETINGS, due not only to the thin population but also to the lack of facilities for making a pleasant camp.[140] As early as 1895, however, revivals became a regular community event. Generally on the last Sunday, but sometimes on both the first and last Sundays, there would be preaching all day and dinner on the ground.[141] For cowboys who rode in for the food, it was preaching on the ground and dinner all day.[142]

Dee McDade remembered the popularity of this day and the excited throng arriving at the small church in wagons, surreys, and on horseback. The men built two sixty-foot-long hitching racks for the horses. "I remember those hitch racks because we hitched our buggy to 'em. . . . Big cedar post with a hole bored through it and a big log chain run through that hole. Well, you'd pull up your wagon and hitch it to this log chain and if that hitch rack was full when you got there, why you just pulled up and hitched your team or buggy or surrey or saddle horse to the back wheels of the wagon that was hitched there, and they'd be double parked and triple parked sometimes."[143]

In the earliest days the food was actually spread on tablecloths laid on the ground; people walked around, knelt, and served themselves. It was literally dinner on the ground.[144] Later, bales of hay covered with towels or tablecloths were used to hold the food. People would not have to stoop down so far to get their servings, and the food was protected from ants and other "varmints."

The seats in the old churches were homemade pews slatted out of one-by-fours, and these were taken from the church and lined up in the shade next to the church to hold the food.[145] "Gosh, they had these ol' straight-back benches that's ten, twelve feet long and they'd pick 'em up and carry 'em outside. They'd face 'em and set 'em double, use tablecloths over those seats, and you'd reach over the back to help yourself."[146] Of course, one or more women had to stand alongside the food with a tree branch and fan the flies off the food.

"Man, you didn't have to be hungry to eat there," Lavert Avent said. "It was really good eat'n."[147] C. B. Witt recalled his mother's fixing a big ham and putting spots of pepper on it for decoration, and that impressed everyone.[148] "We had *lots* of fried chicken and ham," Lita Witt reminisced. "You'd have that table just loaded down. I mean it was loaded *down* with good food."[149] Ruby Archer said that people raised hogs and chickens, and they served red ham gravy. "You poured coffee in the gravy and made the red ham gravy—and rice. That was another big dish you'd bring. Rice was a good meal to carry—potatoes and rice."[150]

"When we got ready to eat," Marcia Caldwell explained, "well we got us a plate and a fork and probably a spoon, if there was enough to go around, and then we just went all over. And Mrs. Brown over yonder would have something that was so good and the women'd whisper to each other, 'Get over there and get some of her potato salad.' Now, one thing that really went well was salmon patties. *My!* There was something special. And I remember just one time that somebody brought a bowlful of salmon salad and they were talking about that. I'd never eaten salmon salad and I wanted that. I heard 'em talk about how good it was, and so I worked just as hard as I could to get over there and get me some of that salmon salad, and it was all gone when I got there. *Oh*, I'm still disappointed. Of course, there was lots of garden stuff by this time. There'd be green beans and black-eyed peas and cabbage—all of those things."[151]

Avent admitted that he was a little particular. "Some people would go around to everybody else's plate, but I always liked to eat what my folks carried because I knew what it was and it was good. My sister [would] make these cakes, cook 'em in cake pans, and be five or six high. Coconut and pineapple and everything good in between 'em, and boy, it was good too!"[152] The pies and cakes were, naturally, a special treat for the children. McDade was partial to the cobbler pies. People could not bring just any kind of dessert, he said. "You'd have to carry 'em in a wagon. You couldn't have a boggy-topped pie with calf slobbers on it because it'd shake it to pieces, but you'd get a cobbler and put it in a apple box."[153]

TO BE SURE, CAMP MEETINGS AND REVIVALS WERE UNIQUE AND EXCITING events, the highlight of the summer. "They didn't think about going to Colorado or to New York City or L.A. or somewhere," Louise Gibson said. "It was right there and it was vital to them to have a part in a religious service, because life went on and death did come and they wanted to be ready for it."[154] These meetings were, therefore, more than a vacation. They were more than a funfest, far more than a food-fest. They were a religious event, "Truly a siege of feasting for the soul."[155]

Chapter 11

Camp Meetings— Half-Revival

They'd try to scare the Devil out of 'em. They'd have a lot of singing of that type—"come, come, come." These preachers were hellfire preachers and they would stir up emotions pretty high.

See, I was a bit of a reprobate when I was a kid because I saw a lot of those things that upset me and there wasn't anybody to talk to. They believed in literal hells and literal heavens. I didn't believe in literal hells or literal heavens. I believe in hell and heaven because I've experienced both a little bit.

Even as a kid I was prejudiced against that stuff. Now, I know that Jonah was in the belly of a big fish. I know that for an eternal truth because I've spent a little time there myself.

Mitchell Jones, Sr.

Perpetual winds. Arid and treeless. The deadening cold of the north; the withering heat of the south. These were some of the features that made life difficult across the early plains.[1]

E. C. Abbott joked about a tough guy who was killed in West Texas, and as soon as he got to hell he wired back for his overcoat. "From what I went through," Abbott wrote, "I believe it. The Rio Grande river was boiling mud."[2] "Hell in Texas," an eleven-verse poem, describes in detail the creation of hell on the Rio Grande, land deeded to the Devil for the express purpose of eternal torment.[3]

> *The heat in the summer is one hundred and ten,*
> *Too hot for the Devil and too hot for the men.*
> *The wild boar roams through the black chaparral;*
> *'Tis a Hell of a Place that he has for a Hell.*

On graduating from the United States Military Academy in 1853, Philip Sheridan served a year at Fort Duncan on the Rio Grande frontier. To General Sheridan is attributed the statement that if he owned both hell and Texas he would rent out Texas and live in hell.[4]

West Texan A. C. Greene is familiar with the torrid quality of the region's summers, land where a surly sun burns hard. His grandmother admonished that he place a handful of green leaves in his hat before going out on a summer day. "The sun," she said, "would cook your brain by pulling out all the moisture and cool from your body. And you would surely die."[5] The sun burns the moisture from the soil, the color out of fabric and paint. "It burns the sin out of people because sin is a moist, soft thing, tinted pretty colors."[6]

ALTHOUGH CAMP MEETINGS COULD INVOLVE AS MANY AS FIVE services a day, most reports suggest sessions were held in the morning, afternoon, and evening.[7] Some kind of shelter was therefore necessary to protect worshipers from the sun's punishing glare and to lessen the heat that could linger into early nighttime. Churches or school houses, where they existed, could not hold large crowds and would have only trapped indoor revivalists in the clutches of the heat. Indoor protracted meetings were held at night, but because it was still warm, there was little choice but to endure the heat.

Born in Central Texas in 1899, Ruby Cole Archer said that fans were cherished gifts. Palm-leaf and pasteboard fans were distributed freely by hardware stores and funeral parlors before a meeting. Fold-up fans attached to long beaded chains hung around the necks of some women, others fanned with their husbands' black felt hats.[8] Elizabeth Hart Chatham, another Central Texas native, born in 1853, remembered going to camp meetings and taking turkey tails or wings for fans. "When we killed a turkey, we always saved the wings and tail and spread them out and put a rock or something heavy on them until they were pressed and dry. These made good fans."[9]

To combat the sun's rays, a common solution was to build a brush arbor, a rude cover that provided shade and allowed any cooling breezes to circulate freely through the open sides and drive the heat upward through the loose, airy network of brush overhead. In some areas of the plains, however, there was scant or no brush to be found.[10] "We did not have any brush," Bertie Culp laughed. "We had pasture. I used to wonder what a brush arbor was."[11] In some circumstances—more likely during the evening or nighttime—services might simply be held out in the open.[12] Benches would be placed in an open field with coal-oil lanterns strung around for light.[13] On other occasions preaching might be held in a grove of trees or under a large tree.[14] A. J. Holt, Texas Baptist minister at the turn of the century, cleared out an area under a large magnolia tree and brought in logs for seats.[15] "We's in a big ol' cottonwood tree," Lee Matney said. "They didn't have no brush, but we's in the shade."[16] Prayer meetings, Bible study, and testimonial meetings ("experience meetings") were held under a tree or in a grove. Men and women often met in separate groups, and the men's prayer tree at the Bloys site was affectionately referred to as the "hitchin' post."[17]

When there were no trees to cut for brush, canvas tents were used, the sides fastened up for ventilation. Archer recalled the traveling shows that would come through the small towns in the early spring and fall. "They'd put on a play and tell a few jokes and maybe they had an animal or two with them." When they were not using these tents they rented them out.[18] The tent was sometimes referred to as an arbor and might be erected in conjunction with a brush arbor.[19] With time, as was the case at the Bloys campsite, most arbors were replaced by the gospel tent or possibly a more permanent, roofed, and open-sided tabernacle.[20]

If, however, an arbor was to be built and a stand of trees was nearby, the structure would be located under these branches to benefit from the additional canopy of shade. In more settled communities the arbor might be constructed next to a church or school house, but it was not unusual for the site to be on an open field or out on the prairie.[21] Opal Berryman recalled the difficulty in getting permission to erect an arbor on someone's pasture.[22] Many of the landowners did not want their grass trampled, leaving the exposed soil to be swirled around in clouds of dust for the rest of the summer.

Thomas Ulvan Taylor—a trained civil engineer born in Parker County, Texas, in 1858—began teaching in 1888 at the University of Texas, where he became dean of the college of engineering. Taylor called the brush arbor a structure of "rare architectural design." Green posts, six to eight inches in diameter and terminating in a fork, were cut approximately twelve feet long. They were placed in the ground about three feet and in rows ten feet apart. Green poles were placed in the forks and other cross poles laid horizontally, creating a perfect matwork. Green brush was then stacked on this structure until a dense shade was formed underneath.[23] Joe Shelton said, "They'd cut cottonwood trees [that] was here—well, any kind of a tree with a fork on it. Of course, they'd lay a log in that fork, across, get all the framework up there and then they'd cut willows usually, about so big around. Then they'd put hay on top of that—ol' weathered straw. Make kind of a roof. They'd have to have them [willows] on there to support that hay because it was solid on there. Then they'd put that hay over it. It might be a foot thick. It'd keep the sun off. Of course, it didn't keep much water off. It didn't turn water too good."[24] Instead of horizontal poles, a latticework of baling wire might be stretched from the tops of the vertical posts and then the brush placed on top of the wire.[25]

"Brush," a general term, included any variety of vegetation: weeds, grass, bear grass, hay, prairie hay, straw, oat straw, kafir corn, broom corn, leafy branches, mesquite, oak, cottonwood, or willow limbs, and shinnery bushes. Men and boys would take wagons and teams and go out and chop down saplings, or, as Albert Byars said, "We'd pick a wagonload of limbs off of four or five trees that needed to be cut off anyway and throw 'em on top of that arbor and make a cover there that would last you ten or fifteen days."[26] Berryman went with her father to the wagon yard where freighters put up for the night, and some of the men agreed to donate one day a week to cutting and hauling brush.[27] Joe Evans recalled cowboys on horseback dragging brush off the hillsides using a rope tied to the horns of their saddles.[28] Brush gathering was a good day's work at a minimum and could sometimes involve several days of cutting, loading, and hauling, especially if scrub and trees were scarce. Berryman remembered the cuts and scratches on her preacher father's delicate hands after several days in the brush.[29]

Once the arbor was completed, then new-mown hay, fresh straw, or pine needles were liberally scattered on the ground for the comfort of the worshipers.[30] A blanket or quilt spread out over this straw became a comfortable bed or nursery for small children, or worshipers could sit on the padding and rest their tired backs against the edge of the simple bench.[31] Services were long, so these benches became very uncomfortable because they often had no backrests—"And, they were very hard too!"[32] The hay also provided a cushion for those kneeling in extended prayer; when sprinkled with water this mat helped control the dust.[33]

Fannie Wyatt cited an unexpected drawback to the thatch—it served as a cover for snakes! Worshipers were kept in a nervous state, because it was not unusual for the snakes to crawl up through the straw at someone's feet. The snakes seemed partial to the altar and appeared there in numbers. "At first I could not muster the courage to go to the altar and kneel above the snakes, but finally I decided if others could, I could too. One man became very efficient in killing snakes. He would grab them by their tails and with a mighty swing pop their heads off. These incidents did not break up the meetings, probably only adding enthusiasm. After a while the snakes became something of a laughing matter."[34]

Seating was required and the earliest solution—one also required in crowded situations—was simply to have people sit on the ground.[35] People might sit on boxes or bales of hay.[36] Trees were cut down and the logs rolled in for a primitive form of seating, or logs were split, the rough places hewed off, and the ends placed crosswise on large logs laid lengthwise.[37] Puncheon benches, sometimes no more than six inches wide and, again, without back supports, could make for a long and miserable service. "They just cut out a tree and split that thing wide open," Sheldon said, "scrape and smooth it off a little and that's your seat. You sat on that thing and sometimes they'd find a splinter or two. You'd better not slide. That wasn't safe."[38]

Rough lumber was hauled in and placed on nail kegs or anything else that would serve as a support. These boards were placed smooth side up, but sometimes a impish cowhand would turn the splinter side up, hoping to catch a fellow hand unaware.[39] If a lumber yard was nearby, meeting organizers borrowed planks to build benches, and after the services were over they returned the lumber, pocked with nail holes, to the yard.[40] Before leaving home for a meeting, people often loaded their chairs into the wagon, wanting to avoid the crude benches, invariably remembered as anything but soft.[41] It was also a common practice to remove the spring seats from wagons and carry them under the arbor.[42]

Facilities in place, people milling around the grounds, the call to service was sounded by something such as the blowing of a cow's or ram's horn, the ringing of a bell, or in one Taylor County, Texas, meeting, striking an old circle saw with a large rock.[43] Before he had a bell, the Reverend Bloys would stand out in the open and with a loud voice call, "Come to Church, Come to Church."[44] At the sound of the signal, all visiting, coffee drinking, cooking, whittling, horseshoe pitching, and other diversions would cease as campers hurried to the worship service. Although there were other sessions during the day, all were a preliminary for the night service when the arbor and grounds were lighted by torches, lamps, and bonfires.[45]

Kerosene lanterns were hung around for these night services. "That was all the light they had," Caldwell said. "Well, you brought yours and I brought mine and all the neighbors around brought 'em, and they'd hang 'em on those poles and sometimes they'd get on fire."[46] One meeting place in Texas was called "Jug Light" because lights were made by extending wicks into jugs of oil and lighting them.[47] To have light, the Reverend Holt erected two scaffolds for holding pine knots, and he stationed a man under each. It was their responsibility to feed these enormous pine torches during the service.[48] A lantern was generally hung over the preacher, so while fighting the Devil he also had to fight off the bugs, undoubtedly making for an animated sermon and making this man behind the pulpit the dramatic focal point of attention.[49]

LIKE OTHER MORTALS, FRONTIER PREACHERS WERE DISSIMILAR. There was no single type, no one mold.[50] In addition to the learned, rational, and modest churchmen, there were the boorish "sons of thunder," the vain showmen, and the weeping prophets.[51] Turn-of-the-century Oklahoma Territory, for example, was a country overrun with self-appointed and self-ordained evangelists: cowboy preachers, female preachers, a Sioux Indian preacher, a fellow promoting himself as "Noah of today," and a black man operating under the title of "Sin-killer Griffin."[52]

As a child, Merle White thought preachers were "pretty smart because they could get up and talk all this time."[53] Some were gifted with such fervid tongue and eloquence of voice that they could excite an audience to near madness.[54] Many others, although not ignorant, were uneducated, and a few bordered on illiteracy, much like frontier society itself where illiteracy was a common commodity.[55] One preacher, typical of his day, had such a limited education that he was able to read his Bible only very "slowly and stumblingly."[56] A man wanting to preach might be advised not to go to college, and in some circles there was an active bias against preachers with too much book learning.[57] After all, one did not get to heaven with a wet finger, that is to say a finger wetted by the tongue in order to turn the pages in a book.[58]

Even though they were modestly trained, most preachers were respected, some regarded with awe. Andrew Jackson Potter was such a man, someone who could read but little and who for years was unable even to write his own name. Yet, Potter was so effective that the very terror of his name became a powerful deterrent to immoral conduct.[59] Early itinerants and circuit riders were especially important to lonely settlers, coping with life far from the reassuring presence of nearby churches.[60] They recognized the need for religion, so preachers were welcomed messengers.[61] Respect was implicit in the great distances people often traveled to hear a sermon. Kansas homesteaders would walk ten miles to hear a sermon described as positively "execrable."[62]

S. F. Sparks, a mid-nineteenth-century Texas settler, related something of the sacrifice people would make for their minister. The "sisters" would spin and weave for him a fine suit of jeans, and although the men wore moccasins and homespun pants and shirts to church, they took their deerskins to town and bartered for a hat and shoes for the preacher.[63] The Reverend Holt spoke of the deference that he received. On many occasions the cowboys insisted on carting him about and would not even allow him to saddle his own horse.[64]

The behavior and activities of spurious preachers, on the other hand, afforded many frontiersmen an excuse for dismissing them as rather nonsensical figures.[65] In addition to the sincere and selfless crusaders, there were the selfish and fleshly, those counted among the worst of impostors, rascals, and rakes.[66] It did not go unnoticed how one preacher's horses trembled and pulled away whenever he stepped close enough to touch them.[67] Even children were upset by the indifference of some preachers to their animals, leaving them out in the wintry cold without blankets while they nuzzled up to a pot-bellied stove and prayed for themselves and the kingdom. John Ise's older sisters found little virtue in church attendance, believing most of the clergy were preaching simply because they were too lazy to do anything else and because they relished the yellow-legged chicken served wherever they went.[68]

Preachers themselves, however, often suffered forbidding lives, laboring under a common lot of privations, poverty, loneliness, and ongoing conflict with a rugged frontier and abusive frontiersmen.[69] At best, the life of an early-day cleric, C. N. Cosby said, "wasn't a very inviting situation. It was a frontier proposition and wasn't any big glory or big deal about it."[70] Extremes of heat and cold, of drought and flood were their portion, and only the bold and hardy went forth.[71] L. R. Millican reminisced about the tribulations of his fifty-five-year West Texas ministry and the long, hazardous trips, many endured with nothing but his saddle blanket for a bed, saddle for a pillow, and the starlit heavens for a covering. He had to swim swollen streams and rivers. His hands and ears were repeatedly frostbitten, his ears and feet badly frozen, and his resolve tested by threats of violence from men who opposed his preaching.[72] More than one preacher probably had an experience similar to that of R. F. Dunn. On attempting to dismount after riding forty-five miles in a blizzard to conduct a service, he found his boot frozen to the stirrup.[73]

The miles covered by the ranging minister could add up quickly. One mid-nineteenth-century Baptist preacher traveled 3,000 miles by horseback over three Texas counties in a single year.[74] M. K. Little's Vernon, Texas, district included the Panhandle and covered 45,000 square miles. During a year's ministry his team of "big blacks" carried him 7,600 miles, and after four years he had logged more than 30,000 miles.[75] Such a ministry required good horses, horses with stamina. "I could always depend on my horses. . . . They'd take me 50 miles any day."[76]

Material rewards for this gospel work were meager, often reducing the minister and his family to a level of poverty unknown by the best class of people he served.[77] Some were grateful for every meal featuring the yellow-legged chicken. There were churches unfamiliar with the practice of paying preachers, so in addition to their ministry some taught school, practiced law or medicine, or worked at one of the more common labors, like carpentry.[78] Edward Baxter Featherston, born in Mississippi in 1850, was brought to Texas at age two. He became a Baptist "corn field preacher," supporting his ministry and family by farming.[79] Featherston was pastor of one small church for four years during which time he received nothing in the way of salary except what he ate at church members' tables.[80] He lamented, "I have had a hard life as a preacher—have preached comparatively without pay and, in some instances, perhaps without appreciation."[81] One man preached for a year in a West Texas community, and his only reimbursement was a cat and a can of soap grease.[82] The preacher might take home little more than a squealing pig in a poke or a couple of hens with their heads sticking through the hole in a sack.[83]

Generally the pay was in the form of eatables or other material goods. One minister made it known that he preferred money, but he would settle for meat, meal, potatoes, or corn.[84] Parishioners with cash, however, were almost unknown. Chickens, eggs, pork, corn, corn meal, potatoes, sorghum molasses, turnips, tomatoes, cabbage, onions, buffalo robes, discarded clothing, and old toys were just some of the donations placed in the preacher's buggy. One Kansas woman thought back on the dolls her circuit-riding father brought home. Although old and worn, they were the only ones she had and were very special.[85] Some of the old, threadbare clothing, however, was not so well received.

LIFE IN EARLY WEST TEXAS WAS COARSE AND SIMPLE. IT WAS A time and place that demanded a plain and straightforward message, one delivered with fiery oratory and based on stern Biblical texts.[86] Much of the revivalism, therefore, was characterized by the fiery preaching style and the stern text messages of these frontier preachers.

Style frequently took on a flamboyant, theatrical flare. Ruth Lowes remembered the revival evangelist as a performer, one whose chances of finding work dependent on his appeal. People would not turn out for a local minister: "They needed somebody who was a little bit more dramatic, and dramatic they were! . . . If the preacher was a good performer, a good actor, why he could fill that tent."[87] Decked out in his frock-tail coat and derby hat, Abe Mulkey was one of the more successful ones. "He'd get up on that stage—he was a show-man," Tom Black said. "He'd run back and forth and he'd tell stories. . . . He was kind of like one of these medicine men that used to go around and sell medicine on the street corners. They used to get up on a wagon and they'd have a big crowd listening and they'd carry on with a whole lot of rigmarole stuff that didn't amount to a damn."[88]

The frontier was a place for those who were assertive, and the preacher of the day was endowed with assertion.[89] He preached force-fully and hard, his sermons "more of a pounding thing."[90] Often un-couth and unlettered, he was, nonetheless, effective. "Some of them damned ol' boys—I only went to one," said Lee Matney, "[but] he was a spellbinder."[91] The most successful in holding attention were those whose vernacular and idiom could "penetrate 'their tangled hair'" and those with whom the people could identify.[92] Emmanuel Dubbs and L. R. Millican were such men. A former cowboy and buffalo hunter, Dubbs was admired for his daring in Indian fights and long treks on the cattle trail. "His language was the typical cowboy slang and his manner altogether western and that of the open range."[93] Millican, the "cowboy preacher," was known for his bronc-riding ability. After seeing him perform, cowboys would nudge one another and whisper, "He's our kind, he'll do."[94]

Preaching was accompanied by much waving and slinging of the arms, behavior likened to that of fighting off swarming bees.[95] As a boy witnessing his first camp meeting, Andrew Davis was startled by the agitated manner of the preacher. "He seemed to be as restless as though he stood on embers. . . . He was talking loudly and his gestures were of the most violent character."[96] Someone gave Ed Trigg a black cub named John that was taught to wrestle. Trigg kept the bear on a twenty-foot chain because of his tendency to wander, but one evening John got loose. A very tall man was holding a service at the Baptist church that night, and, searching for John, Trigg was attracted by the unusual noise coming from the church. When he reached the building a crowd was wedged around the doors and windows. The bear had lumbered up the aisle dragging his twenty-foot chain. Having mistaken the preacher's gestures as an invitation to wrestle, he was walking around the pulpit on his hind legs, communicating in his own way for the preacher to come on and wrestle. "This was one time preaching was dismissed without singing."[97]

Sermons were also long and loud. A preacher in orbit was difficult to land. It was as though he preached all day—on and on and on, preach and preach and preach.[98] During one of these prolonged services Inez Doshier's father took a younger brother out and she followed. A woman who was also leaving asked her father if he was going home. "'No, I'm just gonna milk and come back for the rest of it.' So I thought, *whee*, he gets tired too."

Morning services were not so long, Caldwell suspected, because the preacher wanted to go to somebody's house for dinner. "But at night—I don't know how long. I heard 'em say three hours. It all seemed like a week or two to me."[99] The Reverend Holt acknowledged that his sermons, as well as those of fellow churchmen, usually lasted from one to two hours.[100] J. A. Hornbeak began his Presbyterian ministry as a circuit rider, and on Sundays he would preach in homes to people who gathered from a radius of ten to fifteen miles. "I preached a short sermon of two and a half hours; there was dinner on the ground and in the afternoon I preached a shorter sermon of one and a half hours."[101]

Preaching could be shrill, the pulpiter shrieking to the point of hoarseness. "*Ohh*, you never saw the like of it," Caldwell exclaimed. "*Oh, my goodness!*"[102] Ira Taylor said, "They'd just shout and holler and beg and one thing and another."[103] One man preached with such force that neighbors more than a mile away could enjoy the message. On quiet evenings, those more than two miles away could sometimes hear him—if their windows were open.[104] G. S. Wyatt felt fortunate to be blessed with a marvelous voice, but the volume of his preaching almost landed him in jail for disturbing the peace.[105]

Undoubtedly, more than one listener was made to cringe by the overpowering style of the frontier pulpit. Combined with a literal hell-fire, brimstone doctrine and "old blood and thunder, molten lead, fiery furnace threats," the consequences could be terrifying.[106] Neverthe-less, these sons of thunder were unwavering in their conviction that all mankind, old and young alike, must be awakened to the horrifying consequences of their sinful ways. The Lord was a consuming fire for all sin, and it was his God-given duty to warn his defenseless flock.[107]

This apocalyptic doctrine in the hands of a committed spokes-man could transform him into a zealot. The conclusion reached on one Kansas evangelist was that he was some kind of fanatic whose irrationality was frightening.[108] However, the observer continued, he was acting as any real Christian must act. He was doing what he could do to save people from hell. "If there is danger of eternal punishment being inflicted upon sinners, every honest Christian should give his whole life to the business of rescuing souls from such terrible fate. Mr. Hammond acts out his doctrine and of course acts like a crazy man. No man of decent heart can believe in the doctrine of eternal punishment without becoming insane."[109]

Deathbed episodes and a succession of lurid narratives were stock tools of the trade. To be sure, these stories had an indelible ef-fect on children, particularly those of a more inhibited disposition.[110] "It was frightening to children, and I was very timid by nature," Edna Bridwell admitted. "It didn't take much to scare me."[111] Joe Shelton acknowledged that there were some people who needed to hear these hell and damnation sermons—"Ol' frontiersmen, you know, Indian fighters and buffalo hunters"—but children were more impression-able. "I remember one feller who preached over there—he was a little feller, weighed about 125 or 130—he had on a hickory shirt and blue jeans and buckle shoes and he had whiskers way down here—heavy whiskers. And you talk about preaching hard, that man did. . . . I sat up on the front seat and I got kind of scared. I thought the ol' bad man was acoming. But those fellers, they really felt that. They shore did. I could just see the ol' man and a red hot pitch fork coming down that aisle almost. I kinda got uneasy. In fact, I'd never heard anybody preach like he did. And he preached for about an hour and a half. *Boy,* he sure did preach."[112]

"Those preachers," Marcia Caldwell avowed, "just scared the pants off of me. They didn't show me any way—this was even when I was little—there wasn't anything I could see that I could do about it. And *waay* off up yonder God knew every naughty thing I ever did and kept a record of it. They never offered my understanding any hope, and I was scared. . . . I couldn't see to save my life how I was gonna avoid hell. Now, hell was a word that wasn't used in my home, not even when you's talking about it. It was the *bad place,* but the preachers would use the word hell. [I'd squirm] for two reasons. It was a bad word and then, I didn't want to go there."[113]

Ruth Lowes was worried because they said everybody was a sinner, and she tried to figure out just what she had done that was a sin—other than quarrel with her brothers. "That was my great fear. I didn't want anything like that to happen. Anything you got at the church was always, if you've sinned you're going to burn the rest of your life, and I didn't know whether I'd sinned or not."[114]

Merle White was afraid to walk home after one of these services "because the man talked so plain telling you that it was probably your last chance if you didn't come up and that you *could* die on the way home. But years ago that was a whole lot of the preaching. It scared people."[115] Ruby Archer had little doubt that when early-day preachers read the Book of Job it was not to understand what Job had done to receive his sores, but to rejoice in the fact that he got exactly what he deserved.[116]

Frank Goodwyn grants that sermons were frightfully graphic, but the ultimate message, he maintains, was one of joy. For sure, sinners were warned about the unspeakable consequences of persisting in their ways, but the emphasis was on the glory of the Christian faith. It was the love and sacrifice of Christ, not the vindictiveness of God that was the primary inducement to conversion.[117] Nevertheless, it is only four paragraphs later that Goodwyn cites the Reverend Francis Wilson's ominous portrayal of Christ's second coming and the last judgment, "how He would leave His place as mediator and ascend the judgment seat; how an angel would sweep across the heavens and blow out the sun; how the living would cringe, the graves would open, and the dead would rise; how the east would be bathed all at once in a new light brighter than a thousand suns. . . . how the wicked would plead in vain from dark depths below; how mountain rocks would fall on them, crushing them, smothering their shrieks, and hiding them from the face of Him that sat on high." Eyewitnesses avowed that the tones of the Reverend Wilson's voice penetrated and froze the very bones of those assembled, and their moans duplicated the groans and wails of those doomed sinners he so vividly described.[118]

It was a steadfast and dauntless soul, indeed, who could stand resolute when confronted with the unimaginable horrors of eternal death, a death that had "ten thousand heads; every head had ten thousand bodies; every body had ten thousand tails; every tail had ten thousand stings; and every sting emitted ten thousand deaths."[119]

The bliss of heaven was not totally ignored, for there was much contrasting of heaven and hell.[120]

> *Broad is the road that leads to death,*
> *And thousands walk together there,*
> *But wisdom shews a narrow path,*
> *With here and there a traveler.*[121]

When one of Texas' "best converters" held a revival meeting on the banks of the Pecos, it was said that cowboys from all around came to

> *hear the pastor tell*
> *Salvation's touching story,*

And how the new road misses hell
And leads you straight to glory.[122]

Pet Ott recalled a preacher's demonstrating what it was going to be like to stand at the final judgment, to have one's name called and not be ready. "He had some that were Christians and some that were not. You had to make your decision right there in the group. If you were not ready to go you went on one side, and if you were ready to go you went to the other, and that's the way it's going to be when the time comes for us to be called to our eternal resting place."[123] Heaven beckoned the redeemed while hell yawned wide for the unrepentant.[124] The damned writhed in hell, the saints shouted in glory.[125]

The choice was simple. Harken to the Scriptures and forsake your sinful path, and a personal God will deliver you from earthly struggles and usher you into an eternal paradise graced by pearly gates. You will wear a crown of stars, ascend golden stairs, and walk streets of gold while angels circle peacefully overhead. But, reject the Word and you are doomed by an equally personal Devil to everlasting torment in a consuming lake of fire and brimstone.[126]

John Lockhart gave a vivid example of this juxtaposing of heaven and hell.

In the opening the preacher first drew a strong and striking likeness of
the habitation of the blessed, the extreme happiness there where every
want was cared for and there was utter freedom from care and trouble.
By much persuasive eloquence he would get the people's feeling enlisted
with him in the desire for good and to be with the angels in heaven.
Thus he would lead them in an unconscious manner into new fields of
thought, like a good shepherd would lead his flock to a beautiful lake of
crystal water surrounded with umbrageous trees, where they could rest
and cool their parched tongues. Then, to the great surprise of his
congregation, when he had gotten them to the brink of the beautiful
water he, with one flight of oratory, would uncover the home of the
"adversary," and bid them behold the souls of the lost. There he would

hold them spellbound, as a master would hold his audience, in
pointing out the horrors of a great painting. There, in imagination,
you could see the doomed souls writhing in mortal agony, deep down in
the pit of sulphurous burning, and perhaps a soul would rise and in
the deepest agony cry for one drop of water, when his cry would be
answered with molten lead poured down his already parched throat.
Then the poor soul would sink out of sight for perhaps a couple of
million years, when perhaps he would reappear to suffer the same
fate. . . . Eternity was compared to a bird from some far-off planet
which should visit this earth once in a million years and carry off one
grain of sand at each visit. When he had carried off this whole world
eternity had just commenced. What an awful picture. And further, the
smoke from this pit shall ascend forever and ever, and be a sweet savor
unto those who are redeemed."[127]

A preacher, however, was more than a prophet of the consuming
fire to come, more than a ranting fanatic threatening frightened mortals with eternal doom. There were those like the Reverend Millican
who neither stormed nor blustered, who used neither whip nor threat.
They instead shared their message in a quiet and friendly voice.[128]
The preacher was also an intercessor, an intermediary between sinful
man and a righteous God. J. B. Cranfill remembered everyone in the
congregation kneeling in prayer and the preacher's earnest voice
cleaving the heavens as he begged for mercy for those in desperate
need of salvation.[129] Much like the frontier doctor, to many the frontier preacher represented hope.

It was possibly out of this same spirit of concern that some members of the church, especially older women, felt compelled to approach suspected sinners in the congregation and plead with them to
kneel before the mourner's bench, renounce their sins, and beseech
forgiveness.[130] With weeping eyes and words of compassion the sinner
was entreated to come to Jesus.[131] One man remembered the soft and
motherly hand on his head as "a good old sister" asked if he had seen
the light.[132] Sometimes the exhorter would kneel before the person

and—maybe tearfully—pray for their salvation.[133] Three or four
church members might "crowd around you and beg you to join the
church," Ira Taylor said. "They'd just hem you up and might near
make you think you's gonna die the next minute and go to hell if you
didn't go up there and join that church."[134]

Mitchell Jones exclaimed:

> *They prayed for me. They'd come and pray for you. I went down to get
> rid of those people. They'd come right around there and—"Are you
> lost?" "Don't you want to be saved?"—and all that stuff. I went
> down and joined the church to get rid of that kind. So after I was
> saved they didn't bother me any more. And I almost resented—my
> mother seemed to go along with that stuff. But I had observed quite a
> bit as a kid, things that were going on, things that happened that I
> couldn't talk about personally. I could have talked to my dad but I
> didn't know it. Even then I resented it and some of the other kids did,
> but we didn't talk about it. Nobody to talk to.*

> Did you talk about it to anyone?

> *Oh yeah, we did that. Oh, we had a Huckleberry Finn in our
> community. He analyzed all of that for us. He was a little older than
> we were, and his family were Presbyterians, so he had a lot of fun
> making fun of the Baptists. We loved Harry McNeil. He chewed
> tobacco and the folks didn't like that—and things like that.*[135]

This very public pressure, of course, left any number of individuals embarrassed and resentful, "buckled up" and "hard hearted."
Caldwell speculated that it was fear of being singled out for this coer-
cion that led some young men to stand around outside the arbor. "The
women'd get 'em and I mean they'd proposition 'em—'Are you a
Christian? Are you saved?' And if they said 'no,' well blah, blah, blah,
blah. I never saw anybody agoing around talking to people except old
women."[136] "Of course," Taylor allowed, "it was all right to talk to 'em
I guess, but they run it in the ground."[137]

THE FERVOR OF THE PREACHING AND THE FIERY-FURNACE SER-
mons always contributed to camp-meeting and revival-meeting emotionalism, and plains meetings were no exception. Although, as
indicated, the grosser hysterics of forest meetings were uncommon,
religious enthusiasm was not totally abandoned. After all, they were
"stir-'em-up camp meetings" conducted by hellfire preachers.[138]

An evening preaching service might begin with a testimony period, and these personal accounts of religious experience were often
emotional. "Anyone who cared to rose up and told his story, [and] the
more outspoken," Archer said, "often shouted and clapped their
hands while walking up and down."[139] These testimonies could pro-
long a service into the late hours and included any variety of experiences. Faye Lewis observed that the more daring stood and confessed
not only to their own indulgence in sin but also to the ultimate victory
of spirit over flesh. She thought of one young couple who electrified
the congregation by tearfully owning up that they had tasted of mari-
tal delights on more than one occasion before their recent marriage.
"At that time, when sex was not recognized openly as existent, much
less talked about, this young couple's disclosure was a real shocker.
The preacher seemed quite nonplussed, having gotten, for once,
more than he had bargained for."[140]

The status of women in frontier religion was similar to their place
in the broader frontier society.[141] Men assumed positions of leadership
and generally were in charge of important affairs of the churches. In
the excitement of revivalism, however, women were able to shed
their subordinate status and exercise a more active and emotional role
in public praying and as convert exhorters, singers, and testifiers. In
some instances they even assumed responsibility for the preaching.[142]

Because they were more prone to emotional displays, women
were often the object of curiosity and amusement for wide-eyed children. Ira Ott recalled two women who would get to shouting and "carrying on" in a service. "It was fun for us kids. We went more for the
fun of it them days than we did [for the religion]." One of his friends,

however, was unimpressed: "If I have to do all of that to go to heaven I don't want to go."[143] Hazel Walsh always looked forward to watching and hearing one particular woman. It was a show for the younger children who delighted in seeing her come up the aisle, shouting and clapping her hands.[144] Mitchell Jones spoke of the excessive hoopla that was not very much related to religion, an opinion evidently shared by others: "Some thought it might not have much religion but all agreed it was great."[145]

These emotional displays could well take on a physical and demonstrative character. Oneita Davidson smiled at the recollection of her father—"He was just so happy!"—walking up and down the aisle, praising God, and shaking hands with the people.[146] People would jump from one seat to another or dance in the aisle and around the pews.[147] C. B. Witt watched in wonder as women rolled in the aisle and in front of the altar. "Now, those women, they may have been putting on a show somewhat, but they were real Christians. I counted them devout, the most devout people in the country."[148] G. B. E. Bourland, a Mississippian who became a cook, drover, and cowboy for the Matador Ranch, recalled the excitement of three or four people shouting and hitting on one another in the fervor of a service. "Sometimes they would nearly beat a fellow to death."[149]

Even though religious experience was sometimes accompanied by weeping and moaning, most emotionalism involved shouting. In a meeting attended by James Vardy, campers were already shouting as they rushed into the brush arbor at the summons of the cow's horn. The preacher simply took his seat and turned the service, or at least a portion of the service, over to the crowd. "It seemed to me that ever [*sic*] one but me was happy and shouting. . . . They were not ashamed of their religion."[150]

People felt free to express themselves, and some of the women became practically exhausted from their animation.[151] Birtie Taylor remembered a large, elderly woman whom people talked about for coming to church without wearing hose. "They used to [laugh and] say, 'Well, we didn't know Mrs. Baker come [*sic*] to church without hose on'—of course, they called 'em stockings then—'until she got to shouting'—when she'd get to shouting and pull her dress [up]."[152]

Men could also contribute to the shouting. When R. E. L. Muncy held an 1897 revival in Matador, Texas, a wagon boss—"one of the hardest cussers one most ever heard"—was converted and his shouting reverberated through the small church.[153] Another old-timer, "Happy Tom," acquired his name because he would "get up shouting, hollering how happy he was and one thing and another."[154] An elderly carpenter in Willie McClary's church would toss his hat in the air and "holler" his joy: "*Glory to the Lord!*" "*Praise the Lord!*" "*Hallelujah!*" The kids, as might be expected, thought it was all great fun.[155]

This shouting, like the preaching, was sometimes so loud as to be heard for great distances, and although some children were entertained, others were frightened.[156] "I'll tell you," Ira Ott contended, "it'd make the hair stand up on your head."[157] The shouting, however, was an expression of happiness and joy. It was a publicly sanctioned opportunity to put aside inhibitions and break forth in loud and animated gladness.

"Now, I never had the inspiration to make noise with my joy," Velma Bell commented. "I was always quiet."[158] For most people, a more common way of expressing emotion was through the music. Various instruments might accompany the singing although in some meetings there was no musical support.[159] The key of the melody was sometimes pitched with a tuning fork, French harp, fiddle, or by a layman "with a lusty voice." A piano was available at times, but the instrument of choice was a pump organ. The vibrations of an organ could be felt in the floor, and the walls of a small building would literally shake from vigorous singing.[160] In combination, these sensations could create the impression, especially among children, that a very real and spiritual force was about.

"There was a lot of hymn singing," Bill Collyns said. "That was very popular. They really sang out. People really went after the hymns."[161] People would, in fact, get so caught up in the act of singing that they might not even be singing the same song. Vardy could hear two or more songs in as many different groups being sung at the same time.[162]

People joined in enthusiastically whether they could carry a melody or not, and, like some sermons, one settler found the singing execrable.[163] Wilbur Coe maintained that the test of a good voice was whether it could be lifted above all the others. Without exception there was one old mother who sang off key and whose shrill voice prevailed over all the others, but J. Marvin Hunter remembered the duel between an high-pitched old grandfather and the elderly sister with a high-cracked voice who tried to outdo him.[164] The singing, therefore, was at best an awful racket, but it was the spirit, Coe concluded, that was important.[165] There might be little talent, but there was always zeal. Where there was no melody, there was always fervor.[166] Loud and lusty, the singing sounded better from afar—dampened by distance.[167]

Like the shouting, the singing was jubilant. "There was a lot of joy," Bell said, "called joy from singing."[168] The Reverend Featherston might interrupt a sermon with a song because he felt better able to express his feelings by singing.[169] Nora Harvey recalled women overcome with happiness. "They weren't possessed with the Spirit or anything of this nature; 'they were just happy.' So, they went up and down the aisles, clapping their hands and singing to show their joy."[170]

Jessie Robinson would stand on the bench, "and boy, when they'd sing 'When the Roll is Called Up Yonder' and things like that—I shouldn't add this but I stuttered and so I couldn't talk. But I could sure sing—I thought I could. But I could sing when I couldn't talk. . . . I'd tell Mama when I'd get up on that and sing, I said, 'Mama, I get happy enough to shout!' And there I was, I guess, four or five years old. *Ohh*, I was so happy. I couldn't talk, you see, and so I could sing and that made me happy."[171]

There was a rousing, almost contagious nature to the singing. Gospel songs were brief and redundant and sung to a quick, lively tempo.[172] Tuneful, they had beautiful melodies and simple refrains, making them easier to remember.[173] Song books were limited or unavailable, but then, some people could not read anyway. "My mother never went to school and didn't know how to read or write," Caldwell said, "but she knew lots of songs and she'd just sing her heart out."[174] Also, it was difficult to read the words by the dim light of the lanterns. When there were hymnals, several people always looked on the same book. Marcia added that she could never recall there being enough song books to go around.

The assurance of salvation was a recurring theme in these choruses, and although expressions of this theme might vary, there was no variation in the certainty of salvation claimed by each voice.[175] "Blessed Assurance," "When the Roll is Called Up Yonder," "In the Sweet By and By," "Rock of Ages," "When We All Get to Heaven," and "Amazing Grace"—these were just some of the popular hymns that declared this confidence. A coarse version of the assurance theme is even found in one of the range ditties:

Talk about your good things,
Talk about your glory,
When you get to Heaven,
You'll be all hunky-dory.[176]

To be sure, the sinner, the one without assurance, was not overlooked in this songfest. When, for example, Gabriel sounds his mighty trumpet at the return of Christ, let the unredeemed be forewarned:

O sinner, you will tremble,
O sinner, you will tremble,
O sinner, you will tremble,
At the old church-yards,
While the band of music,
While the band of music,

While the band of music
Shall be sounding through the air. [177]

Another hymn exhorts the sinner:

Think, O sinner, on thy end;
See the judgment day appear!
Thither must thy spirit wend;
There thy righteous sentence hear. [178]

The final verse ends with one, last, desperate appeal:

Fly to Jesus, sinner, fly!

Austin and Alta Fife examine cowboy idiom in revivalist songs, and in the life to come, "celestialized cowboys" could anticipate golden spurs and heavenly ranges, "glorified plots of the western cattle country—a land of green pastures and rolling hills where cattle graze untouched by adversity." [179] But for the mavericks, those strays tainted by the "mange of sin," another, less celestial image was more fitting: "The throes of death are likened to the milling of nervous cattle prior to stampede, and the human body divested of the soul is a shriveled thing—like the camp cook's curled bacon." [180]

ONE OF THE MOST REMARKABLE ASPECTS OF REVIVAL SINGING, however, was the way it contrasted with the intense sermons on the wages of sin. People were enthusiastic and happy when they sang. They were not cringing or sweating with fear. They did not sing about burning brimstone or sulfurous lakes of fire or the wrath of God. Rather, their singing welled with the glories and joys of the life to come—"The Home Over There," "In the Sweet By and By," "There Is a Green Hill Far Away," and "I'm on My Way to Canaan."

Although death is the great conveyer to that heavenly home, Isaac Watts's hymn questioned why death should be cause for fear:

Why do we mourn departing friends,
Or shake at death's alarms?
'Tis but the voice that Jesus sends,
To call them to his arms.

Why should we tremble to convey
Their bodies to the tomb?
There the dear flesh of Jesus lay,
And left a long perfume.[181]

Another Watts revival favorite repeated this sense of assurance in the face of death:

When I can read my title clear,
To mansions in the skies,
I'll bid farewell to ev'ry fear,
And wipe my weeping eyes.

There, anchor'd safe, my weary soul
Shall find eternal rest;
Nor storms shall beat, nor billows roll
Across my peaceful breast.[182]

There should be no dread of death. The Christian could only anticipate a land that is fairer than day, a land where "tears and sighing are forevermore unknown" and friends and family ever near:

Let me go where saints are going
To the mansions of the blest;
Let me go where my Redeemer
Has prepared his people rest.

I would gain the realms of brightness,
Where they dwell forevermore;
I would join the friends that wait me
Over on the other shore.

Chorus:
Let me go, 'tis Jesus calls me;
Let me gain the realms of day;
Bear me over angel pinions,
Longs my soul to be away.[183]

Another revival hymn confronts the ever-present nearness of death:

My latest sun is sinking fast,
My race is nearly run;
My strongest trials now are past
My triumph is begun.

I know I'm nearing the holy ranks
Of friends and kindred dear,
For I brush the dews on Jordan's banks,
The crossing must be near.

But the songsters are not cowed by death's menace. Each verse is attended by the confident and resounding words of the chorus:

O come, angel band,
Come and around me stand,
O, bear me away on your snowy wings
To my immortal home.[184]

The theme of separation was explicit in one other popular revival hymn:

God be with you till we meet again,
By His counsels guide, uphold you,
With His sheep securely fold you;
God be with you till we meet again.

Chorus:
Till we meet, till we meet,
Till we meet at Jesus' feet;
Till we meet, till we meet,
God be with you till we meet again.[185]

The separation in this instance is not one occasioned by death, but rather by the conclusion of the camp meeting. For Minnie Clifton the final service was the most moving of all the week's experiences. Emotions, she said, were thinly veiled. "It meant a time of leave-taking and goodbyes; in years past it meant parting between friends and loved ones for long intervals, a time for expression of sentiment, of benefits received and vows renewed."[186] Immediately following the benediction, many of the older men could be seen quietly slipping out of the arbor, too emotional to exchange final good-byes.

The closing also saddened the young. One participant looked back on the camp meeting as the greatest annual event of his boyhood, and he retained a reverence for the old brush arbor that he said would last as long as life. "When the last Sunday night would come and 'God Be With You Till We Meet Again,' sung, there would be an aching void in my mind from which it would take many days to free myself."[187]

John Lockhart concluded his 1879 camp meeting article in *The Galveston Daily News* with a portrayal of the camp-ground scene on that final day. All the camps were torn down and the furniture loaded into wagons for the trip homeward. Several hours were devoted to "good-byes" and "God bless yous" as the women moved from campsite to campsite, embracing friends old and new. "For many it is the last until the next camp meeting, and with others until the sad hour when to their honest belief they will be awakened by the blast of the trump which will call all to the great resurrection, when, according to the preacher, each shall receive the final parting which to them will be forever. May God enlighten our minds more fully on this momentous subject, so mote it be. Amen. Soon the campers are all at home once more and feel better for their week's outing."[188]

Chapter 12

Fellowship of the Lonely

We had lived in our new home about three years when a Methodist Circuit rider drove into the country, and word was sent out everywhere to come to the camp meeting. . . . Pioneer life was so hard, so uncompromising, and so lonely. I had many long days of solitude behind me, but I was still a young woman, and I enjoyed so much the companionship of other women during that meeting. I wanted that meeting to go on forever.

Sarah Duncan,
"Memoirs of a Pioneer Woman:
Mrs. A. B. Duncan, Floydada, Texas,"
by Polly A. Kimmis, 1938

There was just fellowship. There was always fellowship.
Anything for fellowship. Any excuse to get together. That's the nice thing when somebody died, you know. It gave you another excuse to get together with people that you knew for fellowship, and fellowship was really a great thing.

Marcia Caldwell

DEATH AND REVIVAL ON THE EARLY PLAINS, AS IN CONTEMPORARY times, shared common features. Camp meetings and revivals were always gatherings for a religious service, and a religious observance generally accompanied burials. There were those burials without any service, religious or otherwise, but there were also aspects of early revival meetings that were less than religious. Various components of these services were similar. Someone typically spoke, maybe only a few words in the case of a graveside service, yet always much verbalizing at a camp meeting or revival. Singing, Scripture reading, and prayers were features in common.

There were also similarities between the major actors in these two events, physicians and preachers. The term "minister" described the doctor's treatment of a patient.[1] Doctors were often just as concerned with the spiritual welfare of their patients as they were with their physical condition. When the struggle to save a patient was a losing one, doctor became clergyman as well as physician and nurse, caring for the spiritual needs of his patient as death approached.[2]

It was also sometimes necessary for the frontier preacher to serve as doctor. Just as some physicians supported their families by preaching, the preacher might practice medicine.[3] Preachers were usually familiar with old home remedies and maybe newer ones, so if a doctor were not available the preacher might well fill this role.[4] Opal Berryman recalled her father's tending the sick and the visible strain created by exhausting hours of nursing.[5]

Doctors and ministers shared in a work that was simultaneously benevolent and unselfish, difficult and trying. They received both adulation and derision from those they served. Some were regarded as heroes, the bearers of consolation and hope; others as impostors, incompetents, or illiterates.

THE ADVERSE CONDITIONS OF FRONTIER LIFE CREATED PRESsures that demanded emotional release, and, as noted, both revivals and funerals were socially sanctioned occasions for catharsis. They were opportunities to discard inhibitions and purge pent-up emotions too long suppressed. The history of revivalism is one of excitement. Camp meetings and revivals were, after all, "stir 'em up" affairs marked by vivid displays of passion. Animated behavior and vocal expressions lent authenticity to spiritual experience. Funerals were likewise affective events with much vocal and public manifestation of feeling. Grief was demonstrative, in part, because public opinion demanded it. Hysteria was kindred to grief. Survivors who did not grieve openly seemingly did not care. The funeral, like the revival, represented an "emotional jumping-off place" for many a stoic and expressionless person.[6]

"God help the lonely."

THIS VOLUME HAS FOCUSED ON ANOTHER COMMONALITY BEtween death and revival—the opportunity afforded for social contact. Early West Texans were desperate for entertainment and any opportunity to socialize.[7] There were those occasional singings, picnics, barbecues, school programs, weddings, and dances, but for most settlers the closest thing to any form of social activity was some kind of religious happening.[8] Religious get-togethers were community gathering times, with camp meetings, brush-arbor meetings, tent revivals, and protracted meetings perhaps the grandest of all early social affairs.[9] People wagoned in from distant farms and ranches not daring to miss this momentous occasion, knowing that they could visit with friends and relatives not to be seen again for months. These meetings were to become almost the only social life available to the far-flung farms and ranches.[10] Surely it was a time of welcomed spiritual renewal, but it was a social gala too.[11]

"Social life," one Panhandle settler conceded, "ebbed very low in the early days," but another was more emphatic: "There was no social thing *whatever*. People [were] just too far apart."[12] Tom Black agreed and elaborated:

They didn't have a damn thing else to go to. Nothing else to do. See?
See, there wasn't any social events in those days like there is now.
They just lived out there in the country and chopped cotton and didn't
go to town once in six months. You see, back there in those days—all
people have to do something for recreation. Anybody that's grown and
able-bodied and got any sense is not agonna just sit down and hold his
hands. They're gonna do something. See, at that time we didn't have
books to read like they have now. You never hardly saw a newspaper.
You wouldn't get no papers. Hell, you had to seek out entertainment
with your neighbors, some kind of entertainment.[13]

Bill Collyns remembered only two outside attractions, tent revivals
and Harley Sadler's tent shows, and both events brought out the
crowds—by crowds, meaning from twenty-five to fifty people.[14]

Percy Ebbutt was ten years old when in 1870 he immigrated
from England with his father, brother, and three other young men.
Three months after landing in America they settled on the Kansas
prairies. Ebbutt remembered that camp meetings were attended by
many people who were not members of any church.[15] It was the sociability that was important, not necessarily the religion.[16] Even "if
they didn't care for their Lord or if they were satisfied with the relationship they had with Him," they attended.[17]

Camp meetings and revivals were recreational—"Just plain
fun," a chance for "pleasurin'."[18] The whole affair took on the nature
of an extended picnic. Along with the plenitude of eats and drinks,
there was considerable amusement for what Ebbutt called "the not
too serious part of the community."[19] Cowboys, especially, were attracted by the festivities. It was someplace to go, a place where there
would be not only the food, but a crowd.[20] Others had similar motives.
Pet Ott was insistent: "We went to be with the crowd. We went because the others went."[21]

Many of the gospel songs that campers and revivalists found so
uplifting had a social origin. Passed down through oral tradition, from
person to person, the singing of these songs retained a social func-

tion.[22] It was an opportunity for group participation, for unity and bonding as people responded in one single voice. Lost in this fellowship of harmony—or disharmony as was often the case—loneliness and hardships were for a brief time forgotten.

Fellowship, friendship, and brotherhood were some of the terms used to describe the best aspect of camp meetings and revivals. Such gatherings were times for renewing or making friendships. Strangers did not remain outsiders for long. Taken in hand they were introduced around and made to feel they were among friends of a lifetime.[23]

For Joe Evans the camp meeting was a "love feast from start to finish," and for some it took on the character of a family reunion.[24] Children felt little hesitation about crawling up in the lap of any adult, knowing that the person would be someone related by blood or marriage, or someone affectionately known as "aunt," "uncle," or "cousin" from familiarity.[25]

Women delighted in mixing and mingling with other women. "You never heard so much talking in your life as [the women'd] do when they's fixing the meals," Joe Shelton said.[26] At the 1886 camp meeting in West Texas' Blanco Canyon, it was reported that the women talked and played like children as they gathered wild plums, currants, and agarita berries for wintertime jelly making.[27] Between services women traded recipes for baking and cooking and shared secrets for treating the sick. They brought along their knitting and pieces of handwork, stitching on these as they talked about quilting and sewing. Patterns were exchanged, fabrics compared, and needlework admired.

It was a time when everyone was keenly interested in everyone else—their deaths, births, marriages, family affairs, fortunes, or failures.[28] They would wonder "if sister so-and-so was in a family way again," Caldwell said. "'Pregnant' wasn't a word in our vocabularies then. She was in 'a family way.'"[29] Child-rearing ideas were shared and they compared notes on the development of their babies, especially when a new tooth appeared.[30] At some point there was anticipation of and preliminary planning for the next meeting, and finally, of course, there had to be "a little gossip, I'm sure, about what this lady did or that man did or something."[31]

The men would stand around or sit in groups smoking, chewing and spitting, or whittling on pieces of wood as they talked about matters of world and area significance. The progress of the railroads, crops, who had the best seed for wheat or corn, ideas about planting and harvesting, and any new implements on the market were surely discussed. Changes in the price of cotton or corn or cattle were everybody's concern, and it was a good opportunity to strike up bargains or do some horse trading with near and distant neighbors.[32] They would swap experiences, learn what they could of the outside world, and exchange a little political "yow yow."

News of current events came primarily by word of mouth. "There wasn't any television," C. N. Cosby stressed. "There wasn't any radio. There wasn't any newspaper pitched around every day. And about the only way you got any news was [by] getting together with your neighbors and finding out what was going on up on the river or what are the boys doing over there."[33] Talking with people other than those from one's immediate neighborhood was like having contact with another part of the world. "That was worth an awful lot to you," Caldwell stated, "just to communicate with people from all around, maybe for ten, fifteen miles away."[34]

Camp meetings were no less than a carnival for children. Bertie Culp remembered the excitement of getting to be with other children. "That was the thrill of our life to get somebody else to play with. We's just thrilled to death to get somebody to play with. You can't imagine what it is to be asetting out—well, just take a ranch setting way out in the middle of a pasture and that's the only place there is around and you had just a small two-room house or such a matter and have somebody, kids to play with you. You couldn't imagine. It was a joy."[35] Joe Shelton was not yet two years old when his mother died, and until his father remarried he stayed in different homes. For a child from an isolated farm with no one to play with, the camp meeting was a field day. "Oh Boy! We'd rip and run around—play. When it come time for

Children at a Texas camp meeting.
Courtesy The Center for American History, The University of Texas at Austin

preaching they took us in and sat us down and we knew darn well we
had to sit there, so we did. But boy, it sure did get tiresome. As soon as
they turned us loose, man, we went out of there on the run."[36]

Children probably enjoyed the simple games popular in that
day—dolls, marbles, drop the handkerchief, playing cowboys and
Indians, or "ranch."[37] Girls, wanting to be lady-like, usually enjoyed
more sedentary activities.[38] Boys were likely found trapping birds,
hunting rattlesnakes, riding stick horses, roping stumps, and climbing
anything above ground level.[39] Riding horses was a favorite of all ages,
and dogs, if present, must have been involved in children's fun. Older
boys found camaraderie in conceiving and carrying out their multitude of pranks.

Although the devout were always interested in the salvation of the youth, the young were more interested in one another.[40] For the sons it was a chance to get close enough to enjoy the fragrance of young girls, and for the daughters a chance to be seen by eyes other than those of family members and the livestock.[41] A camp meeting or revival was, therefore, a unique opportunity for frenzied courting and laying the groundwork for future households.[42] Dora Slade's definition of a good "pertracted meeting" was one that netted at least two weddings; a real good one, maybe three.[43]

It was pointed out that as settlers established churches, these became the centers of social activity. People found church and Sunday school attendance their closest approximation to any form of regular socializing.[44] Weary wife and husband might have to sit on a hard bench and listen to an excruciatingly long sermon, but it was a measure of relaxation from the toil of the homestead. Best of all, it was an opportunity to see friends.

Sunday visiting was intense—"They'd just visit all to pieces."[45] People would socialize before and after preaching, but it was following the service that the serious visiting started and might well last as long as the church service itself.[46] To dash out and scurry home was uncommon, and if so, explained and understood.[47] One settler spoke of everyone gathering at the school house once a month for preaching and visiting, suggesting that the two were almost expected to occur in tandem.[48]

SICKNESS AND DEATH DID NOT SERVE AS OCCASIONS FOR ENTER-tainment and extended socializing as did camp meetings and revivals. Never were these misfortunes regarded as opportunities for recreational diversion, but sickness and death served a social function by bringing people together, albeit maybe only briefly, and making for closer relations. Marcia Caldwell recalled small groups standing around or sitting on their heels outside the home of sickness or death.

"Funny things would come up but they'd laugh kind of quietly." If they were sitting up with a body, "There wasn't anything they could do except visit with each other. That was a wonderful occasion."[49]

A. W. Young described a custom in the latter part of the nineteenth century of holding funerals long after the corpse had been buried. Generally, they held these services from three to six months following the burial, but in some instances the service was a year later. These funerals were advertised, or norated, for weeks in advance so that people from across the country might be present, and they usually were. Such events were among the most popular gatherings of the day, a kind of family reunion and place where people could learn the latest news. Announcements of common interest were made by the reverend before or after the funeral sermon. There was courting among the young people, horse trading between the men.[50]

Frontier settlers viewed funerals as respected occasions, and although only a dozen people might attend, that was a good crowd. Everybody "took out and went." Jennie Holcomb said, "If there was to be a funeral, most everybody quit and went 'cause there wasn't very many people here. Most people would feel it was their duty to quit and go to the funeral."[51] Willie McClary's parents believed that they should go no matter when or where the person died. There were so few people, each neighbor owed that to the other.[52] Lavert Avent recalled the death of a stranger in the community and his burial in the potter's field. "There wasn't many people that went, but my mother and dad and me went out there. Dad said, 'Well, there won't be very many there. Somebody ought to go along and be there.'"[53] Asked if people would attend a funeral or burial service, Joe Shelton was quick to respond: "Oh, yes! They sure would. You bet they would. If there's any hard feelings around you never knew it then, 'cause no matter what had happened between any two people, when a thing like that happened that was all [put aside]."[54]

Schools sometimes closed and the children would march from the building, maybe two-by-two, enter the small church, and march around the coffin.[55] If a town was nearby, some of the residents out of respect might attend the funeral for a migrant, unknown to them, who had died on the trail. Out on the range, neighboring outfits would gather to pay homage to one of their fellow cowhands.[56]

In these times of coming together, there was more of a focus on helping than in socializing or simply enjoying one another's company. Loyalty to and responsibility for distant neighbors has been discussed. Scattered though they were, cords of interdependency made it a duty to assist in times of distress.[57] They went without being asked. "Your neighbors," Black emphasized, "hell, they was just like part of your family almost."[58] Just as news got around that new bolts of calico had arrived at the general store, a dance was to be held at one of the ranches, or a preacher was on his way, settlers learned of neighbors in need. "'Twas with great sympathy and feeling at heart," one pioneer said, "that one would see a neighbor driving up in a big wagon when there was sickness, with a castor oil bottle in one hand and a box of salts in another."[59]

Ad Spaugh had just finished supper late one evening when a cowboy rode into camp and in frightened voice said that the five-year-old in a cabin some eight miles away was very ill, dying from a fever. "Would someone come and help?" Spaugh had been on horseback since early morning, but he caught a fresh horse and told the rider he was on his way. He and a partner, Dogie Robinson, reached the two-room cabin just as the moon was appearing, but on seeing them, the father could only shake his head in a pitiful gesture of loss. A few quiet and solemn words were exchanged. "We'll be stayin' with you tonight, and tomorrow the rest a' the boys'll come over," Dogie said. "I'm goin' to fix you a cup o' coffee now."[60]

That night Ad Spaugh and Dogie Robinson made a crude little coffin from boards found in a lean-to and dug a grave on a nearby hill. They returned to the roundup camp at daybreak, arriving just as the cook was calling out breakfast. "'We'll knock off the circle today,' [Ad] announced. 'That little Harkness girl died last night. Reckon you men want to help out any way you can.'"[61] The men standing around the campfire nodded their heads. They would clean up a bit and be ready to go in an hour. Later that morning a half-hundred men stood with hats in hands on the brow of a knoll for the simple service. Without doubt, they neither forgot nor neglected the grieving parents in the days that followed.

In times of sickness or death it was this sense of helping out "any way you can" that seemed so characteristic of early plains settlers. Neighbors, for sure, would have visited and been companionable in these circumstances, but the social benefits came primarily from deeds rather than words.

Riding for help was one way to assist. When a doctor was needed, "you'd just get on your horse and go," and no one would ride farther or faster than a cowboy.[62] Although the heroic run made by B. A. Oden was for a fellow cowhand, it could just as well have been for a neighbor. Eighteen years old and sickly—weighing only around seventy-five pounds—Oden joined up with a cattle drive passing through San Angelo, Texas, on the way to New Mexico. Eating antelope meat and roughing it in the open air made him look like a man and, Oden believed, saved his life, so when his companion suffered a relapse after taking all of his prescription, Oden was fit enough to ride for the refill. He rode seventy miles the first day, stopping only to borrow a fresh horse at one of the ranches on the way. Loping along a rocky hill the horse slipped, fell, and badly crushed Oden's thumb between the saddle and a rock. He returned to the ranch in three days, during which time he had ridden 180 miles.[63]

S. K. Bynum was age eighteen when he signed on with a West Texas ranch in 1881. He and a partner rode to see a friend camped nearly six miles away and found the man sick abed. They stayed until late in the night—"about as cold a night as a man could go up against"—but before leaving asked if there were anything they could do for their friend. "Well he said groaningly I would sure like to have a box of pils [*sic*] and a bottle of tonic, so we said all right, then late as it was at night we mounted and headed for Dockum's store some fifty moles [*sic*] away. . . . About day light we came to Dockum's store, got the pills but not the tomic [*sic*]. I would like to know if any of the readers would ride a night and day to get a pal a box of pills."[64]

If needed, friends assisted the doctor in the primitive surgery of the day, brushing away flies or administering anesthesia. If the patients or surviving members were very poor, neighbors provided for them until they were able to get back on their feet, or they made arrangements for them to return home—"That was common back there."[65] They did all the chores, and that meant, among other things, milking a bunch of cows. "It was a lot of work!"[66] "Sometimes," according to Gladys Deitiker, "they'd come in and say, 'Can we take some laundry you need done?' Now, I'm not talking about an automatic washer either. I mean they would take it home and [wash it] in a tub and washboard."[67] They would clean the house, bring in baked goods, feed the stock, hang a screen door, plow a field, ride for groceries, go for fresh water—do just whatever needed to be done. When a neighbor's child lingered between life and death for several months, Albert Byars's father called him aside and said, "Now, we're going over and plow his field for him because he's grieving and he wants to stay with her."[68]

This help was provided without any thought of pay. People knew that when the shadows fell on them, these services would be returned in kind. That was their only remuneration, and it was sufficient.[69] Expressions of gratitude, however, were not neglected. Black spoke of his aunt nursing a little girl through what was thought would be a fatal case of measles. "I remember then the ol' man Brakemore brought up a—they didn't have any money in those days—he brought a hog up there and gave it to my aunt and uncle. The neighbor, he wanted to give her something and he gave her a hog. Yeah, gave her a hog."[70]

SICKNESS AND DEATH IN EARLY WEST TEXAS, AS IN OTHER PARTS OF THE plains, were not private tragedies confined to the immediate family.

They were community concerns, and people stepped forward. As he approached his final hours of life in 1856, Kansas settler William Colt had no fear of death for himself, believing that beyond the dark vale opened gates of pearl to a heavenly mansion.[71] His source of distress, though, was the thought of leaving behind his wife and small daughter in a land of strangers. The Colts had only recently lost their young son, so Mrs. Colt was in the depths of despondency when after her husband's death she closed his eyes and despaired aloud, "My God! My God! why hast Thou forsaken me?" Unaware of the man standing nearby, she felt his hand on her shoulder as he said, "My dear woman, though God has taken your husband, He is able to raise up friends for you."[72]

More than one plains settler doubtless had occasion to take comfort from a reassuring voice and a hand on the shoulder. It was a time and place uniquely beholden to friends and neighbors.

The plain lay under the cloudless sky
In utter and terrible silence.
Not a sound, not a living soul, not a voice
Broke from the russet reach of sod
Save a cricket that cried from the deep
Of his loneliness, like a lost soul.[73]

STATIONED IN COLEMAN COUNTY, TEXAS, IN 1870, S. P. ELKINS NOTED THAT settlers had much to endure. Among other hardships, there was the constant threat of Indians and no close neighbors to lend a helping hand. Any stranger who showed up was welcomed and made to feel at home. If settlers did live close enough, they might have preaching services once a month, the men arriving armed, wearing their pistols as naturally as their clothes. Inside, they stacked their guns in the corner of the house until the meeting was over. "They were glad to see each other," Elkins said, "and would shake hands when they met, and also when they parted, thinking maybe for the last time."[74]

With settlement and the passage of time, life in West Texas became less desperate. The dangers subsided, the isolation and loneliness lessened. There was no longer that starvation for contacts with other people. Not to be forgotten, however, are those bygone days when it was "Anything for fellowship. Any excuse to get together . . . with people that you knew for fellowship, and fellowship was really a great thing."[75]

Notes

INTRODUCTION

1. Marcia Caldwell, recorded interview with author, Mar. 1, 1984, Canyon, Tex., Research Center, Panhandle-Plains Historical Museum [hereafter RCP-PHM].

2. Caldwell, recorded interview with author, Mar. 17, 1986, Canyon, Tex., RCP-PHM.

3. Joanna L. Stratton, *Pioneer Women: Voices from the Kansas Frontier,* p. 10.

4. Ibid., pp. 24–25.

5. Walter Nugent, *Structures of American Social History,* p. 24.

6. Fite maintains that precise dating is not meaningful when talking about the frontier experience. Gilbert C. Fite, *The Farmers' Frontier: 1865–1900,* p. ix.

7. Garry Nall, "The Farmers' Frontier in the Texas Panhandle," *Panhandle-Plains Historical Review* 45: 1–20; Jayme A. Sokolow, "The Demography of a Ranching Frontier: The Texas Panhandle in 1880," *Panhandle-Plains Historical Review* 60: 79; Jan Blodgett, *Land of Bright Promise: Advertising the Texas Panhandle and South Plains, 1870–1917,* p. 99.

8. Frederick W. Rathjen, personal communication with author, Dec. 12, 2000.

9. Garry Nall, "Panhandle Farming in the "Golden Era" of American Agriculture" *Panhandle-Plains Historical Review* 46: 68–76; Blodgett, *Land of Bright Promise,* p. 82.

10. Joseph Conrad, *Victory,* p. 234.

11. John L. Allen, "The Garden-Desert Continuum: Competing Views of the Great Plains in the Nineteenth Century," *Great Plains Quarterly* 5 (fall): 207–20.

12. Ibid., p. 209.

13. Lillian Schlissel, Byrd Gibbens, and Elizabeth Hampsten, *Far From Home: Families of the Westward Journey*, p. 242.

14. Susan Armitage, "Women and Men in Western History: A Stereoptical Vision," *The Western Historical Quarterly* 16, no. 1 (1985): 382; Julie Roy Jeffrey, "'There Is Some Splendid Scenery': Women's Responses to the Great Plains Landscape," *Great Plains Quarterly* 8, no. 2 (1988): 69–70.

15. David Thelen, "Memory and American History" *The Journal of American History* 75, no. 4 (Mar.): 1117.

16. William Cronon, "A Place for Stories: Nature, History, and Narrative," *The Journal of American History* 78, no. 4 (Mar.): 1349.

17. Paul Fussell, *The Great War and Modern Memory*, p. 218.

18. Tamara K. Hareven, "The Search for Generational Memory: Tribal Rites in Industrial Society," *Daedalus* 107, no. 4 (fall): 142.

19. John Bodnar, "Power and Memory in Oral History: Workers and Managers at Studebaker," *The Journal of American History* 75, no. 4 (Mar.): 1202. A summary of recent research on collaborative memory is found in Bruce Bower, "Partners in Recall: Elderly Spouses Build Better Memories through Collaboration," *Science News* 152 (Sept. 13, 1997): 174–75.

20. Barbara Allen, "Shaping History: The Creation of a Collective Pioneer Experience," *Columbia* 7, no. 4 (winter, 1993–94): 6–13.

21. Cronon, "Place for Stories," p. 1373.

22. Investigations on the effects of aging on memory for remote events are contradictory. Studies report effects ranging from diminished to superior performance in elderly subjects when compared to the young. Morris Moscovitch and Gordon Winocur, "The Neuropsychology of Memory and Aging," in *The Handbook of Aging and Cognition*, ed. by Fergus I. M. Craik and Timothy A. Salthouse, pp. 315–72. Craik and Jennings suggest that although memory for factual historic events appears to decline with increasing age, it is possible that personal, autobiographical experiences are affected differently. Fergus I. M. Craik and Janine M. Jennings, "Human Memory," in Craik and Salthouse, *Handbook of Aging and Cognition*, pp. 51–110. Bodnar concludes that despite the complexity surrounding human recollection, oral histories are trustworthy because the historical facts tend to survive (p. 1221). Thelen would appear to agree, citing opinion that although memory of details may become obscured by time, the basic accuracy of historical events is preserved (p. 1121).

23. Julie Roy Jeffrey, *Frontier Women: The Trans-Mississippi West, 1840–1880*, p. 53; Jeffrey, "'There Is Some Splendid Scenery,'" p. 70; Fite, *Farmers' Frontier*, p. 216; Sokolow, "Demography," pp. 80–81.

24. Nugent, *Structures*, p. 24. Roger Barker discusses the influence of frontier environments on behavior, emphasizing that similar conditions made

for similar behaviors. Roger G. Barker, "The Influence of Frontier Environments on Behavior," in *The American West: New Perspectives, New Dimensions*, Ed. by Jerome O. Steffen, pp. 61–93.

25. John W. Lockhart, "Old Fashioned Camp Meetings," *The Galveston Daily News* 56, no. 53 (Sun., May 16, 1897): 19.

26. Nebraska Society of the Daughters of the American Revolution, *Collection of Nebraska Pioneer Reminiscences*, p. 22.

27. Ruth Tressman, "Home on the Range," *New Mexico Historical Review* 26, no. 1 (1951): 14. William Tanner, turn-of-the-century southwestern cowboy and Oklahoma Territory homesteader, seemed constantly lonely, even after a night of fun or during a Fourth of July picnic. William W. Tanner, papers, 1898–1912, RCP-PHM.

28. Fite, *Farmers' Frontier*, p. 200.

29. Seymour V. Connor, "The West Is for Us: The Reminiscences of Mary A. Blankenship," *The Museum Journal* 2 (1958): 70.

30. Charles Dudley Eaves and C. A. Hutchinson, *Post City, Texas*, p. 35. Dorothy Schwieder and Deborah Fink found isolation still a problem in rural counties of Nebraska and South Dakota in the 1930s. Dorothy Schwieder and Deborah Fink, "Plains Women: Rural Life in the 1930s," *Great Plains Quarterly* 8, no. 2 (1988): 79–88. Katherine Jellison includes the issue of isolation in her article "Women and Technology on the Great Plains, 1910–1940," *Great Plains Quarterly* 8, no. 3 (1988): 145–57.

31. Nebraska Society of the DAR, *Collection*, p. 165.

32. Frank Goodwyn, *Lone-Star Land: Twentieth-Century Texas in Perspective*, p. 237.

33. H. G. Bedford, "Memoirs," n.d., RCP-PHM.

34. Samuel P. and Susan E. Newcomb, "Diaries" (1865–73), JEHC—Midland. [hereafter JEHC—Midland].

CHAPTER I

1. "Short Life History of Mrs. Phebe K. Warner," *Claude News*, Feb., 1935, RCP-PHM.

2. The twenty northern counties of West Texas, the Panhandle, and the adjoining seventeen southern counties, the South Plains, comprise what is called the Llano Estacado or Staked Plains. B. R. Brunson, *The Texas Land and Development Company: A Panhandle Promotion, 1912–1956*, p. 6.

3. Nall discusses other early barriers to the settlement of the Texas Panhandle in "The Farmers' Frontier in the Texas Panhandle," *Panhandle-Plains Historical Review* 45 (1972): 1–2.

4. Ibid., pp. 1–20.

5. Walter Prescott Webb, *The Great Plains*, p. 152.

6. William Hard, "The Disappearance of the Great American Desert," *Munsey's Magazine* 40, no. 1 (1908): 71–75.

7. Keene Abbott, "The Great Plains," in *The Prairie Schooner*, Vol. 1, p. 94.

8. Garry Nall, "Panhandle Farming in the 'Golden Era' of American Agriculture," *Panhandle-Plains Historical Review* 46 (1973): 70. The first railroad to cross the Panhandle, the Fort Worth and Denver City, originated in Fort Worth, laying tracks through the towns of Wichita Falls, Quanah, Childress, Clarendon, and Texline. The line reached the Texas–New Mexico border in 1888. Blodgett, *Land of Bright Promise*, p. 27.

9. Blanche Scott Rutherford, *One Corner of Heaven*, p. 16.

10. Margaret Locke Kirk, "The Story of a Gentle Lady Who Pioneered the Panhandle in 1882," 1938, p. 1, RCP-PHM.

11. Walter N. Vernon, Robert W. Sledge, Robert C. Monk, and Norman W. Spellman, *The Methodist Excitement in Texas: A History*, p. 156.

12. Mrs. N. S. Bagwell, interview by Zella Hollingsworth, 1938, RCP-PHM.

13. Mrs. Frank Metcalf, "The White Family," n.d., RCP-PHM. Miner reports the account of a young girl who was warned by her grandmother that if she went to Kansas she would have to eat grasshopper soup. Craig Miner, *West of Wichita: Settling the High Plains of Kansas, 1865–1890*, p. 134.

14. Connor, "The West Is for Us," p. 23. Faye Cashatt Lewis was thirteen years old when in 1909 her family left Iowa for South Dakota. She recalled seeing her mother "sitting in a corner with three other women and from the worried little frown on her face I knew they were talking again about the dangers that threatened us in the new country. 'Just don't listen to such talk,' Father had told her more than once. . . . but her vulnerability must have been apparent in her face, for she seemed unable to escape this scaremongering. Prairie fires and rattlesnakes were favorite topics in these conversations, but now they were talking about Indians." All the observing child could envision was "An unknown blankness, dotted with hazards," a land with no schools, no books, and maybe no neighbors. Faye C. Lewis, *Nothing to Make a Shadow*, pp. 8, 10.

15. John M. Faragher, *Women and Men on the Overland Trail*, p. 208; Jayme A. Sokolow, "The Demography of a Ranching Frontier: The Texas Panhandle in 1880," *Panhandle-Plains Historical Review* 60 (1982): 86–87; Glenda Riley, *Frontierswomen: The Iowa Experience*, p. 18.

16. Riley, *Frontierswomen*, p. 18.

17. Nancy Ross, *Westward the Women*, p. 11.

18. Riley, *Frontierswomen*, p. 14.

19. Mrs. Edward Neal Burrus, interview by Pollyanna B. Hughes, 1964, p. 1, RCP-PHM.

20. James I. Fenton, "Critters, Sourdough, and Dugouts: Women and Im-

itation Theory on the Staked Plains, 1875–1910," in *At Home on the Range: Essays on the History of Western Social and Domestic Life*, ed. by John R. Wunder, p. 27; W. C. Holden, *Alkali Trails: Or Social and Economic Movements of the Texas Frontier 1846–1900*, p. 72.

21. Rutherford, *One Corner*, p. 16. Amelia Hadley was married in Illinois in April, 1851, and four days later she and her husband were on a honeymoon trip to Oregon that would last 130 days. She intended her account to read "Journal of Travels," but her spelling error resulted in a "Journal of Travails," and Kenneth Holmes notes the point in her record when the travails became regular inclusions. Kenneth L. Holmes, *Covered Wagon Women: Diaries & Letters from the Western Trails 1840–1890*, Vol. 3 (1851), p. 53.

22. Holden, *Alkali Trails*, p. 72.

23. Gracy Henderson, "A Month on Wheels: From the Diary of Mrs. Davidson and Interviews with Mr. Gracy Henderson," n.d., p. 13, RCP-PHM.

24. Mary Hudson Brothers, *A Pecos Pioneer*, p. 158. Mrs. George Legg was a child in the mid-1860s when her family was on their way to the Northwest. A stranger they happened upon persuaded her father to turn south into Texas, and although disappointed about the change of plans, she had pleasant memories of the journey. "How I loved the lull and sway of the wagon, hour after hour slowly moving along. . . . Nothing in my life has ever been quite the free easy pleasure of this trip." C. O. Lanman, "Memoirs of Mrs. George E. Legg," n.d., RCP-PHM.

25. Phebe Kerrick Warner, "Mary Ann Goodnight," n.d., RCP-PHM. Miner (*West of Wichita*, p. 133) notes that regardless how excited all or some of the family members were about migration, leaving was still very difficult.

26. Jeffrey, *Frontier Women*, p. 37.

27. Connor, "The West Is For Us," p. 86.

28. Lodisa Frizzell, *Across the Plains to California in 1852: Journal of Mrs. Lodisa Frizzell*, p. 5. Miriam Davis Colt left New York with her husband and two children for Kansas in 1856. She sensed that those final moments with her mother were the last "we shall have until we meet *where parting never comes.*" She later pondered: "Why must friends be so endeared? why [*sic*] must they meet only to part, perhaps forever, in this world?" Miriam Davis Colt, *Went to Kansas*, pp. 25, 122. Mary Riddle was a thirty-eight-year-old Iowan who migrated to Oregon in 1878. Her diary acknowledged the difficulty of looking back at the "weeping ones," but she fortified herself with the knowledge that "it has to be parting and meeting and meeting and parting in this life." Holmes, *Covered Wagon Women*, Vol. 10 (1875–83), p. 18.

29. Holmes, *Covered Wagon Women*, Vol. 5 (1852, The Oregon Trail), pp. 27–28.

30. Rutherford, *One Corner*, p. 17.

31. Phoebe Goodell Judson was twenty years old when she migrated from Ohio to Oregon in 1853. She remembered the parting that was "very affecting," and she anguished over the parents left to grieve in their lonely home. Her husband was an only son, and their two-year-old daughter was the idol of her grandparents. "The tender 'good-byes' were said with brave cheers in the voices, but many tears from the hearts." Emotions peaked when the child held out her arms for her grandfather to take her, and he begged that the child be left with them. Mrs. Judson would later write that along the way her mind was preoccupied with many sad reflections. Phoebe Goodell Judson, *A Pioneer's Search for an Ideal Home*, p. 11. It was in Iowa that Gro Svendsen settled after leaving her native Norway in 1862. She was despondent over having left her parents behind, and her sleep was tortured by disturbing dreams, often sad and foreboding. After crossing the Atlantic she wrote home acknowledging the "unspeakable sorrow" she knew that she had caused her parents and siblings. Pauline Farseth and Theodore C. Blegen, *Frontier Mother: The Letters of Gro Svendsen*, p. 7.

32. Faragher, *Women and Men*, p. 208; Riley, *Frontierswomen*, p. 18. A few of the Riddle's friends accompanied them for five days down the trail before regretfully taking their leave, and the final link with home was not broken until the seventh day. Holmes, *Covered Wagon Women*, Vol. 10, p. 18.

33. Dora Merrell Stroup, "Memories From Years 7 to 17," 1965, RCP-PHM.

34. Lillian Schlissel, *Women's Diaries of the Westward Journey*, p. 14.

35. Jeffrey, *Frontier Women*, p. 38.

36. Faragher states (*Women and Men*, pp. 82–83) that men rarely rode in the wagons, but women frequently did. "This distinction between riding and walking was so basic that it came close to a role-defining division between the sexes." Nevertheless, some of the women walked; many much of the time. To lighten the load, there is reason to believe that as the journey progressed many women walked as a matter of course.

37. Schlissel, *Women's Diaries*, p. 28; Faragher, *Women and Men*, pp. 110–12.

38. Women also suffered separations on the trail. Clarissa Shipley, her husband, and two daughters left Iowa destined for Idaho in 1864. She recorded in her diary: "I thought it was hard to part with friends at home, but it is nothing compared to parting with them out here." Holmes, *Covered Wagon Women*, Vol. 9 (1864–68), pp. 42–43. Parties broke off, pursuing different destinations, taking different routes, and "When friends parted, women wept." Jeffrey, *Frontier Women*, p. 41. Separations by death were all too common. For Mrs. Frizzell, "it is very sad to part with them here, for the heart can hardly support the addition, of so much grief, for there are few whose hearts are not already pained, by leaving so many behind." Frizzell, *Across the Plains*, p. 14.

39. Jeffrey, *Frontier Women*, p. 36. Myers cites the case of a young man who

slipped behind the barn before his grandmother could see his tears when he bid her a final farewell. Sandra L. Myres, *Westering Women and the Frontier Experience 1800–1915*, p. 101.

40. James H. Baker, "Diary (1858–1872)," p. 23, JEHC—Midland.

41. Charles R. Warren, "Pioneer Life in Armstrong County, Texas, As Remembered by Charles R. Warren, of Amarillo [Texas]," n.d. RCP-PHM. Isham Reavis stepped off a Missouri River steamboat onto Nebraska soil in 1858. "As I stood on the bank of the fast-flowing river, and saw the steamboat that had born me there, cast off her moorings and slowly float out into the stream to resume her voyage northward against the turbid flood of the Missouri, an indescribable feeling of lonesomeness came over me, which I shall never forget. For the first time I realized what it was to break off the associations of a lifetime. . . . Every tie that bound me to the old life and the old home [and] . . . all the sacred memories that cluster around them, were severed once and forever." John S. Goff, "Isham Reavis, Pioneer Lawyer and Judge," *Nebraska History* 54, no. 1 (1973): 8–9.

42. Colt, *Went to Kansas*, p. 123.

43. Fite, *Farmers' Frontier*, p. 217. Passionate pleas for family and friends to join settlers in the new land resounded in letters home, but if destiny decreed these earthly relationships severed, some took comfort in believing that come the end of time all would meet again in heaven. The morale of many a pioneer woman was sustained by her faith that the eternal network of family and friends would be restored in the life hereafter. Jeffrey, *Frontier Women*, p. 75.

44. "Short Life History of Mrs. Phebe K. Warner." Women yearned for family and companions left behind. Letters and diaries acknowledged new friends and the attractions of the West, but Myres finds these acknowledgments juxtaposed with both a forlorn longing for home and family and bitter expressions of loneliness, homesickness, and depression. Myres, *Westering Women*, p. 168. Abigail Scott was seventeen and one of nine children when her family migrated from Illinois to Oregon in 1852. She wrote from the trail to a friend left behind: "Your likeness is lying on the stand before me, it does look '*so*' natural, When I gaize [*sic*] on the likenesses of any of our friends it is impossible to discribe [*sic*] my feelings, In one instant, my whole (*past*) life rushes upon my almost frensied [*sic*] mind, and, although such scenes are past and gone forever from my sight, I can but think of them '*with a quivering lip and throbing brow.*' Many persons may say it is folly and deem me weak but under such circumstances it is impossible to control my feelings." Holmes, *Covered Wagon Women*, Vol. 5, p. 170. It was not unusual for the image of far-removed relations to appear repeatedly in dreams. Phoebe Judson described a dream in which she was with a companion of younger days. "She wandered with me on Lake Erie's beach; a soft south wind was blowing; the little

ripples came creeping over the shells and pebbles; my hungry heart was feeding on the joys of bygone days . . . I extended my hands over the clear waters . . . and exclaimed 'Beautiful, beautiful Lake Erie.' I awoke with my
hands outspread, my pillow wet with tears, and my heart aching with a lonely
longing for the scenes and friends of the 'days of yore.'" Judson, *Pioneer's
Search*, pp. 222–23.

W. B. Benton's parents migrated from Missouri to the Texas Panhandle in
1903. He told how his mother would go to the gate, look toward Missouri and
wish for some trees. Then, as if it were an afterthought, Mr. Benton added:
"When the trains went by they had such a lonesome whistle." W. B. Benton,
"This Is the Partial Story of My Father's Early Life in the Panhandle As He
Had Started to Write It," 1940, RCP-PHM.

45. Tanner papers.

46. Dorothy Scarborough, *The Wind*, p. 33.

47. Holmes, *Covered Wagon Women*, Vol. 7 (1854–60), p. 130. *Courtesy
Arthur H. Clark Company, Glendale, California.*

CHAPTER 2

1. Rudolph H. Moos, ed., *Human Adaptation: Coping with Life Crises*,
p. 189. Marc Fried maintains that the emotional response to resettlement and
the loss of familiar physical surroundings and social ties can take on features
resembling the sorrow and mourning of grief. Marc Fried, "Grieving for a
Lost Home," in *Human Adaptation: Coping with Life Crises*, ed. by Rudolf H.
Moos, pp. 192–201. H. B. M. Murphy concludes that studies in the United
States suggest a relationship between migration and more serious mental
disorders. H. B. M. Murphy, "Migration and the Major Mental Disorders:
A Reappraisal," in *Mobility and Mental Health*, ed. by Mildred B. Kantor,
p. 24.

2. Judith Stevens-Long and Michael Commons, *Adult Life*, p. 484.

3. Eugene B. Brody, ed., *Behavior in New Environments*, p. 14.

4. Miner, *West of Wichita*, p. 133.

5. Jeffrey, "'There Is Some Splendid Scenery,'" p. 73.

6. Buren Sparks, "An Apostle to the Cowboys," *Farm and Ranch*, Sept. 9,
1931.

7. Ernest R. Archambeau, "The First Federal Census in the Panhandle,
1880," *Panhandle-Plains Historical Review* 23 (1950): 22.

8. L. F. Sheffy, "The Experimental Stage of Settlement in the Panhandle
of Texas," *Panhandle-Plains Historical Review* 3 (1930): 78.

9. Sandra L. Myres, *Westering Women and the Frontier Experience 1800–
1915*, 15.

10. T. Guy Willis, interview by Hazel Willis, 1946, RCP-PHM.

11. Mildred R. Bennett, "Willa Cather and the Prairie," *Nebraska History* 56, no. 2 (1975): 231.

12. Vera Meredith, "Memoirs of Bob Brewer and W. B. Clark," 1936, pp. 11–12, RCP-PHM. A 1936 Pioneer Day speech by J. C. Estlack at the Tri-State Fair in Amarillo was unrestrained in its poetic passion for the Panhandle: "The glory of your mornings when the sun bursts forth from a mantle of dawn tinting the horizon with new hope of a better day . . . the splendor and glitter of millions of diamonds made through the night when the evening stars bend low and kiss to tears the grains and grasses . . . the mysterious night voices as the wind whispers a benediction among the quivering leaves of the craggy cottonwoods . . . the symphonies, sweet and dim, as the long-needed rain patters down producing a sound sweeter than chimes of an ancient cathedral; your gorgeous sunsets veiled in ruby fires greeted by an audience of a multitude of stars of mystical patterns." J. C. Estlack, "My Panhandle I Salute You: Speech on Pioneer Day at the Tri-State Fair in Amarillo [Texas], Sept. 23, 1936," p. 1, RCP-PHM.

13. Temple Ann Ellis, n.d. "Texas Plains Pioneers" [Microfilm E47], SCTTU. Following her husband's death Mrs. Ellis began writing under the name of Temple Ann Ellis. "Sunrise on Plains," *Amarillo Sunday News-Globe* 13, no. 33 (Aug. 14, 1938): Section D, p. 14.

14. Maude Smith Galloway, "Fifty Years in the Texas Panhandle," n.d., RCP-PHM. According to Robert Sawvell, retired professor of geography at West Texas A&M University, "The terms 'plain' and 'prairie' are often used to describe the same earth feature. Both are a tract or area of slightly rolling or near level land, typically of great extent or size. For many the term 'plain' emphasizes the shape of the surface, namely the flatness of the feature. The term 'prairie,' on the other hand, gives greater emphasis to what is on the surface, namely the vegetation. Thus when using 'prairie,' most see a large and extended grassland often, but not always, devoid of clusters of trees or forests." Robert D. Sawvell, personal communication, Sept., 1998. One of the reviewers of this manuscript pointed out that the term "prairie" is used almost exclusively in Canadian English to refer to the Great Plains in Canada.

15. "Hardships and Happiness Tell Story of Mrs. Arthur Duncan, First Lady of Floyd County [Texas]," n.d., RCP-PHM.

16. Evalyn W. Rasmussen, "Memoirs of Ed B. Trigg," 1939, RCP-PHM.

17. Billy M. Jones, "West Texas: A Haven for Health Seekers," *West Texas Historical Association Year Book* 42 (1966): 5.

18. Medicine during the period of westward expansion has been described as primitive and ineffective, a tragic and colossal failure. Billy M. Jones, *Health-Seekers in the Southwest, 1817–1900*, pp. 24, 26. Early Parker County, Texas, physician Dr. W. M. Campbell graduated from Vanderbilt Medical College around 1890. "I didn't know a thing in the world about medi-

cine, and I didn't know anybody that did. I never had a teacher that knew the cause of a single disease." Medicine, he continued, suffered from shameful ignorance. Doctoring was crude stuff. W. M. Campbell, "Medicine Then and Now," *West Texas Historical Association Year Book* 32 (Oct., 1956): 50.

19. Jones, *Health-Seekers*, p. 37.

20. Ibid., p. 39.

21. Ibid., p. 45; Barbour, *Westward to Health*, p. 40.

22. Psychological well-being might also benefit. In 1846 Susan Shelby Magoffin, a young lady of wealth and status, left Missouri with her trader husband for New Mexico and Mexico, possibly the first white American female to travel the Santa Fe Trail. Five days out of Independence, Mrs. Magoffin recorded in her diary: "Oh, this is a life I would not exchange for a good deal! There is such independence, so much free uncontaminated air, which impregnates the mind, the feelings, nay every thought, with purity. I breathe free without that oppression and uneasiness felt in the gossiping circles of a settled home." Susan Shelby Magoffin, *Down the Santa Fe Trail and Into Mexico*, p. 10.

23. Asthma, hay fever, rheumatism, and certain skin diseases and internal disorders were thought to respond positively to living in a more favorable climate. Jones, *Health-Seekers*, pp. 144–45.

24. Hellen Heath, "Memoirs of Mrs. J. W. Hough," 1936, RCP-PHM.

25. Jones, *Health-Seekers*, p. viii; "When Death Rate Was High," *Amarillo Sunday News and Globe* 13, no. 33 (Aug. 14, 1938): Section D, p. 13. Health motivated nearly all overland emigrants. Faragher, *Women and Men*, pp. 17–18.

26. Jones, "West Texas," pp. 3–14.

27. Opal Leigh Berryman, *Pioneer Preacher*, p. 95.

28. Agnes Morley Cleaveland, *No Life for a Lady*, p. 182.

29. Blodgett, *Land of Bright Promise*, p. 92.

30. "Consumptives Unwelcome in Texas," *Journal of the American Medical Association* 53 (Apr. 3, 1909): 1118.

31. Jones, "West Texas," p. 14. Jones gives another version of this myth in *Health-Seekers*, pp. 107–108: "Some emigrants . . . were entering Texas via the Red River and met a very old man whose features were 'seared and shrunken by the hand of time.' He was rushing with all speed to the boundary of the state, and when asked the reason for such haste, he neither stopped nor paused but murmured in passing: 'I am tired of life and of the monotony of the ages, I am weary of the slow steps of time and the dragging march of the centuries, and I am hurrying out of Texas that I may find some place where people can die.'"

32. Allan R. Bosworth, *Ozona Country*, p. 1.

33. Mattie L. Grant, "Miss Addie Rosalee Whitcomb Tells of Life in Amarillo [Texas]," 1939, RCP-PHM.

34. Nellie Witt Spikes, "The Early Days on the South Plains," n.d., SCTTU.

35. Jones, "West Texas," p. 9.

36. Mrs. Clyde W. Warwick, *The Randall County [Texas] Story*, p. 267.

37. W. Hubert Curry, *Sun Rising on the West: The Saga of Henry Clay and Elizabeth Smith*, p. 236.

38. Hazel Whited, "Memoirs of Herbert M. Timmons," 1936, RCP-PHM.

39. "When Death Rate Was High," p. 13.

40. Wallace Stegner, *Wolf Willow: A History, a Story, and a Memory of the Last Plains Frontier*, p. 7.

41. National Live Stock Association, *Prose and Poetry of the Live Stock Industry of the United States*, vol. 1, p. 550.

42. W. H. Auden, "Plains," in *The Shield of Achilles*, p. 25. Anna Langhorne Waltz was a native of Philadelphia who was married to a Baptist missionary assigned to South Dakota. Traveling by train to their mission field, she could see nothing but sky and land and endless miles of cactus and tumbleweed in every direction. Disembarking in the small town of Burke in 1911 she gathered up her baggage and a few loose bundles. "A great lump came in my throat. For some strange reason I couldn't see things very clearly and I had to pinch myself to realize that I had any feeling left. I just felt numb all over. How can I actually live in this wild and lonely looking country?" Anna Langhorne Waltz, "West River Pioneer: A Woman's Story, 1911–1915," *South Dakota History* 17, no. 1 (1987): 46–47.

43. Galloway, "Fifty Years."

44. Berryman, *Pioneer Preacher*, p. 83.

45. Ibid., pp. v, 1, 63.

46. Una M. Brooks, "The Influence of the Pioneer Women Toward A Settled Social Life on the Llano Estacado," 1941, p. 47, master's thesis, West Texas State Teachers College. Wallace Stegner describes the emptiness of the plains as being almost frighteningly total. Stegner, *Wolf Willow*, p. 3. Laurence Ricou reviews references to landscape in recent Canadian prairie fiction. One author writes of the "terror of infinite space." For others cited by Ricou it is a land of "frightening sterility"; as "empty as nightmare"; a place of "stupefying space"; "inscrutable and unsmiling"; "grey and severe"; "life-denying." Laurence Ricou, "Empty As Nightmare: Man and Landscape in Recent Canadian Prairie Fiction," *Mosaic* 6, no. 22 (1973): 143–60.

47. S. B. Fedric, "The Panhandle Fifty-Two Years Ago," n.d., RCP-PHM, p. 4.

48. Wm. K. Britton, "Memoirs of C. E. Cheyne," 1937, RCP-PHM. Faye Lewis (*Nothing to Make a Shadow*, pp. 33, 132) remembered her family being tired and hot when her mother despaired, "There's nothing to make a

shadow." It was not the heat that oppressed her so much as the vast unshel-
teredness all around them. "Nothing to make a shadow, as far as the eye could
see, had been her first fearful impression of this new land."

49. Bennett, "Willa Cather," p. 231.

50. Holmes, *Covered Wagon Women*, Vol. 2 (1850), p. 79.

51. Stegner, *Wolf Willow*, p. 8.

52. David Dary, *Cowboy Culture*, pp. 164–65.

53. Mrs. T. W. Tomlinson, "A Brief and Partial History of Swisher County
[Texas]," 1922, p. 5, RCP-PHM.

54. Elizabeth Hampsten, *Read This Only to Yourself: The Private Writings of
Midwestern Women, 1880–1910*, p. 39.

55. V. H. Whitlock, *Cowboy Life on the Llano Estacado*, p. ix.

56. Mrs. Ralph E. Randel, ed., *A Time to Purpose: A Chronicle of Carson
County*, Vol. 1, p. 14.

57. Vance Johnson, "This Was a Wide Open Country, and a Lonesome
One Too, When Mitch Bell Arrived; Got First Job Cutting Cedar Posts,"
Amarillo Daily News 29, no. 51 (Jan. 3, 1938): 5.

58. A. C. Greene, *A Personal Country*, p. 129.

59. Nellie Witt Spikes, "Old Settlers Reunion Draws Old Timers Together," *The Crosbyton Review* 28, no. 12 (Mar. 20, 1936): Section 2, p. 1. According to Jonathan Raban, new arrivals in the northern plains found themselves in an openness of country that defeated their best efforts to bring it into
focus. The land fanned out continuously in every direction. Raban comments
on one young man's "blue-eyed, long-distance, prairie stare." Jonathan Raban, *Bad Land: An American Romance*, p. 246.

60. M. K. Wisehart, "'Wichita Bill,'" Cowboy Artist, Rode Into The Halls
Of Fame," *The American Magazine*, Aug., 1927, pp. 34–70. Anna Waltz recalled
South Dakota in 1911: "There was nothing to break your gaze—the ground
just went on and on and on and so did the sky." Waltz, "West River Pioneer,"
p. 50.
In 1872 J. H. Tice described the forbidding and oppressively monotonous
appearance of the Kansas landscape. "Your eye sweeps in vain around the
horizon for an object to rest upon, nor shrub, nor tree, nor rock is visible at any
point or in any direction." J. H. Tice, *Over the Plains—and—On the Mountains
or Kansas and Colorado*, p. 84. Neil Evernden argues, however, that the prairie
can never be a visual resource, because it fails the "thing test." Travelers
crossing the plains will "hold their visual breath for a thousand miles."
Tourists, he continues, will complain because there is nothing to focus on, but
"We can only accept the gentle onslaught of the prairie. The prairie is an experience, not an object—a sensation, not a view. The prairie is a way of being
and not a thing at all." Neil Evernden, "Beauty and Nothingness: Prairie as
Failed Resource," *Landscape* 27, no. 3 (1983): 2, 8.

61. Nebraska Society of the Daughters of the American Revolution, *Collection*, "Forethought."

62. Malcolm Lewis reviews how this relationship coalesced in the minds of early plains travelers. The constant winds and fields of swaying grass, the buoyant clouds sweeping the boundless sky, the uninterrupted view and absence of upright objects, the sense of emptiness—all left the impression of an ocean of land. "The central Great Plains were said to be 'swept by winds as freely as the ocean.' The shadows of moving clouds gave a sense of motion similar to that at sea and this was emphasized by the waves in the wind-blown grass. Clumps of trees were likened to islands, bluffs to coastlines, and isolated groups of hills and mountains to archipelagos. Immigrants came in waves, many of them in wagons called prairie schooners. . . . Isolated trees served as lighthouses and the rotting carcasses of buffalo were looked upon as wrecks. It was even predicted that domestic cattle would multiply in the region as the fish in the sea." G. Malcolm Lewis, "The Great Plains Region and Its Image of Flatness," *Journal of the West* 6, no. 1 (1967): 21; Jones, "West Texas," p. 4.

63. Hamlin Garland, "Moods of the Plain," in *Prairie Songs*, p. 117.

64. Miriam Colt (*Went to Kansas*, pp. 70–71) began to suspect soon after arrival that her family's move to Kansas was a grim mistake. She would later write: "The dark storm-clouds, (to my mind's eye,) are gathering in our horizon. . . . I am so impressed some nights with this feeling, that I sit up in bed for hours, and fairly cringe from some unknown terror. I tell my husband, 'We are a doomed ship; unless we go away, some great calamity will come upon us; and it is on me that the storm will burst with all its dark fury.' Sometimes a voice speaks to me in thunder tones, saying, 'Rise, rise! Flee to the mountains,—tarry not in all the plain. Haste away! Destruction's before thee, and sorrow behind;' and, 'you never will be a happy family again.'"

65. According to Walter Prescott Webb, the wind is more constant and forceful on the plains than in any other section of the United States, save the seashore. The average wind velocity is the same for both regions. Webb continued: "The hot winds, chinooks, northers, and blizzards are the most novel features of United States weather. . . . [and] they all find their habitat in the Great Plains . . . An arid region to begin with, it is burnt by hot winds, chilled by northers, frozen by blizzards, and flailed with ice stones." Webb referred to the blizzard as the "grizzly of the Plains." Walter Prescott Webb, "The Land and the Life of the Great Plains," *West Texas Historical Association Year Book* 4 (1928): 67, 71.

66. Garland, "Lost in a Norther," in *Prairie Songs*, p. 119.

67. Ibid.

68. Duff Green, "Memoirs of Duff Green," *Panhandle-Plains Historical Review* 17 (1944): 83. According to one report, the etymology of the word

"Kansas" includes the meaning, "people of the South wind." Kansans claimed that it was the only place in the country where the wind could blow on all four sides of a house at the same time. Stuart Henry, *Conquering Our Great American Plains*, p. 58. John Ise (*Sod and Stubble: The Story of a Kansas Homestead*, p. 44) gave voice to his Kansas mother's despair: "The incessant, wearying wind! How it knocked and pounded at the windows and at the sod roof, scattering dust and pebbles over the floor, flapping the curtains, the towel hanging on the door, and the sheet that hung down over the side of the bed, rattling the saw that hung on the wall, banging the door back against the wood box, pulling and twisting the flower plants on the window shelf."

69. Stegner, *Wolf Willow*, p. 3.

70. Hamlin Garland, "Do You Fear the Force of the Wind?" in *Prairie Song and Western Story*, p. 272.

71. Ibid., p. 84.

72. Nebraska Society of the Daughters of the American Revolution, *Collection*, p. 33; Isaac M. Cline, "Hot Winds in Texas, May 29 and 30, 1892," *The American Meteorological Journal* 9, no. 10 (Feb., 1893): 440; Isaac M. Cline, "Summer Hot Winds on the Great Plains," *Bulletin* [Philosophical Society of Washington] 12 (1894): 317.

More renowned as the U.S. Weather Bureau's chief meteorologist in Galveston during the fateful 1900 hurricane, Cline experienced the plains hot winds while stationed in Abilene, Texas, in 1886. These hot currents left swaths in fields that looked burned by fire, plants crisp and curled (p. 331). In Kansas hot winds came in puffs and rolls, striking the face like heat from the open door of a hot oven; crops were turned to parched fodder (pp. 332, 321).

Chinook winds, mentioned in note 65 above, are warm, dry winds that descend down the eastern slopes of the Rockies. As the air moves down the slopes of the mountains it is heated by compression, and within minutes of its arrival ground temperatures may increase 20°C (36°F). Frederick K. Lutgens and Edward J. Tarbuck, *The Atmosphere: An Introduction to Meteorology*, p. 165.

73. Cline, "Summer Hot Winds," p. 336.

74. Anna Waltz's husband came rushing into the house one summer day and told her, "You better not go out of the house today. There is a hot wind blowing." Mrs. Waltz had never heard of a hot wind before. She noticed that his face was very red but thought he was just overly warm from the hot day. When he went into the bedroom to rinse his face she quietly opened the front door, and after going a short distance, "I was hit in the face with such a terrific gust of heat that I thought I was on fire. I covered my face with my hands and ran back in the house as quickly as I could. In that short time my face was burned red. When my husband came in from the bedroom, he was convulsed with laughter when he saw my face. He . . . just stood there and laughed and

wanted to know why I was blushing such a deep red." Waltz, "West River Pioneer," p. 52.

75. Berryman, *Pioneer Preacher*, p. 43.

76. Mrs. Stubbs said, however, that none of the women she knew ever had
this kind of reaction. Lou Caraway Stubbs, recorded interview with Sylvan
Dunn, Aug. 27, 1957, Lubbock, Tex., SCTTU.

77. Scarborough, *The Wind*, p. 175.

78. Isaac Moffatt, "The Kansas Prairie: Or, Eight Days on the Plains,"
Kansas Historical Quarterly 2 (1937): 184. Faye Lewis (*Nothing to Make a
Shadow*, p. 37) wrote, "Quietude" was a feature of the virgin prairie that Faye
Lewis found "difficult to recall accurately, impossible to describe." It was as
though they were interlopers in this vast realm of silence.

79. National Live Stock Association, *Prose and Poetry*, p. 550.

80. Garland, "The Hush of the Plains—July," in *Prairie Songs*, p. 28.

81. Stratton, *Pioneer Women*, p. 80.

82. Temple A. Ellis, *Road to Destiny*, pp. 8–9.

83. Nancy W. Robertson, "John Howard Lyles: Archer County [Texas] Pioneer," 1970, p. 3, RCP-PHM.

84. T. J. Powell, "Samuel Burk Burnett," n.d., p. 15, RCP-PHM.

85. Tice, *Over the Plains*, p. 54.

CHAPTER 3

1. Bedford, "Memoirs," p. 11.

2. James H. Nunn, Sr., interview by Omah Ryan, 1937, p. 3, RCP-PHM.

3. Ibid., p. 5.

4. Virginia Miksch Branscum, "Some Aspects of the Life of Women in
Eastern New Mexico and the Texas Panhandle-Plains Area from 1875 to
1905," 1949, p. 3, master's thesis, University of Texas; Mary Anne Norman,
"Childhood on the Southern Plains Frontier," *The Museum Journal* 18 (1979):
54.

5. Carl Coke Rister, *Southern Plainsmen*, p. 160.

6. Archambeau, "First Federal Census," pp. 22, 25.

7. Texas State Historical Association, *The New Handbook of Texas*, Vol. 5,
p. 37.

8. Mrs. W. G. Conner, interview with L. F. Sheffy, 1934, RCP-PHM.

9. John Robert Henry, interview with Marie Farrington, 1941, p. 6, RCP-
PHM. The Dakotas were so isolated, so desolate that Faye Lewis's family
fantasized they were in a world of their own, a land known only to themselves.
Lewis, *Nothing to Make a Shadow*, p. 40.

10. Charles A. Siringo, "The End of the Cowboy," in *Riata and Spurs*,
p. 261.

11. Cowboys, prospectors, trappers, buffalo hunters, and sheepherders were some of the early pioneers on the southwestern plains. Their migratory existence did not lend itself to family life and the presence of women. Norman, "Childhood on the Southern Plains," p. 55.

12. Spikes, "Old Settlers Reunion," p. 1.

13. C. F. Doan, interview with J. Evetts Haley, 1926, RCP-PHM.

14. Archambeau, "First Federal Census," pp. 48–132. J. Evetts Haley, "Panhandle Notes," Vol. 2, L–W, n.d., JEHC—Midland. Mary May came to the Panhandle in 1879 and married a cowboy in Old Tascosa in 1887. They lived on a ranch, and she remembered being told that she was the belle of ten counties, but the compliment was followed closely by the reminder that she was the only girl in those ten counties. Mary Ada May, responses to a questionnaire, 1939, RCP-PHM.

15. Lother Stephenson, "Reminiscences of Early Pioneer Days in the Panhandle from 1833–1940," 1940, RCP-PHM.

George Abbott was from South Carolina and came to Texas in 1886. He went to work on the sprawling, three-million-acre XIT Ranch around 1890, and over one twenty-four-month period he did not catch glimpse of one woman. Mrs. O. B. Ginn, 1936. George T. Abbott on XIT, RCP-PHM.

Jim Hastings's family migrated to Texas from Tennessee when he was ten years old, and he moved to the Panhandle in 1889 where he worked on several ranches. Hastings remembered there being few women on the ranches, but his explanation for so few women would doubtless be challenged— "Women were obstacles." Alberta Davis, "Memoirs of a JA Cowboy: Jim Hastings," 1939, p. 4, RCP-PHM. Men working cattle out on the range were often isolated. L. P. Trumble was herding cattle in West Texas in the 1880s and over one two-year period the only sign of habitation he encountered was his own dugout and the ranch headquarters. Evelyn Hood, "Viewing a Half-Century of Plains Progress [L. P. Trumble]," 1933, RCP-PHM. John Robert Henry camped on McClelland Creek in Gray County, Texas, in the summer of 1884 and for two months he never saw another human being—male or female. Henry, interview, p. 6.

16. Brooks, "Influence of the Pioneer Women," p. 97; Mrs. Arthur B. Duncan, "Recollections of a Pioneer Mother," n.d., RCP-PHM; C. O. Lanman, "Memoirs of Mrs. George E. Legg," n.d., RCP-PHM; Mrs. Alice Young, "Some Recollections of Coleman County: Mrs. Alice Young As Told to Georgene Falls," 1941, RCP-PHM.

17. Michael L. Odom, "The Recollections of a Pioneer Woman: Sarah Belle Madden Willoughby," 1969, RCP-PHM.

18. Photograph of the H. A. Russell family, *Amarillo Sunday News-Globe* 13, no. 33 (Aug. 14, 1938): Section D, p. 26.

19. Archambeau, "First Federal Census," pp. 48–132.

20. Mrs. N. S. Bagwell, interview with Zella Hollingsworth, 1938, RCP-PHM. In 1887, at the age of fourteen, Mrs. J. H. Gorin left Maryland for her sister and brother-in-law's ranch outside of Old Clarendon, Texas. She was the only girl within a radius of thirty miles. "The Life of Mr. and Mrs. J. H. Gorin," n.d., RCP-PHM.

21. Earl Stagner, "Reminiscences of An 'Old Timer' of the Panhandle Plains," 1941, p. 6, RCP-PHM.

22. Elizabeth Montgomery Neelley, "Pioneering in Young County Sixty Years Ago: As Told by Claude L. Neelley," n.d., RCP-PHM.

23. Dulcie Sullivan, "Celebration," *The Cattleman* 42, no. 6 (1960): 29.

24. Ellis, "Texas Plains Pioneers."

25. G. H. Jones, "Reminiscences of Happy [Texas] Pioneers," 1940, p. 34, RCP-PHM; James N. Browning, "Western Ranch Life in Indian Times," n.d., p. 6, RCP-PHM.

26. Cleaveland, *No Life for a Lady*, p. 50. After her 1853 crossing of the plains and settlement in the Northwest, Phoebe Judson would later write: "In those days anyone residing within twenty miles was considered a neighbor." Judson, *Pioneer's Search*, p. 91.

27. Curry, *Sun Rising on the West*, p. 155.

28. Hood, Evelyn. 1933. Viewing a Half-Century of Plains Progress [L. P. Trumble], RCP-PHM.

29. Connor, "The West Is for Us," p. 70.

30. For Salome Cashatt, however, religious though she was, the isolation of South Dakota was so pervasive that there were times when even God did not seem near. Lewis, *Nothing to Make a Shadow*, p. 132.

31. Women were comforted if they knew there were neighbors within a few miles. Brooks, "Influence of the Pioneer Women," p. 97. One Kansas settler felt so isolated that it were as if there was no neighbor within miles. Not a dwelling could be seen. All the time she lived on the farm she never saw a light from another home at night. Stratton, *Pioneer Women*, p. 86.

32. Gladys Jamison, "A Short History of Lipscomb County," 1936, RCP-PHM.

33. Lillian Hagins Deahl, "Mr. and Mrs. John F. Weatherly, Prominent Pioneer Carson County Citizens," n.d., RCP-PHM.

34. James D. Vardy, "Reminiscences of Jas. [James] D. Vardy," n.d., p. 10, RCP-PHM; Alma McGowen Thompson, "Witherspoon Spins Them Wide," *Amarillo Sunday News-Globe* 13, no. 33 (1938): Section D, p. 14.

35. Thompson, "Witherspoon Spins," p. 14.

36. Mrs. Charley Ross Cowan, interview with R. W. Stewart, 1946, RCP-PHM.

37. Sallie Reynolds Matthews, *Interwoven: A Pioneer Chronicle*, p. 150.

38. Mrs. Clyde Cave, interview with Sharon Corica, 1969, p. 4, RCP-PHM.

39. Joy Mills, "Nazareth [Texas]—1892–1902," n.d., p. 7, RCP-PHM. Nannie Alderson was a West Virginia native who migrated to Montana with her husband following their marriage in 1883. She could remember that seeing men from neighboring ranches five to ten miles away was not uncommon. Ranchers were always riding around looking for drifting cattle or lost horses. Although her children saw these neighboring ranchmen, seeing someone else outside of the family was unusual. A visitor was a grand event. "They would follow him around without a moment's let-up and chatter at him until he was worn out. Women visitors were still more of a novelty, so the little girls tagged after them even more, and thought them all beautiful. Mr. Alderson said that our children never even allowed a guest a necessary moment's privacy—but they were so happy in the chance to talk to a stranger that I hadn't the heart to discipline them." Nannie T. Alderson and Helena Huntington Smith, *A Bride Goes West*, p. 227.

40. Ray Allen Billington, *America's Frontier Heritage*, p. 214.

41. Wilbur Coe, *Ranch on the Ruidoso: The Story of a Pioneer Family in New Mexico, 1871–1968*, pp. 125–26.

42. Nunn, interview, p. 5.

43. Tommy J. Boley, ed., *Ella Elgar Bird Dumont: An Autobiography of a West Texas Pioneer*, pp. 38–39.

44. Billington, *America's Frontier Heritage*, p. 214. There was also, undoubtedly, inhospitality. Blanche Scott Rutherford (*One Corner of Heaven*, p. 16) reported on their family stopping along the trail at a farm house to request milk for the family's sick infant. Although the milk was eventually given, the initial response was surly and inhospitable.

45. Millie Porter, *Memory Cups of Panhandle Pioneers*, p. 125.

46. Elizabeth Montgomery Neelley, "Known as Pioneers—Life of Early Settlers," n.d., p. 36, RCP-PHM.

47. Frederick W. Rathjen, *The Texas Panhandle Frontier*, p. 246.

48. Ibid.

49. Ira Taylor, recorded interview with the author, Aug. 9, 1985, Amarillo, Tex., RCP-PHM.

50. Joe Shelton, recorded interview with the author, Mar. 15, 1984, Pampa, Tex., RCP-PHM.

51. Spikes, "Old Settlers Reunion," p. 1. Carl Rister (*Southern Plainsmen*, pp. 135–36) cited the inscription over the door of one isolated dwelling: "Hotel de starvation; 1,000 miles from hay and grain, 70 miles from wood, and 15 miles from water."

Wayne Gard (*Rawhide Texas*, p. 12) reports that on a cabin abandoned in

Blanco County, Texas, around 1886, someone had written in chalk on a board nailed to the door:

250 miles to nearest post office.
100 miles to wood.
20 miles to water
6 inches to hell.
God bless our home.
Gone to live with the wife's folks.

52. Tom Black, recorded interview with the author, July 20, 1984, Canyon, Tex., RCP-PHM.

53. Buster Barker, "Memoirs of Sara Leon Coleman," 1940, p. 2, RCP-PHM. Hooking up a team of horses was a chore, and this was another incentive to stay home. Mrs. Ernest White, recorded interview with the author, Aug. 10, 1984, Canyon, Tex., RCP-PHM.

54. Rathjen, *Texas Panhandle Frontier,* p. 229.

55. Randel, ed., *A Time to Purpose,* p. 201.

56. Temple Ann Ellis, "Trails of Long Ago," n.d., SCTTU.

57. Cora Mellon Cross, "An Old Trail Driver Talks About Early Days" [From *Dallas Semi-Weekly News*] *Frontier Times* 1, no. 8 (1924): 26; Aulton Durham, "Memoirs of M. C. Potter," 1936, RCP-PHM; Sammie Roach, "Forty Years in the Texas Panhandle," 1938, p. 1, RCP-PHM.

58. Ethel Wells, "The Disappearance of the Frontier," 1933, RCP-PHM.

59. George M. Hunt, *Early Days Upon the Plains of Texas,* p. 26. In the mid-1800s, Isham Reavis found Nebraska as completely isolated from the world as Alaska, the land of the midnight sun, at the beginning of the nineteenth century. Goff, "Isham Reavis," pp. 1–46.

Hobart McManigal of Happy, Texas, and his father used to ride over to Hereford, Texas, to fish. Until around 1915 there was one place along the trail where all that was visible was a lone windmill. "You couldn't see another house. You couldn't see a fence. You couldn't see nothing but that windmill. You couldn't see nothing but a pasture." Mr. and Mrs. Hobart McManigal, recorded interview with the author, Aug. 3, 1984, Happy, Tex., RCP-PHM.

60. Hunt, *Early Days,* p. 27.

61. Connor, "The West Is for Us," p. 39.

62. Wells, "Disappearance of the Frontier."

63. Mrs. T. W. Tomlinson, "A Brief and Partial History of Swisher County [Texas]," 1922, p. 6, RCP-PHM.

64. Mr. and Mrs. Joe Gibson, recorded interview with the author, Oct. 7, 1986, Canyon, Tex., RCP-PHM.

65. Mr. and Mrs. Ira Ott, recorded interview with the author, Dec. 9, 1993, Hereford, Tex., RCP-PHM.

66. Ochiltree County Historical Survey Committee, *Wheatheart of the Plains*, p. 212.

67. Cross, "Old Trail Driver," p. 26. Ella Elgar Bird Dumont's family settled south of Fort Worth in 1867. In 1877 at age sixteen she married Texas Ranger Tom Bird and they moved to King County. She spoke of the day when three wagons with families and cattle came driving into their isolated camp. They were glad to see them as these were the first women she had seen in some twelve months. That afternoon three large tents were erected, and "It seemed almost like living in town." Boley, ed., *Ella Elgar Bird Dumont*, p. 39.

Towns were sometimes little more than the outgrowth of former ranches. After his family's move to Kansas in 1893, Ed Lord continued on to Kenton, Oklahoma, a few years later. He claimed that Hooker, Oklahoma, began as a single ranch house. LaVerne Hanners, *The Lords of the Valley: Including the Complete Text of Our Unsheltered Lives by Ed Lord*, p. 37. William Simpson witnessed the dividing and fencing off of open grass range into enormous pastures. These pastures, in turn, were sectioned into moderate-sized stock farms, which in some cases later became towns. Cross, "Old Trail Driver," p. 26.

68. Edmond and Rosa Belle Strange moved to the Childress area in 1906. Their son, Clarence, said, "Mama didn't care much about going to town unless she needed something like material that Papa couldn't get. Sometimes she would only go once a year." Rosa Lee Griffin, "A Strange Story," 1978, RCP-PHM.

69. Jessie de Prado Farrington, "Rocking Horse to Cow Pony (Continued)," *New Mexico Historical Review* 30, no. 4 (1955): 320.

70. Martha and John Arnot, married in 1889, lived eight miles northwest of Amarillo where he worked for the Frying Pan Ranch. Mrs. Arnot said she had no money to spend and she could not go to the saloon, so she stayed home. Stevenson, Carrie Pauley. 1933. Those Who Went Up the Long Trail, RCP-PHM.

71. Philip Ashton Rollins, *The Cowboy: An Unconventional History of Civilization on the Old-Time Cattle Range*, p. 35; Laura V. Hamner, *Short Grass and Longhorns*, p. 42.

72. Hamner, *Short Grass and Longhorns*, p. 13.

73. Colt, *Went to Kansas*, p. 123. Spirits would sag and anxieties increase without word from home. Settlers, and especially the women, could not help ruminating over the well-being and health of those left behind. If correspondence was cut off for an extended period of time, then a new fear might become a source of torment—Was it was possible that those at home had ceased to care? Jeffrey, *Frontier Women*, p. 74. The diary of Ada Colvin included the brooding entry: "Nary a letter. The folks grow worse all the time about writing. Gone two months and forgotten so soon by those that pretended to be my

best friends." Holmes, *Covered Wagon Women*, Vol. 11 (1879–1903), p. 47. Gro
Svendsen wrote to her parents that it had been three months since she had
sent her last letter without receiving a reply. She then added: "My yearning
grows stronger as the days pass by with no word from you." Farseth and Blegen, *Frontier Mother*, p. 47.

Letters could also make for homesickness and loneliness. Tanner received
a letter on June 23, 1907, that "caused a lump big as a base ball [*sic*], to rise in
my throat. I could not swallow, neither can I cough it up and I feel that it will
be many days before it will melt or disapeare [*sic*]." William W. Tanner, papers, 1898–1912, Book 3, p. 3, RCP-PHM.

74. Edgar Beecher Bronson, *The Red-Blooded Heroes of the Frontier*, p. 173.

75. S. K. Bynum, "Recollections," n.d., RCP-PHM; Boley, ed., *Ella Elgar
Bird Dumont*, p. 39.

76. L. F. Sheffy, "Mr. N. F. Locke, Miami, Texas," 1925, RCP-PHM, 3.
Early mail service was frequently provided by the "Tom, Dick and Harry"
system; cowboys or one of the neighbors would take turns about going after
it. "Mrs. Ellen Carter," n.d., RCP-PHM. This mail run might entail a trip of
over thirty miles or several days. Anyone in a section who happened to be going to town would bring back not only his own mail but his neighbor's as well,
and this practice would be observed even if the distance was ten miles from
the settler's home. Virginia Morton, "Early Settlement of Quay County, New
Mexico," n.d., RCP-PHM.

77. Branscum, "Some Aspects of Life," p. 84.

78. Ruth Tressman, "Home on the Range," *New Mexico Historical Review*
26, no. 1 (1951): 14; Cleaveland, *No Life for a Lady*, p. 47.

79. Randel, ed., *A Time to Purpose*, p. 202.

80. Cleaveland, *No Life for a Lady*, p. 69.

81. Ellis, "Texas Plains Pioneers."

CHAPTER 4

1. David L. Cohn, "Mr. Speaker," *The Atlantic Monthly* 170, no. 4, (1942): 76.
Faye Lewis (*Nothing to Make a Shadow*, p. 57) wrote of the occasion when
her brother saw two wagons approaching down the road. "'Look! There's two
rigs coming down from the Smith Hill!'

"Two vehicles on the road past our house at the same time were an almost
unheard of amount of traffic. We all stopped what we were doing and watched
them approach. Father even delayed getting back to his plowing to watch
with us."

2. Colt, *Went to Kansas*, p. 123.

3. Everett Dick, *The Sod-House Frontier 1854–1890*, p. 235; Harry E.
Chrisman, *The 1,001 Most-Asked Questions About the American West*, p. 282;

James I. Fenton, "Critters, Sourdough, and Dugouts: Women and Imitation Theory on the Staked Plains, 1875–1910," in *At Home on the Range: Essays on the History of Western Social and Domestic Life,* John Wunder, ed., p. 23. Agnes Morley Cleaveland (*No Life for a Lady,* p. 157) recalled the passive and un-spectacular heroism of one woman who with her small son endured endless months alone in a New Mexico canyon. It was a rare visitor, a cowboy perhaps riding the range, who stopped by long enough for a greeting.

4. Mrs. T. W. Tomlinson, "A Brief and Partial History of Swisher County [Texas]," 1922, p. 6, RCP-PHM.

5. Ellis, "Texas Plains Pioneers."

6. Richard A. Bartlett, *The New Country: A Social History of the American Frontier, 1776–1890,* p. 354.

7. Ricou, "Empty As Nightmare," pp. 154, 156.

8. Berryman, *Pioneer Preacher,* p. 83.

9. Newcomb diaries, p. 70.

10. Whitlock, *Cowboy Life,* p. 190.

11. Connor, "The West Is for Us," p. 41.

12. Jennie Holcomb, recorded interview with the author, July 5, 1984, Wellington, Tex., RCP-PHM.

13. Sandra L. Myres, *Westering Women and the Frontier Experience 1800–1915,* pp. 167–68.

14. Ibid.; Dick, *Sod-House Frontier,* p. 235.

15. Joseph W. Snell, "Roughing It on Her Claim: The Diary of Abbie Bright, 1870–1871," *The Kansas Historical Quarterly* 37, no. 3 (1971): 255.

16. Joseph W. Snell, "Roughing It on Her Claim: The Diary of Abbie Bright, 1870–1871—Concluded," *The Kansas Historical Quarterly* 37, no. 4 (1971): 414.

17. Randel, ed., *A Time to Purpose,* p. 36.

18. Harriette Andreadis, "True Womanhood Revisited: Women's Private Writing in Nineteenth-Century Texas," *Journal of the Southwest* 31, no. 2 (1989): 204.

19. Ibid., p. 188.

20. Newcomb diaries.

21. C. Dwight Dorough, *Mr. Sam,* p. 66.

22. Margaret Armstrong, Diary, 1872–77, p. 4, JEHC—Midland.

23. Howard Ruede and John Ise, eds., *Sod-House Days: Letters from a Kansas Homesteader 1877–78,* p. xi.

24. William W. Tanner, Papers, 1898–1912, n.d., RCP-PHM.

25. Andreadis, "True Womanhood," p. 186.

26. Hamlin Garland, "A Human Habitation," in *Prairie Songs,* pp. 75–76.

27. Billy M. Jones, "Walter Dibrell: Early Methodist Circuit Rider in the

Concho Basin," *West Texas Historical Association Year Book* 48 (1972): 111; Orrie Clark, "Autobiography of Orrie Clark," n.d., p. 1, RCP-PHM; Ellis, "Texas Plains Pioneers."

28. Taylor, interview. According to the web site of the National Cowboy Hall of Fame and Western Heritage Center, Oklahoma City, cowboys grumbled that they had to work from "can't see to can't see," from before sunrise till after sunset.

29. Faragher, *Women and Men*, p. 176.

30. Bartlett, *New Country*, p. 354; Violet E. King, "Sweet Rest," in *Bethel Chimes: A Collection of New Songs for the Sabbath School, Church, and Home*, ed. by Charles K. Langley and R. H. Randall, pp. 114–15.

31. Colt, *Went to Kansas*, p. 89.

32. Edith Duncan Pitts, "At Home in a Dugout," n.d., RCP-PHM.

33. Ibid.

34. Faragher maintains (*Women and Men*, p. 112) that this was the single-most important distinction between the social and cultural worlds of men and women—the isolation and immobility of wives in comparison to their husbands.

35. June Sochen, "Frontier Women: A Model for All Women," *South Dakota History* 7, no. 1 (1976): 42.

36. McManigal, interview.

37. Joe Killough, interview with Mrs. D. T. Leachman, 1945, p. 5, RCP-PHM.

38. Ellis, "Texas Plains Pioneers." Ira Taylor commented that "Women didn't shop very much in them days. Women'd write out the grocery bill and the man'd go to town and get it and bring it home." Taylor, interview.

39. Lucille Park, "A Pioneer [Mrs. S. E. Askren] of Deaf Smith County [Texas]," n.d., p. 7, RCP-PHM.

40. Lula Mae Farley, "Women Rode the Range," *Amarillo Sunday News-Globe* 13, no. 33 (Aug. 14, 1938): Section D, p. 25.

41. Ellis, "Texas Plains Pioneers."

42. Boley, ed., *Ella Elgar Bird Dumont*, p. 64.

43. Emma Boles Burns, "Diary of Mrs. Emma Boles Burns," 1889, SCTTU. When the husband was gone, a woman could get "powerful lonesome sittin' all day waitin' for her man to come home." Berryman, *Pioneer Preacher*, p. 41.

44. Wayne Gard, *The Chisholm Trail*, p. 155.

45. Connor, "The West Is for Us," p. 44.

46. Newcomb diaries, p. 53.

47. Ibid., p. 80. Freight wagon drivers were also absent for extended periods. Lea Paine left home at age twelve to work for a horse wrangler. Later,

after marrying and settling in Dickens County, Texas, he drove a freight wagon between Dickens County and Quanah, Texas, a distance of 110 miles. He freighted for three years but then decided to buy a livery stable. "This change," he said, "was chiefly because of the fact that I was away from home practically all the time, and it was very hard going on my wife and children." Winston Wofford, "Memoirs of Lea Paine," 1937, RCP-PHM.

48. Maggie Lee Holden, "Memoirs, 1944–48," Charlie Baldwin Papers, SCTTU.

49. Scarborough, *The Wind*, p. 22.

50. Ellis, "Texas Plains Pioneers." Mary Blankenship acknowledged that everyone talked their "thoughts" to the cows. Connor, "The West Is for Us," p. 80.

51. Stratton, *Pioneer Women*, p. 80.

52. Ellis, "Texas Plains Pioneers." Following their marriage in 1894 Mrs. J. N. Ivy and her husband ranched and farmed in Deaf Smith County, Texas. Because of the isolation, she was another who would climb the windmill to see if by chance anyone was in sight. Mary M. Henderson, "Mrs. J. N. Ivy," 1938, RCP-PHM.

53. Phebe Kerrick Warner, "The Wife of a Pioneer Ranchman," *The Cattleman* 7, no. 10 (1921): 69.

54. Colt, *Went to Kansas*, p. 104.

55. Effyle Whitsett, "Memoirs of Mrs. Jim W. Carter," n.d., RCP-PHM; Virginia Morton, "Early Settlement of Quay County, New Mexico," *Panhandle-Plains Historical Review* 19 (1946): 81. Some lonely women became desperate in their quest for relief. Elizabeth Hampsten reports that loneliness drove one woman into the fields where she would roll in the grass and scream out her anguish. Elizabeth Hampsten, *Settlers' Children: Growing Up on the Great Plains*, p. 200. Another account tells of women walking ten miles just to see the faces in a passing train. Schlissel, Gibbens, and Hampsten, *Far From Home*, p. 78. Stratton (*Pioneer Women*, p. 80) also includes the account of a pioneer who told his wife he was going to town for wood, whereupon she asked to go with him. She had not seen trees for two years, so when they arrived she put her arms around a tree and hugged it hysterically.

56. Mrs. Thomas Currie, interview, 1938, RCP-PHM.

57. Armstrong, Diary, p. 3. Glenda Riley ("Women's Responses to the Challenges of Plains Living," *Great Plains Quarterly* 9, no. 3 (1989): 174–84) provides a summary of the various activities used by plains women to maintain a positive outlook and cope. Writing, reading whatever they could find, music, rituals, and cultural conservation were just some of the activities in which they participated. These attempts helped many to survive, some even to flourish.

58. Mr. and Mrs. Joe E. Engelbrecht, recorded interview with the author,

July 11, 1994, Amarillo, Tex., RCP-PHM; Hazel Cottrell Whited, "Memoirs of Mrs. I. W. Foreman," 1939, RCP-PHM. One document included the comment: "Folks in this County had lots of children." Then followed a listing of families and children:

Farnsworth—9
Bussard, brother of Lloyd—9
Scotts—10
Weavers—10
Bussards—10
Hurley (pronounced Hurli, long "i") 15—8 grew up
Two Widmers—ten each
Roth—9 perhaps 10

W. H. Keffers, Sept. 25. 1940, RCP-PHM.

Sam Rayburn grew up in a family of fourteen. In addition to his parents there were ten siblings and an uncle. His brother and sisters made light of the possibility that his childhood could have been lonely, surrounded as he was by such a large and vital family. D. B. Hardeman and Donald C. Bacon, *Rayburn: A Biography*, pp. 17–18.

59. Paul Patterson, *Crazy Women in the Rafters*, p. 9.

60. Faragher, *Women and Men*, p. 58; Myres, *Westering Women*, p. 170.

61. Tanner, Papers.

62. T. C. Oatts, "Diary of T. C. Oatts," 1871, pp. 21–22, JEHC—Midland.

63. Wells, "Disappearance of the Frontier," p. 12.

64. J. H. Weems, interview with Mary H. Gaetz, 1941, RCP-PHM.

65. Walter Posey, interview with Seymour V. Connor, 1956, p. 23, SCTTU.

66. Mrs. Claude Boone, "Mrs. Claude Boone," n.d., RCP-PHM.

67. Dary, *Cowboy Culture*, p. 276.

68. J. Vinson Younger, "Memoir of Frank Exum," 1936, p. 7, RCP-PHM.

69. Rister, *Southern Plainsmen*, p. 125.

70. Rollins, *The Cowboy*, p. 74.

71. Connor, "The West Is for Us," p. 80.

72. Rollins, *The Cowboy*, p. 60.

73. Ben C. Mayes, "Reminiscences of Ben C. Mayes," 1932, JEHC—Midland.

74. J. Evetts Haley, "The XIT Ranch; As Remembered by Its Cowboys," Vol. 4, Mc–Y, n.d., pp. 94–95, JEHC—Midland.

75. Adelle Howell, "Memoirs of William Carey Newton," n.d., RCP-PHM.

76. J. Evetts Haley, "Cowboy-Sheriff," *The Shamrock*, summer, 1963, p. 3, JEHC—Midland.

77. M. K. Wisehart, "'Wichita Bill,' Cowboy Artist, Rode Into The Halls Of Fame," *The American Magazine*, Aug., 1927, p. 68.

78. Coleman Jones, "Writings of Coleman Jones," n.d., p. 21, RCP-PHM.

79. National Live Stock Association. *Prose and Poetry of the Live Stock Industry of the United States*, p. 550.

80. C. C. Rister, "Social Activities of the Southwestern Cowboy," *The West Texas Historical Association Year Book* 7 (1931): 45.

81. Rister, *Southern Plainsmen*, p. 125.

82. Carrie Pauley Stevenson, "Those Who Went Up the Long Trail," 1933, RCP-PHM.

CHAPTER 5

1. Dick, *Sod-House Frontier*, p. 232; Bartlett, *New Country*, p. 364; Schlissel, *Women's Diaries*, p. 28; Faragher, *Women and Men*, pp. 18–19; Archambeau, "First Federal Census," pp. 23, 30.

2. Schlissel, *Women's Diaries*, p. 51.

3. Jayme A. Sokolow, "The Demography of a Ranching Frontier: The Texas Panhandle in 1880," *Panhandle-Plains Historical Review* 60 (1982): 83.

4. Newton Harrell, recorded interview with the author, Nov. 9, 1984, Claude, Tex., RCP-PHM.

5. McManigal, interview.

6. Archambeau, "First Federal Census," p. 28.

7. Sokolow, Demography of a Ranching Frontier, p. 90. Eventually, more than fifty European "folk islands" were established in northwestern Texas. "European Folk Islands in Northwest Texas: Introduction," *Panhandle-Plains Historical Review* 56 (1983): v.

8. Alabama, Georgia, Missouri, Kentucky, Kansas, Illinois, Indiana, Ohio, Pennsylvania, Iowa, Wisconsin, and the Carolinas were other states that provided large numbers of migrants. Holden, *Alkali Trails*, p. 71.

9. Blodgett, *Land of Bright Promise*, p. 97. It was common for newcomers from older, established states to settle in East or Central Texas for a while, then move to the West Texas frontier where land prices were an inducement. Holden, *Alkali Trails*, p. 71.

10. David B. Gacy II, "Selling the Future: A Biography of William Pulver Soash," *Panhandle-Plains Historical Review* 50 (1977): 31.

11. Lee Matney, recorded interview with the author, June 14, 1984, Amarillo, Tex., RCP-PHM; Shelton, interview, Mar. 15, 1984; Mr. and Mrs. J. N. Bridwell, recorded interview with the author, Oct. 28, 1994, Texoma, Tex., RCP-PHM; C. N. Cosby, recorded interview with the author, Feb. 28, 1986,

Canyon, Tex., RCP-PHM; B. A. Oden, "Early Cowboy Days in New Mexico and Texas," n.d., JEHC—Midland; Taylor, interview.

12. McManigal, interview; Mitchell Jones, Sr., recorded interview with the author, Mar. 8, 1984, Canyon, Tex. RCP-PHM; George W. Moore, recorded interview with the author, Jan. 11, 1985, Canyon, Tex., RCP-PHM.

13. George W. Moore, interview; Ed Ramey, recorded interview with the author, Aug. 7, 1984, Dimmitt, Tex., RCP-PHM.

14. Clark, "Autobiography."

15. Addie Whitcomb, interview with L. E. Moyer, 1958, RCP-PHM.

16. Mitchell Jones, Sr., interview, Mar. 8, 1984.

17. Percy G. Ebbutt, *Emigrant Life in Kansas*, p. 211; Bridwell, interview.

18. Lavert Avent, recorded interview with the author, June 10, 1985, Canyon, Tex., RCP-PHM.

19. Some communities had the reputation for violence. Joe Shelton said that the bullets in Dodge City, Kansas, were so thick that a man who was not fast with a gun had best stay in his wagon. Shelton, interview, Mar. 15, 1984.

20. Holcomb, interview.

21. Mildred Winkleman, recorded interview with the author, May 9, 1984, Amarillo, Tex., RCP-PHM.

22. Avent, interview, June 10, 1985. Jess Barker recalled the discovery in a small cabin the bodies of three neighbors who had died from influenza in 1918. Jess Barker, recorded interview with the author, Sept. 27, 1984, Canyon, Tex., RCP-PHM.

23. Lewis, *Nothing to Make a Shadow*, p. 106.

24. Claude Biddy, interview with Christopher Biddy, 1969, p. 2, RCP-PHM.

25. Metcalf, "The White Family," p. 1, RCP-PHM. Nannie Alderson attributed the lack of illness to the healthy climate and the rarity of "disease germs." When someone went for a doctor, she wrote, it was generally for one of two reasons—an accident or childbirth. Alderson and Smith, *Bride Goes West*, p. 195.

26. Eula Hartman, "Reminiscence of Mr. [Fred] Scott," 1933, RCP-PHM. As a group, cowboys were undoubtedly a hearty group, but as is noted later in this chapter, they were not immune to sickness or to impaired health due to injuries. Over time, the nature of the work took it toll on their bodies.

27. C. R. Wilson, "An Interview with an Early Settler," 1933, RCP-PHM.

28. Matthews, *Interwoven*, p. 44.

29. Rister, *Southern Plainsmen*, p. 160.

30. Cleaveland, *No Life for a Lady*, p. 164. James and Robert Cator, northern Texas Panhandle buffalo hunters in the early 1870s and '80s, later established the first trading post in the region north of the Canadian River. Receipts for foodstuffs purchased from 1872–74 included: coffee, sugar, onions,

potatoes, flour, canned tomatoes and fruit, pepper, vinegar, yeast, salt, lard, bacon, cornmeal, syrup, beans, pickles, and mustard. By 1896 their purchases had expanded to include: cabbage, soda crackers, candy, currants, raisins, cranberries, lemons, oranges, nectarines, prunes, apricots, dried apples and peaches, ginger, mixed nuts, bonbons, popcorn, chili sauce, catsup, oysters, and salmon. Cator Family Papers, RCP-PHM.

When one family moved to Castro County, Texas, in 1884 they took with them: 1,000 pounds of flour, a barrel each of brown sugar, white sugar, and molasses, 500 pounds of bacon, and beans, hominy, and coffee. Whitsett, "Memoirs of Mrs. Jim W. Carter."

31. Jones, *Health-Seekers*, p. 85.

32. Charles R. King, "The Woman's Experience of Childbirth on the Western Frontier," *Journal of the West* 29, no. 1 (1990): 79. Miner (*West of Wichita*, p. 169) identifies the greatest terrors to pioneers as pneumonia (lung fever), appendicitis (inflammation of the bowels), diphtheria, cholera, spinal meningitis, and the flu.

33. E. C. Abbott and Helena Huntington Smith, *We Pointed Them North*, p. 96.

34. Born in 1859 and reared on an Indiana farm, Andy Adams went to Texas as a youth where he began a ten-year stretch as a cowboy. Adams later wrote a number of popular novels based on his cattle-driving experiences in Texas and on the plains. Adams treated fiction as fact, and he branded his own writings as a form of fictitious realism. Andy Adams, *Cattle Brands: A Collection of Western Camp-Fire Stories*, p. 207.

35. Bartlett, *New Country*, p. 364.

36. Rister, *Southern Plainsmen*, p. 160.

37. Mitchell Jones, Sr., interview, Mar. 8, 1984.

38. "When Death Rate Was High," p. 13.

39. Merrill J. Mattes, *The Great Platte River Road: The Covered Wagon Mainline Via Fort Kearny to Fort Laramie*, p. 90.

40. Crudgington said,

> *Usually, the "privy" was placed as far from the house as the size of the family's lot would allow because of the odor which was particularly strong in the summer time or when the wind was in the wrong direction.*
>
> *But when the winter came on with its rain and snow and below-freezing temperatures, the thinking was different. Waking up in the middle of a below-zero night with a "pressing urge" and faced with a fifty or sixty (and sometimes even as much as a hundred) yard run through such weather was enough to make a "Spartan sob."*
>
> *I have heard medical doctors say that the inconvenience of the out door [sic] toilet caused unnecessary constipation, the results of which brought on earlier deaths for both men and women. This, however, is far secondary to the*

fact that the "outhouse" was a built-in disease breeder on every homestead that used them.

John W. Crudgington, interview with John B. Hines, n.d., RCP-PHM.

One pioneer recalled that in 1903 Callahan County, Texas, they did not have the luxury of an outdoor toilet. When nature beckoned the person was forced to scurry to a small grove of trees some distance from the cabin. Mrs. W. A. Everett, interview with Mike Everett, 1975, RCP-PHM.

41. Mrs. Harvey Cash, interview with James Webb, 1965, RCP-PHM.

42. Rollins, *The Cowboy*, p. 191.

43. Hanners, *Lords of the Valley*, p. 73.

44. Ibid.

45. Ibid., p. 74.

46. Dick, *Sod-House Frontier*, p. 240; Okla Mae Lawrence, "The Life of Mrs. Alice Tubb," 1935, RCP-PHM.

47. Mattes, *Great Platte River Road*, pp. 81–82.

48. Cash, interview, p. 4; Holden, "Memoirs," p. 22; Rister, *Southern Plainsmen*, p. 160.

49. Lesley Brown, ed., *The New Shorter Oxford English Dictionary*, Vol. 1, p. 690.

50. Jeffrey, *Frontier Women*, p. 69. Susan Magoffin wrote in her 1847 diary of the constant sickness of pregnancy, of the heartburn, the headaches, and the cramping. She concluded her entry with the comment that "this thing of marrying is not what it is cracked up to be." Magoffin, *Down the Santa Fe Trail*, p. 245.

51. Faragher, *Women and Men*, p. 58.

52. Schlissel, Gibbens, and Hampsten, *Far From Home*, p. 45.

53. Norman, "Childhood on the Southern Plains," p. 74.

54. Edward Everett Dale, *Frontier Ways: Sketches of Life in the Old West*, p. 194.

55. James I. Fenton, "Critters, Sourdough, and Dugouts: Women and Imitation Theory on the Staked Plains, 1875–1910," in *At Home on the Range: Essays on the History of Western Social and Domestic Life*, ed. by John R. Wunder, p. 31.

56. C. N. Cosby, recorded interview with the author, Sept. 5, 1986, Canyon, Tex., RCP-PHM.

57. Jeffrey, *Frontier Women*, p. 69.

58. Faragher, *Women and Men*, p. 58.

59. Gladys Deitiker, recorded interview with the author, July 24, 1984, Amarillo, Tex., RCP-PHM.

60. Greene, *A Personal Country*, pp. 254–55.

61. Schlissel, Gibbens, and Hampsten, *Far From Home*, p. 108.

62. Ibid., pp. 153–54.

63. Deitiker, interview.

64. Frank Collinson, *Life in the Saddle*, p. 161.

65. Mattes (*Great Platte River Road*, p. 90) attributes most of the trail accidents to shootings. Wagons were rolling arsenals and men were armed to the teeth with everything from rifles to shotguns to revolvers.

66. Sallie Matthews (*Interwoven*, p. 61) shares the account of a young man riding alongside a wagon in which a young mother was riding, her infant in her arms. His pistol accidentally discharged, killed the baby, "and almost crazed the young man for a time. They had to stop and bury the baby as that was all they could do. There was absolutely nothing out of which to make even a crude box; they could only wrap the little body in a quilt and commit it to the ground."

67. William Curry Holden, *The Spur Ranch*, p. 108.

68. "When Death Rate Was High," p. 13.

69. Ibid.

70. Mattes, *Great Platte River Road;* Bridwell, interview.

71. Rosalind Knupp, interview with Karen Cornelius, 1980, RCP-PHM.

72. Boley, ed., *Ella Elgar Bird Dumont*, p. 136.

73. Connor, "The West Is for Us," p. 91.

74. Ibid., p. 93.

75. Rollins, *The Cowboy*, p. 296.

76. Holden, *Spur Ranch*, pp. 104–106.

77. Ibid., p. 104; Mrs. Frank Bonnifield, interview with Donna Chambers, n.d., RCP-PHM.

78. H. E. Crowley, "The Wife of the Pioneer," *The Cattleman* 1, no. 10 (1915): 95.

79. Billie Lloyd Jackson, "M. J. 'Uncle Dock' McCoy," 1940, RCP-PHM.

80. Cordia Duke and Joe B. Frantz, *6,000 Miles of Fence: Life on the XIT Ranch of Texas*, p. 213.

81. Ellis, "Texas Plains Pioneers."

82. Ibid., p. 298.

83. Dary, *Cowboy Culture*, p. 298.

84. J. Marvin Hunter, *The Trail Drivers of Texas*, p. 458.

85. Coe, *Ranch on the Ruidoso*, pp. 91–92.

86. Esther Jane Wood Hall, "Cowboy Remedies on the Trail (Pharmaceuticals Since 1865)," *The West Texas Historical Association Year Book* 41 (Oct., 1965): 33.

87. Bartlett, *New Country*, p. 228.

88. Gard, *Chisholm Trail*, pp. 125–26.

89. Abbott and Smith, *We Pointed Them North*, p. 80.

90. Ibid., p. 81.

91. Ibid.

92. Gard, *Chisholm Trail*, p. 133.

93. Abbott and Smith, *We Pointed Them North*, p. 42.

94. Mattes, *Great Platte River Road*, p. 91.

95. Gard, *Chisholm Trail*, p. 132. Andy Adams's *The Log of a Cowboy* is regarded as a classic of western fiction. In this story of life on a cattle drive he described the Red River as a "terror to trail drovers . . . That she was merciless was evident, for although this crossing had been in use only a year or two when we forded, yet five graves, one of which was less than ten days made, attested her disregard for human life." Adams's narrative included the drowning tragedy of the foreman of an outfit that was swimming a Colorado herd across the North Platte River at Forty Islands, Wyoming. Among papers taken from the victim's pockets was a letter from his mother warning him to guard against just such an event. He was her third son to be lost by drowning. Andy Adams, *The Log of a Cowboy: A Narrative of the Old Trail Days*, p. 121.

96. Gard, *Chisholm Trail*, p. 132.

97. Glenn R. Ellison, *Cowboys Under the Mongollon Rim*, p. 1.

98. "When Death Rate Was High," p. 13.

99. Mitchell Jones, Sr., interview, Mar. 8, 1984.

100. Cleaveland, *No Life for a Lady*, p. 66.

101. Joe B. Frantz and Julian Ernest Choate, Jr., *The American Cowboy: The Myth and the Reality*, p. 22.

102. Timmie Brown, recorded interview with the author, Oct. 28, 1994, Stratford, Tex., RCP-PHM; Barker, interview.

103. Adelle Howell, "Memoirs of John Gibson," n.d., RCP-PHM; Boley, ed., *Ella Elgar Bird Dumont*, p. 60.

104. Emerson Hough, *The Story of the Cowboy*, p. 88.

105. Rollins, *The Cowboy*, p. 294.

106. Boley, ed., *Ella Elgar Bird Dumont*, p. 59.

107. Jackson, "Uncle Dock McCoy."

108. Ramon Adams, *Cowboy Lingo*, p. 95; Duke and Frantz, *6,000 Miles*, p. 120.

109. Ibid.

110. Rollins, *The Cowboy*, p. 303.

111. Howell, "Memoirs of William Carey Newton."

112. Rollins, *The Cowboy*, p. 293.

113. Adams, *Cowboy Lingo*, p. 104.

114. Shelton, interview, Mar. 15, 1984.

115. Crowley, "Wife of the Pioneer," p. 96.

116. Hough, *Story of the Cowboy*, p. 89.

117. Mrs. J. Evetts Haley, personal communication with author, May 5, 1994.

118. Rollins, *The Cowboy*, p. 314.

119. Lewis, *Nothing to Make a Shadow*, p. 131.
120. Alderson and Smith, *Bride Goes West*, p. 203.

CHAPTER 6

1. Albert S. Gilles, Sr., "Death's First Visit to Old Faxon," *The Chronicles of Oklahoma* 44, no. 3 (1966): 309.
2. Ise, *Sod and Stubble*, p. 46.
3. Rutherford, *One Corner*, p. 146.
4. Warwick, *Randall County [Texas] Story*, p. 249. Furniture stores were one of the first businesses to sell caskets, and some of these naturally evolved into providing funeral services.
5. Willie Newbury Lewis, *Between Sun and Sod*, p. 177; Schlissel, Gibbens, and Hampsten, *Far From Home*, p. 154.
6. Maris A. Vinovskis, "Angels' Heads and Weeping Willows: Death in Early America," in *The American Family in Social Historical Perspective*, 2nd ed., ed. by Michael Gordon, p. 558.
7. Ibid., p. 560.
8. Adelheid Albers, recorded interview with the author, June 22, 1984, Canyon, Tex., RCP-PHM.
9. Schlissel, *Women's Diaries*, p. 131; Schlissel, Gibbens, and Hampsten, *Far From Home*, p. 154.
10. Judson, *Pioneer's Search*, p. 35; Schlissel, Gibbens, and Hampsten, *Far From Home*, p. 154.
11. Elizabeth Hampsten notes that turn-of-the-century Midwestern women nearly always knew someone who was dying, and because they were the ones who tended the sick and the ones who wrote the letters, some of their finest literary compositions were devoted to death scenes. Virtually no other topic evoked such impassioned writing. Hampsten, *Read This Only to Yourself*, p. 123.
12. Julia Louisa Lovejoy, "Letters from Kansas," *The Kansas Historical Quarterly* 11, no. 1 (1942): 37.
13. Hunt, *Early Days*, p. 51.
14. Colt, *Went to Kansas*, p. 170.
15. Randel, ed., *A Time to Purpose*, p. 101; Ramon F. Adams, *Western Words: A Dictionary of the Range, Cow Camp and Trail*, p. 136.
16. Adams, *Western Words*, p. 136.
17. Colt, *Went to Kansas*, p. 205.
18. Deitiker, interview; Jack Goody, "Death and the Interpretation of Culture: A Bibliographic Overview," *American Quarterly* 26, no. 5 (1974): 455.
19. Mrs. Hud Prichard, recorded interview with the author, Oct. 18, 1984, Canyon, Tex., RCP-PHM.

20. Schlissel, Gibbens, and Hampsten, *Far From Home*, p. 44. Informed of the death of her sister's baby in 1854, Rachel Malick Biles wrote, "So the world goes—one minute in good health and the next in eturnity [*sic*]." Ibid., p. 40. Polly Coon migrated to Oregon from Wisconsin in 1852. After observing the tragedy at a river crossing when a member of the emigrant train drowned in the rapid water, she recorded in her diary: "What a brittle thread has life and how uncertain that another moment is ours." Holmes, *Covered Wagon Women*, Vol. 5 (1852, The Oregon Trail), p. 183.

21. Mrs. A. L. Walsh, recorded interview with the author, Dec. 3, 1984, Canyon, Tex., RCP-PHM.

22. Kenneth Wiggins Porter, ed., "'Holding Down' a Northwest Kansas Claim, 1885–1888," *The Kansas Historical Quarterly* 12, no. 3 (1956): 224.

23. "A Texas Cowboy's Funeral," [from *The Cattleman*] *Frontier Times* 16, no. 8 (1939): 350.

24. Ibid., p. 351.

25. Eva Pendleton Henderson, *Wild Horses: A Turn-Of-The-Century Prairie Girlhood*, p. 21.

26. Frazier Hunt, *The Long Trail from Texas: The Story of Ad Spaugh, Cattleman*, p. 54.

27. Adams, *Log of a Cowboy*, p. 276.

28. Gard, *Chisholm Trail*, p. 247.

29. Holmes, *Covered Wagon Women*, Vol. 7 (1854–60), p. 130.

30. Newcomb diaries, p. 26.

31. Vinovskis, "Angels' Heads," p. 560.

32. Boone McClure, recorded interview with the author, Nov. 6, 1984, Canyon, Tex., RCP-PHM.

33. Taylor, interview.

34. Abbott and Smith, *We Pointed Them North*, p. 33. Dave McCormick left Missouri for Colorado in 1872 where he went to work for Charles Goodnight. McCormick remembered the Methodist and Baptist revivals of his childhood and his fear of going to hell if he did not get his sins forgiven. "I could not see what I had done to be burned for eternity. I wanted to try and avoid that God." D. R. McCormick, "D. R. McCormick Manuscripts," 1933, JEHC—Midland.

35. Ruth Lowes, recorded interview with the author, Oct. 17, 1986, Canyon, Tex., RCP-PHM.

36. Ruth Lowes, recorded interview with the author, Mar. 23, 1984, Canyon, Tex., RCP-PHM.

37. Lewis, *Between Sun and Sod*, p. 174; Willie McClary, recorded interview with the author, July 10, 1984, Dumas, Tex., RCP-PHM; Mitchell Jones, Sr., interview, Mar. 8, 1984, RCP-PHM; Miner, *West of Wichita*, p. 158.

38. Henderson, *Wild Horses*, p. 42.

39. Matney, interview.

40. Edward Everett Dale, *Cow Country,* p. 131.

41. Thomas A. Muzzall, "Across the Plains in 1866," *New Mexico Histori-cal Review* 32, no. 3 (1957): 247, 250–51. At one point, depressed and plagued with thoughts of death, Nannie Alderson entreated her husband, upon her death, to carry her in and bury her in a place where there were water, flowers, and trees—not on some lonely hill. "He said he didn't feel that way about death. He wanted to be buried where he was, not carted around. He felt that when you died, it was just like throwing away an old coat. I knew he was right; yet I couldn't help shivering when I thought of those lonely graves out west, so far from friends." Alderson and Smith, *Bride Goes West,* p. 198.

42. Nature provided Louise Gibson with ample evidence that death was a part of this cycle, and "it's what my daddy always said, we were born and we were going to die." Mr. and Mrs. Joe Gibson, interview with the author, Nov. 28, 1984, Canyon, Tex., RCP-PHM.

43. Cosby, interview, Feb. 28, 1986. Ruth Lowes recalled their funerals for childhood pets, "And if we didn't have a pet of our own that was accom-modating enough to die for a funeral when we wanted one we'd go out in the alley and look for a dead cat or a dead dog or a dead bird and bring them in and have quite a ceremony on the cellar door, the dugout door." Lowes, interview, Mar. 23, 1984.

44. Ramey, interview.

45. Cosby, interview, Feb. 28, 1986.

46. Knupp, interview, p. 2.

47. Gibson, interview, Nov. 28, 1984; Deitiker, interview; Caldwell, inter-view, Mar. 1, 1984.

48. Albers, interview.

49. Bridwell, interview. Margaret Fullerton Frost writes about the death of her family's hired man in 1906. For days she and her brother "bombarded" their parents with questions about "funerals, souls, Heaven and why did nice people have to die? They told us about life after death, how people's souls lived on, and discussed many other pseudo-comforting theories which really didn't impress us." Margaret Fullerton Frost, "Small Girl in a New Town," *The Great Plains Journal* 19 (1980): 21.

50. George W. Moore, interview.

51. Lowes, interview, Mar. 23, 1984. Dr. Lowes went with her mother to a home in which there had been a death. It was the thing to do, she was told. People were sitting very quietly around the room, talking in subdued voices, and this mood made the young caller apprehensive. "This was such a solemn, quiet occasion, and I couldn't understand why they'd go and just sit."

52. Newcomb diaries, p. 70.

53. Schlissel, Gibbens, and Hampsten, *Far From Home*, p. 154.

54. Ise, *Sod and Stubble*, p. 62.

55. Ed R. Wallace, *Parson Hanks: Fourteen Years in the West*, p. 162. For Abigail Scott, death carried her small son "beyond the reach of mortal suffering, [and] in my heart I praise the Lord, who gave and who has taken away." She found reassurance in the belief that he would now "vie with angels around the throne of God." Holmes, *Covered Wagon Women*, Vol. 5, p. 117.

56. Angie Debo, "The Diary of Charles Hazelrigg," *The Chronicles of Oklahoma* 25, no. 3 (1947): 254.

57. R. F. Dunn, "First Evangel For Methodist Church in This Section Recalls Day of Pulpit Pioneering," unidentified, undated newspaper article, Dunn Papers, SCTTU.

58. Colt, *Went to Kansas*, p. 169.

59. Schlissel, Gibbens, and Hampsten, *Far From Home*, p. 154.

60. J. Marvin Hunter, *The Trail Drivers of Texas*, p. 928.

61. Weymouth T. Jordan, "A Soldier's Life on the Indian Frontier, 1876–1878: Letters of 2Lt. C. D. Cowles," *The Kansas Historical Quarterly* 28, no. 1 (1972): 152.

62. Colt, *Went to Kansas*, p. 170.

63. Ibid., p. 205.

64. Dunn, "First Evangel."

65. Debo, Diary of Charles Hazelrigg, 255. Writing from Iowa in 1877 to her parents in Norway, Gro Svendsen informed them of her young daughter's death. She too saw this tragedy as a manifestation of God's wisdom, His act to draw their thoughts closer to Him. She also took comfort in what was now to be the child's intercessory role. "With my sisters and brothers I, too, have one of mine who has gone to intercede for us at the throne of mercy. We must not let them pray in vain. May we be united with them beyond death and the grave!" Farseth and Blegen, *Frontier Mother*, p. 130.

Phoebe Judson (*Pioneer's Search*, p. 35) found it an awful thought to contemplate burial and finality alongside some obscure, mid-nineteenth-century overland trail. But with time she was to be assured that the "mystery which we call death is but a transition of the spiritual from the mortal, and it matters but little where the body lies; buried on the mountain top, in the briny deep, or consumed by fire, it is of no more account than the shell, or chrysalis, from which the bird or butterfly have flown; for we shall be clothed with a glorious spiritual body and be more ourselves than ever before."

Lodisa Frizzell (*Across the Plains*, p. 23) wrote that scarcely a day passed that some migrant was not left on the plains to return to mother dust. After the wagon train passed the grave digging for a twelve-year-old girl she could only imagine how hard it would be to leave one's children behind on the desolate plains. But she felt secure in her belief that "God will watch over all their dust till He shall bid it rise."

66. Miner, *West of Wichita*, p. 169.

67. Goff, "Isham Reavis," p. 29.

68. Jeffrey, *Frontier Women*, p. 70.

69. May Davison Rhodes, *The Hired Horseman: My Story of Eugene Manlove Rhodes*, p. 109.

70. Boley, ed., *Ella Elgar Bird Dumont*, p. 52.

71. Ise, *Sod and Stubble*, pp. 62–63.

72. Colt, *Went to Kansas*, p. 191.

73. McCormick, Manuscripts, p. 2.

74. Berryman, *Pioneer Preacher*, pp. 72–73.

75. Abbott and Smith, *We Pointed Them North*, p. 33. Abbott went on to suggest that the life cowboys led had a lot to do with their infidelity. "After you come in contact with nature you get all that stuff knocked out of you— praying to God for aid, divine Providence and so on—because it don't work. You could pray all you damn pleased, but it wouldn't get you water where there wasn't water. Talk about trusting in Providence, hell, if I'd trusted in Providence I'd have starved to death." Ibid.

76. Hough, *Story of the Cowboy*, pp. 198–99.

77. Adams, *Log of a Cowboy*, p. 297.

CHAPTER 7

1. Montene Merchant and Paul Engelbrecht, recorded interview with the author, Amarillo, Tex., May 26, 1994, RCP-PHM; Max Albright, "Daughter Fulfills Father's Wish," *Amarillo Globe-News*, 84, no. 184, Mar. 28, 1994, Section C, p. 1.

2. Reactions of friends varied. "I can't believe you're doing this." "Are you crazy?" "I couldn't do that at all. I can't believe it." Others were more sympathetic: "That's a great idea."

3. Robert Kastenbaum and Ruth Aisenberg, *The Psychology of Death*, pp. 238–39.

4. Ibid., p. 385. Robert Blauner, "Death and Social Structure," *Psychiatry* 29 (1966): 379.

5. Herman Fiefel, *New Meanings of Death*, p. 5.

6. Goody, "Death and the Interpretation of Culture," p. 454.

7. Blauner, "Death and Social," p. 389.

8. Bruce Kiskaddon, "A Cowboy Funeral," in *Rhymes of the Ranges and Other Poems*, p. 13.

9. Crosby County Pioneer Memorial in Cooperation with Crosby County

Historical Commission, *Gone, But Not Forgotten: A Cemetery Survey of Crosby County*, p. 9. Jess Barker remembered sitting with a sick professor one night, then sitting up with his body the following night. Barker, interview.

10. Spikes, "Early Days."

11. McClary, interview, July 10, 1984.

12. Jones, "Walter Dibrell," p. 111.

13. E. M. Fender, interview with Roy Poff, 1969, RCP-PHM.

14. T. U. Taylor, "A Frontier Home," *Frontier Times* 2, no. 6 (1925): 16–17. Ira Taylor remembered: "Everybody went in and waited on 'em while they's sick—tried to do something for 'em. Go in and bring 'em chuck." Taylor, interview.

15. Lennie Harter, recorded interview with the author, Sept. 21, 1984, Canyon, Tex., RCP-PHM.

16. Caldwell, interview, Mar. 1, 1984.

17. Taylor, interview.

18. Dick, *Sod-House Frontier*, p. 253; McClary, interview, July 10, 1984.

19. Mrs. Neil F. Fotheringham, "The Memoirs of Mrs. Lilian Bell, Dimmitt, Texas," 1936, RCP-PHM.

20. Crosby County, *Gone, But Not Forgotten*, p. 9; Albers, interview; Marilyn Albert, ed., *God, Grass, and Grit, Vol. II: History of the Sherman County Trade Area*, p. 11.

21. Mr. and Mrs. Joe E. Engelbrecht, recorded interview with the author, July 11, 1994, Amarillo, Tex., RCP-PHM.

22. Dick, *Sod-House Frontier*, p. 253.

23. Ibid.; Randel, ed., *A Time to Purpose*, p. 36; Crosby County, *Gone, But Not Forgotten*, p. 9.

24. Schlissel, *Women's Diaries*, p. 131; McClary, interview, July 10, 1984.

25. Hanners, *Lords of the Valley*, p. 128.

26. Ise, *Sod and Stubble*, p. 142.

27. Crosby County, *Gone, But Not Forgotten*, p. 9.

28. Goff, "Isham Reavis," p. 31.

29. Herbert Timmons and Carolyn Timmons, "'Those Are Our Boys on Boot Hill,'" *Amarillo Sunday News-Globe* 13, no. 33 (Aug. 14, 1938): Section D, p. 32. Riders were sent to Tulia, Texas, for "the best clothes that could be bought" for two cowboys killed by lightning in an 1895 roundup. Inez Christian Doshier, "Lone Prairie Graves," *Amarillo Sunday Globe-News* 13, no. 33 (Aug. 14, 1938): Section B, p. 26.

30. Frost, "Small Girl," p. 20.

31. May, responses to questionnaire.

32. Frost, "Small Girl," p. 20.

33. Rutherford, *One Corner*, p. 147.

34. Hough, *Story of the Cowboy*, p. 198.

35. Randel, ed., *A Time to Purpose*, p. 36; Rose Mary Johns, interview with Valerie Pogue, 1984, RCP-PHM.

36. White, interview, June 10, 1985; Bridwell, interview; Miner, *West of Wichita*, p. 170.

37. Caldwell, interview, Mar. 1, 1984. Even on the trail emigrants might sit overnight with a dead member of the wagon train. Mary Riddle wrote in her diary about sitting up with a dead boy: "no one can begin to tell the awfull [*sic*] dreariness of setting up with a corps in a tent in a wild country. It is so sad and lonesome to set and hear the silent gards [*sic*] keep up their steady tramp around the camp." Holmes, *Covered Wagon Women*, Vol. 10 (1875–83), p. 52.

38. Crosby County, *Gone, But Not Forgotten*, p. 9; Ochiltree County Historical Survey Committee, *Wheatheart*, p. 179.

39. Crosby County, *Gone, But Not Forgotten*, p. 9. Joanna Stratton (*Pioneer Women*, p. 81) cites S. N. Hoisington's spine-tingling experience with wolves. Mr. Hoisington and his mother were sitting up with a lonely, sick neighbor whose husband was away and who became terrified by the scratching of wolves on the door, sod, and windows of her sod house. Going to her house he carried with him his revolver, extra ammunition, an ax, and several large clubs. "The odor from the sick woman seemed to attract the wolves, and they grew bolder and bolder. I would step out, fire off the revolver and they would settle back for a while when they would start a new attack. I shot one through the window and I found him dead in the morning." Eventually the woman died and the wolves became even more aggressive in their attempts to get in the house. One forced his head between the door and door casing and as he was trying to squirm through Hoisington's mother struck him on the head with an ax and killed him. Another was shot while trying to come through a window. Mr. Hoisington and his mother fought the wolves for five successive nights, killing or wounding five gray wolves and two coyotes. When the woman's husband returned home and found his wife dead and his house ravaged by the wolves, he fainted and later sold out and left the area.

40. Barker, interview.

41. McClure, interview.

42. Ott, interview.

43. Mary Ella Peters, interview with Dwight Howard, 1942, RCP-PHM.

44. Hanners, *Lords of the Valley*, pp. 40–41. The cats were killed, LaVerne Hanners explains, because of the common belief in that part of the Southwest that any animal known to have eaten human flesh had to be destroyed. The idea of having one's body consumed by animals was horrifying to westerners. Ibid.

45. Mariett Foster Cummings and her husband left Illinois for California

in April, 1852. In June, ten days out of Fort Laramie, Wyoming, they passed Bitter Cottonwood Creek and observed on a bank of the creek a woman's burial. She recorded the scene in her diary: "The little children were sitting in the wagon, and the husband at the head of the grave, weeping bitterly over the uncoffined burial." Holmes, *Covered Wagon Women*, Vol. 4 (1852, The California Trail), p. 144.

In order to lose as little time as possible, a death on the trail might demand that the grave be dug even before the person died. Because embalming services were generally not available during this era, it was important that the body be prepared and buried as quickly as possible. Several comments emphasized the importance of a prompt burial: "Had to rush right around and get him buried"; "Dead one day, buried the next"; "Had to bury quick or be odor." In some cases, promptness necessitated burial at night. Louis Fairchild, "Death and Dying on the Southern Great Plains Around 1900," *Panhandle-Plains Historical Review* 59 (1986): 45.

46. Alfred I. Moye, "Chuck Wagon Stories by Texas Pioneers," *The Cattleman* 7, no. 10 (1921): 174.

47. Ibid.

48. Collinson, *Life in the Saddle*, p. 167.

49. John P. Bloom, "New Mexico Viewed by Americans 1846–1849," *New Mexico Historical Review* 34, no. 3 (1959): 185.

50. Alexander Majors and Colonel Prentiss Ingraham, eds., *Seventy Years on the Frontier: Alexander Majors' Memoirs of a Lifetime on the Border*, p. 262.

51. Shelton, interview, Mar. 15, 1984.

52. Mack Jones, "'Mack' Jones," 1940, RCP-PHM.

53. J. Frank Dobie, *The Longhorns*, p. 136; Frank Collinson, "Tongue River's First Ranch," n.d., RCP-PHM; Schlissel, *Women's Diaries*, pp. 226–27.

54. Baylis John Fletcher, *Up the Trail in '79*, p. 49.

55. Dick, *Sod-House Frontier*, p. 253; Shelton, interview, Mar. 15, 1984; Collinson, "Tongue River's First Ranch"; Collinson, *Life in the Saddle*, p. 125; Ott, interview.

56. Adams, *Log of a Cowboy*, p. 303.

57. William Timmons, *Twilight on the Range: Recollections of a Latterday Cowboy*, p. 80; Grace T. Lewellen, "Memoirs of J. C. Estlack," 1937, RCP-PHM.

58. Collinson, *Life in the Saddle, p.* 164; Dobie, *Longhorns*, p. 236.

59. Knupp, interview, p. 2; Jean Garnsey, "First Family of Amarillo [Mrs. Clarke H. Garnsey]," 1952, p. 2, RCP-PHM; Schlissel, *Women's Diaries*, p. 183.

60. Holmes, *Covered Wagon Women*, Vol. 3, 1851, p. 132; Whitlock, *Cowboy Life*, p. 42; Dee Brown, *The Gentle Tamers: Women of the Old Wild West*, p. 26.

61. Claude Hall, *The Early History of Floyd County*, p. 37; Collinson, *Life in*

the Saddle, p. 94; Dick, *Sod-House Frontier*, p. 253; Fannie G. Chisholm, "The True Story of the Chisholm Trail," *The Cattleman* 42, no. 6 (1960): 52.

62. Hall, *Early History*, pp. 37–38.

63. Dick, *Sod-House Frontier*, p. 447.

64. August Santleben, "Perils of Early Day Freighting," *Frontier Times* 21, no. 5 (1944): 227. Hannah King's diary recorded a death on the trail to Utah, and the corpse was laid on a bed of leaves and then covered with boughs before the grave was filled. Holmes, *Covered Wagon Women*, Vol. 6 (1853–54), p. 193.

Abigail Scott never forgot leaving her mother's body behind wrapped in a blanket and buried in a lonely, shallow grave beside the road. A feather mattress served as her coffin. Holmes, *Covered Wagon Women*, Vol. 5 (1852, The Oregon Trail), p. 72.

65. Cosby, interview, Feb. 28, 1986.

66. Mary A. E. Shearer, "Pioneer Life in Grayson County," *Frontier Times* 22, no. 11 (1945): 325.

67. Brown, *Gentle Tamers*, p. 41.

68. Donald W. Stewart, "Memoirs of Watson Stewart: 1855–1860," *The Kansas Historical Quarterly* 18, no. 4 (1950): 391.

69. Shelton, interview, Mar. 15, 1984.

70. McManigal, interview.

71. Majors and Ingraham, eds., *Seventy Years*, p. 262; Savage, Winston. 1941. Life on the "F" Ranch, RCP-PHM. Dora Stroup ("Memories") said that when men were working cattle, hammer, nails, and saw were always carried in the chuck wagon, so these would be handy for making a quick coffin. All that was needed was wood.

Mary Surfus remembered their wagon was new, made of oak, and freshly painted, so the boards made a sturdy coffin when one was later required. Holmes, *Covered Wagon Women*, Vol. 10, 1875–1883, p. 271.

72. H. L. Daily, "Higgins [Texas]," 1940, RCP-PHM. Elizabeth Hampsten relates the experience of one North Dakota settler who, at his wife's request, bought boards while in town to build a larger table, but in the short time he was gone his wife became deathly ill. On returning home, "That very night our dad and this good neighbor took that lumber and made our mother a coffin." Hampsten, *Settlers' Children*, p. 76.

73. Dick, *Sod-House Frontier*, p. 253.

74. Rhodes, *The Hired Horseman*, p. 50.

75. Whitlock, *Cowboy Life*, p. 73.

76. Caldwell, interview, Mar. 1, 1984.

77. Bob Beverly, "Lonely Graves in Lonely Places," *Frontier Times* 26, no. 9 (1949): 234.

78. Boley, ed., *Ella Elgar Bird Dumont*, p. 50.

79. Stroup, "Memories."

80. Timmons and Timmons, "'Those Are Our Boys'"; Ise, *Sod and Stubble,* p. 47.

81. Avent, interview, June 10, 1985.

82. Ott, interview.

83. Dick (*Sod-House Frontier,* p. 253) cites one early Kansas settler's recollection of a boy who rode up on horseback to the coffin maker and gave him a stick with marks on it indicating the shoulder width and length of the corpse.

84. Holcomb, interview; Fotheringham, "Memoirs of Mrs. Lilian Bell"; Timmons and Timmons, "'Those Are Our Boys.'"

85. J. W. Whitehead, interview with Mildred Hobbs, 1941, RCP-PHM; Ise, *Sod and Stubble,* p. 88; Holcomb, interview.

86. Nellie Witt Spikes and Temple Ann Ellis, *Through the Years: A History of Crosby County, Texas,* p. 467; Stratton, *Pioneer Women,* p. 81.

87. Lena Mae Stephens, "Doans, A Trading Post on a Texas Cattle Drive, 1876–1895," 1940, RCP-PHM.

88. Hunt, *The Long Trail from Texas,* pp. 254–55.

89. Lillian Carlile Swartz, "Life in the Cherokee Strip," *The Chronicles of Oklahoma* 42, no. 2 (1964): 68; Spikes and Ellis, *Through the Years,* p. 292.

90. Hanners, *Lords of the Valley,* p. 128.

91. Dick, *Sod-House Frontier,* p. 253. Soot or lampblack was often used to blacken the boards. Ibid.

92. Metcalf, "The White Family."

93. Juanita Daniel Zachry, *The Settling of a Frontier: A History of Rural Taylor County,* p. 118.

94. Mitchell Jones, Sr., interview, Mar. 8, 1984.

95. Gibson, interview, Nov. 28, 1984.

96. McClure, interview.

97. Gilles, Sr., "Death's First Visit," p. 311.

98. Schlissel, *Women's Diaries,* p. 132; Laura V. Hamner, *Light 'N Hitch: A Collection of Historical Writing Depicting Life on the High Plains,* p. 169.

99. Hamner, *Light 'N Hitch,* p. 169.

100. Gard, *Chisholm Trail,* p. 139.

101. Abbott and Smith, *We Pointed Them North,* pp. 43–44.

102. Collinson, *Life in the Saddle,* pp. 162–63. Merrill Mattes points out (*Great Platte River Road,* p. 88) that grave digging along the Great Platte River Road was handicapped by a number of factors: the hurried nature of the trip, a shortage of spades, and sand so shallow that any hole dug could hardly be called a grave.

103. Holmes, *Covered Wagon Women,* Vol. 5, p. 47.

104. Brown, *Gentle Tamers,* p. 26; Schlissel, *Women's Diaries,* pp. 226–27; Majors and Ingraham, eds., *Seventy Years,* p. 260.

105. Holmes, *Covered Wagon Women,* Vol. 3, p. 76. Majors and Ingraham,

eds., *Seventy Years*, p. 260. Mattes reports (*Great Platte River Road*, p. 91) the comments of David Cartwright about coyotes fighting and howling on a nearby knoll during the midst of a funeral service. "They were doubtless in scent of the corpse, and in angry waiting for a chance to tear it to pieces."

106. Jamison, "A Short History of Lipscomb County."

107. Hanners, *Lords of the Valley*, p. 41.

108. Greene, *A Personal Country*, p. 255.

109. Berryman, *Pioneer Preacher*, p. 74.

110. Burrus, Mrs. Edward Neal. 1964. interview with Pollyanna B. Hughes., pp. 8–9, RCP-PHM.

111. Crosby County, *Gone, But Not Forgotten*, p. 12; Santleben, "Perils of Early Day Freighting," p. 227.

112. Charles A. Siringo, "The End of the Cowboy," in *Riata and Spurs*, p. 261.

113. Mary M. Henderson, "Mrs. J. N. Ivy," 1938, RCP-PHM.

114. Majors and Ingraham, eds., *Seventy Years*, p. 266.

115. Mattes, *Great Platte River Road*, p. 89. Schlissel, *Women's Diaries*, p. 131; Matthews, *Interwoven*, p. 61.

116. According to Schlissel, one of the most unshakable anxieties of overlanders was that their grave, or the grave of a loved one, might be dug up by wolves or Indians. Irrespective of how stoic they might otherwise have been, this fear stalked them relentlessly. Schlissel, *Women's Diaries*, p. 47. In order to obscure a grave it was sometimes placed in the middle of the road and the wagons repeatedly driven over it, or in the corral to be tromped by the hooves of the stock. The sod and vegetation might even be replaced, all in an attempt to make the spot look as natural and undisturbed as possible. Brown, *Gentle Tamers*, p. 26.

117. Schlissel, *Women's Diaries*, p. 131.

118. Holmes, *Covered Wagon Women*, Vol. 2 (1850), p. 214.

119. Everett Dick, *The Story of the Frontier*, p. 241.

120. Adams, *Log of a Cowboy*, p. 276. Mattes makes mention (*Great Platte River Road*, p. 89) of various other grave markers: elk horns, wooden crosses, and the iron rim from a wagon wheel.

121. Schlissel, *Women's Diaries*, p. 131.

122. Hamner, *Light 'N Hitch*, p. 42.

123. Greene, *A Personal Country*, p. 258.

124. Ibid., p. 260.

125. Silas Amon, "Daguerreotype On A Tombstone," *The Prairie Schooner*, Vol. 1, p. 268.

126. Boley, *Ella Elgar Bird Dumont*, p. 63; Mary Whatley Clarke, "The Founding of the Matador," *The Cattleman* 43, no. 5 (1956): 62; Marguerite Wallace Kennedy, *My Home on the Range*, p. 325; Zachry, *Settling of a Frontier*, p. 43.

127. Laura V. Hamner, *Short Grass and Longhorns*, p. 42.

128. Warwick, *Randall County [Texas] Story*, p. 133.

129. Greene, *A Personal Country*, pp. 254–55.

130. Berryman, *Pioneer Preacher*, p. 74.

131. Stroup, "Memories."

132. "Grave on a Lonely Rise," *Amarillo Sunday News-Globe* 13, no. 33 (Aug. 14, 1938): Section E, p. 21.

133. Jack Loftin, *Trails Through Archer: A Centennial History—1880–1980*, p. 433.

134. Ralph Allred, recorded interview with the author, May 4, 1984, Amarillo, Tex., RCP-PHM.

135. Henderson, *Wild Horses*, p. 93. This excerpt from *Wild Horses* by Eva Pendleton Henderson appears courtesy of Sunstone Press, Box 2321, Sante Fe, New Mexico, 75044-2321.

136. Miner, *West of Wichita*, p. 171.

137. John Clay, *My Life on the Range*, p. 46.

138. Younger, "Memoir of Frank Exum."

139. Dobie, *Longhorns*, pp. 136–37.

140. Edward Everett Dale, "Riders of the Range," in *Cow Country*, p. 112.

141. Majors and Ingraham, eds., *Seventy Years*, pp. 262–63.

142. Dick, *Sod-House Frontier*, p. 236; Mrs. Bessie Irene Montgomery, responses to a questionnaire, 1939, RCP-PHM; Jamison, "A Short History of Lipscomb County."

143. Adams, *Cattle Brands*, p. 211; Jones, "'Mack' Jones."

144. Shelton, interview, Mar. 15, 1984; Doshier, "Lone Prairie Graves."

145. Holmes, *Covered Wagon Women*, Vol. 5, p. 72.

146. Miner, *West of Wichita*, p. 159.

147. Whitlock, *Cowboy Life*, p. 268.

148. Hamlin Garland, "A Brother's Death-Search," in *Prairie Songs*, p. 84.

CHAPTER 8

1. Lewellen, "Memoirs of J. C. Estlack." Estlack's parents were among the earliest settlers in the Panhandle, settling in Tascosa in 1883. "The several years to follow," Estlack said, "taught me much about the 'wild west' as it was, rather than what modern writers have to say about it."

2. Abbott and Smith, *We Pointed Them North*, p. 45.

3. [As told by] Fred E. Sutton [And written down by] A. B. MacDonald, "The Cowboy's Dream," in *Hands Up! Stories of the Six-Gun Fighters of the Old Wild West*, p. 148.

4. Ibid., pp. 148–49.

5. Howard C. Raether and Robert C. Slater, "Immediate Postdeath Ac-

tivities in the United States," in *New Meanings of Death*, ed. by Herman Fiefel, p. 234.

6. Ibid., p. 239.

7. Colt, *Went to Kansas*, p. 199.

> *There was once a cow boy funeral that I many times recall,*
> *A bad hoss killed a feller on a beef work late one fall.*
> *We hadn't any coffin, and there was no bell to toll.*
> *We went up on a hill side and we dug a narrow hole.*
> *We wrapped him up inside his bed and laid him in the shale;*
> *His saddle onderneath [sic] his head, to ride the last long trail.*
> *We had no book where we could look and read of from its pages.*
> *No one was there to say a prayer, or sing the "Rock of Ages."*
> *I recollect nobody spoke. We didn't care to talk.*
> *We filled the hole and took a smoke, and raised a pile of rock.*
> *And when the thing was over, it was soter [sic] like a dream,*
> *How we helped the cook and wrangler while they harnessed up the team.*
> *We got the day herd movin' and departed on our way.*
> *And left that cow boy there to sleep, till resurrection day.*

Kiskaddon, "A Cowboy Funeral," in *Rhymes of the Ranges and Other Poems*, p. 13.

8. Loretta Harrison, "The Story of Mrs. Velma Heathington," 1970, p. 5, RCP-PHM.

9. Snell, "Roughing It on Her Claim," p. 240.

10. Josie Baird, "The Two Circles Bar Ranch," 1935, RCP-PHM.

11. Sutton, *Hands Up!* p. 148; Sutton went on to say that following the burial, "we returned to town, thirsty, and the glasses tinkled, chips rattled on the gaming tables, the fiddles tuned up, and life went on again as before." Possibly it was this manner of burial that prompted the criticism to which Mary Ada May was responding in Chapter 7.

12. Mrs. T. D. Hobart, "Pioneer Days in the Panhandle Plains," *Panhandle-Plains Historical Review* 8 (1935): 75–76.

13. Rollins, *The Cowboy*, pp. 273–74.

14. Ibid., p. 274.

15. Henry, *Conquering Our Great American Plains*, p. 207.

16. Kennedy, *My Home*, p. 333.

17. Hunt, *The Long Trail from Texas*, p. 256.

18. Kennedy, *My Home*, p. 331. Andy Adams's narrative (*Log of a Cowboy*, p. 305) recorded in detail the funeral for the trail boss following his watery death on the North Platte. As the notes of an old hymn slowly died away, there lingered, he wrote, a profound stillness. No sounds of movement were heard from the heavy-hearted trail drivers.

19. Shelton, interview, Mar. 15, 1984.

20. Dale, *Cow Country*, p. 63; Sylvia Ann Grider and Sara Jarvis Jones, "The Cultural Legacy of Texas Cemeteries," *The Texas Humanist* 6, no. 5 (May–June, 1984): 34.

21. Albert W. Thompson, *They Were Open Range Days: Annals of a Western Frontier*, p. 41.

22. Shelton, interview, Mar. 15, 1984.

23. Dick, *Sod-House Frontier*, p. 254; Porter, *Memory Cups of Panhandle Pioneers*, p. 476; Buster Barker, "Days with My Father (Story of Judge P. W. Myers): Mrs. Hugh Longino to Buster Barker," 1940, RCP-PHM; Snell, "Roughing It on Her Claim."

24. A. W. Young, "Thirty Years in Texas Pulpit and School," *Frontier Times* 6, no. 8 (1929): 347.

25. Spikes, "Early Days."

26. Mrs. Cline Gilbert, interview with Winnie Davis Hale, 1941, p. 2, RCP-PHM.

27. Marie Hess, interview with Pollyanna Hughes, 1956, pp. 5–6, RCP-PHM.

28. McClary, interview, July 10, 1984.

29. Mitchell Jones, Sr., interview, Mar. 8, 1984; Shelton, interview, Mar. 15, 1984.

30. Hunt, *The Long Trail from Texas*, p. 254.

31. Laura Mabel Widmer King, "Laura Mabel Widmer King," 1940, RCP-PHM; Clarke, "Founding of the Matador," p. 62.

32. Whitlock, *Cowboy Life*, p. 42; Mrs. Mervin Wilterding, interview with Gayla Wagnon, 1976, RCP-PHM.

33. Stroup, "Memories."

34. Clayton W. Williams, *Texas' Last Frontier: Fort Stockton and the Trans-Pecos, 1861–1895*, p. 315; Goff, "Isham Reavis," p. 31. Mattes writes (*Great Platte River Road*, p. 87) of a gradual change in emigrant attitudes toward the deaths of fellow travelers as the journey progressed. In the early stages the dead were buried with as much reverence and dignity as possible, but farther along the trail these last rites were performed indifferently, sometimes with callous haste. A numbing, dehumanizing process seemed to set in that well-nigh depleted the emigrants of all sentiment.

35. Mrs. J. T. Jowell, "Recollections of Mrs. J. T. Jowell as Related to Lucile Hughes," 1938, p. 5, RCP-PHM.

36. Gilbert, interview.

37. Rollins, *The Cowboy*, p. 274.

38. McClary, interview, July 10, 1984.

39. Alma Pafford, recorded interview with the author, Apr. 13, 1984, Amarillo, Tex., RCP-PHM.

40. May, responses to questionnaire.

41. Timmons, *Twilight on the Range*, p. 81.

42. Mitchell Jones, Sr., interview, Mar. 8, 1984; Black, interview, July 20, 1984.

43. Mary J. Jaques, *Texan Ranch Life; With Three Months Through Mexico in a "Prairie Schooner,"* p. 223.

44. Kennedy, *My Home*, p. 333.

45. Winkleman interview.

46. Stroup, "Memories."

47. Porter, ed., "'Holding Down' a Northwest Kansas Claim," p. 224. Andy Adams's story (*Log of a Cowboy*, p. 304) of the Platte River funeral included what was for him the unforgettable last verse of the "Portuguese Hymn," sung by two young girls:

> *When through the deep waters I call thee to go,*
> *The rivers of sorrow shall not overflow;*
> *For I will be with thee thy troubles to bless,*
> *And sanctify to thee thy deepest distress.*

48. Timmons, *Twilight on the Range*, p. 81; Dale, *Cow Country*, pp. 128–29. Eva Henderson (*Wild Horses*, p. 21) could remember seeing old women wiping tears from their eyes at the singing of "Little Joe the Wrangler," perhaps thinking of a son or brother killed in a cattle stampede.

49. Gard, *Chisholm Trail*, p. 285.

50. Vinovskis, "Angels' Heads," p. 558.

51. Dick, *Sod-House Frontier*, p. 254.

52. Kennedy, *My Home*, p. 327.

53. George W. Tucker, personal communication with author, Sept. 12, 1984.

54. Hess, interview.

55. Fairchild, "Death and Dying," p. 49.

56. McManigal, interview.

57. Walsh, interview, Dec. 3, 1984.

58. McClure, interview.

59. Bill Collyns, recorded telephone interview with the author, May 27, 1994, RCP-PHM.

60. Ott, interview.

61. Caldwell, interview, Mar. 1, 1984. On the other hand, Ira Ott was of the opinion that "When somebody dies that didn't belong to a church or something, he was preached into hell, you might say. That's the way it sounded to me." Ott, interview.

62. Jaques, *Texan Ranch Life*, p. 223. An aged minister from a nearby emigrant train was called on to conduct Adams's Platte River funeral, and the old

man's words were a source of comfort: "he spoke as though he might have been holding family worship and we had been his children." Adams, *Log of a Cowboy*, p. 305.

63. Stephens, "Doans, A Trading Post."

64. Metcalf, "The White Family."

65. McClary, interview, July 10, 1984; Deitiker, interview.

66. Caldwell, interview, Mar. 1, 1984.

67. Ibid.

68. Lowes, interview, Mar. 23, 1984.

69. Ibid.

70. Black, interview, July 20, 1984.

71. Winkleman, interview. Mrs. Winkleman said that she and the other children present were allowed to play outside during the service for her grandmother, "and there were some comments about that."

72. Kennedy, *My Home*, p. 331.

73. Ise, *Sod and Stubble*, p. 47.

74. Whitlock, *Cowboy Life*, p. 42.

75. Ibid.

76. Ise, *Sod and Stubble*, p. 47.

77. Kennedy, *My Home*, p. 332.

78. Crosby County, *Gone, But Not Forgotten*, p. 9.

79. Tucker, interview.

80. Dick, *Sod-House Frontier*, p. 254.

81. Matney, interview.

82. George W. Moore, interview; Rutherford, *One Corner*, p. 147; Gibson, interview, Nov. 28, 1984.

83. Goff, "Isham Reavis," p. 32; Berryman, *Pioneer Preacher*, p. 73.

84. Zachry, *Settling of a Frontier*, p. 177; Lewis, *Between Sun and Sod*, p. 177.

85. Kennedy, *My Home*, p. 332.

86. Jaques, *Texan Ranch Life*, p. 223.

87. Spikes and Ellis, *Through the Years*, p. 292.

88. Gibson, interview, Nov. 28, 1984; Deitiker, interview.

89. Shelton, interview, Mar. 15, 1984. Possibly it was because comfort was so hard to find just at the moment it was most needed that children found funerals disturbing. "The greatest experience for a young child then," according to Joe Gibson, "was the death of a close person, a family member or a member of the community. That was a tragedy, the most trying experience I had as a child. If a child drowned or a mother died in childbirth, [it was] the greatest tragedy in the world." Gibson, interview, Nov. 28, 1984.

90. Kennedy, *My Home*, p. 324.

91. Rollins, *The Cowboy*, p. 274.

92. Hampsten, *Settlers' Children*, p. 178.

93. Ruth Cross, recorded interview with the author, Apr. 20, 1984, Canyon, Tex., RCP-PHM.

94. Walsh, interview, Dec. 3, 1984.

95. Gibson, interview, Nov. 28, 1984.

96. Winkleman, interview.

97. Caldwell, interview, Mar. 1, 1984.

98. Walsh, interview, Dec. 3, 1984.

99. Lowes, interview, Mar. 23, 1984.

100. A collection of western campfire stories by Andy Adams (*Cattle Brands*, p. 210) included Billy Edwards's account of the young tubercular who joined the outfit. "We always gave him gentle horses to ride, and he would go with us on trips that we were afraid would be his last. There wasn't a man on the range who ever said 'No' to him. He was one of those little men you can't help but like; small physically, but with a heart as big as an ox's. He lived about three years on the range, was welcome wherever he went, and never made am enemy or lost a friend. He couldn't; it wasn't in him." When the end came, Edwards said, "I did something for him that I've often wondered who would do the same for me—I closed his eyes when he died." Voice quavering, the storyteller concluded his tale with the men's distress at the loss of their friend. "Of all the broke-up outfits, we were the most. Dead tough men bawled like babies. I had a good one myself."

101. Deitiker, interview.

102. Matney, interview.

103. Harter, interview.

104. Frank S. Hastings, *A Ranchman's Recollections: An Autobiography*, p. 124.

105. Holcomb, interview; Deitiker, interview; Gibson, interview, Nov. 28, 1984; Caldwell, interview, Mar. 1, 1984; Mitchell Jones, Sr., interview, Mar. 8, 1984.

106. McClary, interview, July 10, 1984.

107. Deitiker, interview.

108. Boley, ed., *Ella Elgar Bird Dumont*, pp. 133–34.

109. Hampsten, *Settlers' Children*, p. 64.

110. Goff, "Isham Reavis," p. 32.

111. Ibid.

112. McClure, interview.

113. Collyns, interview.

114. Deitiker, interview.

115. Colt, *Went to Kansas*, p. 181.

116. Berryman, *Pioneer Preacher*, p. 74.

117. Rutherford, *One Corner*, pp. 148–49.

118. Deitiker, interview.

CHAPTER 9

1. Greene, *A Personal Country,* pp. 3, 128.
2. Ricou, "Empty As Nightmare," p. 148.
3. Powell, "Samuel Burk Burnett."
4. Pitts, "At Home in a Dugout."
5. Ramon F. Adams, *The Old-Time Cowhand,* p. 48.
6. Abbott and Smith, *We Pointed Them North,* p. 33.
7. Badger Clark, "A Cowboy's Prayer," in *Sun and Saddle Leather,* pp. 50–51.
8. Charles A. Johnson, *The Frontier Camp Meeting,* p. 104.
9. Rister, *Southern Plainsmen,* p. 185.
10. Walter Brownlow Posey, *Frontier Mission: A History of Religion West of the Southern Appalachians to 1861,* p. 23.
11. Nebraska Society of the Daughters of the American Revolution. *Collection of Nebraska Pioneer Reminiscences,* p. 85.
12. Andreadis, "True Womanhood," p. 184.
13. Emory Lindquist, "Religion in Kansas During the Era of the Civil War," *The Kansas Historical Quarterly* 25, no. 4 (1959): 431.
14. Abbott recalled the terrible storms on the North and South Platte and one in particular. "One man was so scared he threw his six-shooter away, for fear it would draw the lightning; and I remember old Matt Winter, with the rain apouring down and the lightning flashing, taking off his hat and yelling at God Almighty: 'All right, you old bald-headed son of a bitch up there, if you want to kill me, come on do it!' It scared the daylights out of the rest of us." Abbott and Smith, *We Pointed Them North,* p. 79.
15. Johnson, *Frontier Camp Meeting,* p. 11.
16. Gilles, Sr., "Death's First Visit," p. 307; Posey, *Frontier Mission,* p. 23.
17. Catherine Andrew, "Frontier Women of the Texas Panhandle," 1973, p. 49, master's thesis, West Texas State University. Alfred Holland arrived in Mobeetie, Texas, in 1882 and called it a typical cowboy village with ten or twelve houses and a business district composed of two hotels, a couple of restaurants, a blacksmith shop, one general store, and seven saloons. Marsene Smith Weaks, "Alfred A. Holland," 1936, RCP-PHM. In 1887, Tascosa, Texas, had a population of around four hundred people, and in Nov. of that year *The Tascosa Pioneer* proclaimed: "Seven saloons. We boom." Charles F. Rudolph, ed., "Saturday, Nov. 26, 1887," [section in "Old Tascosa: Selected News Items from *The Tascosa Pioneer,* 1886–88"] *Panhandle-Plains Historical Review* 39 (1966): 134.

Saloons were about the only recreational spots for cowboys to spend their wages, so a common recollection concerning the small West Texas and New Mexico towns was the number of saloons. Cecil Briggs, "Recollections of a

Frontier Merchant—George Clairborne Harris to Cecil Briggs," 1937, RCP-PHM; J. S. Wynne, interview with J. Evetts Haley, 1926, RCP-PHM; George Sidney Hatch, interview with E. L. Hammit, 1946, RCP-PHM; The Rev. [T. F.] Robeson, interview with L. S. Baker, 1924, RCP-PHM; Mrs. Ed. Harrell, interview with Dorothy Warwick, 1942, RCP-PHM.

18. Brooks, "Influence of the Pioneer Women," p. 109.

19. Andrew, "Frontier Women," p. 35.

20. Ibid., p. 48. Ruby Cole Archer said: "Often a lone cowboy preacher on horseback would ride into a ranch. He would stay over a few days free to rest up his horse, and you got the ranches near to come to your home to hear him. When he left he took a flour sack of sourdough biscuits, side of bacon, coffee, and tin cup of wild plumb jelly to eat. He could stop, build a campfire, brew some coffee in a tin syrup bucket, let the horse graze, and then saddle up and move on. A few traveled in a one-horse, top buggy. He could carry some religious books to sell. *Pilgrim's Progress* by John Bunyan was one book. One book was on phrenology telling what the bumps on your head meant—like a high brow, etc." Ruby Cole Archer, recorded interview with the author, June 4, 1993, Amarillo, Tex., RCP-PHM.

21. Deitiker, interview.

22. Norman, "Childhood on the Southern Plains," p. 55.

23. Andrew, "Frontier Women," p. 61. Jessica Young, daughter of a Methodist minister, came to Texas in 1875 when she was three years of age. The family moved to the Panhandle in 1880, and she recalled the cowboys riding up and down the main street of Mobeetie, whooping and shooting up the town. "A child or woman never dreamed of going alone on the streets in the evening. The town was practically turned over to the sporting element." She also spoke of the "unmentionable women slipping in the back door of the Saloon, and gambling and drinking with the men." Jessica Morehead Young, "Pioneer Days," n.d., RCP-PHM.

24. Samuel Newcomb recorded in his diary: "It is very seldom that the people of this country have an opportunity of going to church, and there are even persons in this place that are grown, married, and are the parents of children and have never been to a religious meeting." Newcomb diaries, p. 63.

Following the first sermon preached in Fort Davis in 1865, Susan Newcomb had a similar entry in her diary: "I understand that there were a few grown persons in this place that never had heard the word of God preached untill [*sic*] today. That looks a little like heathenism, but here on the frontier where the people are so scattered, if there was preaching in the country, it would hardly be practicable for many to attend with their families." Newcomb diaries, p. 84. S. K. Bynum said he never attended a real Sunday school "in all my days." He was in a church sometimes once or twice a year but might go two or three years without ever seeing a church. S. K. Bynum, notes to J. Evetts Haley, 1925, RCP-PHM.

25. Mrs. John B. Harvey, 1937. "Early Settler Tells How First Post Office Came to Be Designated 'Shamrock.'" *The Shamrock Texan* 34, no. 103 (Sept. 7, 1937): Section 4, p. 2.

26. Inez Christian Doshier, "The Cowboy's Association with the Nester," 1937, RCP-PHM.

27. John Ise (*Sod and Stubble*, p. 24) wrote that people would come from over twelve miles to attend one of these meetings, riding in their wagons or walking—some even barefooted.

28. Andrew, "Frontier Women," p. 72.

29. Joe Shelton, recorded interview with the author, Dec. 18, 1986, Pampa, Tex., RCP-PHM. At one night meeting held in the Ise home, so many people crowded inside that the floor began to sag. Henry Ise asked the worshippers to step outside while he went down to the cellar to brace up the floor with poles. Ise, *Sod and Stubble*, p. 24.

30. Brooks, "Influence of the Pioneer Women," p. 112. In some areas where there were no churches, a circuit rider might come through anywhere from twice a month to twice a year. Frances Edwards Hall, interview with Rebecca Carnes, 1980, RCP-PHM; J. W. Pierce, "Memoirs of Mrs. Cora Miller Kirkpatrick," 1938, RCP-PHM.

31. Shelton, interview, Dec. 18, 1986.

32. Brooks, "Influence of the Pioneer Women," p. 114.

33. Max Bentley, "The 'Little Minister' Who First Carried the Gospel into the Cow Camps of the West," *Fort Worth Star-Telegram*, Aug. 25, 1923, p. 4.

34. Gard, *Rawhide Texas*, p. 128.

35. Posey, *Frontier Mission*, p. 23; William Ransom Hogan, *The Texas Republic: A Social and Economic History*, p. 21; W. Eugene Hollon, *The Southwest: Old and New*, p. 143; Coe, *Ranch on the Ruidoso*, p. 112.

36. Ross Phares, *Bible in Pocket, Gun in Hand*, p. 77.

37. Dickson D. Bruce, Jr., *And They All Sang Hallelujah: Plain-Folk Camp-Meeting Religion, 1800–1845*, p. 51; Johnson, *Frontier Camp Meeting*, p. 26.

38. Roger Finke and Rodney Stark, *The Churching of America, 1776–1990*, p. 46; Johnson, *Frontier Camp Meeting*, pp. 25, 27.

39. Goodwyn, *Lone-Star Land*, pp. 231–32.

40. Catharine C. Cleveland, *The Great Revival in the West 1797–1805*, p. 52.

41. Ibid., p. 54.

42. Bernard A. Weisberger, *They Gathered at the River: The Story of the Great Revivalists and Their Impact Upon Religion in America*, p. 24.

43. Cleveland, *Great Revival*, p. 52.

44. Johnson, *Frontier Camp Meeting*, p. 36.

45. Weisberger, *They Gathered*, p. 26.

46. Johnson, *Frontier Camp Meeting*, p. 98.

47. Charles Johnson, "The Frontier Camp Meeting: Contemporary and Historical Appraisals, 1805–1840," *Mississippi Valley Historical Review* 37 (1950–51): 100.

48. Ibid., p. 98.

49. Nancy Tatom Ammerman, *Baptist Battles: Social Change and Religious Conflict in the Southern Baptist Convention*, pp. 27–28; Bruce, Jr., *And They All Sang*, p. 53.

50. "The Old-Time Campmeeting," *Frontier Times* 3, no. 1 (1925): 9.

51. Jessie Robinson, recorded interview with the author, Jan. 30, 1987, Claude, Tex., RCP-PHM.

52. Lewis, *Nothing to Make a Shadow*, p. 84.

53. Johnson, *Frontier Camp Meeting*, p. 4.

54. Lockhart, "Old Fashioned Camp Meetings," p. 19.

55. Johnson, *Frontier Camp Meeting*, p. 64; Phares, *Bible in Pocket*, p. 79.

56. William G. McLoughlin, Jr., *Modern Revivalism: Charles Grandison Finney to Billy Graham*, p. 170.

57. Johnson, *Frontier Camp Meeting*, p. 57; Finke and Stark, *Churching of America*, 93; Bruce, Jr., *And They All Sang*, p. 53.

58. Posey, *Frontier Mission*, pp. 26–27.

59. Finke and Stark, *Churching of America*, pp. 92–93.

60. Cleveland, *Great Revival*, p. 59.

61. Ibid., p. 51.

62. Ibid., p. 118.

63. Rister, *Southern Plainsmen*, p. 185; Bruce, Jr., *And They All Sang*, p. 6; Zane Mason, "Some Thoughts on Frontier Religion in Texas after the Civil War," *West Texas Historical Association Year Book* 57 (1981): 45; Johnson, "Frontier Camp Meeting: Contemporary and Historical," pp. 108–109; Lewis, *Nothing to Make a Shadow*, p. 84.

64. Lewis, *Nothing to Make a Shadow*, p. 84.

65. J. Marvin Hunter, "A Campmeeting at Menardville in 1886," *Frontier Times* 18, no. 10 (1941): 435–436.

66. W. Henry Miller, *Pioneering in North Texas*, p. 196.

67. Bruce, Jr., *And They All Sang*, p. 53; Cleveland, *Great Revival*, p. 119.

68. "The First Camp Meeting in America," *Frontier Times* 26, no. 7 (1949): 170.

69. Johnson, "Frontier Camp Meeting: Contemporary and Historical," p. 102; Vernon, et al., *The Methodist Excitement*, p. 181.

70. Phares, *Bible in Pocket*, p. 85.

71. Bruce, Jr., *And They All Sang*, p. 56.

72. J. B. Cranfill (*From Memory: Reminiscences, Recitals, and Gleanings From*

a Bustling and Busy Life, p. 45) wrote of his first visit to the brush-arbor meeting that would later change his life. "I went with Miss Mamie Pickens to this revival service. Neither of us had any religious impressions whatsoever. We went to the public gathering as young people will. We sat far back almost on the very last seat. . . . when the service was over, I went back to where the young lady sat and escorted her home. It was a six-mile ride across the country."

73. Gard, *Rawhide Texas*, p. 132.

74. Finke and Stark, *Churching of America*, 96; Brown, *Gentle Tamers*, p. 140; Hogan, *Texas Republic*, p. 216.

75. Johnson, "Frontier Camp Meeting: Contemporary and Historical," p. 98.

76. Ammerman, *Baptist Battles*, p. 27.

77. Hogan, *Texas Republic*, p. 210; Goodwyn, *Lone-Star Land*, p. 123; Texas State Historical Association, *The New Handbook of Texas*, Vol. 5, pp. 523–29.

78. Vernon, et al., *The Methodist Excitement*, p. 182; Carter E. Boren, *Religion on the Texas Frontier*, p. 287. As late as 1909 the camp meeting in Newberry, Parker County, Texas, had been held every year for thirty-seven years. James D. Newberry, (1909) Chapter 8, in *Pioneer Days in the Southwest from 1850 to 1879: Thrilling Descriptions of Buffalo Hunting, Indian Fighting and Massacres, Cowboy Life and Home Building*, contributed to by Charles Goodnight, Emanuel Dubbs, John A. Hart and others, p. 225.

The Bloys camp meeting continues to be a five-day annual affair, usually starting on the second Tuesday of August and continuing through the following Sunday. The Hill County meeting is held each August near Ingram, Texas. Texas State Historical Association, *New Handbook*, Vol. 1., p. 601.

79. Holden, *Alkali Trails*, pp. 175–85.

80. Bruce, Jr., *And They All Sang*, p. 56.

81. Johnson, "Frontier Camp Meeting: Contemporary and Historical," p. 100.

82. McLoughlin, *Modern Revivalism*, pp. 92–93.

83. Vernon, et al., *The Methodist Excitement*, p. 175.

84. Mason, "Some Thoughts," p. 45.

85. Goodwyn, *Lone-Star Land*, p. 233.

86. Vernon, et al., *The Methodist Excitement*, p. 181.

CHAPTER 10

1. Johnson, *Frontier Camp Meeting*, p. 120.

2. Bruce, Jr., *And They All Sang*, pp. 70–71.

3. In the early days of plains settlement, according to Joe Evans, "Our greatest handicap . . . was the water question. There were no well machines

and we had to dig for water with pick and shove." Joe M. Evans, *Bloys: Cowboy Camp Meeting*, p. 14.

A bookkeeper with a yen to ranch, P. H. Gates arrived in Pecos, Texas, in 1910. Four years later he became a minister. Gates said that water was "scarcer than hen's teeth," and during his years on the range, "it never rained enough to wet my shirt." The Rev. P. H. Gates, interview with Charles R. Gates, 1936. RCP-PHM. Merle White knew something about arid conditions. "I thought today, we were married sixty-five years and farmed all the time, and I feel like nearly the whole sixty-five years we's looking for rain." White, interview, June 10, 1984.

4. Jennie Baker, recorded interview with the author, Oct. 3, 1986, Canyon, Tex., RCP-PHM; Brown, interview; Ochiltree County Historical Survey Committee, *Wheatheart*, p. 250; W. C. Gilmore, "Memoirs of P. L. Vardy, M.D.," 1936, pp. 49–50, RCP-PHM; Mrs. H. L. Holland, recorded interview with the author, Dec. 18, 1986, Happy, Tex., RCP-PHM; Bertie Culp, recorded interview with the author, Dec. 18, 1986, Happy, Tex., RCP-PHM.

5. Bruce, Jr., *And They All Sang*, p. 71.

6. Ann Gallaway, "Speaking of Texas: Keeping the Faith," *Texas Highways* 48, no. 1 (Jan., 2001): 3.

7. Matthews, *Interwoven*, p. 71.

8. Carter Matthews, recorded interview with the author, Oct. 31, 1986, Amarillo, Tex., RCP-PHM.

9. Ella Dumont spoke of going to one of the ranch dances and then she followed with the comment that it would be the last one attended for some time, "as warm weather was coming on and big meetings beginning." Boley, ed., *Ella Elgar Bird Dumont*, p. 15.

10. Goodwyn, *Lone-Star Land*, p. 233.

11. Vernon, et al., *The Methodist Excitement*, p. 175; Lita Witt, recorded telephone interview with the author, Apr. 20, 1987, RCP-PHM.

12. Rister, *Southern Plainsmen*, p. 184; Walter Prescott Webb, "Some Vagaries of the Search for Water in the Great Plains," *Panhandle-Plains Historical Review* 3 (1930): 28.

13. Mr. and Mrs. Ira Taylor, recorded interview with the author, Oct. 24, 1986, Amarillo, Tex., RCP-PHM. It was Tom Black's recollection that "Along about Aug. the first they'd what they called 'lay the crop by.' They'd lay it by, they'd plow it the last time and wouldn't have anything to do then till time to gather the crop, so then they'd have these big meetings." Tom Black, recorded interview with the author, Sept. 12, 1986, Canyon, Tex., RCP-PHM.

14. Caldwell, interview, Mar. 17, 1986.

15. Goodwyn, *Lone-Star Land*, p. 234; Zachry, *Settling of a Frontier*, p. 110; Paul McClung, "Papa Jack: The Adventures of a Pioneer Cowman," *Great Plains Journal* 12, no. 2 (1973): 123.

16. Johnson, "Frontier Camp Meeting: Contemporary and Historical," p. 100; Gard, *Rawhide Texas,* p. 129.

17. Taylor, interview, Oct. 24, 1986.

18. Pecos Higgins and Joe Evans, *Pecos' Poems,* preface. The second of nine children, Evans remembered his father calling the eight boys together and telling them their mother had tried to teach them to be religious and he had tried to teach them how to work, now "that's all we can do for you."

19. Evans, *Bloys: Cowboy.*

20. Berryman, *Pioneer Preacher,* p. 110.

21. Minnie D. Clifton, "The Bloys Camp Meeting," *Sul Ross State Teachers College Bulletin* 27, no. 2 (1958): 27. JEHC—Midland.

22. Evans, *Bloys: Cowboy,* p. 5.

23. Ibid., p. 36; Vardy, "Reminiscences."

24. Gard, *Rawhide Texas,* p. 124. One Kansas settler never knew what time it was when he got out of bed every morning, "Because clocks are like angels' visits—few and far between." Ruede and Ise, eds., *Sod-House Days,* p. 85.

25. Caldwell, interview, Mar. 17, 1986.

26. Faye Morrison, "Forty-Seven Years in Floyd County [Texas] (Story of Mrs. W. A. Shipley)," 1937, RCP-PHM.

27. Robeson, interview, p. 2.

28. Gates, interview.

29. Mrs. William Dixon, "Reminiscences of a Pioneer As Told to Wilda Talbot," 1938, p. 2, RCP-PHM.

30. Taylor, interview.

31. Hunter, "A Campmeeting at Menardville," p. 434.

32. Berryman, *Pioneer Preacher,* p. 104.

33. Vernon, et al., *The Methodist Excitement,* pp. 181–82; Lockhart, "Old Fashioned Camp Meetings," p. 19.

34. Taylor, interview.

35. Mitchell Jones, Sr., interview, Sept. 19, 1986.

36. Ochiltree County Historical Survey Committee, *Wheatheart,* p. 250; Neelley, "Pioneering in Young County."

37. Lockhart, "Old Fashioned Camp Meetings," p. 19.

38. Mrs. W. B. Burkhalter, "A Pioneer Woman Recalls the Old Time Religion: The Life Story of Mrs. Fannie Maude Wyatt," 1938, RCP-PHM; Matthews, *Interwoven,* p. 68; Ochiltree County Historical Survey Committee, *Wheatheart,* p. 250.

39. Faragher, *Women and Men,* p. 119.

40. Gard, *Rawhide Texas,* p. 131.

41. Hester Moore suggested it was even work for a mother to get her children ready for a nighttime revival service. "I guess that was a lot of trouble for [Mother] to get the kids all ready to go and see that they stayed out of mis-

chief. . . . To get four kids ready to go somewhere after a long day's hard work was an undertaking, and I don't think she looked forward to it." Hester Moore, recorded interview with the author, Nov. 12, 1993, Hereford, Tex., RCP-PHM.

42. Burkhalter, "Pioneer Woman"; Lockhart, "Old Fashioned Camp Meetings," p. 19; Ochiltree County Historical Survey Committee, *Wheatheart*, p. 250.

43. Ott, interview.

44. Gibson, interview, Oct. 7, 1986; Delbert Trew discusses wash-day routines in "Wash Day on the Farm Always Fell on Monday," *Amarillo Globe-News* 1, no. 29 (2001): Section C, p. 2.

45. McManigal, interview.

46. Myrtle Murray, "Home Life on Early Ranches of Southwest Texas: Ernst Jordan, Gillespie County," *The Cattleman* 26, no. 10 (1940): 136.

47. Ibid.

48. Berryman, *Pioneer Preacher*, p. 111.

49. Lockhart, "Old Fashioned Camp Meetings," p. 19.

50. Shelton, interview, Dec. 18, 1986.

51. Connor, "The West Is for Us," p. 67.

52. Ibid., pp. 67–68.

53. Oneita Davidson, recorded interview with the author, Nov. 12, 1994, Hereford, Tex., RCP-PHM; Mr. and Mrs. Albert Byars, recorded interview with the author, Oct. 10, 1986, Canyon, Tex., RCP-PHM.

54. Byars, interview, Oct. 10, 1986.

55. Lockhart, "Old Fashioned Camp Meetings," p. 19.

56. Ibid.

57. Berryman, *Pioneer Preacher*, p. 111. C. B. Witt seemed proud that he was the one who did the "hitchin'" in his family. "Pretty early in my life, by the time I was eight years old I was a good farm hand." C. B. Witt, recorded interview with the author, Apr. 8, 1987, Amarillo, Tex., RCP-PHM.

58. William Stubblefield, recorded interview with the author, Mar. 21, 1986, White Deer, Tex., RCP-PHM.

59. Hogan, *Texas Republic*, p. 211.

60. Herbert Timmons and Carolyn Timmons, "Veteran Preacher Tells of Early Experiences," *Amarillo Sunday News-Globe* 14, no. 6 (Feb. 5, 1939): Section 2, p. 10. The Reverend Little remembered one man and his son rode over 200 miles on horseback, sleeping at night on the prairie, to attend district conference.

61. Evans, *Cowboys' Hitchin' Post*, p. 21; Matthews, *Interwoven*, pp. 70–71.

62. Clifton, "Bloys Camp Meeting," p. 28.

63. Evans, *Cowboys' Hitchin' Post*, p. 22.

64. Matthews, *Interwoven*, p. 71. Minnie Clifton cited another account of campground arrivals: "In old days . . . boys astride their pet cow ponies or broncs and girls with long riding skirts on side saddles came galloping into camp. Others came in hacks, buckboards, or buggies, followed by chuck wagons with baggage, tents, and bed rolls and camping supplies." Clifton, "Bloys Camp Meeting," p. 26.

65. Matthews, *Interwoven*, p. 71.

66. Lockhart, "Old Fashioned Camp Meetings," p. 19.

67. Murray, Home Life, 136; John A. Hart, "History of Pioneer Days in Texas and Oklahoma," Chapter 7 in *Pioneer Days in the Southwest from 1850 to 1879*, p. 145.

68. Berryman, *Pioneer Preacher*, p. 133.

69. Matthews, interview.

70. Shelton, interview, Dec. 18, 1986.

71. Dee McDade, recorded interview with the author, Jan. 2, 1987, Wildorado, Tex., RCP-PHM.

72. Spikes and Ellis, *Through the Years*, p. 332.

73. Matney, interview; Baker, interview; J. S. Wynne, interview with J. Evetts Haley, 1926, RCP-PHM; Shelton, interview, Dec. 18, 1986; Robinson, interview; Willie McClary, recorded interview with the author, Dec. 16, 1986, Dumas, Tex., RCP-PHM.

74. Neelley, "Pioneering in Young County," p. 46.

75. Brown, interview.

76. Matthews, interview.

77. Bentley, "'Little Minister,'" p. 4.

78. Melton McGehee, recorded interview with the author, Mar. 26, 1987, Wayside, Tex., RCP-PHM.

79. C. B. Witt, interview.

80. Rex E. Galloup, Sr., "Dasie Martin Currie—Pioneers of Amarillo," 1939, RCP-PHM; Newberry, Chapter 8, in *Pioneer Days in the Southwest from 1850 to 1879*, p. 219.

81. Bentley, "'Little Minister,'" p. 4.

82. Evans, *Bloys: Cowboy*, p. 13.

83. Matthews, *Interwoven*, p. 72.

84. Neelley, "Pioneering in Young County"; Naceeb Abraham, recorded interview with the author, Nov. 5, 1993, Amarillo, Tex., RCP-PHM; Ollie Jones, recorded telephone interview with the author, Dec. 10, 1986, RCP-PHM; Mrs. Payne and Mrs. Rowsey—Joint interview, 1940, RCP-PHM.

85. Coe, *Ranch on the Ruidoso*, p. 113.

86. Phares, *Bible in Pocket*, pp. 85–86.

87. Barker, "Memoirs of Sara Leon Coleman."

88. Berryman, *Pioneer Preacher,* p. 112.

89. N. Howard Thorp, *Partner of the Wind: Story of the Southwestern Cowboy,* p. 140.

90. Evans, *Cowboys' Hitchin' Post,* p. 33; R. L. Jones, "Folk Life in Early Texas, Part II: The Autobiography of Andrew Davis," *The Southwestern Historical Quarterly* 43, no. 3 (1940): 339.

91. Haley, "Panhandle Notes," Vol. 2, L–W, n.d., JEHC—Midland.

92. Neelley, "Pioneering in Young County," p. 45.

93. David Bowen, interview with Maud Lummus, 1939, p. 5, RCP-PHM.

94. Payne and Rowsey, interview.

95. Mitchell Jones, Sr., interview, Sept. 19, 1986; Caldwell, interview, Mar. 17, 1986.

96. McClary, interview, Dec. 16, 1986.

97. Willis, interview, p. 6.

98. Taylor, interview.

99. Caldwell, interview, Mar. 17, 1986.

100. Willis, interview, p. 6.

101. Ise, *Sod and Stubble,* p. 243.

102. Inez Christian Doshier, recorded interview with the author, Nov. 7, 1986, Amarillo, Tex., RCP-PHM.

103. Mary Griffith, "Memories of Charles Jackson Mapes," 1938, RCP-PHM.

104. McClary, interview, Dec. 16, 1986.

105. Connor, "The West Is for Us," p. 69.

106. Bedford, "Memoirs."

107. Evans pointed out that camp meetings were a wonderful trip for dogs because they got all the scraps they wanted, including lots of fresh antelope meat. Evans, *Cowboys' Hitchin' Post,* p. 31.

108. Bedford, "Memoirs"; Horace Bailey Carroll, "Social Life in West Texas From 1875 to 1890," p. 19, master's thesis, Texas Tech College, 1928. Oneita Davidson told of her uncle's habit of wearing a long-tailed coat when he preached. During one service he knelt in the straw to pray, and a small dog went to barking and biting at the twitching coattail. Unable to continue, the frustrated preacher called on someone in the congregation to finish the prayer while "I kick the Devil out of this dog." Davidson, interview.

109. Evans, *Bloys: Cowboy,* pp. 9–10.

110. Ibid., p. 9.

111. Dale, *Frontier Ways,* p. 223.

112. Bedford, "Memoirs."

113. Taylor, interview.

114. Ott, interview. Pet Ott's brother broke his wrist in a fight. It did not

matter that it was a revival. "This was a chance to get together and have it out with so and so."

115. Miller, *Pioneering in North Texas*, p. 196.

116. Zachry, *Settling of a Frontier*, p. 177.

117. Clifton, "Bloys Camp Meeting," p. 41. C. N. Cosby, age eighty-nine, recited from memory the lyrics to a song popular around the turn of the century:

> *Two lovers rode upon their steeds,*
> *Light-hearted, homeward bound,*
> *For sacred songs had died away*
> *Upon the old camp ground.*
>
> *Two hearts were glad, two souls rejoiced,*
> *And in the still night air,*
> *They whispered tender words of love*
> *And breathed a solemn prayer.*
>
> *From out the forest's dismal shade*
> *A jealous lover came,*
> *With fire of vengeance in his breast*
> *That burned him like a flame.*
> *Soon on the bosom of the earth*
> *Three lifeless bodies lay,*
> *A raging suitor slew his friends*
> *And stole his life away.*

Cosby, interview, Sept. 5, 1986.

118. Johnson, *Frontier Camp Meeting*, p. 210; Goodwyn, *Lone-Star Land*, p. 233.

119. Shelton, interview, Dec. 18, 1986. Ira Taylor said these bedrolls were "just like we used on the ranch—sleeping." Taylor, interview. Hendrix provides a more complete description of the bedroll. John M. Hendrix, "The Bed Roll," *The Cattleman* 21, no. 4 (Sept., 1934): 10.

120. Evans, *Bloys: Cowboy*, pp. 27–28. Evans said the only bath they had was in a water hole before they left the ranch and it had to last until they got back home. Sometimes the water hole dried up and they had to postpone their baths until it rained again. Ibid.

121. Mr. and Mrs. Posey Bonds, recorded interview with the author, Dec. 18, 1986, Happy, Tex., RCP-PHM.

122. Taylor, interview.

123. Coe, *Ranch on the Ruidoso*, p. 112; Evans, *Cowboys' Hitchin' Post*, p. 30.

124. Stubblefield, interview.

125. Shelton, interview, Dec. 18, 1986.

126. Berryman, *Pioneer Preacher,* p. 134.

127. Lavert Avent, recorded interview with the author, Dec. 18, 1986, Amarillo, Tex., RCP-PHM.

128. Coe, *Ranch on the Ruidoso,* p. 112; Clifton, "Bloys Camp Meeting," p. 34; Hart, "History of Pioneer Days," p. 145.

129. Clifton, "Bloys Camp Meeting," p. 112.

130. Evans, *Bloys: Cowboy,* p. 15.

131. Shelton, interview, Dec. 18, 1986.

132. Clifton, "Bloys Camp Meeting," pp. 34–35.

133. Bentley, "'Little Minister,'" p. 8.

134. Evans, *Bloys: Cowboy,* p. 43.

135. Born in Mississippi, Fannie Maude Wyatt came to Texas in 1887, the wife of a circuit-riding preacher. She said that because her husband was a preacher no one expected them to bring any supplies. "We would be invited from tent to tent to partake of the best that could be cooked by those good women." Burkhalter, "Pioneer Woman."

136. "Old-Time Campmeeting," p. 9.

137. Byars, interview, Oct. 10, 1986.

138. Oneita Davidson's husband was a Methodist preacher, and when they went to a small community they would eat with different families during the day. They would eat fried chicken for breakfast, fried chicken at noon, and again for supper. "I've seen them go out after we came in from a service— a woman go out and get a chicken and wring its head and have it for lunch." Davidson, interview; Adams, *Old-Time Cowhand,* p. 50.

139. Jo Stewart Randel, interview with Ruth Parker, 1977, RCP-PHM.

140. H. B. Carroll, "Coronado's Step-Children: Social Life in the Early South Plains," *The West Texas Historical Association Year Book* 9 (1933): 66.

141. Doshier, interview.

142. Gladys Jamison, "Short Sketches of History of Ochiltree County, Texas: Story of Life of Mrs. B. J. Jackson," 1937, p. 13, RCP-PHM. These cowboys, C. B. Witt said, would bring corn for their horses. "They had this little sack of corn that their horse could stick his head in. We called it a moral. They'd hang that around his head and he'd eat his dinner there. And so the horses were taken care of too because we'd have a big dinner too." C. B. Witt, interview.

143. McDade, interview.

144. Mrs. Dick McElroy, recorded interview with the author, Nov. 21, 1986, Claude, Tex., RCP-PHM.

145. McDade, interview; McGehee, interview; Avent, interview, Dec. 18, 1986.

146. McGehee, interview.

147. Avent, interview, Dec. 18, 1986.

148. C. B. Witt, interview.

149. Lita Witt, interview.

150. Archer, interview.

151. Caldwell, interview, Mar. 17, 1986.

152. Avent, interview, Dec. 18, 1986.

153. It was after Mr. McDade's death that I asked Mrs. McDade what was meant by a "boggy-topped pie with calf slobbers on it." She laughed and said that a calf, when it is milking, will make a lot of froth. Her father-in-law referred to meringue as "calf-slobbers."

154. Gibson, interview, Oct. 7, 1986.

155. Rutherford, *One Corner,* p. 26.

CHAPTER II

1. Dick, *Sod-House Frontier,* p. 233.

2. Abbott and Smith, *We Pointed Them North,* p. 50.

3. "Hell in Texas," n.d., RCP-PHM. (A shorter version is found in John A. Lomax, *Cowboy Songs: And Other Frontier Ballads,* pp. 222–23.)

4. Walter Prescott Webb, ed., *The Handbook of Texas: A Dictionary of Essential Information,* Vol. 2, pp. 602–603.

5. Greene, *A Personal Country,* p. 130.

6. Ibid., p. 127.

7. Evans, *Cowboys' Hitchin' Post,* p. 21; Ott, interview; Shelton, interview Dec. 18, 1986; Rister, *Southern Plainsmen,* p. 184; Hogan, *Texas Republic,* p. 211; Rutherford, *One Corner,* p. 26.

8. Archer, interview.

9. Maxine Sloneker, "Recollections of a Pioneer Woman: Mrs. Elizabeth Hart Chatham," 1938, pp. 9–10, RCP-PHM.

10. Hester Moore, interview; Culp, interview; Cosby, interview, Sept. 5, 1986.

11. Culp, interview.

12. Mr. and Mrs. Ira Taylor, interview; Brown, *Gentle Tamers,* p. 139.

13. Mary Garner, recorded interview with the author, Jan. 30, 1987, Claude, Tex., RCP-PHM.

14. Matney, interview; "Emma A. Wynett-Booker," 1940, RCP-PHM; A. J. Holt, *Pioneering in the Southwest,* p. 71.

15. Holt, *Pioneering in the Southwest,* p. 71.

16. Matney, interview.

17. Evans, *Cowboys' Hitchin' Post,* p. 48. One first-time participant followed the men to what he thought was going to be a pear tree, expecting to bring back a bucketful of pears.

18. Archer, interview.

19. Velma Bell, recorded interview with the author, Jan. 30, 1987, Claude, Tex., RCP-PHM; Berryman, *Pioneer Preacher*, p. 111.

20. Clifton, "Bloys Camp Meeting."

21. Webb, "Some Vagaries of the Search for Water," p. 28.

22. Berryman, *Pioneer Preacher*, p. 99.

23. Taylor, "A Frontier Home," p. 19.

24. Shelton, interview, Dec. 18, 1986. Ira Taylor agreed. "It'd knock off the sun but it wouldn't knock off the rain." Taylor, interview, Oct. 24, 1986.

25. Taylor, interview, Oct. 24, 1986; Caldwell, interview, Mar. 17, 1986.

26. Mr. and Mrs. Albert Byars, interview.

27. Berryman, *Pioneer Preacher*, p. 94.

28. Evans, *Cowboys' Hitchin' Post*, p. 12.

29. Berryman, *Pioneer Preacher*, p. 97.

30. "First Camp Meeting," p. 169; Taylor, interview; C. B. Witt, interview; Burkhalter, "Pioneer Woman"; Rister, *Southern Plainsmen*, p. 184.

31. Henry Ham, recorded interview with the author, Dec. 16, 1986, Dumas, Tex., RCP-PHM; Sloneker, "Recollections."

32. Beulah Carter, recorded interview with the author, Nov. 11, 1993, Amarillo, Tex., RCP-PHM.

33. "Old-Time Campmeeting," p. 8; Mitchell Jones, Sr., interview, Sept. 19, 1986.

34. Burkhalter, "Pioneer Woman."

35. Lita Witt, interview; Evans, *Bloys: Cowboy*, p. 8.

36. Culp, interview; Evans, *Bloys: Cowboy*, p. 8; Ethel Mullins, recorded interview with the author, May 20, 1987, Canyon, Tex., RCP-PHM.

37. Holt, *Pioneering in the Southwest*, p. 71; Lockhart, "Old Fashioned Camp Meetings," p. 19.

38. Shelton, interview, Dec. 18, 1986.

39. Adams, *Old-Time Cowhand*, p. 51.

40. Carter, interview; Berryman, *Pioneer Preacher*, p. 93.

41. Taylor, interview; Stroup, "Memories"; Robeson, interview.

42. Taylor, interview; Fred Whetstone, "Memoirs of Ernest Warren," 1936, RCP-PHM; Stroup, "Memories"; Spikes and Ellis, *Through the Years*, p. 332.

43. Vardy, "Reminiscences"; Hogan, *Texas Republic*, p. 211; Zachry, *Settling of a Frontier*, p. 110.

44. Evans, *Bloys: Cowboy*, p. 13.

45. Hogan, *Texas Republic*, p. 211.

46. Caldwell, interview, Mar. 17, 1986.

47. Zachry, *Settling of a Frontier*, p. 103.

48. Holt, *Pioneering in the Southwest*, p. 71.

49. Mason, "Some Thoughts," p. 44.

50. Johnson, "Frontier Camp Meeting: Contemporary and Historical," p. 103.

51. Ibid.

52. Franklin C. Smith, "Pioneer Beginnings at Emmanuel, Shawnee," *The Chronicles of Oklahoma* 24, no. 1 (1946): 7.

53. White, interview, Nov. 3, 1986.

54. Jaques, *Texan Ranch Life*, p. 256.

55. Johnson, "Frontier Camp Meeting: Contemporary and Historical," p. 103.

56. Ise, *Sod and Stubble*, p. 23.

57. Cave, interview.

58. Bartlett, *New Country*, p. 377.

59. Ibid., p. 9.

60. J. Evetts Haley, "Andrew Jackson Potter: Fighting Parson!" *The Shamrock*, summer, 1961, p. 7, JEHC—Midland.

61. McClary, interview, Dec. 16, 1986.

62. Ruede and Ise, eds., *Sod-House Days*, p. xi.

63. S. F. Sparks, "Recollections of S. F. Sparks," *The Quarterly of the Texas State Historical Association* 12, no. 1 (1908): 78.

64. Holt, *Pioneering in the Southwest*, p. 68.

65. Hogan, *Texas Republic*, p. 210.

66. Ise, *Sod and Stubble*, pp. 23–24.

67. Ibid., p. 245.

68. Ibid., p. 246.

69. Hogan, *Texas Republic*, p. 206; T. R. Havins, "Frontier Missionary Difficulties," *West Texas Historical Association Year Book* 15, 1939, p. 56.

70. Cosby, interview, Sept. 5, 1986.

71. Havins, "Frontier Missionary Difficulties," p. 56; Young, "Thirty Years in Texas Pulpit and School," p. 350.

72. L. R. Millican, "Sermon and Very Short Life Sketch of L. R. Millican, Over Fifty Years a Missionary in West Texas," n.d., pp. 8–9, JEHC—Midland.

73. Dunn, "First Evangel."

74. Havins, "Frontier Missionary Difficulties," p. 56. Hogan (*Texas Republic*, p. 207) cited the autobiography of Francis Wilson, a Methodist preacher in East Texas, in which the Reverend Wilson claimed a career total of 7,000 sermons delivered and 150,000 miles traveled.

75. Timmons and Timmons, "Veteran Preacher."

76. Ibid. The men too had to be hardy. "Father" John L. Dyer, the "Snowshoe Itinerant," was an early-day western frontier preacher. It was reported that he walked forty miles each Sunday in order to serve three con-

gregations. Gordon Langley Hall, *The Sawdust Trail: The Story of American Evangelism.* (Photo caption on second photograph page following text page 32.)

77. Rister, *Southern Plainsmen*, p. 77; Havins, "Frontier Missionary Difficulties," p. 73.

78. Edward Baxter Featherston, *A Pioneer Speaks*, p. 66; Mason, "Some Thoughts," p. 41.

79. Rutherford, *One Corner*, p. 25.

80. Featherston, *Pioneer Speaks*, p. 122.

81. Ibid., p. 27. The Reverend Featherston added: "I believe this hard life has been punishment sent on me for not answering the call [to preach] earlier in my youth. I try to submit cheerfully to this chastisement, remembering the experience of the Prophet Jonah and that the Apostle Paul said, 'Whom the Lord loveth He chastiseth, and scorcheth every son that he receiveth.'"

82. Spikes, "Early Days."

83. Parmer County [Texas] Historical Commission, *Prairie Progress*, p. 22.

84. Gard, *Rawhide Texas*, p. 128.

85. Stratton, *Pioneer Women*, p. 180.

86. Sparks, "An Apostle to the Cowboys," p. 9.

87. Lowes, interview, Oct. 17, 1986.

88. Black, interview, Sept. 12, 1986.

89. Phares, *Bible in Pocket*, p. 47.

90. Mullins, interview.

91. Matney, interview.

92. Johnson, "Frontier Camp Meeting: Contemporary and Historical," p. 104.

93. Grace Tyree Lewellen, "Memoirs: Mrs. Luella Harrah Macintire," 1937, p. 14, RCP-PHM; Emanuel Dubbs, (1909) Chapters 2 and 3, in *Pioneer Days in the Southwest from 1850 to 1879*, pp. 29–99.

94. Sparks, "An Apostle to the Cowboys," p. 9.

95. Adams, *Old-Time Cowhand*, pp. 51–52.

96. R. L. Jones, "Folk Life," p. 338.

97. Evalyn W. Rasmussen, "Memoirs of Ed B. Trigg," 1939, RCP-PHM.

98. Black, interview, Sept. 12, 1986; Doshier, interview. "Some of them," Ira Ott said, "they wouldn't know when to quit, especially if they got one to come up to the rail." Ott, interview. Eva Henderson (*Wild Horses*, p. 34) found town preaching "entirely too long-winded."

99. Caldwell, interview, Mar. 17, 1986.

100. Holt, *Pioneering in the Southwest*, p. 56.

101. Alberta Davis, "Memoirs of J. A. Hornbeak, Hereford, Texas," 1937, RCP-PHM.

102. Caldwell, interview, Mar. 17, 1986.

103. Taylor, interview.

104. Ise, *Sod and Stubble*, p. 24.

105. Burkhalter, "Pioneer Woman."

106. Richards, O. H. "Memories of an 89'er," *The Chronicles of Oklahoma* 26, no. 1 (1948): 10; William Curry Holden, *Alton Hutson: Reminiscences of a South Plains Youth*, p. 144.

107. Russell K. Hickman, "Lewis Bodwell, Frontier Preacher: The Early Years," *The Kansas Historical Quarterly* 12, no. 3 (1943): 290.

108. William E. Berger, "A Kansas Revival of 1872," *The Kansas Historical Quarterly* 13, no. 4 (1957): 378.

109. Ibid.

110. Archer, interview; Berryman, *Pioneer Preacher*, p. 138.

111. Bridwell, interview. Henry A. Miller was eleven years of age when he attended an 1865 Methodist revival in Iowa. The sermon, he said, left him frantic. "[P]erdition was not described by the preacher as simply a mental condition after death. . . . the unregenerate would be literally roasted in Hell over a hot fire—hotter than any fire I had ever seen. And that fire would never go out either, or even die down a little. I wouldn't have a chance to get out of it even for a little while and put a wet rag on the burned places (as I had done when I burned my hand so bad trying to mold some hot lead into a ferrule . . . at the blacksmith shop). No, I would just keep on burning, forever and ever. And forever was a long time. I had never realized before what a long time forever would be. The brimstone would be furnished by the Devil, and he had unlimited supplies. Brimstone was supposed to make a hotter fire than any other fuel." Henry A. Miller, "Methodist Revival Meeting: Remembering a Boyhood Experience in 1865," *The Palimpsest* 71, no. 1 (1990): 13–14.

112. Shelton, interview, Dec. 18, 1986.

113. Caldwell, interview, Mar. 17, 1986.

114. Lowes, interview, Oct. 17, 1986.

115. White, interview, Nov. 3, 1986. Velma Bell feared rather than loved God. "I thought He was a condemning person, but now I think of God as being love. But then as a child, I feared the wrath of God. . . . I think the preachers then preached God as a powerful person and . . . it would be hard to get forgiveness. You really had to be sorry for your sins." Velma Bell, interview.

Dave McCormick's youthful reasoning was that "if a God had created me and all other things it certainly was not just to punish us when we had not done anything very wrong. I have not changed my mind since." D. R. McCormick, McCormick Manuscripts, 1933, p. 2, JEHC—Midland.

Oneita Davidson confided that her Uncle Dick was pretty rough in the way he got people into the kingdom. "He scared 'em in there. When he got through preaching about hell you didn't want to go there." Davidson, interview.

116. Archer, interview.

117. Goodwyn, *Lone-Star Land*, p. 235.

118. Ibid., p. 237.

119. Hogan, *Texas Republic*, p. 214.

120. Gard, *Rawhide Texas*, p. 129.

121. Isaac Watts, "Broad Is the Road," in William Allen, *Psalms and Hymns for Public Worship*, p. 471.

122. Thorp, *Partner of the Wind*, p. 140.

123. Ott, interview.

124. Dan McAllister, "Pioneer Woman," *New Mexico Historical Review* 34, no. 3 (1991): 163.

125. Berryman, *Pioneer Preacher*, p. 114.

126. Phares, *Bible in Pocket*, p. 77; Archer, interview.

127. Lockhart, "Old Fashioned Camp Meetings," p. 19.

128. Sparks, "An Apostle to the Cowboys," p. 9.

129. Cranfill, *From Memory*, p. 51.

130. Norman, "Childhood on the Southern Plains," p. 80.

131. Wallace, *Parson Hanks*, p. 66.

132. Miller, "Methodist Revival," p. 14.

133. Mitchell Jones, Sr., interview; Ollie Jones, interview.

134. Taylor, interview.

135. Mitchell Jones, Sr., interview.

136. Caldwell, interview, Mar. 17, 1986. Dee McDade said this approach by a well-meaning woman drove his best friend from the church. "He hated that lady until she died on that account. She would not leave him alone. She'd go pick him out every time." McDade, interview. Mary Garner said, "People would have their mind on one certain one and they'd go to 'em every night. . . . hound 'em all the time." Garner, interview.

137. Taylor, interview.

138. Bob Pendleton, recorded interview with the author, 1994, RCP-PHM; Mitchell Jones, Sr., interview, Sept. 19, 1986.

139. Archer, interview.

140. Lewis, *Nothing to Make a Shadow*, p. 84. Ira Ott said, "I can remember one ol' guy, he lived down in Arkansas and every Saturday he'd go to town to get the mail and buy groceries and he rode a mule. . . . He'd get a mile or so away from home and the burro would want to go back home. And he whipped and he whipped and the more he whipped the [more] stubborn the mule would get. And finally he got down off of the mule and prayed that that mule would go, and he got back on that mule and never had no more trouble.

I heard him testify several different times and that's the way he told it." Ott, interview.

141. Bruce, Jr., *And They All Sang*, p. 76.

142. Neelley, "Pioneering in Young County."

143. Ott, interview.

144. Mrs. A. L. Walsh, recorded interview with the author, Nov. 13, 1986, Canyon, Tex., RCP-PHM.

145. Mitchell Jones, Sr., interview, Sept. 19, 1986; Murray, "Home Life on Early Ranches," p. 13.

146. Davidson, interview.

147. Bridwell, interview; Black, interview, Sept. 12, 1986.

148. C. B. Witt, interview. Some, Mary Garner said, would fall down and lie on the ground "trying to get the Holy Ghost—or whatever you call it. They hypnotized 'em." Garner, interview.

149. Ruth Crabtree, "The Memoirs of Mr. G. B. E. Bourland," 1937, RCP-PHM.

150. Vardy, "Reminiscences," p. 10.

151. Stubblefield, interview.

152. Taylor, interview.

153. Maudie Meredith, "Memoirs of Rev. R. E. L. Muncy," 1936, p. 6, RCP-PHM.

154. C. R. Walser, recorded interview with the author, Aug. 18, 1993, Hereford, Tex., RCP-PHM.

155. McClary, interview, Dec. 16, 1986.

156. Holmes, *Covered Wagon Women*, Vol. 9 (1864–68), p. 200; Garner, interview; "The Biography of Edward Baxter Featherston," n.d., RCP-PHM.

157. Ott, interview.

158. Velma Bell, interview.

159. Irbin H. Bell, interview with J. Evetts Haley, 1927, RCP-PHM; Neelley, "Pioneering in Young County"; Sammie Roach, "Forty Years in the Texas Panhandle," 1938, RCP-PHM.

160. Doshier, interview.

161. Collyns, interview.

162. Vardy, "Reminiscences." At the same time others were singing, mischievous boys often enjoyed singing their own lyrics to the songs.

163. Ruede, *Sod-House Days*, p. 75.

164. Dale, *Frontier Ways*, p. 219; Hunter, "A Campmeeting at Menardville," p. 434.

165. Coe, *Ranch on the Ruidoso*, p. 112.

166. Stratton, *Pioneer Women*, p. 174.

167. Adams, *Old-Time Cowhand*, p. 52.

168. Velma Bell, interview.

169. "Biography of Edward Baxter Featherston."

170. Anna Lou German, "The Harveys: Plains People," 1970, RCP-PHM.

171. Robinson, interview.

172. Bruce, Jr., *And They All Sang*, p. 91; Goodwyn, *Lone-Star Land*, p. 236.

173. Christ-Janer, Hughes, and Smith, *American Hymns*, p. 365.

174. Caldwell, interview, Mar. 17, 1986.

175. Bruce, Jr., *And They All Sang*, p. 96.

176. J. M. Boswell, "The Development of Mobeetie, Oldest Town in the Panhandle, and Its Social Activities," n.d., p. 15, RCP-PHM.

177. Anonymous, "You Will See Your Lord A-Coming," in Christ-Janer, Hughes, and Smith, *American Hymns*, p. 377.

178. Jared B. Waterbury, "Sinner, Is Thy Heart at Rest?" in Christ-Janer, Hughes, and Smith, *American Hymns*, p. 373.

179. Austin Fife and Alta Fife, *Heaven on Horseback: Revivalist Songs and Verse in the Cowboy Idiom*, p. 3.

180. Ibid.

181. Isaac Watts, "Why Do We Mourn Departed Friends?" in *Psalms and Hymns* [Presbyterian Church in the United States], p. 412.

182. Isaac Watts, "When I Can Read My Title Clear," in *The Book of Common Prayer* [Protestant Episcopal Church in the United States of America], p. 228.

183. L. Hartsough, "Let Me Go," in *Church and Sunday School Hymnal*, ed. by J. D. Brunk, p. 174.

184. Jefferson Hascall, "My Latest Sun Is Sinking Fast," in *New Baptist Hymnal*, p. 313.

185. J. E. Rankin, "God Be With You," in B. B. McKinney, ed., *Voice of Praise*, p. 299.

186. Clifton, "Bloys Camp Meeting," p. 40.

187. "Old-Time Campmeeting," p. 9.

188. Lockhart, "Old Fashioned Camp Meetings," p. 19.

CHAPTER 12

1. Dale, *Frontier Ways*, p. 204; P. C. Coleman, "Experiences of a Pioneer Doctor," *The West Texas Historical Association Year Book* 7 (1931): 37.

2. Dick, *Sod-House Frontier*, p. 441. Dr. George Hare, born in Ireland in 1842, followed his brothers to America after the Civil War. He drifted through Ohio, Nebraska, and Arkansas supporting himself by preaching, but after marrying, he and his wife contracted malaria and this illness gave him the incentive to attend medical school. In 1889 Dr. Hare moved his family from Arkansas to Childress County, Texas, where for fifteen years he was the only

doctor within a radius of forty miles. A devoted physician, he would stay with a patient for days until their crisis had passed, but Dr. Hare was just as attentive to the spiritual well-being of his patients. When one patient, not known for his Christian virtues, was fatally ill he told the man in plain language that there was no chance for his recovery. "'Make your peace with God, for your time is near! And there is nothing I can do for you, I am going home!'. . . . Dr. Hare was really interested in saving souls, and he could not allow one to depart unwarned." "Dr. George Hare," n.d, RCP-PHM.

3. Zane Mason, "Some Experiences of Baptists on the Texas Frontier," *West Texas Historical Association Year Book* 36 (1960): 62.

4. Ibid.

5. Berryman, *Pioneer Preacher*, p. 72.

6. Lewis, *Nothing to Make a Shadow*, p. 84.

7. Parmer County [Texas] Historical Commission. *Prairie Progress*, p. 118.

8. Dale, *Frontier Ways*, p. 219.

9. Carroll, "Social Life," p. 17.

10. Parmer County [Texas] Historical Commission, *Prairie Progress*, p. 22.

11. Rutherford, *One Corner*, p. 26.

12. Margaret Locke Kirk, "Memorable Extracts from Mrs. M. B. Wright's Experiences in the North Panhandle," n.d., RCP-PHM; Holland, interview; L. E. Jones was equally adamant: "There just wasn't much to [go to] back in them days, I'll tell you. Everybody'd go." L. E. Jones, recorded interview with the author, Dec. 16, 1986, Amarillo, Tex., RCP-PHM.

Joe Gibson said that because of their isolation, families had to entertain themselves, so if the opportunity came to attend a camp meeting "it was really a highlighting thing in their lives." Gibson, interview, Oct. 7, 1986, RCP-PHM.

13. Black, interview, Sept. 12, 1986.

14. Collyns, interview.

15. Ebbutt, *Emigrant Life*, p. 124.

16. Holland, interview.

17. Caldwell, interview, Mar. 17, 1986.

18. Walsh, interview, Nov. 13, 1986; Phares, *Bible in Pocket*, p. 90.

19. Ebbutt, *Emigrant Life*, p. 124.

20. Doshier, interview.

21. Ott, interview.

22. Bruce, Jr., *And They All Sang*, p. 91; Arthur Austin, *The Family Book of Hymns*, p. 13.

23. Hunter, "A Campmeeting at Menardville," p. 434; S. P. Elkins, Chapter 12, in *Pioneer Days in the Southwest from 1850 to 1879*, p. 270.

24. Evans, *Cowboys' Hitchin' Post*, p. 21; Mr. and Mrs. Newton Harrell, recorded interview with the author, Mar. 14, 1986, Canyon, Tex., RCP-PHM.

25. Minnie D. Clifton, "The Bloys Camp Meeting," *Sul Ross State Teachers College Bulletin* 27, no. 2 (1958): 43, JEHC—Midland; Hart, "History of Pioneer Days," p. 145.

26. Shelton, interview, Dec. 18, 1986.

27. Pitts, "At Home in a Dugout"; Duncan, "Recollections of a Pioneer Mother."

28. Dana Harmon Trent, "The Gay Nineties in the Panhandle," n.d., p. 1, RCP-PHM.

29. Caldwell, interview, Mar. 17, 1986.

30. Margaret A. Elliot, "A Visit With a Daughter of the Great Plains: Memoirs of Mrs. Fred Hornsbrugh," 1936, p. 8, RCP-PHM.

31. Davidson, interview.

32. Goodwyn, *Lone-Star Land*, p. 233.

33. Cosby, interview, Sept. 5, 1986.

34. Caldwell, interview, Mar. 17, 1986.

35. Culp, interview.

36. Shelton, interview, Dec. 18, 1986.

37. Norman, "Childhood on the Southern Plains," p. 106.

38. Ibid., p. 110.

39. Evans, *Cowboys' Hitchin' Post*, p. 13.

40. Miller, *Pioneering in North Texas*, p. 196.

41. Goodwyn, *Lone-Star Land*, p. 233.

42. Ammerman, *Baptist Battles*, p. 28.

43. Berryman, *Pioneer Preacher*, p. 98.

44. Dale, *Frontier Ways*, p. 219.

45. Roy Ransom, recorded interview with the author, Apr. 3, 1987, Claude, Tex., RCP-PHM.

46. Dale, *Frontier Ways*, p. 219; Mary Fannie Miles, "My First Days in Texas," n.d., RCP-PHM; Ochiltree County Historical Survey Committee, *Wheatheart*, p. 190.

47. Ochiltree County Historical Survey Committee, *Wheatheart*, p. 190.

48. Willis, interview.

49. Caldwell, interview, Mar. 1, 1984.

50. Young, "Thirty Years in Texas Pulpit and School," p. 347.

51. Holcomb, interview.

52. McClary, interview, July 10, 1984.

53. Avent, interview, June 10, 1985.

54. Shelton, interview, Mar. 15, 1984.

55. Gibson, interview, Nov. 28, 1984; Lowes, interview, Mar. 23, 1984; McClure, interview; Pendleton, interview.

56. Holmes, *Covered Wagon Women*, Vol. 10 (1875–83), p. 79; Willis, interview.

57. Hart, "History of Pioneer Days," p. 147.

58. Black, interview, July 20, 1984.

59. Jamison, "Short Sketches of History of Ochiltree County."

60. Hunt, *The Long Trail from Texas*, p. 254.

61. Ibid., p. 255.

62. John Myers Myers, *The Westerners: A Roundup of Pioneer Reminiscences*, p. 20; Hart, "History of Pioneer Days," p. 164. Barbara Allen finds in western legends the common motif of a young man on horseback riding a very long distance, in an exceptionally short time, and under difficult circumstances, carrying an important message or seeking help in an emergency. Barbara Allen, "Story in Oral History: Clues to Historical Consciousness," *The Journal of American History* 79, no. 2 (Sept., 1992): 607.

63. B. A. Oden, "Early Cowboy Days in New Mexico and Texas," n.d., p. 20, JEHC—Midland.

64. Bynum, notes to J. Evetts Haley.

65. Mitchell Jones, Sr., interview, Mar. 8, 1984.

66. White, interview, Aug. 10, 1984.

67. Deitiker, interview.

68. Albert Byars, recorded interview with the author, July 27, 1984, Canyon, Tex., RCP-PHM. Although it occurred more recently, one Panhandle resident spoke of a time her uncle was in the hospital, very ill, and it came time for harvest. She looked out one morning a little after daybreak, and down the road came binders and other equipment to harvest his crop. "It was just his friends and neighbors. . . . just those upper old timers you know and they did that. . . . Some came up to ten miles to help Uncle Ed and harvest Uncle Ed's crop." Ruth Glail, interview with Michael C. Young, 1990, RCP-PHM.

69. Rutherford, *One Corner*, p. 137.

70. Black, interview, July 20, 1984.

71. Colt, *Went to Kansas*, p. 178.

72. Ibid., p. 180.

73. Hamlin Garland, "The Noonday Plain," in *Prairie Songs*, p. 89.

74. Elkins, Chapter 12, in *Pioneer Days in the Southwest from 1850 to 1879*, p. 270.

75. Caldwell, interview, Mar. 1, 1984.

Bibliography

Abbott, E. C., and Helena Huntington Smith. *We Pointed Them North.* New York: Farrar and Rinehart, Inc., 1939.

Abbott, Keene. "The Great Plains." *The Prairie Schooner.* Vol. 1. New York: Kraus Reprint Corporation, 1927, pp. 93–94.

Abraham, Naceeb. Recorded interview with the author. November 5, 1993. Amarillo, Tex. Tape recording, Research Center, Panhandle-Plains Historical Museum, Canyon, Tex.

Adams, Andy. *The Log of a Cowboy: A Narrative of the Old Trail Days.* Boston: Houghton Mifflin Company, 1931.

———. *Cattle Brands: A Collection of Western Camp-Fire Stories.* Freeport, N.Y.: Books for Libraries Press, 1971.

Adams, Ramon F. *Cowboy Lingo.* Boston: Houghton Mifflin Company, 1936.

———. *Western Words: A Dictionary of the Range, Cow Camp and Trail.* Norman: University of Oklahoma Press, 1944.

———. *The Old-Time Cowhand.* New York: The Macmillan Company, 1961.

Albers, Adelheid. Recorded interview with the author. Canyon, Tex. June 22, 1984. Tape recording, Research Center, Panhandle-Plains Historical Museum, Canyon, Tex.

Albert, Marilyn, ed. *God, Grass, and Grit, Vol. II: History of the Sherman County Trade Area.* [Hereford, Tex.]: Pioneer Book Publishers, Inc., 1975.

Albright, Max. "Daughter Fulfills Father's Wish." *Amarillo Globe-News* 84, no. 184 (March 28, 1994): Section C, p. 1.

Alderson, Nannie T., and Helena Huntington Smith. *A Bride Goes West.* Lincoln: University of Nebraska Press, 1942.

Allen, Barbara. "Story in Oral History: Clues to Historical Consciousness." *The Journal of American History* 79, no. 2 (September, 1992): 606–11.

————. "Shaping History: The Creation of a Collective Pioneer Experience." *Columbia* 7, no. 4 (winter, 1993–94): 6–13.

Allen, John L. "The Garden-Desert Continuum: Competing Views of the Great Plains in the Nineteenth Century." *Great Plains Quarterly* 5 (fall, 1985): 207–20.

Allred, Ralph. Recorded interview with the author. May 4, 1984. Amarillo, Tex. Tape recording, Research Center, Panhandle-Plains Historical Museum, Canyon, Tex.

Alvis, Berry Newton. "History of Union County, New Mexico." *New Mexico Historical Review*, vol. 22, no. 3 (1947): 247–73.

Ammerman, Nancy Tatom. *Baptist Battles: Social Change and Religious Conflict in the Southern Baptist Convention*. New Brunswick, N.J.: Rutgers University Press, 1990.

Amon, Silas. "Daguerreotype on a Tombstone." *The Prairie Schooner.* Vol. 1. New York: Kraus Reprint Corporation, 1927.

Andreadis, Harriette. "True Womanhood Revisited: Women's Private Writing in Nineteenth-Century Texas." *Journal of the Southwest* 31, no. 2 (1989): 179–204.

Andrew, Catherine. "Frontier Women of the Texas Panhandle." Master's Thesis, West Texas State University, 1973.

Archambeau, Ernest R. "The First Federal Census in the Panhandle, 1880." *Panhandle-Plains Historical Review* 23 (1950): 22–132.

Archer, Ruby Cole. Recorded interview with the author. June 4, 1993. Amarillo, Tex. Tape recording, Research Center, Panhandle-Plains Historical Museum, Canyon, Tex.

Armitage, Susan. "Women and Men in Western History: A Stereoptical Vision." *The Western Historical* Quarterly 16, no. 1 (1985): 382–95.

Armstrong, Margaret. "Diary of Margaret Armstrong." J. Evetts Haley Collection, Nita Stewart Haley Memorial Library, Midland, Tex.

Auden, W. H. *The Shield of Achilles*. New York: Random House, 1955.

Austin, Arthur. *The Family Book of Hymns*. New York: Funk & Wagnalls Company, 1950.

Avent, Lavert. Recorded interviews with the author. June 10, 1985, and December 18, 1986. Canyon, Tex. Tape recordings, Research Center, Panhandle-Plains Historical Museum, Canyon, Tex.

Bagwell, Mrs. N. S. Interview with Zella Hollingsworth. 1938. Research Center, Panhandle-Plains Historical Museum, Canyon, Tex.

Baird, Josie. 1935. The Two Circles Bar Ranch. Research Center, Panhandle-Plains Historical Museum, Canyon, Tex.

Baker, James H. Diary. 1858–1872. J. Evetts Haley Collection, Nita Stewart Haley Memorial Library, Midland, Tex.

Baker, Jennie. Recorded interview with the author. October 3, 1986. Canyon,

Tex. Tape recording, Research Center, Panhandle-Plains Historical Museum, Canyon, Tex.

Balderston, Lucile. "Recollections of a Cowboy, Mr. R. E. (Bob) Foster." 1940. Research Center, Panhandle-Plains Historical Museum, Canyon, Tex.

Baldwin, Byron. Interview with Kay Lincycomb. 1977. Research Center, Panhandle-Plains Historical Museum, Canyon, Tex.

Baldwin, Mrs. Charlie. Charlie Baldwin Papers. 1898. Southwest Collection, Texas Tech University, Lubbock.

Barbour, Barton H. "Westward to Health: Gentlemen Health-Seekers on the Santa Fe Trail." *Journal of the West* 28, no. 2 (1989): 39–43.

Barker, Buster. "Days with My Father (Story of Judge P. W. Myers): Mrs. Hugh Longino to Buster Barker." 1940. Research Center, Panhandle-Plains Historical Museum, Canyon, Tex.

———. "Memoirs of Sara Leon Coleman." 1940. Research Center, Panhandle-Plains Historical Museum, Canyon, Tex.

Barker, Jess. Recorded interview with the author. September 27, 1984. Canyon, Tex. Tape recording, Research Center, Panhandle-Plains Historical Museum, Canyon, Tex.

Barker, Roger G. "The Influence of Frontier Environments on Behavior." In *The American West: New Perspectives, New Dimensions*, ed. Jerome O. Steffen. Norman: University of Oklahoma Press, 1979.

Bartlett, J. H. Interview with Louise Keaton. 1966. Research Center, Panhandle-Plains Historical Museum, Canyon, Tex.

Bartlett, Richard A. *The New Country: A Social History of the American Frontier 1776–1890*. New York: Oxford University Press, 1974.

Bedford, H. G. "Memoirs." n.d. Research Center, Panhandle-Plains Historical Museum, Canyon, Tex.

Bell, Irbin H. Interview with J. Evetts Haley. 1927. Research Center, Panhandle-Plains Historical Museum, Canyon, Tex.

Bell, Velma. Recorded interview with the author. January 30, 1987. Claude, Tex. Tape recording, Research Center, Panhandle-Plains Historical Museum, Canyon, Tex.

Bennett, Mildred R. "Willa Cather and the Prairie." *Nebraska History* 56, no. 2 (1975): 231–36.

Bentley, Max. "The Gospel West of the Pecos." *Frontier Times* 1, no. 6 (1924): 4–7.

———. "The 'Little Minister' Who First Carried the Gospel into the Cow Camps of the West." *Fort Worth Star-Telegram*, August 25, 1923, pp. 4–8.

Benton, W. B. "This Is the Partial Story of My Father's Early Life in the Panhandle As He Had Started to Write It." 1940. Research Center, Panhandle-Plains Historical Museum, Canyon, Tex.

Berger, William E. "A Kansas Revival of 1872." *The Kansas Historical Quarterly* 13, no. 4 (1957): 368–81.

Berryman, Opal Leigh. *Pioneer Preacher.* New York: Thomas Y. Crowell Company, 1948.

Beverly, Bob. "Lonely Graves in Lonely Places." *Frontier Times* 26, no. 9 (1949): 232–34.

Biddy, Claude. Interview with Christopher Biddy. 1969. Research Center, Panhandle-Plains Historical Museum, Canyon, Tex.

Billington, Ray Allen. *America's Frontier Heritage.* New York: Holt, Rinehart and Winston, 1966.

"The Biography of Edward Baxter Featherston." n.d. Research Center, Panhandle-Plains Historical Museum, Canyon, Tex.

Black, Tom. Recorded interviews with the author. July 20, 1984, and September 12, 1986. Canyon, Tex. Tape recordings, Research Center, Panhandle-Plains Historical Museum, Canyon, Tex.

Blauner, Robert. "Death and Social Structure." *Psychiatry* 29 (1966): 378–94.

Blodgett, Jan. *Land of Bright Promise: Advertising the Texas Panhandle and South Plains, 1870–1917.* Austin: University of Texas Press, 1988.

Bloom, John P. "New Mexico Viewed by Americans 1846–1849." *New Mexico Historical Review* 34, no. 3 (1959): 165–98.

Bodnar, John. "Power and Memory in Oral History: Workers and Managers at Studebaker." *The Journal of American History* 75, no. 4 (March, 1989): 1201–21.

Boley, Tommy J., ed. *Ella Elgar Bird Dumont: An Autobiography of a West Texas Pioneer.* Austin: University of Texas Press, 1988.

Bonds, Mr. and Mrs. Posey. Recorded interviews with the author. October 1, 1984, and December 18, 1986. Happy, Tex. Tape recordings, Research Center, Panhandle-Plains Historical Museum, Canyon, Tex.

Bonnifield, Mrs. Frank. Interview with Donna Chambers. n.d. Research Center, Panhandle-Plains Historical Museum, Canyon, Tex.

Boone, Mrs. Claude. "Mrs. Claude Boone." n.d. Research Center, Panhandle-Plains Historical Museum, Canyon, Tex.

Boren, Carter E. *Religion on the Texas Frontier.* San Antonio: The Naylor Company, 1968.

Boswell, G. C. "James Abercrombie Hyder, Dean of West Texas Preachers." *West Texas Historical Association Year Book* 11 (1935): 38–46.

Boswell, J. M. "The Development of Mobeetie, Oldest Town in the Panhandle, and Its Social Activities." n.d. Research Center, Panhandle-Plains Historical Museum, Canyon, Tex.

Bosworth, Allan R. *Ozona Country.* New York: Harper and Row, 1964.

Bourland, G. B. E. Interview with Ruth Crabtree. 1937. Research Center, Panhandle-Plains Historical Museum, Canyon, Tex.

Bowen, David. Interview with L. F. Sheffy. 1939. Research Center, Panhandle-Plains Historical Museum, Canyon, Tex.

———. Interview with Maud Lummus. 1939. Research Center, Panhandle-Plains Historical Museum, Canyon, Tex.

Bower, Bruce. "Partners in Recall: Elderly Spouses Build Better Memories through Collaboration." *Science News* 152 (September 13, 1997): 174–75.

Branscum, Virginia Miksch. "Some Aspects of the Life of Women in Eastern New Mexico and the Texas Panhandle-Plains Area from 1875 to 1905." Master's Thesis, University of Texas, 1949.

Bridwell, Mr. and Mrs. J. N. Recorded interview with the author. October 28, 1994. Texoma, Tex. Tape recording, Research Center, Panhandle-Plains Historical Museum, Canyon, Tex.

"A Brief Life Sketch of Dr. J. C. Bagwell and Family in Texas, and the Early Panhandle, As Told to His Children, and As Remembered by the Children." n.d. Research Center, Panhandle-Plains Historical Museum, Canyon, Tex.

Briggs, Cecil. "Recollections of a Frontier Merchant. George Clairborne Harris to Cecil Briggs." 1937. Research Center, Panhandle-Plains Historical Museum, Canyon, Tex.

Britton, Wm. K. "Memoirs of C. E. Cheyne." 1937. Research Center, Panhandle-Plains Historical Museum, Canyon, Tex.

Brody, Eugene B., ed. *Behavior in New Environments*. Beverly Hills: Sage Publications, 1970.

Bronson, Edgar. *Reminiscences of a Ranchman*. New York: The McClure Company, 1908.

———. *The Red-Blooded Heroes of the Frontier*. New York: George H. Duran Company, 1910.

Brooks, Una M. "The Influence of the Pioneer Women Toward a Settled Social Life on the Llano Estacado." Master's Thesis, West Texas State Teachers College, 1941.

Brothers, Mary Hudson. *A Pecos Pioneer*. Albuquerque: The University of New Mexico Press, 1943.

Brown, Dee. *The Gentle Tamers: Women of the Old Wild West*. New York: Bantam Books, 1958.

Brown, Lesley. *The New Shorter Oxford English Dictionary*. Oxford: Clarendon Press, 1993.

Brown, Timmie. Recorded interview with the author. October 28, 1994. Stratford, Tex. Tape recording, Research Center, Panhandle-Plains Historical Museum, Canyon, Tex.

Browning, James N. "Western Ranch Life in Indian Times." n.d. Research Center, Panhandle-Plains Historical Museum, Canyon, Tex.

Bruce, Dickson D., Jr. *And They All Sang Hallelujah: Plain-Folk Camp-Meeting Religion, 1800–1845*. Knoxville: The University of Tennessee Press, 1974.

Burkhalter, Mrs. W. B. "A Pioneer Woman Recalls the Old Time Religion: The Life Story of Mrs. Fannie Maude Wyatt." 1938. Research Center, Panhandle-Plains Historical Museum, Canyon, Tex.

Burns, Emma Boles. "Diary of Mrs. Emma Boles Burns, 1889." 1889. Southwest Collection, Texas Tech University, Lubbock.

Brunson, B. R. *The Texas Land and Development Company: A Panhandle Promotion, 1912–1956*. Austin: University of Texas Press, 1970.

Burrus, Mrs. Edward Neal. Interview with Pollyanna B. Hughes. 1964. Research Center, Panhandle-Plains Historical Museum, Canyon, Tex.

Byars, Albert. Recorded interview with the author. July 27, 1984. Canyon, Tex. Tape recording, Research Center, Panhandle-Plains Historical Museum, Canyon, Tex.

Byars, Mr. and Mrs. Albert. Recorded interview with the author. October 10, 1986. Canyon, Tex. Tape recording, Research Center, Panhandle-Plains Historical Museum, Canyon, Tex.

Bynum, S. K. Notes to J. Evetts Haley from S. K. Bynum. 1925. Research Center, Panhandle-Plains Historical Museum, Canyon, Tex.

———. "Recollections." n.d. Research Center, Panhandle-Plains Historical Museum, Canyon, Tex.

Caldwell, Marcia. Recorded interviews with the author. March 1, 1984, and March 17, 1986. Canyon, Tex. Tape recordings, Research Center, Panhandle-Plains Historical Museum, Canyon, Tex.

Carr, Robert V. *Cowboy Lyrics*. Chicago: W. B. Conkey Company, 1908.

Carroll, H. B. "Coronado's Step-Children: Social Life in the Early South Plains." *West Texas Historical Association Year Book* 9 (1933): 60–68.

———. "Social Life in West Texas From 1875 to 1890." Master's Thesis, Texas Tech College, 1928.

Carter, Beulah. Recorded interview with the author. November 11, 1993. Amarillo, Tex. Tape recording, Research Center, Panhandle-Plains Historical Museum, Canyon, Tex.

"Carter, Mrs. Ellen." n.d. Research Center, Panhandle-Plains Historical Museum, Canyon, Tex.

Cash, Mrs. Harvey. Interview with James Webb. 1965. Research Center, Panhandle-Plains Historical Museum, Canyon, Tex.

Cator Family Papers. 1871–1927. Research Center, Panhandle-Plains Historical Museum, Canyon, Tex.

Cave, Mrs. Clyde. Interview with Sharon Corica. 1969. Research Center, Panhandle-Plains Historical Museum, Canyon, Tex.

Chisholm, Fannie G. "The True Story of the Chisholm Trail." *The Cattleman* 42, no. 6 (1960): 26–52.

Chrisman, Harry E. *The 1,001 Most-Asked Questions About the American West.* Athens: Ohio University Press, 1982.

Christ-Janer, Albert, Charles W. Hughes, and Carleton S. Smith. *American Hymns Old and New.* New York: Columbia University Press, 1980.

Clark, Badger. "A Cowboy's Prayer." In *Sun and Saddle Leather.* Boston: Richard G. Badger, The Gorham Press, 1922.

Clark, Orrie. "Autobiography of Orrie Clark." n.d. Research Center, Panhandle-Plains Historical Museum, Canyon, Tex.

Clarke, Mary Whatley. "The Founding of the Matador." *The Cattleman* 43, no. 5 (1956): 42–63.

Clay, John. *My Life on the Range.* Norman: University of Oklahoma Press, 1962.

Cleaveland, Agnes Morley. *No Life for a Lady.* Boston: Houghton Mifflin Company, 1941.

Cleveland, Catharine C. *The Great Revival in the West 1797–1805.* Chicago: The University of Chicago Press, 1916.

Clifton, Minnie D. "The Bloys Camp Meeting." *Sul Ross State Teachers College Bulletin* 27, no. 2 (1958): 17–46. J. Evetts Haley Collection, Nita Stewart Haley Memorial Library, Midland, Tex.

Cline, Isaac M. "Hot Winds in Texas, May 29 and 30, 1892." *The American Meteorological Journal* 9, no. 10 (February, 1893): 437–43.

———. "Summer Hot Winds on the Great Plains." *Bulletin* [Philosophical Society of Washington] 12 (March, 1894): 309–48.

Coe, Wilbur. *Ranch on the Ruidoso: The Story of a Pioneer Family in New Mexico, 1871–1968.* New York: Alfred A. Knopf, 1969.

Cohn, David L. "Mr. Speaker." *The Atlantic Monthly* 170, no. 4 (1942): 73–78.

Coleman, P. C. "Experiences of a Pioneer Doctor." *West Texas Historical Association Year Book* 7 (1931): 35–39.

Collinson, Frank. Letter. August 25, 1939. "Work Projects Administration" File. Research Center, Panhandle-Plains Historical Museum, Canyon, Tex.

Collinson, Frank. *Life in the Saddle.* Norman: University of Oklahoma Press, 1963.

———. "Tongue River's First Ranch." n.d. Research Center, Panhandle-Plains Historical Museum, Canyon, Tex.

Collyns, Bill. Recorded telephone interview with the author. May 27, 1994. Tape recording, Research Center, Panhandle-Plains Historical Museum, Canyon, Tex.

Colt, Miriam Davis. *Went to Kansas.* Ann Arbor, Mich.: University Microfilms, Inc., 1966; Waterford: L. Ingals and Company, 1862.

Conner, Mrs. W. G. Interview with L. F. Sheffy. 1934. Research Center, Panhandle-Plains Historical Museum, Canyon, Tex.

Connor, Seymour V. "The West Is for Us: The Reminiscences of Mary A. Blankenship." *The Museum Journal* [Texas Technological College] 2 (1958): 70.

Conrad, Joseph. *Victory.* New York: The Modern Library, 1915.

"Consumptives Unwelcome in Texas." *Journal of the American Medical Association* 52 (April 3, 1909): 1118.

Cosby, C. N. Recorded interviews with the author. February 28 and September 5, 1986. Canyon, Texas. Tape recordings, Research Center, Panhandle-Plains Historical Museum, Canyon, Tex.

Cowan, Mrs. Charley Ross. Interview with R. W. Stewart. 1946. Research Center, Panhandle-Plains Historical Museum, Canyon, Tex.

Cox, Mrs. Bob. "Biography of Martha Lou Wesley." n.d. Research Center, Panhandle-Plains Historical Museum, Canyon, Tex.

Cox, Vera. Interview with Karen Gilmore. 1967. Research Center, Panhandle-Plains Historical Museum, Canyon, Tex.

Crabtree, Ruth. The Memoirs of Mr. G. B. E. Bourland. 1937. Research Center, Panhandle-Plains Historical Museum, Canyon, Tex.

Craik, Fergus I. M., and Janine M. Jennings. "Human Memory." In *The Handbook of Aging and Cognition*, ed. Fergus I. M. Craik and Timothy A. Salthouse. Hillsdale, N.J.: Lawrence Erlbaum Associates, Publishers, 1992.

Cranfill, J. B. *From Memory: Reminiscences, Recitals, and Gleanings From a Bustling and Busy Life.* Nashville: Broadman Press, 1937.

Cronon, William. "A Place for Stories: Nature, History, and Narrative." *The Journal of American History* 78, no. 4 (March, 1992): 1347–76.

Crosby County Pioneer Memorial in Cooperation with Crosby County Historical Commission. *Gone, But Not Forgotten: A Cemetery Survey of Crosby County.* Crosbyton, Tex.: Quality Printers and Typographers, 1983.

Cross, Cora Mellon. "An Old Trail Driver Talks About Early Days" [From *Dallas Semi-Weekly News*] *Frontier Times* 1, no. 8 (1924): 26–27.

Cross, Ruth. Recorded interview with the author. April 20, 1984. Canyon, Tex. Tape recording, Research Center, Panhandle-Plains Historical Museum, Canyon, Tex.

Crowley, H. E. "The Wife of the Pioneer." *The Cattleman* 1, no. 10 (1915): 59–97.

Crudgington, John W. Interview with John B. Hines. n.d. Research Center, Panhandle-Plains Historical Museum, Canyon, Tex.

Culp, Bertie. Recorded interview with the author. December 18, 1986. Happy, Tex. Tape recording, Research Center, Panhandle-Plains Historical Museum, Canyon, Tex.

Currie, Mrs. Thomas. Interview. 1938. Research Center, Panhandle-Plains Historical Museum, Canyon, Tex.

Curry, W. Hubert. *Sun Rising on the West: The Saga of Henry Clay and Elizabeth Smith.* Crosbyton, Tex.: Quality Printers and Typographers, 1979.

Dale, Edward Everett. *Cow Country.* Norman: University of Oklahoma Press, 1965.

———. *Frontier Ways: Sketches of Life in the Old West.* Austin: University of Texas Press, 1959.

Daily, H. L. "Higgins [Texas]." 1940. Research Center, Panhandle-Plains Historical Museum, Canyon, Tex.

Dary, David. *Cowboy Culture: A Saga of Five Centuries.* New York: Alfred A. Knopf, 1981.

Davidson, Oneita. Recorded interview with the author. November 12, 1994. Hereford, Tex. Tape recording, Research Center, Panhandle-Plains Historical Museum, Canyon, Tex.

Davis, Alberta. "Memoirs of a JA Cowboy: Jim Hastings." 1939. Research Center, Panhandle-Plains Historical Museum, Canyon, Tex.

———. "Memoirs of J. A. Hornbeak, Hereford, Texas." 1937. Research Center, Panhandle-Plains Historical Museum, Canyon, Tex.

Deahl, Lillian Hagins. "Mr. and Mrs. John F. Weatherly, Prominent Pioneer Carson County Citizens." n.d. Research Center, Panhandle-Plains Historical Museum, Canyon, Tex.

Debo, Angie. "The Diary of Charles Hazelrigg." *The Chronicles of Oklahoma* 25, no. 3 (1947): 229–70.

Deitiker, Gladys. Recorded interview with the author. July 24, 1984. Amarillo, Tex. Tape recording, Research Center, Panhandle-Plains Historical Museum, Canyon, Tex.

Dick, Everett. *The Sod-House Frontier 1854–1890.* Lincoln, Nebr.: Johnsen Publishing Company, 1954.

———. *The Story of the Frontier.* New York: Tudor Publishing Company, 1941.

Dixon, Mrs. William. "Reminiscences of a Pioneer As Told to Wilda Talbot." 1938. Research Center, Panhandle-Plains Historical Museum, Canyon, Tex.

Doan, C. F. Interview with J. Evetts Haley. 1926. Research Center, Panhandle-Plains Historical Museum, Canyon, Tex.

Dobie, J. Frank. *The Longhorns.* New York: Bramhall House, 1941.

Dorough, C. Dwight. *Mr. Sam.* New York: Random House, 1962.

Doshier, Inez Christian. "Lone Prairie Graves." *Amarillo Sunday Globe-News* 13, no. 33 (August 14, 1938): Section B, p. 26.

———. Recorded interview with the author. November 7, 1986. Amarillo, Tex. Tape recording, Research Center, Panhandle-Plains Historical Museum, Canyon, Tex.

"Dr. George Hare." n.d. Research Center, Panhandle-Plains Historical Museum, Canyon, Tex.

Dubbs, Emanuel. Chapter 2: "Personal Reminiscences" and Chapter 3 in *Pioneer Days in the Southwest from 1850 to 1879: Thrilling Descriptions of Buffalo Hunting, Indian Fighting and Massacres, Cowboy Life and Home Building*, contrib. Charles Goodnight, Emanuel Dubbs, John A Hart and others. Guthrie, Okla.: The State Capital Company, 1909.

Duke, Cordia, and Joe B. Frantz. *6,000 Miles of Fence: Life on the XIT Ranch of Texas*. Austin: University of Texas Press, 1961.

Duncan, Mrs. Arthur B. "Recollections of a Pioneer Mother." n.d. Research Center, Panhandle-Plains Historical Museum, Canyon, Tex.

Dunn, R. F. Dunn Papers. n.d. Southwest Collection, Texas Tech University, Lubbock.

Dunn, R. F. "First Evangel For Methodist Church in This Section Recalls Day of Pulpit Pioneering." [Unidentified, undated newspaper article.] Dunn Papers. Southwest Collection, Texas Tech University, Lubbock.

Durham, Aulton. "Memoirs of M. C. Potter." 1936. Research Center, Panhandle-Plains Historical Museum, Canyon, Tex.

Eaves, Charles Dudley, and C. A. Hutchinson. *Post City, Texas*. Austin: Texas State Historical Association, 1952.

Ebbutt, Percy G. *Emigrant Life in Kansas*. New York: Arno Press, 1975.

Elkins, S. P. Chapter 12. In *Pioneer Days in the Southwest from 1850 to 1879: Thrilling Descriptions of Buffalo Hunting, Indian Fighting and Massacres, Cowboy Life and Home Building*, contrib. Charles Goodnight, Emanuel Dubbs, John A. Hart and others. Guthrie, Okla.: The State Capital Company, 1909.

Elliot, Margaret A. "A Visit With a Daughter of the Great Plains: Memoirs of Mrs. Fred Hornsbrugh." 1936. Research Center, Panhandle-Plains Historical Museum, Canyon, Tex.

Ellis, Temple A. *Road to Destiny*. San Antonio: Naylor Company, 1939.

———. "Texas Plains Pioneers" [Microfilm E47]. n.d. Southwest Collection, Texas Tech University, Lubbock.

———. "Trails of Long Ago." n.d. Southwest Collection, Texas Tech University, Lubbock.

Ellison, Glenn R. *Cowboys Under the Mongollon Rim*. Tucson: The University of Arizona Press, 1968.

"Emma A. Wynett-Booker." 1940. Research Center, Panhandle-Plains Historical Museum, Canyon, Tex.

Emrich, Duncan. *American Folk Poetry: An Anthology*. Boston: Little, Brown, and Company, 1974.

Engelbrecht, Mr. and Mrs. Joe E. Recorded interview with the author. July 11, 1994. Amarillo, Tex. Tape recording, Research Center, Panhandle-Plains Historical Museum, Canyon, Tex.

Estlack, J. C. "My Panhandle I Salute You: Speech on Pioneer Day at the Tri-

State Fair in Amarillo [Texas], September 23, 1936." 1936. Research Center, Panhandle-Plains Historical Museum, Canyon, Tex.

"European Folk Islands in Northwest Texas: Introduction." *Panhandle-Plains Historical Review* 41 (1983): iv–v.

Evans, Joe M. *Bloys: Cowboy Camp Meeting.* El Paso: Guynes Printing Company, 1959.

———. *The Cowboys' Hitchin' Post.* El Paso: Joe Evans, n.d.

Everett, Mrs. W. A. Interview with Mike Everett. 1975. Research Center, Panhandle-Plains Historical Museum, Canyon, Tex.

Evernden, Neil. "Beauty and Nothingness: Prairie as Failed Resource." *Landscape* 27, no. 3 (1983): 1–8.

Fairchild, Louis. "Death and Dying on the Southern Great Plains Around 1900." *Panhandle-Plains Historical Review* 59 (1986): 35–53.

Faragher, John M. *Women and Men on the Overland Trail.* New Haven: Yale University Press, 1979.

Farley, Lula Mae. "Women Rode the Range." *Amarillo Sunday News-Globe* 13, no. 33 (August 14, 1938): Section D, p. 25.

Farrington, Jessie de Prado. "Rocking Horse to Cow Pony (Continued)." *New Mexico Historical Review* 30, no. 4 (1955): 313–39.

Farseth, Pauline, and Theodore C. Blegen. *Frontier Mother: The Letters of Gro Svendsen.* Northfield, Minn.: The Norwegian-American Historical Association, 1950.

Featherston, Edward Baxter. *A Pioneer Speaks.* Dallas: Cecil Baugh and Company, 1940.

Fedric, S. B. The Panhandle Fifty-Two Years Ago. n.d. Research Center, Panhandle-Plains Historical Museum, Canyon, Tex.

Fender, E. M. Interview with Roy Poff. 1969. Research Center, Panhandle-Plains Historical Museum, Canyon, Tex.

Fenton, James I. "Critters, Sourdough, and Dugouts: Women and Imitation Theory on the Staked Plains, 1875–1910." In *At Home on the Range: Essays on the History of Western Social and Domestic Life,* ed. John R. Wunder, p. 27. Westport, Conn.: Greenwood Press, 1985.

Fiefel, Herman. *New Meanings of Death.* New York: McGraw-Hill Book Company, 1977.

Fife, Austin, and Alta Fife. *Heaven on Horseback: Revivalist Songs and Verse in the Cowboy Idiom.* Logan: Utah State University Press, 1970.

Finke, Roger, and Rodney Stark. *The Churching of America, 1776–1990.* New Brunswick, N.J.: Rutgers University Press, 1992.

"The First Camp Meeting in America." *Frontier Times* 26, no. 7 (1949): 167–71.

Fite, Gilbert C. *The Farmers' Frontier: 1865–1900.* New York: Holt, Rinehart and Winston, 1966.

Fletcher, Baylis John. *Up the Trail in '79*. Norman: University of Oklahoma Press, 1968.

Fotheringham, Mrs. Neil F. "The Memoirs of Mrs. Lilian Bell, Dimmitt, Texas." 1936. Research Center, Panhandle-Plains Historical Museum, Canyon, Tex.

Frantz, Joe B., and Julian Ernest Choate, Jr. *The American Cowboy: The Myth and the Reality*. Norman: University of Oklahoma Press, 1955.

Fried, Marc. "Grieving for a Lost Home." In *Human Adaptation: Coping with Life Crises*, ed. Rudolf H. Moos, pp. 192–201. Lexington, Mass.: D. C. Heath and Company, 1976.

Frizzell, Lodisa. *Across the Plains to California in 1852: Journal of Mrs. Lodisa Frizzell*. New York: Public Library, 1915.

Frost, Margaret Fullerton. "Small Girl in a New Town." *Great Plains Journal* 19 (1980.): 2–73.

Fussell, Paul. *The Great War and Modern Memory*. New York: Oxford University Press, 1975.

Gacy, David B., II "Selling the Future: A Biography of William Pulver Soash." *Panhandle Plains Historical Review* 50 (1977): 1–75.

Gallaway, Ann. "Speaking of Texas: Keeping the Faith." *Texas Highways* 48, no. 1 (January, 2001): 3.

Galloup, Rex, Sr. "Dasie Martin Currie—Pioneers of Amarillo. 1939. Research Center, Panhandle-Plains Historical Museum, Canyon, Tex.

Galloway, Maude Smith. "Fifty Years in the Texas Panhandle." n.d. Research Center, Panhandle-Plains Historical Museum, Canyon, Tex.

Gard, Wayne. *The Chisholm Trail*. Norman: University of Oklahoma Press, 1954.

———. *Rawhide Texas*. Norman: University of Oklahoma Press, 1965.

Garland, Hamlin. *Prairie Song and Western Story*. Freeport, N.Y.: Books for Libraries Press, 1928.

———. *Prairie Songs*. Chicago: Stone and Kimball, 1893.

Garner, Mary. Recorded interview with the author. January 30, 1987. Claude, Tex. Tape recording, Research Center, Panhandle-Plains Historical Museum, Canyon, Tex.

Garnsey, Jean. "First Family of Amarillo [Mrs. Clarke H. Garnsey]." 1952. Research Center, Panhandle-Plains Historical Museum, Canyon, Tex.

Gates, The Rev. P. H. Interview with Charles R. Gates. 1936. Research Center, Panhandle-Plains Historical Museum, Canyon, Tex.

German, Anna Lou. "The Harveys: Plains People." 1970. Research Center, Panhandle-Plains Historical Museum, Canyon, Tex.

Gibson, Mr. and Mrs. Joe. Recorded interviews with the author. November 28, 1984, and October 7, 1986. Canyon, Texas. Tape recordings, Research Center, Panhandle-Plains Historical Museum, Canyon, Tex.

Gilbert, Mrs. Cline. Interview with Winnie Davis Hale. 1941. Research Center, Panhandle-Plains Historical Museum, Canyon, Tex.

Gilles, Albert S., Sr. "Death's First Visit to Old Faxon." *The Chronicles of Oklahoma* 44, no. 3 (1966): 307–12.

Gilmore, W. C. "Memoirs of P. L. Vardy, M.D." 1936. Research Center, Panhandle-Plains Historical Museum, Canyon, Tex.

Ginn, Mrs. O. B. "George T. Abbott on XIT." 1936. Research Center, Panhandle-Plains Historical Museum, Canyon, Tex.

Glail, Ruth. Interview with Michael C. Young. 1990. Research Center, Panhandle-Plains Historical Museum, Canyon, Tex.

Goff, John S. "Isham Reavis, Pioneer Lawyer and Judge." *Nebraska History* 54, no. 1 (1973): 1–46.

Goodnight, Charles, Emanuel Dubbs, John A. Hart and others, contribs. *Pioneer Days in the Southwest from 1850 to 1879: Thrilling Descriptions of Buffalo Hunting, Indian Fighting and Massacres, Cowboy Life and Home Building.* Guthrie, Okla.: The State Capital Company, 1909.

Goodwyn, Frank. *Lone-Star Land: Twentieth-Century Texas in Perspective.* New York: Alfred A. Knopf, 1955.

Goody, Jack. "Death and the Interpretation of Culture: A Bibliographic Overview." *American Quarterly* 26, no. 5 (1974): 448–55.

Grant, Mattie L. "Memoirs of R. E. (Ranch) and Julia Smith McQueen." 1939. Research Center, Panhandle-Plains Historical Museum, Canyon, Tex.

———. 1939. "Miss Addie Rosalee Whitcomb Tells of Life in Amarillo [Texas]." Research Center, Panhandle-Plains Historical Museum, Canyon, Tex.

"Grave on a Lonely Rise." *Amarillo Sunday News-Globe* 13, no. 33 (August 14, 1938): Section E, p. 21.

Green, Duff. "Memoirs of Duff Green." *Panhandle-Plains Historical Review* 17 (1944): 68–93.

Greene, A. C. *A Personal Country.* College Station: Texas A&M University Press, 1969.

Grider, Sylvia Ann, and Sara Jarvis Jones. "The Cultural Legacy of Texas Cemeteries." *The Texas Humanist* 6, no. 5 (May–June, 1984): 34–39.

Griffin, Rosa Lee. "A Strange Story." 1978. Research Center, Panhandle-Plains Historical Museum, Canyon, Tex.

Griffith, Mary. "Memories of Charles Jackson Mapes." 1938. Research Center, Panhandle-Plains Historical Museum, Canyon, Tex.

Haley, J. Evetts. "Andrew Jackson Potter: Fighting Parson!" *The Shamrock*, summer, 1961, pp. 8–11. J. Evetts Haley Collection, Nita Stewart Haley Memorial Library, Midland, Tex.

———. "Cowboy-Sheriff." *The Shamrock*, summer, 1963, pp. 2–6. J. Evetts Haley Collection, Nita Stewart Haley Memorial Library, Midland, Tex.

———. "Panhandle Notes," Vol. 2, L–W. n.d. J. Evetts Haley Collection, Nita Stewart Haley Memorial Library, Midland, Tex.

———. "The XIT Ranch; As Remembered by Its Cowboys," Vol. 1, A–D. n.d. J. Evetts Haley Collection, Nita Stewart Haley Memorial Library, Midland, Tex.

———. "The XIT Ranch; As Remembered by its Cowboys," Vol. 4 (Mc–Y). n.d. J. Evetts Haley Collection, Nita Stewart Haley Memorial Library, Midland, Tex.

Haley, Mrs. J. Evetts. Personal communication with author. May 5, 1994.

Hall, Claude. *The Early History of Floyd County.* Canyon, Tex.: Research Center, Panhandle-Plains Historical Society, 1947.

Hall, Esther Jane Wood. "Cowboy Remedies on the Trail (Pharmaceuticals Since 1865)." *West Texas Historical Association Year Book* 41 (1965): 31–37.

Hall, Frances Edwards. Interview with Rebecca Carnes. 1980. Research Center, Panhandle-Plains Historical Museum, Canyon, Tex.

Hall, Gordon Langley. *The Sawdust Trail: The Story of American Evangelism.* Philadelphia: Macrae Smith Company, 1964.

Ham, Henry. Recorded interview with the author. December 16, 1986. Dumas, Tex. Tape recording, Research Center, Panhandle-Plains Historical Museum, Canyon, Tex.

Hamner, Laura V. *Light 'N Hitch: A Collection of Historical Writing Depicting Life on the High Plains.* Dallas: American Guild Press, 1958.

———. *Short Grass and Longhorns.* Norman: University of Oklahoma Press, 1943.

Hampsten, Elizabeth. *Read This Only to Yourself: The Private Writings of Midwestern Women, 1880–1910.* Bloomington: Indiana University Press, 1982.

———. *Settlers' Children: Growing Up on the Great Plains.* Norman: University of Oklahoma Press, 1991.

Hanners, LaVerne. *The Lords of the Valley: Including the Complete Text of* Our Unsheltered Lives *by Ed Lord.* Norman: University of Oklahoma Press, 1996.

Hard, William. "The Disappearance of the Great American Desert." *Munsey's Magazine* 40, no. 1 (1908): 71–75.

Hardeman, D. B., and Donald C. Bacon. *Rayburn: A Biography.* New York: Madison Books, 1987.

"Hardships and Happiness Tell Story of Mrs. Arthur Duncan, First Lady of Lloyd County [Texas]." n.d. Research Center, Panhandle-Plains Historical Museum, Canyon, Tex.

Hareven, Tamara K. "The Search for Generational Memory: Tribal Rites in Industrial Society." *Daedalus* 107, no. 4 (fall, 1978): 137–49.

Harrell, Mr. and Mrs. Newton. Recorded interview with the author. March 14,

1986. Canyon, Tex. Tape recording, Research Center, Panhandle-Plains Historical Museum, Canyon, Tex.

Harrell, Mrs. Ed. Interview with Dorothy Warwick. 1942. Research Center, Panhandle-Plains Historical Museum, Canyon, Tex.

Harrell, Newton. Recorded interview with the author. November 9, 1984. Claude, Tex. Tape recording, Research Center, Panhandle-Plains Historical Museum, Canyon, Tex.

Harrison, Loretta. "The Story of Mrs. Velma Heathington." 1970. Research Center, Panhandle-Plains Historical Museum, Canyon, Tex.

Hart, John A. "History of Pioneer Days in Texas and Oklahoma." Chapter 7 in *Pioneer Days in the Southwest from 1850 to 1879: Thrilling Descriptions of Buffalo Hunting, Indian Fighting and Massacres, Cowboy Life and Home Building*, contrib. Charles Goodnight, Emanuel Dubbs, John A. Hart and others. Guthrie, Okla.: The State Capital Company, 1909.

Harter, Lennie. Recorded interview with the author. September 21, 1984. Canyon, Tex. Tape recording, Research Center, Panhandle-Plains Historical Museum, Canyon, Tex.

Hartman, Eula. "Reminiscence of Mr. [Fred] Scott." 1933. Research Center, Panhandle-Plains Historical Museum, Canyon, Tex.

Hartsough, L. "Let Me Go." In *Church and Sunday School Hymnal*, ed. J. D. Brunk, p. 174. Scottsdale, Pa.: Mennonite Publishing House, 1902.

Harvey, Mrs. John B. "Early Settler Tells How First Post Office Came To Be Designated 'Shamrock.'" *The Shamrock Texan* 34, no. 103 (September 7, 1937): Section 4, p. 2.

Hascall, Jefferson. "My Latest Sun Is Sinking Fast." In *New Baptist Hymnal*, p. 313. Philadelphia: The American Baptist Publication Society, 1926.

Hastings, Frank S. *A Ranchman's Recollections: An Autobiography*. Chicago: The Breeder's Gazette, 1921.

Hatch, George Sidney. Interview with E. L. Hammit. 1946. Research Center, Panhandle-Plains Historical Museum, Canyon, Tex.

Havins, T. R. "Frontier Missionary Difficulties." *West Texas Historical Association Year Book* 15 (1939): 54–74.

Heath, Hellen. "Memoirs of Mrs. J. W. Hough." 1936. Research Center, Panhandle-Plains Historical Museum, Canyon, Tex.

"Hell in Texas." n.d. Research Center, Panhandle-Plains Historical Museum, Canyon, Tex.

Henderson, Eva Pendleton. *Wild Horses: A Turn-Of-The-Century Prairie Girlhood*. Santa Fe: Sunstone Press, 1983.

Henderson, Gracy. "A Month on Wheels: From the Diary of Mrs. Davidson and Interviews with Mr. Gracy Henderson." n.d. Research Center, Panhandle-Plains Historical Museum, Canyon, Tex.

Henderson, Mary M. "Mrs. J. N. Ivy." 1938. Research Center, Panhandle-Plains Historical Museum, Canyon, Tex.

Hendrix, John M. "The Bed Roll." *The Cattleman* 21, no. 4 (September, 1934): 10.

Henry, John Robert. Interview with Marie Farrington. 1941. Research Center, Panhandle-Plains Historical Museum, Canyon, Tex.

Henry, Stuart. *Conquering Our Great American Plains.* New York: E. P. Dutton and Company, Inc., 1930.

Hess, Marie. Interview with Pollyanna Hughes. 1956. Research Center, Panhandle-Plains Historical Museum, Canyon, Tex.

Hickman, Russell K. "Lewis Bodwell, Frontier Preacher; The Early Years." *The Kansas Historical Quarterly* 12, no. 3 (1943): 269–99.

Higgins, Pecos, and Joe Evans. *Pecos' Poems.* El Paso: Pecos Higgins and Joe Evans, 1956.

Hobart, Mrs. T. D. "Pioneer Days in the Panhandle Plains." *Panhandle-Plains Historical Review* 8 (1935): 65–78.

Hogan, William Ransom. *The Texas Republic: A Social and Economic History.* Norman: University of Oklahoma Press, 1946.

Holcomb, Jennie. Recorded interview with the author. July 5, 1984. Wellington, Tex. Tape recording, Research Center, Panhandle-Plains Historical Museum, Canyon, Tex.

Holden, Maggie Lee. "Memoirs." 1944–48. Charlie Baldwin Papers, Southwest Collection, Texas Tech University, Lubbock.

Holden, William Curry. *Alkali Trails: Or Social and Economic Movements of the Texas Frontier 1846–1900.* Dallas: The Southwest Press, 1930.

———. *Alton Hutson: Reminiscences of a South Plains Youth.* San Antonio: Trinity University Press, 1975.

———. *The Spur Ranch.* Boston: The Christopher Publishing House, 1934.

Holland, Mrs. H. L. Recorded interview with the author. December 18, 1986. Happy, Tex. Tape recording, Research Center, Panhandle-Plains Historical Museum, Canyon, Tex.

Hollon, W. Eugene. *The Southwest: Old and New.* New York: Alfred A. Knopf, 1961.

Holmes, Kenneth L. *Covered Wagon Women: Diaries & Letters from the Western Trails 1840–1890,* Vol. 1, 1840–49; Vol. 2, 1850; Vol. 3, 1851; Vol. 4, 1852, The California Trail; Vol. 5, 1852, The Oregon Trail; Vol. 6, 1853–54; Vol. 7, 1854–60. Glendale, Calif.: The Arthur H. Clark Company, 1983–88.

———. 1989. *Covered Wagon Women: Diaries & Letters from the Western Trails 1840–1890,* Vol. 8, 1862–65; Vol. 9, 1864–68; Vol. 10, 1875–83; Vol. 11, 1879–1903. Spokane, Wash.: The Arthur H. Clark Company, 1989–93.

Holt, A. J. *Pioneering in the Southwest.* Nashville: Sunday School Board of the Southern Baptist Convention, 1923.

Hood, Evelyn. "Viewing a Half-Century of Plains Progress [L. P. Trumble]." 1933. Research Center, Panhandle-Plains Historical Museum, Canyon, Tex.

Hough, Emerson. *The Story of the Cowboy.* New York: Grosset and Dunlap, 1879.

Howell, Adelle. "Memoirs of John Gibson." n.d. Research Center, Panhandle-Plains Historical Museum, Canyon, Tex.

———. n.d. "Memoirs of William Carey Newton." Research Center, Panhandle-Plains Historical Museum, Canyon, Tex.

Hunt, Frazier. *The Long Trail from Texas: The Story of Ad Spaugh, Cattleman.* New York: Doubleday, Doran, and Company, Inc., 1940.

Hunt, George M. *Early Days Upon the Plains of Texas.* Lubbock, Tex.: George M. Hunt, 1919.

Hunter, J. Marvin. *The Trail Drivers of Texas.* Nashville: Cokesbury Press, 1925.

———. "A Campmeeting at Menardville in 1886." *Frontier Times* 18, no. 10 (1941): 433–36.

———. "The Early Day Doctors." *Frontier Times* 24, no. 10 (1947): 469–71.

Ise, John. *Sod and Stubble: The Story of a Kansas Homestead.* Lincoln: University of Nebraska Press, 1936.

Jackson, Billie Lloyd. "M. J. 'Uncle Dock' McCoy." 1940. Research Center, Panhandle-Plains Historical Museum, Canyon, Tex.

Jamison, Gladys. "A Short History of Lipscomb County." 1936. Research Center, Panhandle-Plains Historical Museum, Canyon, Tex.

———. "Short Sketches of History of Ochiltree County, Texas: Story of Life of Mrs. B. J. Jackson." 1937. Research Center, Panhandle-Plains Historical Museum, Canyon, Tex.

Jaques, Mary J. *Texan Ranch Life; With Three Months Through Mexico in a "Prairie Schooner."* College Station: Texas A&M University Press, 1989.

Jeffrey, Julie Roy. *Frontier Women: The Trans-Mississippi West 1840–1880.* New York: Hill and Wang, 1979.

———. "'There is Some Splendid Scenery': Women's Responses to the Great Plains Landscape." *Great Plains Quarterly* 8, no. 2 (1988): 69–78.

Jellison, Katherine. "Women and Technology on the Great Plains, 1910–1940." *Great Plains Quarterly* 8, no. 3 (1988): 145–57.

Johnson, Charles. "The Frontier Camp Meeting: Contemporary and Historical Appraisals, 1805–1840." *Mississippi Valley Historical Review* 37 (1950–51): 91–110.

———. *The Frontier Camp Meeting.* Dallas: Southern Methodist University Press, 1955.

Johnson, Vance. "This Was a Wide Open Country, and a Lonesome One Too, When Mitch Bell Arrived; Got First Job Cutting Cedar Posts." *Amarillo Daily News* 29, no. 51 (January 3, 1938): 5.

Jones, Billy M. *Health-Seekers in the Southwest, 1817–1900.* Norman: University of Oklahoma Press, 1967.

———. "Walter Dibrell: Early Methodist Circuit Rider in the Concho Basin." *West Texas Historical Association Year Book* 48 (1972): 111–22.

———. "West Texas: A Haven for Health Seekers." *West Texas Historical Association Year Book* 42 (1966): 3–14.

Jones, Coleman. "Writings of Coleman Jones." n.d. Research Center, Panhandle-Plains Historical Museum, Canyon, Tex.

Jones, G. H. "Reminiscences of Happy [Texas] Pioneers." 1940. Research Center, Panhandle-Plains Historical Museum, Canyon, Tex.

Jones, L. E. Recorded interview with the author. December 16, 1986. Amarillo, Tex. Tape recording, Research Center, Panhandle-Plains Historical Museum, Canyon, Tex.

Jones, Mack. "'Mack' Jones." 1940. Research Center, Panhandle-Plains Historical Museum, Canyon, Tex.

Jones, Mitchell, Sr. Recorded interviews with the author. March 8, 1984, and September 19, 1986. Canyon, Tex. Tape recordings, Research Center, Panhandle-Plains Historical Museum, Canyon, Tex.

Jones, Ollie. Recorded telephone interview with the author. December 10, 1986. Tape recording, Research Center, Panhandle-Plains Historical Museum, Canyon, Tex.

Jones, R. L. "Folk Life in Early Texas, Part II: The Autobiography of Andrew Davis." *The Southwestern Historical Quarterly* 43, no. 3 (1940): 323–41.

Jordan, Weymouth T. "A Soldier's Life on the Indian Frontier, 1876–1878: Letters of 2Lt. C. D. Cowles." *The Kansas Historical Quarterly* 28, no. 1 (1972): 144–55.

Jowell, Mrs. J. T. "Recollections of Mrs. J. T. Jowell as Related to Lucile Hughes." 1938. Research Center, Panhandle-Plains Historical Museum, Canyon, Tex

Judson, Phoebe Goodell. *A Pioneer's Search for an Ideal Home.* Lincoln: University of Nebraska Press, 1925.

Kastenbaum, Robert, and Ruth Aisenberg. *The Psychology of Death.* New York: Springer Publishing Company, Inc., 1972.

"Keffers, W. H." September 25, 1940. WPA Files, Research Center, Panhandle-Plains Historical Museum, Canyon, Tex.

Kennedy, Marguerite Wallace. *My Home on the Range.* Boston: Little, Brown and Company, 1951.

Killough, Joe. Interview with Mrs. D. T. Leachman. 1945. Research Center, Panhandle-Plains Historical Museum, Canyon, Tex.

Kimmis, Polly A. "Memoirs of a Pioneer Woman: Mrs. A. B. Duncan, Floydada, Texas." 1938. Research Center, Panhandle-Plains Historical Museum, Canyon, Tex.

King, Charles R. "The Woman's Experience of Childbirth on the Western Frontier." *Journal of the West* 29, no. 1 (1990): 76–84.

King, Laura Mabel Widmer. "Laura Mabel Widmer King." 1940. Research Center, Panhandle-Plains Historical Museum, Canyon, Tex.

King, Violet E. "Sweet Rest." In *Bethel Chimes: A Collection of New Songs for the Sabbath School, Church, and Home,* ed. Charles K. Langley and R. H. Randall, pp. 114–15. Marion, Iowa: R. H. Randall, 1891.

Kirk, Margaret Locke. "Memorable Extracts from Mrs. M. B. Wright's Experiences in the North Panhandle." n.d. Research Center, Panhandle-Plains Historical Museum, Canyon, Tex.

———. "The Story of a Gentle Lady Who Pioneered the Panhandle in 1882." 1938. Research Center, Panhandle-Plains Historical Museum, Canyon, Tex.

Kiskaddon, Bruce. *Rhymes of the Ranges and Other Poems.* n.p.: Bruce Kiskaddon, 1947.

Knupp, Rosalind. Interview with Karen Cornelius. 1980. Research Center, Panhandle-Plains Historical Museum, Canyon, Tex.

Lanman, C. O. "Memoirs of Mrs. George E. Legg." n.d. Research Center, Panhandle-Plains Historical Museum, Canyon, Tex.

Lawrence, Okla Mae. "The Life of Mrs. Alice Tubb." 1935. Research Center, Panhandle-Plains Historical Museum, Canyon, Tex.

Lewellen, Grace T. "Memoirs of J. C. Estlack." 1937. Research Center, Panhandle-Plains Historical Museum, Canyon, Tex.

———. "Memoirs: Mrs. Luella Harrah Macintire." 1937. Research Center, Panhandle-Plains Historical Museum, Canyon, Tex.

Lewis, Faye C. *Nothing to Make a Shadow.* Ames: The Iowa State University Press, 1971.

Lewis, G. Malcolm. "The Great Plains Region and Its Image of Flatness." *Journal of the West* 4, no. 1 (1967): 11–26.

Lewis, Willie Newbury. *Between Sun and Sod.* Clarendon, Tex.: Clarendon Press, 1938.

"The Life of Mr. and Mrs. J. H. Gorin." n.d. Research Center, Panhandle-Plains Historical Museum, Canyon, Tex.

Lindquist, Emory. "Religion in Kansas During the Era of the Civil War." *The Kansas Historical Quarterly* 25, no. 4 (1959): 407–37.

Lockhart, John W. "Old Fashioned Camp Meetings." *The Galveston Daily News* 56, no. 53 (Sunday, May 16, 1897): 19.

Loftin, Jack. *Trails Through Archer: A Centennial History—1880–1980.* Burnet, Tex.: Eakin Publications, 1979.

Lovejoy, Julia Louisa. "Letters from Kansas." *The Kansas Historical Quarterly* 11, no. 1 (1942): 29–44.

Lowes, Ruth. Recorded interviews with the author. March 23, 1984, and October 17, 1986. Canyon, Tex. Tape recordings, Research Center, Panhandle-Plains Historical Museum, Canyon, Tex.

Lutgens, Frederick K., and Edward J. Tarbuck. *The Atmosphere: An Introduction to Meteorology*. Upper Saddle River, N.J.: Prentice Hall, 1998.

Magoffin, Susan Shelby. *Down the Santa Fe Trail and Into Mexico*. New Haven: Yale University Press, 1926.

Majors, Alexander, and Colonel Prentiss Ingraham, eds. *Seventy Years on the Frontier: Alexander Majors' Memoirs of a Lifetime on the Border*. Columbus, Ohio: Long's College Book Company, 1950.

Mason, Zane. "Some Experiences of Baptists on the Texas Frontier." *West Texas Historical Association Year Book* 36 (1960): 51–62.

———. "Some Thoughts on Frontier Religion in Texas after the Civil War." *West Texas Historical Association Year Book* 47 (1981): 40–46.

Matney, Lee. Recorded interview with the author. June 14, 1984. Amarillo, Tex. Tape recording, Research Center, Panhandle-Plains Historical Museum, Canyon, Tex.

Mattes, Merrill J. *The Great Platte River Road: The Covered Wagon Mainline Via Fort Kearny to Fort Laramie*. Lincoln: Nebraska State Historical Society, 1969.

Matthews, Carter. Recorded interview with the author. October 31, 1986. Amarillo, Tex. Tape recording, Research Center, Panhandle-Plains Historical Museum, Canyon, Tex.

Matthews, Sallie Reynolds. *Interwoven: A Pioneer Chronicle*. College Station: Texas A&M University Press, 1936.

May, Mary Ada. Responses to a Questionnaire. 1939. Research Center, Panhandle-Plains Historical Museum, Canyon, Tex.

Mayes, Ben C. "Reminiscences of Ben C. Mayes." 1932. J. Evetts Haley Collection, Nita Stewart Haley Memorial Library, Midland, Tex.

McAllister, Dan. "Pioneer Woman." *New Mexico Historical Review* 34, no. 3 (1991): 161–64.

McClary, Willie. Recorded interviews with the author. July 10, 1984, and December 16, 1986. Dumas, Tex. Tape recordings, Research Center, Panhandle-Plains Historical Museum, Canyon, Tex.

McClung, Paul. "Papa Jack: The Adventures of a Pioneer Cowman." *Great Plains Journal* 12, no. 2 (1973): 100–45.

McClure, Boone. Recorded interview with the author. November 6, 1984. Canyon, Tex. Tape recording, Research Center, Panhandle-Plains Historical Museum, Canyon, Tex.

McCormick, D. R. D. R. McCormick Manuscripts. 1933. J. Evetts Haley Collection, Nita Stewart Haley Memorial Library, Midland, Tex.

McDade, Dee. Recorded interview with the author. January 2, 1987. Wildorado, Tex. Tape recording, Research Center, Panhandle-Plains Historical Museum, Canyon, Tex.

McElroy, Mrs. Dick. Recorded interview with the author. November 21,

1986. Claude, Tex. Tape recording, Research Center, Panhandle-Plains Historical Museum, Canyon, Tex.

McGehee, Melton. Recorded interview with the author. March 26, 1987. Wayside, Tex. Tape recording, Research Center, Panhandle-Plains Historical Museum, Canyon, Tex.

McKinney, B. B., ed. *Voice of Praise*. Nashville: Broadman Press, 1947.

McLoughlin, William G., Jr. *Modern Revivalism: Charles Grandison Finney to Billy Graham*. New York: The Ronald Press Company, 1959.

McManigal, Mr. and Mrs. Hobart. Recorded interview with the author. August 3, 1984. Happy, Tex. Tape recording, Research Center, Panhandle-Plains Historical Museum, Canyon, Tex.

Merchant, Montene, and Paul Engelbrecht. Recorded interview with the author. May 26, 1994. Amarillo, Tex. Tape recording, Research Center, Panhandle-Plains Historical Museum, Canyon, Tex.

Meredith, Maudie. "Memoirs of Rev. R. E. L. Muncy." 1936. Research Center, Panhandle-Plains Historical Museum, Canyon, Tex.

Meredith, Vera. "Memoirs of Bob Brewer and W. B. Clark." 1936. Research Center, Panhandle-Plains Historical Museum, Canyon, Tex.

Metcalf, Mrs. Frank. "The White Family." n.d. Research Center, Panhandle-Plains Historical Museum, Canyon, Tex.

Miles, Mary Fannie. "My First Days in Texas." n.d. Research Center, Panhandle-Plains Historical Museum, Canyon, Tex.

Miller, Andrew Marshall. Responses to a Questionnaire. 1939. Research Center, Panhandle-Plains Historical Museum, Canyon, Tex.

Miller, Henry A. "Methodist Revival Meeting: Remembering a Boyhood Experience in 1865." *The Palimpsest* 71, no. 1 (1990): 25–26.

Miller, W. Henry. *Pioneering in North Texas*. San Antonio: The Naylor Company, 1953.

Millican, L. R. "Sermon and Very Short Life Sketch of L. R. Millican, Over Fifty Years a Missionary in West Texas." J. Evetts Haley Collection, Nita Stewart Haley Memorial Library, Midland, Tex.

Mills, Joy. "Nazareth [Texas]—1892–1902." n.d. Research Center, Panhandle-Plains Historical Museum, Canyon, Tex.

Miner, Craig. *West of Wichita: Settling the High Plains of Kansas, 1865–1890*. Lawrence: University Press of Kansas, 1986.

Moffatt, Isaac. "The Kansas Prairie: Or, Eight Days on the Plains." *The Kansas Historical Quarterly* 2 (1937): 147–74.

Montgomery, Mrs. Bessie Irene. Responses to a Questionnaire. 1939. Research Center, Panhandle-Plains Historical Museum, Canyon, Tex.

Moore, George W. Recorded interview with the author. January 11, 1985. Canyon, Tex. Tape recording, Research Center, Panhandle-Plains Historical Museum, Canyon, Tex.

Moore, Hester. Recorded interview with the author. November 12, 1993. Hereford, Tex. Tape recording, Research Center, Panhandle-Plains Historical Museum, Canyon, Tex.

Moos, Rudolph H., ed. *Human Adaptation: Coping with Life Crises.* Lexington, Mass.: D. C. Heath and Company, 1976.

Morrell, Z. N. "Happy Days on the Frontier." *Frontier Times* 20, no. 6 (1943): 80–82.

Morrison, Faye. "Forty-Seven years in Floyd County [Texas] (Story of Mrs. W. A. Shipley)." 1937. Research Center, Panhandle-Plains Historical Museum, Canyon, Tex.

Morton, Virginia. "Early Settlement of Quay County, New Mexico." n.d. Research Center, Panhandle-Plains Historical Museum, Canyon, Tex.

———. "Early Settlement of Quay County, New Mexico." *Panhandle-Plains Historical Review* 19 (1946): 73–85.

Moscovitch, Morris, and Gordon Winocur. "The Neuropsychology of Memory and Aging." In *The Handbook of Aging and Cognition,* ed. Fergus I. M. Craik and Timothy A. Salthouse. Hillsdale, N.J.: Lawrence Erlbaum Associates, Publishers, 1992.

Moye, Alfred I. "Chuck Wagon Stories by Texas Pioneers." *The Cattleman* 7, no. 10 (1921): 169–74.

"Mrs. Payne—Mrs. Rowsey—Joint interview." 1940. Research Center, Panhandle-Plains Historical Museum, Canyon, Tex.

Mullins, Ethel. Recorded interview with the author. May 20, 1987. Canyon, Tex. Tape recording, Research Center, Panhandle-Plains Historical Museum, Canyon, Tex.

Murphy, H. B. M. "Migration and the Major Mental Disorders: A Reappraisal." In *Mobility and Mental Health,* ed. Mildred B. Kantor. Springfield, Ill.: Charles C. Thomas, Publisher, 1965.

Murray, Myrtle. "Home Life on Early Ranches of Southwest Texas: Joel D. Fenley, Uvalde County." *The Cattleman* 24, no. 9 (1938): 13–16.

———. "Home Life on Early Ranches of Southwest Texas: Ernst Jordan, Gillespie County." *The Cattleman* 26, no. 10 (1940): 133–36.

Muzzall, Thomas A. "Across the Plains in 1866." *New Mexico Historical Review* 32, no. 3 (1957): 246–58.

Myers, John Myers. *The Westerners: A Roundup of Pioneer Reminiscences.* Englewood Cliffs, N.J.: Prentice-Hall, Inc., 1969.

Myres, Sandra L. *Westering Women and the Frontier Experience 1800–1915.* Albuquerque: University of New Mexico Press, 1982.

Nall, Garry. "The Farmers' Frontier in the Texas Panhandle." *Panhandle-Plains Historical Review* 45 (1972): 1–20.

———. "Panhandle Farming in the 'Golden Era' of American Agriculture." *Panhandle-Plains Historical Review* 46 (1973): 68–93.

National Live Stock Association. *Prose and Poetry of the Live Stock Industry of the United States.* Denver: National Live Stock Historical Association, 1959.

Nebraska Society of the Daughters of the American Revolution. *Collection of Nebraska Pioneer Reminiscences.* Cedar Rapids, Iowa: Torch Press, 1916.

Neelley, Elizabeth Montgomery. "Pioneering in Young County Sixty Years Ago: As Told by Claude L. Neelley." n.d. Research Center, Panhandle-Plains Historical Museum, Canyon, Tex.

———. "Known as Pioneers—Life of Early Settlers Told by Native Daughter of State." n.d. Research Center, Panhandle-Plains Historical Museum, Canyon, Tex.

Newberry, James D. Chapter 8 in *Pioneer Days in the Southwest from 1850 to 1879: Thrilling Descriptions of Buffalo Hunting, Indian Fighting and Massacres, Cowboy Life and Home Building,* contrib. Charles Goodnight, Emanuel Dubbs, John A. Hart and others. Guthrie, Okla.: The State Capital Company, 1909.

Newcomb, Samuel P., and Susan E. Newcomb. Diaries (1865–73). J. Evetts Haley Collection, Nita Stewart Haley Memorial Library, Midland, Tex.

Norman, Mary Anne. "Childhood on the Southern Plains Frontier." *The Museum Journal* [West Texas Museum Association, Texas Tech University] 18 (1979): 48–142.

Nugent, Walter. *Structures of American Social History.* Bloomington: Indiana University Press, 1981.

Nunn, James H., Sr. Interview with Omah Ryan. 1937. Research Center, Panhandle-Plains Historical Museum, Canyon, Tex.

Oatts, T. C. "Diary of T. C. Oatts." 1871. J. Evetts Haley Collection, Nita Stewart Haley Memorial Library, Midland, Tex.

Ochiltree County Historical Survey Committee. *Wheatheart of the Plains: An Early History of Ochiltree County.* n.p.: The Ochiltree County Historical Survey Committee, 1969.

Oden, B. A. "Early Cowboy Days in New Mexico and Texas." n.d. J. Evetts Haley Collection, Nita Stewart Haley Memorial Library, Midland, Tex.

———. "Midland Papers." n.d. Research Center, Panhandle-Plains Historical Museum, Canyon, Tex.

Odom, Michael L. "The Recollections of a Pioneer Woman: Sarah Belle Madden Willoughby." 1969. Research Center, Panhandle-Plains Historical Museum, Canyon, Tex.

"The Old-Time Campmeeting." *Frontier Times* 3, no. 1 (1925): 8–10.

Ott, Mr. and Mrs. Ira. Recorded interview with the author. December 9, 1993. Hereford, Tex. Tape recording, Research Center, Panhandle-Plains Historical Museum, Canyon, Tex.

Pafford, Alma. Recorded interview with the author. April 13, 1984. Amarillo,

Tex. Tape recording, Research Center, Panhandle-Plains Historical Museum, Canyon, Tex.

Park, Lucille. "A Pioneer [Mrs. S. E. Askren] of Deaf Smith County [Texas]." n.d. Research Center, Panhandle-Plains Historical Museum, Canyon, Tex.

Parmer County [Texas] Historical Commission. *Prairie Progress.* Dallas: Taylor Publishing Company, 1981.

Patterson, Paul. *Crazy Women in the Rafters.* Norman: University of Oklahoma Press, 1976.

Pendleton, Bob. Recorded interview with the author. October 28, 1994. Stratford, Tex. Tape recording, Research Center, Panhandle-Plains Historical Museum, Canyon, Tex.

Peters, Mary Ella. Interview with Dwight Howard. 1942. Research Center, Panhandle-Plains Historical Museum, Canyon, Tex.

Phares, Ross. *Bible in Pocket, Gun in Hand.* Garden City, N.Y.: Doubleday and Company, Inc., 1964.

Phillips, Evelyn C. "The Memoirs of George Hollin Phillips." 1938. Research Center, Panhandle-Plains Historical Museum, Canyon, Tex.

Pierce, J. W. "Memoirs of Mrs. Cora Miller Kirkpatrick." 1938. Research Center, Panhandle-Plains Historical Museum, Canyon, Tex.

Pitts, Edith Duncan. "At Home in a Dugout." n.d. Research Center, Panhandle-Plains Historical Museum, Canyon, Tex.

Porter, Kenneth Wiggins, ed. "'Holding Down' a Northwest Kansas Claim, 1885–1888." *The Kansas Historical Quarterly* 22, no. 3 (1956): 220–35.

Porter, Millie. *Memory Cups of Panhandle Pioneers.* Clarendon, Tex.: Clarendon Press, 1945.

Posey, Walter. Interview with Seymour V. Connor. 1956. Southwest Collection, Texas Tech University, Lubbock.

Posey, Walter Brownlow. *Frontier Mission: A History of Religion West of the Southern Appalachians to 1861.* Lexington: University of Kentucky Press, 1966.

Powell, T. J. "Samuel Burk Burnett." n.d. Research Center, Panhandle-Plains Historical Museum, Canyon, Tex.

Powell, W. D., and Rubert Richardson. "A Baptist Preacher on the Texas Frontier." *West Texas Historical Association Year Book* 9, (October, 1933): 48–59.

Prichard, Mrs. Hud. Recorded interview with the author. October 18, 1984. Canyon, Tex. Tape recording, Research Center, Panhandle-Plains Historical Museum, Canyon, Tex.

Raban, Jonathan. *Bad Land: An American Romance.* New York: Pantheon Books, 1996.

Raether, Howard C., and Robert C. Slater. "Immediate Postdeath Activities in the United States." In *New Meanings of Death,* ed. Herman Fiefel. New York: McGraw-Hill Book Company, 1977.

Ramey, Ed. Recorded interview with the author. August 7, 1984. Dimmitt, Tex. Tape recording, Research Center, Panhandle-Plains Historical Museum, Canyon, Tex.

Randel, Jo Stewart. Interview with Ruth Parker. 1977. Research Center, Panhandle-Plains Historical Museum, Canyon, Tex.

Randel, Mrs. Ralph E., ed. *A Time to Purpose: A Chronicle of Carson County, Vol. I*. [Hereford, Tex.]: Pioneer Publishers, 1966.

Ransom, Roy. Recorded interview with the author. April 3, 1987. Claude, Tex. Tape recording, Research Center, Panhandle-Plains Historical Museum, Canyon, Tex.

Rasmussen, Evalyn W. "Memoirs of Ed B. Trigg." 1939. Research Center, Panhandle-Plains Historical Museum, Canyon, Tex.

Rathjen, Frederick W. Personal communication with author. December 12, 2000.

———. *The Texas Panhandle Frontier*. Austin: University of Texas Press, 1973.

Rhodes, May Davison. *The Hired Horseman: My Story of Eugene Manlove Rhodes*. Boston: Houghton Mifflin Company, 1938.

Richards, O. H. "Memories of an 89'er." *The Chronicles of Oklahoma* 26, no. 1 (1948): 2–12.

Ricou, Laurence. "Empty As Nightmare: Man and Landscape in Recent Canadian Prairie Fiction." *Mosaic* 6, no. 22 (1973): 143–60.

Riley, Glenda. *Frontierswomen: The Iowa Experience*. Ames: The Iowa State University Press, 1981.

———. "Women's Responses to the Challenges of Plains Living." *Great Plains Quarterly* 9, no. 3 (1989): 174–84.

Rister, Carl Coke. *Southern Plainsmen*. Norman: University of Oklahoma Press, 1938.

———. "Social Activities of the Southwestern Cowboy." *West Texas Historical Association Year Book* 7 (1931): 40–55.

Roach, Sammie. "Forty Years in the Texas Panhandle." 1938. Research Center, Panhandle-Plains Historical Museum, Canyon, Tex.

Robertson, Nancy W. "John Howard Lyles: Archer County [Texas] Pioneer." 1970. Research Center, Panhandle-Plains Historical Museum, Canyon, Tex.

Robeson, the Rev. [T. F.]. Interview with L. S. Baker. 1924. Research Center, Panhandle-Plains Historical Museum, Canyon, Tex.

Robinson, Jessie. Recorded interview with the author. January 30, 1987. Claude, Tex. Tape recording, Research Center, Panhandle-Plains Historical Museum, Canyon, Tex.

Rollins, Philip Ashton. *The Cowboy: An Unconventional History of Civilization on the Old-Time Cattle Range*. Albuquerque: University of New Mexico Press, 1936.

Ross, Nancy. *Westward the Women*. Freeport, N.Y.: Books for Libraries Press, 1944.

Rudolph, Charles F., ed. "Saturday, Nov. 26, 1887." [Section in "Old Tascosa: Selected News Items from *The Tascosa Pioneer,* 1886–88"]. *Panhandle-Plains Historical Review* 39 (1966): 136–37.

Ruede, Howard, and John Ise, eds. *Sod-House Days: Letters from a Kansas Homesteader 1877–78*. New York: Cooper Square Publishers, Inc., 1966.

Russell, Charles M. *Trails Plowed Under.* New York: Doubleday, Doran, & Company, Inc., 1927.

[Russell, H. A.] Photograph of the H. A. Russell family. *Amarillo Sunday News-Globe* 13, no. 33 (August 14, 1938): Section D, p. 26.

Rutherford, Blanche Scott. *One Corner of Heaven*. San Antonio: The Naylor Company, 1964.

Santleben, August. "Perils of Early Day Freighting." *Frontier Times* 21, no. 5 (1944): 226–28.

Savage, Winston. "Life on the 'F' Ranch." 1941. Research Center, Panhandle-Plains Historical Museum, Canyon, Tex.

Sawvell, Robert D. Personal communication with author. September, 1998.

Scarborough, Dorothy. *The Wind*. 1925. Reprint, Austin: University of Texas Press, 1979.

Schlissel, Lillian. *Women's Diaries of the Westward Journey*. New York: Schocken Books, 1982.

———, Byrd Gibbens, and Elizabeth Hampsten. *Far From Home: Families of the Westward Journey*. New York: Schocken Books, 1989.

Schwieder, Dorothy, and Deborah Fink. "Plains Women: Rural Life in the 1930s." *Great Plains Quarterly* 8, no. 2 (1988): 79–88.

Shearer, Mary A. E. "Pioneer Life in Grayson County." *Frontier Times* 22, no. 11 (1945): 324–27.

Sheffy, L. F. "The Experimental Stage of Settlement in the Panhandle of Texas." *Panhandle-Plains Historical Review* 3 (1930): 78–103.

———. "Mr. N. F. Locke, Miami, Texas." 1925. Research Center, Panhandle-Plains Historical Museum, Canyon, Tex.

Shelton, Joe. Recorded interviews with the author. March 15, 1984, and December 18, 1986. Pampa, Tex. Tape recordings, Research Center, Panhandle-Plains Historical Museum, Canyon, Tex.

"Short Life History of Mrs. Phebe K. Warner." *Claude News*, February, 1935, n.p.

Siringo, Charles A. *Riata and Spurs*. Boston: Houghton and Mifflin Company, 1927.

Sloneker, Maxine. "Recollections of a Pioneer Woman: Mrs. Elizabeth Hart Chatham." 1938. Research Center, Panhandle-Plains Historical Museum, Canyon, Tex.

Smith, Franklin C. "Pioneer Beginnings at Emmanuel, Shawnee." *The Chronicles of Oklahoma* 24, no. 1 (1946): 2–14.

Snell, Joseph W. "Roughing It On Her Claim: The Diary of Abbie Bright, 1870–1871." *The Kansas Historical Quarterly* 27, no. 3 (1971): 233–68.

———. "Roughing It on Her Claim: The Diary of Abbie Bright, 1870–1871—Concluded." *The Kansas Historical Quarterly* 27, no. 4 (1971): 394–428.

Sochen, June. "Frontier Women: A Model for All Women." *South Dakota History* 7, no. 1 (1976): 36–56.

Sokolow, Jayme A. "The Demography of a Ranching Frontier: The Texas Panhandle in 1880." *Panhandle-Plains Historical Review* 60 (1982): 73–125.

Sparks, Buren. "An Apostle to the Cowboys." *Farm and Ranch*, 1931, pp. 3–20.

Sparks, S. F. "Recollections of S. F. Sparks." *The Quarterly of the Texas State Historical Association* 12, no. 1 (1908): 61–79.

Spikes, Nellie Witt. "The Early Days on the South Plains." n.d. Southwest Collection, Texas Tech University, Lubbock.

———. "Old Settlers Reunion Draws Old Timers Together." *The Crosbyton Review* 28, no. 12 (March 20, 1936): Section 2, pp. 1, 7.

———, and Temple Ann Ellis. *Through the Years: A History of Crosby County, Texas.* San Antonio: The Naylor Company, 1952.

Stagner, Earl. "Reminiscences of An 'Old Timer' of the Panhandle Plains." 1941. Research Center, Panhandle-Plains Historical Museum, Canyon, Tex.

Stegner, Wallace. *Wolf Willow: A History, a Story, and a Memory of the Last Plains Frontier.* New York: The Viking Press, 1962.

Stephens, Lena Mae. "Doans, A Trading Post on a Texas Cattle Drive, 1876–1895." 1940. Research Center, Panhandle-Plains Historical Museum, Canyon, Tex.

Stephenson, Lother. "Reminiscences of Early Pioneer Days in the Panhandle from 1833–1940." 1940. Research Center, Panhandle-Plains Historical Museum, Canyon, Tex.

Stevens-Long, Judith, and Michael Commons. *Adult Life*, Fourth Edition. Mountain View, Calif.: Mayfield Publishing Company, 1992.

Stevenson, Carrie Pauley. "Those Who Went Up the Long Trail." 1933. Research Center, Panhandle-Plains Historical Museum, Canyon, Tex.

Stewart, Donald W. "Memoirs of Watson Stewart: 1855–1860." *The Kansas Historical Quarterly* 18, no. 4 (1950): 376–404.

Stratton, Joanna L. *Pioneer Women: Voices from the Kansas Frontier.* New York: Simon and Schuster, 1981.

Stroup, Dora Merrell. "Memories From Years 7 to 17." 1965. Research Center, Panhandle-Plains Historical Museum, Canyon, Tex.

Stubblefield, William. Recorded interview with the author. March 21, 1986.

White Deer, Tex. Tape recording, Research Center, Panhandle-Plains Historical Museum, Canyon, Tex.

Stubbs, Lou Caraway. Recorded interview with Sylvan Dunn. August 27, 1957. Lubbock, Tex. Tape recording, Southwest Collection, Texas Tech University, Lubbock.

Sullivan, Dulcie. "Celebration." *The Cattleman* 42, no. 6 (1960): 26–52.

"Sunrise on Plains." *Amarillo Sunday News-Globe* 13, no. 33 (August 14, 1938): Section D, p. 14.

Sutton, Fred E. *Hands Up! Stories of the Six-Gun Fighters of the Old Wild West.* ["Written down" by A. B. MacDonald.] Indianapolis: The Bobbs-Merrill Company, 1927.

Swartz, Lillian Carlile. "Life in the Cherokee Strip." *The Chronicles of Oklahoma* 42, no. 2 (1964): 62–74.

Tanner, William W. Papers, 1898–1912. Research Center, Panhandle-Plains Historical Museum, Canyon, Tex.

Taylor, Ira. Recorded interview with the author. August 9, 1985. Amarillo, Tex. Tape recording, Research Center, Panhandle-Plains Historical Museum, Canyon, Tex.

Taylor, Mr. and Mrs. Ira. Recorded interview with the author. October 24, 1986. Amarillo, Tex. Tape recording, Research Center, Panhandle-Plains Historical Museum, Canyon, Tex.

Taylor, T. U. "A Frontier Home." *Frontier Times* 2, no. 6 (1925): 15–22.

"A Texas Cowboy's Funeral" [From *The Cattleman*]. *Frontier Times* 16, no. 8 (1939): 349–51.

Texas State Historical Association. *The New Handbook of Texas.* Austin: Texas State Historical Association, 1996.

Thelen, David. "Memory and American History." *The Journal of American History* 75, no. 4 (March, 1989): 1117–29.

Thompson, Albert W. *They Were Open Range Days: Annals of a Western Frontier.* Denver: The World Press, Inc., 1946.

Thompson, Alma McGowen. "Witherspoon Spins Them Wide." *Amarillo Sunday News-Globe* 13, no. 33 (August 14, 1938): Section A, p. 32.

Thorp, N. Howard. *Partner of the Wind: Story of the Southwestern Cowboy.* Caldwell, Idaho: The Caxton Printers, 1945.

Tice, J. H. *Over the Plains—and—On the Mountains or Kansas and Colorado.* St. Louis: The St. Louis Book and News Company, 1872.

Timmons, Herbert, and Carolyn Timmons. "Circuit Rider's Wife: As Told by Mrs. R. M. Morris of Clarendon." *Amarillo Sunday News-Globe* 13, no. 35 (August 14, 1938): Section C, p. 10.

———. "'Those Are Our Boys on Boot Hill.'" *Amarillo Sunday News-Globe* 13, no. 33 (August 14, 1938): Section D, p. 32.

————. "Veteran Preacher Tells of Early Experiences." *Amarillo Sunday News-Globe* 14, no. 6 (February 5, 1939): Section 2, p. 10.

Timmons, William. *Twilight on the Range: Recollections of a Latterday Cowboy.* Austin: University of Texas Press, 1962.

Tomlinson, Mrs. T. W. "A Brief and Partial History of Swisher County [Texas]." 1922. Research Center, Panhandle-Plains Historical Museum, Canyon, Tex.

Trent, Dana Harmon. "The Gay Nineties in the Panhandle." n.d. Research Center, Panhandle-Plains Historical Museum, Canyon, Tex.

Tressman, Ruth. "Home on the Range." *New Mexico Historical Review* 26, no. 1 (1951): 1–17.

Trew, Delbert. "Wash Day on the Farm Always Fell on Monday." *Amarillo Globe-News* 1, no. 29 (May 28, 2001): Section C, p. 2.

Tucker, George W. Personal communication with author. September 12, 1984.

Vardy, James D. "Reminiscences of Jas. [James]. D. Vardy." n.d. Research Center, Panhandle-Plains Historical Museum, Canyon, Tex.

Vernon, Walter N., Robert W. Sledge, Robert C. Monk, and Norman W. Spellman. *The Methodist Excitement in Texas: A History.* Dallas: The Texas United Methodist Historical Society, 1984.

Vinovskis, Maris A. "Angels' Heads and Weeping Willows: Death in Early America." In *The American Family in Social Historical Perspective*, 2nd ed., ed. Michael Gordon. New York: St. Martin's Press, 1978.

Wallace, Ed R. *Parson Hanks: Fourteen Years in the West.* Arlington, Tex.: Journal Print, 1906. J. Evetts Haley Collection, Nita Stewart Haley Memorial Library, Midland, Tex.

Walser, C. R. Recorded interview with the author. August 18, 1993. Hereford, Tex. Tape recording, Research Center, Panhandle-Plains Historical Museum, Canyon, Tex.

Walsh, Mrs. A. L. Recorded interviews with the author. December 3, 1984, and November 13, 1986. Canyon, Tex. Tape recordings, Research Center, Panhandle-Plains Historical Museum, Canyon, Tex.

Waltz, Anna Langhorne. "West River Pioneer: A Woman's Story, 1911–1915." *South Dakota History* 17, no. 1 (1987): 42–77.

Warner, Phebe Kerrick. "Mary Ann Goodnight." n.d. Research Center, Panhandle-Plains Historical Museum, Canyon, Tex.

————. "The Wife of a Pioneer Ranchman." *The Cattleman* 7, no. 10 (1921): 65–71.

Warren, Charles R. "Pioneer Life in Armstrong County, Texas, As Remembered by Charles R. Warren, of Amarillo [Texas]." n.d. Research Center, Panhandle-Plains Historical Museum, Canyon, Tex.

Warwick, Mrs. Clyde W. *The Randall County [Texas] Story*. Hereford, Tex.: Pioneer Book Publishers, Inc., 1969.

Watts, Isaac. "Broad Is the Road." In William Allen, *Psalms and Hymns for Public Worship*, p. 471. Boston: Wm. Pierce; New York: Leavitt, Lord, & Company; Hartford: D. Burgess, & Company, 1835.

———. "When I Can Read My Title Clear." In *The Book of Common Prayer* [Protestant Episcopal Church in the United States of America], p. 228. Philadelphia: Thomas Wardle, 1847.

———. "Why Do We Mourn Departing Friends?" In *Psalms and Hymns* [Presbyterian Church in the United States], p. 412. Philadelphia: Presbyterian Board of Publication, 1843.

Weaks, Marsene Smith. "Alfred A. Holland." 1936. Research Center, Panhandle-Plains Historical Museum, Canyon, Tex.

Webb, Walter Prescott. "The Land and the Life of the Great Plains." *West Texas Historical Association Year Book* 4 (1928): 58–85.

———. "Some Vagaries of the Search for Water in the Great Plains." *Panhandle-Plains Historical Review* 3 (1930): 28–37.

———, editor-in-chief. *The Handbook of Texas: A Dictionary of Essential Information*. Austin: The Texas State Historical Association, 1952.

———. *The Great Plains*. Waltham, Mass.: Blaisdell Publishing Company, 1959.

Weems, J. H. Interview with Mary H. Gaetz. 1941. Research Center, Panhandle-Plains Historical Museum, Canyon, Tex.

Weisberger, Bernard A. *They Gathered at the River: The Story of the Great Revivalists and Their Impact Upon Religion in America*. Boston: Little, Brown and Company, 1958.

Wells, Ethel. "The Disappearance of the Frontier." 1933. Research Center, Panhandle-Plains Historical Museum, Canyon, Tex.

"When Death Rate Was High." *Amarillo Sunday News-Globe* 13, no. 33 (August 14, 1938): Section D, p. 13.

Whetstone, Fred. "Memoirs of Ernest Warren." 1936. Research Center, Panhandle-Plains Historical Museum, Canyon, Tex.

Whitcomb, Addie. Interview with L. E. Moyer. 1958. Research Center, Panhandle-Plains Historical Museum, Canyon, Tex.

White, Mrs. Ernest. Recorded interviews with the author. August 10, 1984, and November 3, 1986. Canyon, Tex. Tape recording, Research Center, Panhandle-Plains Historical Museum, Canyon, Tex.

Whited, Hazel. Memoirs of Herbert M. Timmons. 1936. Research Center, Panhandle-Plains Historical Museum, Canyon, Tex.

Whitehead, J. W. Interview with Mildred Hobbs. 1941. Research Center, Panhandle-Plains Historical Museum, Canyon, Tex.

Whitlock, V. H. *Cowboy Life on the Llano Estacado*. Norman: University of Oklahoma Press, 1970.

Whitsett, Effyle. "Memoirs of Mrs. Jim W. Carter." n.d. Research Center, Panhandle-Plains Historical Museum, Canyon, Tex.

Williams, Clayton W. *Texas' Last Frontier: Fort Stockton and the Trans-Pecos, 1861–1895*. College Station: Texas A&M University Press, 1982.

Willis, T. Guy. Interview with Hazel Willis. 1946. Research Center, Panhandle-Plains Historical Museum, Canyon, Tex.

Wilson, C. R. "An Interview with an Early Settler." 1933. Research Center, Panhandle-Plains Historical Museum, Canyon, Tex.

Wilterding, Mrs. Mervin. Interview with Gayla Wagnon. 1976. Research Center, Panhandle-Plains Historical Museum, Canyon, Tex.

Winkleman, Mildred. Recorded interview with the author. May 9, 1984. Amarillo, Tex. Tape recording, Research Center, Panhandle-Plains Historical Museum, Canyon, Tex.

Wisehart, M. K. "'Wichita Bill,' Cowboy Artist, Rode Into The Halls Of Fame." *The American Magazine*, August, 1927, pp. 34–70.

Witt, C. B. Recorded interview with the author. April 8, 1987. Amarillo, Tex. Tape recording, Research Center, Panhandle-Plains Historical Museum, Canyon, Tex.

Witt, Lita. Recorded telephone interview with the author. April 20, 1987. Tape recording, Research Center, Panhandle-Plains Historical Museum, Canyon, Tex.

Wofford, Winston. "Memoirs of Lea Paine." 1937. Research Center, Panhandle-Plains Historical Museum, Canyon, Tex.

Wynne, J. S. Interview with J. Evetts Haley. 1926. Research Center, Panhandle-Plains Historical Museum, Canyon, Tex.

Young, A. W. "Thirty Years in Texas Pulpit and School." *Frontier Times* 6, no. 8 (1929): 347–50.

Young, Jessica Morehead. "Pioneer Days." n.d. Research Center, Panhandle-Plains Historical Museum, Canyon, Tex.

Young, Mrs. Alice. "Some Recollections of Coleman County, Mrs. Alice Young As Told to Georgene Falls." 1941. Research Center, Panhandle-Plains Historical Museum, Canyon, Tex.

Younger, J. Vinson. "Memoir of Frank Exum." 1936. Research Center, Panhandle-Plains Historical Museum, Canyon, Tex.

Zachry, Juanita Daniel. *The Settling of a Frontier: A History of Rural Taylor County*. Burnet, Tex.: Nortex Press, 1980.

Index

Abbott, E. C., 62, 68, 69, 78, 84, 98, 108, 130, 169, 246n. 75, 259n. 14
Abbott, George, 226n. 15
Abilene, Kans., 111
Abilene, Tex., 21, 51
Adams, Andy, 62, 76, 85, 238n. 34, 241n. 95, 254n. 18, 256n. 47, 256n. 62, 258n. 100
Adams, Ramon, 130
Albers, Adelheid, 74, 80
Albuquerque, N. Mex., 39
alcoholism, 69
Alderson, Nannie, 72, 228n. 39, 237n. 25, 244n. 41
Allen, Barbara, xix, 281n. 62
Allen, John, xviii
Allred, Ralph, 102
Altus, Okla., 33
Amarillo, Tex., xv, 60, 63, 66, 69, 80
Andreadis, Harriette, 44, 45, 131
animals, 20, 27, 67, 79, 92, 234n. 50, 248n. 44, 270n. 142
Archer County, Tex., 25, 102
Archer, Ruby Cole, 167, 170, 171, 182, 187, 260n. 20
Armstrong County, Tex., 11, 29
Armstrong, Margaret, 45, 50
Arnot, John, 230n. 70
Arnot, Martha (Mrs. John), 230n. 70
Artesia, N. Mex., 107
Avent, Lavert, 61, 96, 167, 205

Bagwell, Mrs. N. S., 5
Baird, Ed, 29
Baker, James, 11
Baptists, 146, 171, 177, 186, 243n. 34
Barker, Jess, 92, 237n. 22, 247n. 9
Barker, Roger, 212n. 24
Bartlett, Richard, 46
Bedford, H. G., xxii, 27, 159
bedrolls, 161, 269n. 119
Bell, Lilian, 90
Bell, Mitch, 21
Bell, Velma, 189, 190, 275n. 115
Benton, W. B., 218n. 44
Berryman, Opal, 19, 23, 42, 84, 100, 102, 126, 147, 148, 150, 152, 156, 162, 172, 173, 198
Beverly, Bob, 96
Biles, Rachel Malick, 243n. 20
Bird, Tom, 32, 230n. 67
Biddy, Claude, 61
Black, Tom, 33, 121, 179, 199, 206, 208, 264n. 13
Blanco Canyon, Tex., 30, 153, 201
Blankenship, Andy, 67
Blankenship, Mary, 5, 13, 30, 42, 48, 67, 149, 234n. 50
"Blessed Assurance," 191
Bloys' Camp Meeting, 145, 146, 153, 164, 171, 263n. 78
Bloys, Rev. W. B., 133, 146, 154, 156, 159, 160, 174

Bodnar, John, 212n. 22
Bonds, Posey, 161
Bonham, Tex., 41, 45
Book of Common Prayer, The, 125
Boone, Mrs. Claude, 52
Boot Hill, 60, 110
Bourland, G. B. E., 188
Bower, Bruce, 212n. 19
Boydstun, Henry, 34, 39
Boydstun, Mary (Mrs. Henry), 39, 43
Boydstun, Ora, 39
Boydstun, Riley, 39
Bradly, J. W., 30
Brazos River, xx
Bridwell, Edna Braswell, 80, 181
Bright, Abbie, 43
Briscoe County, Tex., 21
Bronson, Edgar, 38, 59
"Brother's Death-Search, A," 106
Brothers, Mary, 7
Brown, Charles, 65
Brown, Maggie (Mrs. Charles), 65
Brown, Timmie, 153
brush arbors, 158, 171–74; 263n. 72;
    272n. 24
Bunyan, John, 260n. 60
burials. *See* funerals
Burns, Emma (Mrs. Rollie), 48
Burns, Rollie, 48
Burrus, Van Dooney, 100
Byars, Albert, 149, 165, 173, 208
Byars, Lillie (Mrs. Albert), 165
Bynum, S. K., 207, 260n. 24

Caldwell, Marcia, xvi, xvii, 92, 96, 119,
    120, 123, 146, 158, 167, 175, 180,
    182, 186, 191, 197, 201, 202, 204
Callahan County, Tex., 239n. 40
Campbell, Dr. W. H., 219n. 18
Campbell, Mrs. Harry, 30
camp meetings: 133, 135–41, 144–46,
    150, 154–56, 159, 166, 168, 174,
    263n. 78; 267n. 64; attendance at,
    xxi–xxii, 153, 156–57; camping out
    at, 135, 160, 269n. 119; and "camp-
    meeting babies," 138; children at,
    148, 161, 202–203; close of, 195–96;
    courting at, 138, 160, 204, 269n. 117;
    duration of, 145, 170; emotionalism
    at, 135, 169, 187, 198–99, 277n. 148;
    fellowship at, 153; food and meals

at, 148, 161–66, 270n. 135; history
    of, 134–35; misbehavior at, 138,
    154–60, 268n. 114, 277n. 162; music
    and singing at, 157, 189–95, 200–
    201, 277n. 162; peddlers at, 156;
    planning and preparations for, 146,
    148–50, 265n. 41, 266n. 57, 269n.
    120; setting up for, 150–52; as social
    events, xxi, 147, 199–204, 279n. 12;
    supplies for, 149, 152, 171
Canadian River, 35
Canadian, Tex., 97
Canyon, Tex., 74, 123
Carson County, Tex., 31, 39
Cartwright, David, 252n. 105
Cash, Hester, 63
Cashatt, Salome Lynette, 227n. 30
Castro County, Tex., 238n. 30
Cather, Willa, 14, 20
Cator, James, 237n. 30
Cator, Robert, 237n. 30
cattle drives, 48, 69, 115
cattle industry, xvii
Cave, Eula, 31
cemeteries, 61, 101–102
Central Texas, 236n. 9
Ceta Glen Canyon, Tex., 144
Chappell Hill, Tex., xx
Chatham, Elizabeth Hart, 171
Cheyne, C. E., 19
childbirth, 59, 64, 237n. 25
children, 31, 228n. 39; mortality of, 64–
    65, 80–82; and playing, 161, 203
Childress County, Tex., 278n. 2
Childress, Tex., 214n. 8
Chillicothe, Tex., 29
Christian Herald, 131
churches, 131, 154, 187, 204, 260n. 24,
    261n. 27
Civil War, 4, 83, 278n. 2
Clarendon, Tex., 214n. 8, 227n. 20
Clark, W. B., 14
Claude, Tex., xv, 11, 15
Clay, John, 103
Cleaveland, Agnes, 30, 39, 62, 69,
    232n. 3
Clifton, Minnie, 195, 267n. 64
Cline, Isaac M., 224n. 72
Coburn, Catherine Scott, 8
Coe, Frank, 32
Coe, Wilbur, 32, 68, 156, 163, 190

coffins, 87, 88, 94–98, 246n. 2; 250nn. 71, 72
Cole, Mrs. John, 105
Coleman County, Tex., 209
Coleman, Sarah, 34
Colorado City, Tex., xvi
Collingsworth County, Tex., 29, 42
Collinson, Frank, 66, 93, 99
Collyns, Bill, 119, 126, 189, 200
Colt, Miriam Davis (Mrs. William), 27, 46, 50, 75, 82, 83, 126, 209, 215n. 28, 223n. 64
Colt, William, 208
Colvin, Ada, 230n. 73
Coon, Polly, 243n. 20
corpses, 88–93, 247n. 9, 249n. 45, 250n. 64; 248n. 37, 248n. 39, 248n. 44
Cosby, C. N., 65, 79, 95, 177, 202, 269n. 117
Cotton, Tom, 108
Cowans, Charley, 31
"Cowboy Funeral, A," 254n. 7
cowboys: and accidents, 52–53, 67, 68, 192, 246n. 75; appearance of, 68; African-American, 57; and ballads, 118, 256n. 48; conflict between, 66; health and hygeine of, 61, 64, 67, 237n. 26; and nicknames, 54; and work, 52
"Cowboy's Dream, The," 108, 118
cow chips, 148
coyotes/wolves, 19, 25, 99, 249n. 39, 252n. 105
Craik, Fergus I. M., 222n. 22
Cranfield, J. B., 185, 263n. 72
crops, 145, 263n. 13
Crosby County, Tex., 29
Crowell, Tex., 76
Cross, Ruth, 123
Crudgington, John, 63, 238n. 40
Culp, Bertie, 171
Cummings, Mariett Foster, 248n. 45

dances, 146
Dary, David, 20
Davidson, Oneita, 188, 268n. 108, 270n. 138, 274n. 115
Davis, Andrew, 179
Davis Mountains, 31, 144, 145, 150, 154
Davis, Shady, 107

Deaf Smith County, Tex., 234n. 52
death, 60, 74, 75, 76–79, 80, 81, 83, 84, 88, 90, 91, 197, 208, 242n. 11, 244nn. 41, 42, 244n. 51, 245n. 55, 245 n. 65; causes of, 62–63; 65; and children, 74, 80, 81–82, 87, 244n. 49; sermons about, 77–78; social aspects of, 204–209, suddenness of, 73, 75–77, 243n. 20, 250n. 72
Deitiker, Gladys, 65, 75, 120, 124, 126, 127, 131, 208
diaries, xix
Dickens County, Tex., 234n. 47
Dick, Everett, 251n. 83
diet, 62–63, 237n. 30
"Dim Narrow Trail, The," 118
dinner on the grounds, 166, 271n. 153
disease/sicknesss, 16, 61, 63, 64, 220n. 23, 238n. 32
Dodge City, Kans., 82, 237n. 19
Doshier, Inez, 180
drownings, 69, 85, 241n. 95
Dubbs, Rev. Emanuel, 179
Dudley, R. M., 67
Dumont, Ella Elgar Bird, 32, 48, 66, 83, 125, 230n. 67, 264n. 9
Duncan, Mrs. A. B., 197
Duncan, Sarah Kay, 47, 197
Dunn, Rev. R. F., 81, 82, 177
Dyer, "Father" John. L., 273n. 76

East Texas, 60, 138, 236n. 9
Ebbutt, Percy G., 200
Edwards, Billy, 258n. 100
Elkins, S. P., 209
Ellis County, Tex., 15
Ellis, Temple, 15
Ellis, Temple Ann (Elizabeth Ann Spikes), 15, 24, 30, 42, 49
Embree, Henrietta, 45
Estlack, J. C., 107, 219n. 12, 253n. 1
Evans, Joe, 129, 145, 150, 155, 159, 161, 163, 164, 165, 173, 201, 263n. 3, 265n. 18, 268n. 107, 269n. 120
Evernden, Neil, 222n. 60
exorters, 185–86, 276n. 136
Exum, Frank, 103

Fairchild, Amy, 21
Faragher, John, 216n. 36, 233n. 34
farming families, xviii, 131

Faxon, Okla., 73, 98
Featherston, Rev. Edward Baxter, 178, 190, 274n. 81
Federal Census of 1880, 28, 33, 59
Fedric, S. B., 19
Fife, Alta, 192
Fife, Austin, 192
Fink, Deborah, 213n. 30
firearms, 66
Fite, Gilbert, 11, 211n. 6
Fletcher, Baylis, 94
Floydada, Tex., 9, 197
Floyd County, Tex., 9, 34–35, 52, 100
food. *See* diet
Fort Davis, Tex., 133, 150, 260n. 24
Fort Laramie, Wyo., 248n. 45
Fort Worth and Denver City Railroad, 214n. 8
Fort Worth, Tex., xxii, 27, 102, 214n. 8
F Ranch, 115
freighters, 35, 173, 23n. 47
Fried, Marc, 218n. 1
Frizzell, Lodisa, 8, 216n. 38, 245n. 65
frontier, xvii, xx–xxi, 63, 187, 211n. 6, 212n. 24, 239n. 40; boredom on, 45; early settlers on, 226n. 11; farming and ranching on, xvii; hardships on, 42, 130, 137, 198, 209
Frost, Margaret Fullerton, 91, 244n. 49
Frye, Henry, 32
Frye, Lulu (Mrs. Henry), 32
Frying Pan Ranch, 35, 230n. 70
funerals/burials, 60, 84–85, 88, 93, 107–109, 111, 144–15, 119–22, 205, 255n. 34; and children, 205, 257n. 71, 257n. 89; emotions at, 119, 123–24, 198–99, 256n. 61, 258n. 100; Scripture-reading at, 116; sermons at, 118, 257n. 62; singing at, 116, 256n. 47; social aspects of, 205
funeral homes, 242n. 4

Gabriel, 191
Galloway, Maude Smith, 15, 19
Galveston Daily News, The, xx, 195
Galveston, Tex., 21, 224n. 72
Garden City, Kans., 97
Gardner, Bill, 54
Gard, Wayne, 69, 228n. 51

Garland, Hamlin, 21, 45
Garner, Mary, 276n. 136, 277n. 148
Gasper River, Ky., 134
Gates, Rev. P. H., 146, 264n. 3
gender roles, 10, 35, 47, 90, 187, 216n. 36, 233n. 34, 233n. 38
Gibson, Joe, 35, 257n. 89, 279n. 12
Gibson, Louise (Mrs. Joe), 123, 148, 168, 244n. 42
Gilbert, Jessie Loomis, 114
Gilles, Albert, 73, 98
"God Be With You," 195
Goodnight, Charles, 33, 61, 243n. 34
Goodnight, Mary Ann "Molly" (Mrs. Charles), 50, 131
Goodwyn, Frank, 182
Goring, Mrs. J. H., 227n. 20
gospel songs. *See* hymns
Graham, W. M., 28
graves, 62, 98–102, 104–105, 107, 252n. 116, 252n. 120; digging and filling of, 88, 98, 125–27, 251n. 102; and isolation, 76, 102, 244n. 41, 245n. 65
Great American Desert, xviii, 4, 16
Great Plains, xviii, 3
"Great Roundup, The," 118
Green, Duff, 22
Greene, A. C., 21, 65, 99, 102, 129, 170
Griswold, J. T., 5
gunfights, 52, 91, 109
Guthrie, Tex., 35

Hadley, Amelia, 215n. 21
Haley, J. Evetts, 71
Haley, Rosalind (Mrs. J. Evetts), 71
Hamilton, Mary, 82
Hampsten, Elizabeth, 20, 125, 234n. 55, 242n. 11, 250n. 72
Hanners, LaVerne, 64, 248n. 44
Hard, William, 4
Hare, Dr. George, 278n. 2
"Hark the Voice of Jesus Is Calling," 117
Harvey, Mrs. John, 131
Harvey, Nora, 190
Harvey Sadler tent shows, 200
Hastings, Frank, 124
Hastings, Jim, 226n. 15
Hazelrigg, Rev. Charles, 81, 82

health, 60
health seekers, 15–18, 220n. 31
heaven, 82
"Hell in Texas," 169
Hemphill County, Tex., 64
Henderson, Eva, 76, 78, 274n. 98
Henderson, Gracy, 7, 256n. 48
Hendrix, John, 269n. 119
Henry, John Robert, 28
Henry, Stuart, 107, 111
Hereford, Tex., 33, 47, 229n. 59
Hess, Marie Barbier, 114, 119
Hill County Camp Meeting, 263n. 78
history, xvii; oral, xix, xx
Hogan, William R., 273n. 74
Hoisington, S. N., 248n. 39
Holcomb, Jennie, 42, 61, 205
Holden, Maggie Lee, 48
Holland, Alfred, 259n. 17
Holt, Rev. A. J., 171, 175, 176, 180
"Home Over There, The," 192
homesickness, 11, 231n. 73
Hood County, Tex., 23, 65
Hooker, Okla., 230n. 67
Hooks, Matthew "Bones," 57
Hornbeak, Rev. J. A., 180
horses, 53, 69–71
hospitality, 32, 228n. 44
Hough, Emerson, 84, 85, 91, 93
houses, 20, 34
Hoyt, Dr. Henry, 60
Hunter, J. Marvin, Sr., 190
Hunt, George, 35
Hutchinson County, Tex., 31
hymnals, 191
hymns, 190–91, 193–94, 200–201

immigration associations, xviii
immortality, 82, 245n. 55, 245n. 65
"I'm on My Way to Canaan," 192
Indians, xvii, 100, 209
infidelity, religious, 131, 246n. 75,
    259n. 14
interment, 93, 94, 109
"In the Sweet By and By," 117, 191, 192
Ise, Henry, 73, 121, 261n. 29
Ise, John, 177, 224n. 68, 261n. 27
Ise, Rosa (Mrs. Henry), 73, 83, 121
isolation, xvi, xxii, 28, 30, 213n. 30,
    225n. 9, 226n. 15, 270n. 30,

228n. 51, 229n. 59, 230n. 67; and
    loneliness, 32, 40–42; and wind, 22
Ivy, Mrs. J. N., 234n. 52

Jack County, Tex., 45
Jaques, Mary, 116, 119, 122
JA Ranch, 131
Jeffrey, Julie, 10
Jellison, Katherine, 213n. 30
Jennings, Janine M., 212n. 22
Job, 182
Johnson, Charles, 135, 140
Johnson County, Tex., 34
Jonah, 169
Jones, Billy, 220n. 31
Jones, Coleman, 55
Jones, L. E., 279n. 12
Jones, Mack, 93
Jones, Mitchell, Sr., 69, 147, 169, 186,
    188
*Journal of the American Medical Associa-
    tion,* 17
Judson, Phoebe Goodell, 3, 216n. 31,
    217n. 44, 227n. 26, 245n. 65
Junction City, Tex., 116, 122

Kansas City Star, 110
Kennedy, Marguerite Wallace, 116, 121,
    122, 123
Kenton, Okla., 230n. 67
Kerrick, Phebe (Mrs. William Arthur
    Warner), 3
Killough, Joe, 47
Kimmis, Polly A., 197
King County, Tex., 230n. 67
King, Hannah, 250n. 64

land boom, xviii
land companies, 60
Las Vegas, N. Mex., 54
laundry, 148, 208, 266n. 44
Legg, Mrs. George, 215n. 24
"Let Me Go Where Saints Are Going,"
    193
Lewis, Faye, 187, 214n. 14, 221n. 48,
    225n. 78, 225n. 95, 231n. 1
Lewis, Malcolm, 223n. 62
line camps, 55
Lincoln, N. Mex., 32
Lipscomb County, Tex., 93

"Little Joe the Wrangler," 256n. 48
Little, Rev. M. K., 150, 177, 266n. 60
Llano Estacado, 3, 19, 29, 223n. 2
Locke, N. F., 38
Lockhart, Dr. John Washington, xx, 136, 137, 149, 184, 195
Logan County, Ky., 134
loneliness, xvi, xx, xxii, 11, 26, 42, 213n. 27, 218n. 44, 232n. 3, 233n. 43, 235n. 58; and sickness, 51; as cause of death, 55; and women, 234n. 55, 234n. 57; and men, 51
Lord, Ed, 63, 90, 92, 97, 230n. 67
Lowes, Dr. Ruth, 78, 80, 120, 179, 182, 244n. 43, 244n. 51
LS Ranch, 91, 131
Lubbock, Tex., xviii, 15, 48
LX Ranch, 60
Lyles, John, 25

McAllister, Annie (Mrs. J. E.), 91, 131
McAllister, J. E., 91
McClary, Willie, 89, 90, 114, 120, 189, 205
McClure, Boone, 77, 92, 98, 119, 126
McCormick, Dave, 83, 243n. 34, 275n. 115
McCormick, Mrs. Mickey "Frenchy," 110, 111
McCoy, Dock, 67, 70
McDade, Dee, 166, 167, 271n. 153, 276n. 136
McDade, Mrs. Dee, 271n. 153
McGready, Rev. James, 134
McManigal, Anna Mae (Mrs. Hobart), 47
McManigal, Hobart, 119, 229n. 59
McMurtry, Lee "LeeMac," 87
McNeil, Harry, 186
Magoffin, Susan Shelby, 220n. 22, 239n. 50
mail service, 38, 48, 231n. 76
Majors, Alexander, 93
malaria, 16
Matador Ranch, 30, 131
Matador, Tex., 188, 189
Matney, Lee, 78, 122, 171, 179
Mattes, Merrill, 240n. 65, 251n. 102, 252n. 105, 252n. 120, 255n. 34
Matthews, Carter, 144, 153
Matthews, Sallie, 31, 62, 144, 150, 240n. 66

Mayes, Ben, 53
May, Mary Ada, 91, 226n. 14
medicine, 16, 17, 219n. 18
memory, xix, 212n. 19, 212n. 22
Menard, Tex., 147
Merrell, Jane, 117
Methodists, 139, 243n. 34, 275n. 111
Miami, Tex., 31
Midland, Tex., xvii
migration, xviii, 4, 6, 7, 9, 10, 13, 60, 216n. 36, 218n. 1, 236nn. 8, 9; fears and hazards of, 62, 4, 214nn. 13, 14, 215n. 15; motives for, xvii, 16, 220n. 25; preparations for, 8–9
Miller, Henry A., 275n. 111
Millican, Rev. L. R., 179, 185
Mineral Wells, Tex., 114
Miner, Craig, 14, 105, 214n. 13, 238n. 32
Mobeetie, Tex., 48, 259n. 17, 260n. 23
monotony, 44
Montague County, Tex., 19
Moore County, Tex., 89
Moore, George, 80
Moore, Hester, 265n. 41
Morrell, Z. Z., 143
Motley County, Tex., 94
Moye, Alfred "Babe," 68, 93
Mulkey, Abe, 179
Muncy, Rev. R. E. L., 189
Murphy, H. B. M., 218n. 1
"My Bonnie Lies Over the Ocean," 108
Myers, Sandra, 216n. 39, 217n. 44
"My Latest Sun Is Sinking Fast," 194

Nall, Garry, 213n. 3
"Nearer My God to Thee," 117
"'Neath the Western Skies on the Lone Prairie," 105
Neelley, Claude, 30
neighbors, xvi, xxi, 11, 89, 100, 206–208, 247n. 14, 281n. 62, 281n. 68; distance from, 30–31, 227n. 26, 227n. 31
Newberry Camp Meeting, 263n. 78
Newcomb, Samuel P., xxii, 260n. 24
Newcomb, Susan E. (Mrs. Samuel P.), xxii, 41, 42, 44, 48, 77, 81, 260n. 24
Noble, John, 21, 54
"Noonday Plain, The," 209
Nugent, Walter, xvii
Nunn, James, Sr., 27, 32

Oatts, T. C., 51
obituary, 116
"O Bury Me Not on the Lone Prairie,"
    103
Oden, B. A., 207
Olney, Tex., 30
Olton, Tex., 31
oral history. *See* history
Ott, Ira, 35, 92, 96, 160, 187, 189,
    256n. 61, 274n. 98, 276n. 140
Ott, Pet (Mrs. Ira), 92, 119, 148, 184,
    268n. 114

Pafford, Alma, 116
Palo Duro Canyon Baptist Association,
    153
Palo Duro Canyon, Tex., 33
Paine, Lea, 233n. 47
Panama Canal, 4
Pancake Ranch, 29
Panhandle-Plains Historical Museum,
    xviii, xxi, 77
Panhandle (Texas), 3, 14, 17, 33, 213n. 3,
    219n. 12; population of, 28, 29, 33;
    females in, 226nn. 14, 15, 227n. 20
Parker County, Tex., 172, 263n. 78
Patrick, W. H., 157
Patterson, Paul, 50
Peters, Mary Ella, 92
Pickens, Mamie, 263n. 72
Pilgrim's Progress, 260n. 20
Pitts, Edith Duncan, 47, 130
plains, xv, xix, 3, 14, 15, 18–27, 35, 54, 103,
    129, 144, 169, 219n. 14, 221n. 42,
    221n. 46, 221n. 48, 222nn. 59, 60;
    weather and climate of, 16, 18, 21,
    223n. 62, 223n. 64, 224n. 72,
    224n. 74, 225n. 76, 237n. 25
Porter, Catherine Wiggins, 76, 117
"Portuguese Hymn," 256n. 47
Posey, Walter, 52
Post, C. W., xxi
Post, Tex., xxi
Potter County, Tex., 17–18, 63
Potter, Rev. Andrew Jackson, 176
Powell, J. C., 55
preachers, 131, 146, 165, 175–79, 185,
    198, 260n. 20; and circuit riding, 81,
    133, 176, 261n. 30; distances trav-
    eled by, 177, 273n. 74, 273n. 76;
    hardships of, 177, 273n. 76, 274n. 81

pregnancy, 59, 64, 201, 239n. 50
Presbyterians, 155, 186
Prichard, Lois, 75
privations, 46–47
protracted meetings, 139, 140, 158

Quanah, Tex., 214n. 8, 234n. 37
Quitaque, Tex., 10

Raban, Jonathan, 222n. 59
railroads, xvii, 4, 16, 60, 214n. 8
Ramey, Ed, 79
ranch cure, 17
ranchers, xvii; wives of, 131
Ranchman's Recollections, A, 124
Randall County, Tex., 18, 63
Ransom, Mrs. Roy, xvi
Ransom, Roy, xv
Rawlins, Rawhide, 73, 104
Rayburn, Sam, 41, 44, 235n. 58
Reavis, Isham, 87, 125, 217n. 41,
    229n. 59
Red River, 97
religion, 131–33
religious services, xxi, 131, 133, 140, 171,
    175; as social events, 132, 199
resettlement, 14, 218n. 1
revivals, xvi, 140, 166; as social events,
    xvi, 200, 201; and dinner on the
    grounds, 166; emotionalism at, 187–
    89, 277n. 148; singing at, 190–91;
    testimonies at, 137, 187, 276n. 14
Ricou, Laurence, 221n. 46
Riddle, Mary, 215n. 28, 216n. 32,
    248n. 37
"Riders of the Range," 104
Riley, Glenda, 234n. 57
Rio Grande River, 169
Rister, C. R., 57, 228n. 51
Road to Destiny, 24
Robinson, Dogie, 206
Robinson, Jessie, 135, 190
Rocking Chair Ranch, 29
Rollins, Philip, 37, 53, 67, 70, 111, 116, 123
Ross, Bertha Doan, 97
Roswell, N. Mex., 32
Ruidoso River, 32
Russell, H. A., 29
Russell, Molly, 29
Rutherford, Blanche, 74, 91, 126,
    228n. 44

"Safe in the Arms of Jesus," 117
saloons, 36, 259n. 17
San Angelo, Tex., 207
San Antonio, Tex., 16, 17, 66
sandstorms, 23
sanitation, 63
San Saba County, Tex., 10
Santa Fe Trail, 220n. 22
Sawvell, Robert D., 219n. 4
Scarborough, Dorothy, 23, 49
Schlesinger, Arthur M., Jr., xvii
Schlissel, Lillian, 10, 252n. 116
Schweider, Dorothy, 213n. 30
Scott, Abigail, 217n. 44, 245n. 55,
    250n. 64
Scott, David, 9
Scott, Fred, 61
Scott, May (Mrs. David), 9
Scurry County, Tex., 27
separation, 5, 8–10, 12, 215n. 28, 216n. 3,
    216n. 32, 216n. 38, 216n. 39,
    217n. 41, 217n. 43, 217n. 44,
    230n. 73
sermons/preaching, 178–85, 243n. 34,
    274n. 98, 275n. 111, 275n. 115; out-
    door, 133, 13
Seymour, Elizabeth Porter, xxi
"Shall We Gather at the River," 117
Shearer, Mary, 95
Shelton, Joe, 33, 71, 93, 95, 104, 113, 114,
    123, 133, 149, 161, 162, 164, 172,
    174, 181, 201, 202, 205, 237n. 19
Sheridan, Philip, 170
Sherman County, Tex., 114
Shipley, Clarissa, 216n. 38
shootings, 66, 240n. 64, 240n. 65
shrouds, 90, 94, 247n. 29
Silverton, Tex., 34
Simpson, William, 230n. 67
singing. *See* hymns
"Sinner is Thy Heart at Rest?" 191
sitting up, 92, 247n. 9, 248n. 37, 248n. 44
Slade, Dora, 204
Slaughter Ranch, 153
Smith, C. R., 54
Smith, Elizabeth, 30
SMS Ranch, 124
snakes, 173
Snyder, Tex., 75
Soash, W. P., 60
Sparks, S. F., 176

Spaugh, A. D., 76, 114, 206
Spikes, Elizabeth Ann (Temple Ann El-
    lis), 15
Spikes, Nellie, 21, 114
Spur Ranch, 53, 67
Staked Plains, 20, 213n. 2
Stamford, Tex., 124
stampedes, 69
Stegner, Wallace, 18, 20
Stephens County, Tex., 9
Stephenville, Tex., 5
stock farms, 30
stoicism, 10
Strange, Clarence, 230n. 67
Strange, Edmond, 230n. 67
Strange, Rosa Belle (Mrs. Edmond),
    230n. 67
Stratton, Joanna, xvii, 234n. 55, 248n. 39
Stroup, Dora Merrill, 10, 96, 102, 115,
    117, 250n. 71
Stubbs, Lou Caraway, 23, 225n. 76
sunday school, 131, 260n. 24
Sutton, Fred, 108, 109, 111
Surfus, Mary, 250n. 71
Svendsen, Gro, 216n. 31, 231n. 73,
    245n. 65
Swisher County, Tex., 20

Tanner, William, 11, 45, 51, 213n. 27,
    231n. 73
Tascosa, Tex., 91, 109, 226n. 14, 253n. 1,
    259n. 17
Taylor, Birtie (Mrs. Ira), 147, 188
Taylor County, Tex., 174
Taylor, Ira, 33, 46, 78, 89, 145, 147, 158,
    160, 161, 186, 233n. 38, 247n. 14,
    269n. 119, 272n. 24
Taylor, Thomas Ulvan, 172
Temple, Okla., 34
Texas Christian Advocate, 131
Texline, Tex., 214n. 8
"There is a Green Hill Far Away," 192
Thomas, C. M., 74
Thompson, Albert, 112
Tice, J. H., 25, 222n. 60
Timmons, Herbert, 18
Tom Green County, Tex., 53
Tomlinson, Mrs. T. W., 20
towns, 35–37, 230n. 67, 230n. 68
trading posts, 35
travel, 7, 33–34

Trew, Delbert, 266n. 44
Trigg, Ed, 15, 179–80
Trumble, L. P., 226n. 15
Tubb, Alice, 64
tuberculosis, 16, 17, 62, 91
Tucker, George, 119, 122
Tulia, Tex., 247n. 29
Turkey, Tex., 21
Turkey Track Ranch, 107
Two Circles Bar Ranch, 109
typhoid fever, 63

University of Texas, 172

Vardy, James, 31, 188, 190, 277n. 162
Vernon, Tex., 177
Victoria, Tex., 94
visitors, 31–33, 228n. 39

wagons, 4, 6, 8, 66, 231n. 1
Walsh, Hazel, 75, 119, 123, 124, 188
Waltz, Anna Langhorne, 221n. 42,
    222n. 60, 224n. 74
Warner, Dr. William Arthur, 3, 11
Warner, Phebe, 8, 11
Warren, Charles, 11
Washington County, Tex., 27
Watts, Isaac, 193
Weatherly, John, 31
Weatherly, Maggie (Mrs. John), 31
Weaver, Jacob, 52
Webb, Walter Prescott, 223n. 65
Weems, J. H., 52
Wesley, Charles, 133
Wesley, John, 133
West Texas, 14, 19, 27–28, 144, 170; so-
    cial life in, 139, 199
Wheeler County, Tex., 28, 32
"When I Can Read My Title Clear," 193
"When the Roll is Called Up Yonder,"
    117, 190, 191

"When the Work is Done This Fall," 53
Whitcomb, Addie, 60
White, Dabney, 18
White, Isaac, 5
White, Merle, 182, 264n. 3
Whitlock, V. H., 20, 96, 105, 121, 122
Wichita Falls, Tex., 14, 25, 214n. 8
Wichita, Kans., 123
"Why Do We Mourn Departed
    Friends?" 193
Wilbarger County, Tex., 97
Willis, J. A., 14
Willis, T. Guy, 14, 158
Willoughby, Sarah, 29
Wilson, Rev. Francis, 183, 273n. 74
windmills, 48, 50, 234n. 52
Wind, The, 23
Winkleman, Mildred, 116, 123, 257n. 71
Winter, Matt, 259n. 14
Witt, Albert, 89
Witt, C. B., 154, 167, 188, 266n. 57,
    270n. 142
Witt, Lita, 167
women, 28, 35, 47, 43; and coping with
    loneliness, 49–50; emotionalism of,
    187–88; isolation of, 27, 29
work, 46
"Work for the Night is Coming," 117
Wyatt, Fannie Maude (Mrs. G. S.), 173,
    270n. 135
Wyatt, Rev. G. S., 181

XIT Ranch, 33, 52, 54, 67, 226n. 15

Young, A. W., 205
Young County Camp Meeting, 153,
    157
Young, Jessica, 23n. 260
youth, 59–60
"You Will See Your Lord A-Coming,"
    191

ISBN 1-58544-182-1